Site Planning and Design Handbook

About the Author

Thomas H. Russ is a licensed landscape architect with more than 20 years of professional experience in both environmental assessment and site design. He has worked as a project manager and as a principal in design firms and is currently Professor of Environmental Technology at the College of Southern Maryland. Russ has written numerous professional papers on site and environmental design topics and is the author of *Redeveloping Brownfields for Landscape Architects, Designers and Developers.*

Site Planning and Design Handbook

Thomas H. Russ, RLA

Second Edition

New York   Chicago   San Francisco
Lisbon   London   Madrid   Mexico City
Milan   New Delhi   San Juan
Seoul   Singapore   Sydney   Toronto

Library of Congress Cataloging-in-Publication Data

Russ, Thomas H.
   Site planning and design handbook / Thomas H. Russ.—2nd ed.
      p.   cm.
   Includes bibliographical references and index.
   ISBN-13: 978-1-265-62042-4
   ISBN-10: 1-26-562042-3
   1. Building sites—Planning.   2. Architecture—Environmental   aspects. I. Title.
NA2540.5.R87   2009
690—dc22

                                                                         2009019106

McGraw-Hill books are available at special quantity discounts to use as premiums and sales promotions, or for use in corporate training programs. To contact a representative please e-mail us at bulksales@mcgraw-hill.com.

Site Planning and Design Handbook, Second Edition

1 2 3 4 5 6 7 8 9 0   DOC/DOC   0 1 4 3 2 1 0 9

ISBN 978-1-265-62042-4
MHID 1-26-562042-3

Sponsoring Editor
   Joy Bramble Oehlkers

Acquisitions Coordinator
   Michael Mulcahy

Editorial Supervisor
   David E. Fogarty

Project Manager
   Anupriya Tyagi, International
   Typesetting and Composition

Copy Editor
   Kay Mikel

Proofreader
   Manish Tiwari, International
   Typesetting and Composition

Indexer
   Robert Swanson

Production Supervisor
   Richard C. Ruzycka

Composition
   International Typesetting and Composition

Art Director, Cover
   Jeff Weeks

For Karla

Contents

Preface

Preparing the second edition of *Site Planning and Design Handbook* has been enlightening in many ways. Perhaps the greatest surprise was how much the world of land development had changed in only 8 years. I ended the Preface of the first edition with the observation that much of the new design paradigm would be written in the next 25 years and that it was an exciting time to be working in the field. I could not have appreciated how much change there would be in such a short time. Many changes have slipped into the routine of day-to-day work in the rush of the marketplace, but these incremental changes may be the foundation for profound shifts in the way our work is performed and evaluated. As our commitment to a sustainable society takes shape, the design professions are undergoing remarkable change. Since publication of the first edition, a number of states and major cities in the United States have adopted policies requiring green roofs on commercial structures and have committed to practices of increased energy efficiency and sustainable development. Purchasing policies of major companies, cities, and states are beginning to require that LEED-certified design professionals are on design teams and that designers reach back into their supply chains for sustainable products and practices.

At a meeting in 2000 the lead design professional of a building project responded to a question from the client's project manager about LEED certification and protocols by saying that the "environmental stuff" was a "passing fad" and "just adds cost to the project." The mechanical engineer for the project admitted he had never heard of the LEED protocol. That was disappointing, but in 2008 I attended another meeting at which the client's accounting people were asking design professionals fairly detailed questions about LEED and the purchasing people were including LEED performance standards in new requests for proposals. Much had changed in only 8 years.

This second edition of *Site Planning and Design Handbook* has expanded sections on issues of sustainable site design throughout. Chapter 1 has been expanded to include issues for an aging population, water conservation, and an expanded discussion of climate change and energy concerns. More attention is given to the implications of these anticipated problems.

Chapter 2 is new and is entirely devoted to the practices of green design. Protocols, particularly LEED, are discussed and supporting arguments are given for choosing such protocols over traditional nonsustainable practices. This support includes economic, operational, and life cycle considerations that contribute to the decision to "go green."

Among the small changes in the last 5 years is the amount of site data available for little or no cost on the Internet. Chapter 3 is concerned with site analysis and has been revised to reflect the availability of online resources, such as aerial photography, topographic maps, and soil maps. In addition, Appendix C has been added, which lists some of the many online resources available to site planners and designers.

Chapter 4 is concerned with community standards. Issues such as community isolation emerging from not connecting adjacent developments and clustering are discussed in greater detail. The section on site security issues has additional information and detail reflecting practices that have been introduced since September 11, 2001. This is more than a discussion on site hardening of institutional sites and is concerned with the design of sites that consider all of the functions of a site. The discussion on defensible space has also been expanded. This chapter includes details on the construction of site features, lighting, and material specifications.

Chapter 5 has a general discussion on "universal design" and how site design has embraced the idea of functionality for the broadest possible number of users. The design of effective walkways that allow for multiple uses and users is included, and the use of porous paving is introduced. New detail and information is presented in the discussion of leisure opportunities in communities. Considerations for selecting and sizing public recreation facilities also have been updated. The section on design for older residents has been expanded to include the result of recent studies and emerging practices. A new section on dog parks has also been added.

The design of streets and parking areas is a critical component of site design. Chapter 6 has been revised to include recent trends in street design. The concerns and practices promoted by successful "Complete Street" initiatives around the United States are discussed, as well as more information on nontraditional options such as the "woonerf." There is a substantive and expanded discussion on the relationship between street design and pedestrian safety as well as strategies for traffic calming. An entirely new discussion on the use of roundabouts is included. This chapter includes the engineering methods for street design and the AASHTO standards relevant to community streets as well as a more detailed discussion on porous paving design.

Chapter 7 is dedicated to issues of site grading and erosion and sediment control. The chapter includes the general principles of planning for a balanced site and the design and stabilization of slopes. The discussion on erosion and sediment control is thorough but is, of course, subject to local regulations and practices. The general practices and strategies of grading and erosion and sediment control are presented in detail.

Planning and design of infrastructure is discussed in Chapter 8. Storm water management, sanitary sewer design, and water distribution are described, but there is also an expanded discussion of on-site sewage disposal, constructed wetlands, and gray water systems. The section on rain gardens has also been expanded.

Chapter 9 addresses landscape restoration. The discussion on brownfields, in particular, has been expanded and now reflects changes in federal law and newer practices that have emerged in recent years. There is more detail on restoration strategies and technologies. The chapter is also concerned with site stabilization and the restoration of streams and includes many details and specifications for techniques and materials.

Plant materials and using plants for effect in design is the focus of Chapter 10. Recognizing that many fine resources exist on this topic, the chapter focuses on less common aspects such as successful strategies for urban street trees, saving trees subject to cuts or fills as part of new development, invasive species, and toxic plants.

The preservation of historic sites involves some special challenges for site planners and designers. These are the subject of Chapter 11. Special aspects of site assessment of the historic site are reviewed as well as issues of adapting the historic site to contemporary use, including ADA concerns. There is an overview of risks and hazards that might be present on the historic sites as well.

Chapter 12 is concerned with the somewhat more esoteric aspects of the design professional's practice. It provides a historic overview not only of professional practice but also of the cultural context for the idea of landscape and the professional's role. It concludes with some thoughts on the state of practice today and in the future.

Chapter 13 concluded the second edition and is concerned with professional practice in both a business sense and in the standard of care expected of a professional.

Much has changed in the profession in the short period of time from the first edition of this book to the second. These changes are for the most part encouraging and offer some promise that society is beginning to recognize and expect a standard of care from design professionals with more regard to functionality and sustainability. Site professionals are adapting to these expectations with more thoughtful and "greener" designs. It is my hope that this second edition of *Site Planning and Design Handbook* will assist them in their efforts.

Tom Russ
May 2009

Acknowledgments

I am grateful to a number of people and organizations that allowed their work to be used in this book, especially Tom Scheuler of The Center for Watershed Protection, Diane Carstens and John Wiley and Sons, American Association of State Highway and Transportation Officials, McGraw-Hill Professional Books, the American Society of Civil Engineers, and Faddis Concrete Products. Charles Miller PE of Roofscapes, Inc. provided valuable details and photographs of green roofs. Ted Reiff of "The Reuse People" headquartered in Oakland, California, gave some real insight into the emerging practices and issues of building deconstruction and material reuse. Andy Evans of Second Chance in Baltimore, Maryland, also lent his expertise and some photographs. In the public domain, much information was available from the agencies of the U.S. government: the Environmental Protection Agency, Department of Commerce, Geological Survey, Department of Agriculture, and the Natural Resource Conservation Service. Additional assistance or materials were provided by Terry Collins of the Portland Cement Association; David Tuch of Equinox Environmental Consultation and Design, Inc.; Shannon Tuch of the Asheville Planning Department, Asheville North Carolina; Ben Hamilton-Baille; Amy Galvin of Clivus Multrum; Ray Mims of the United States Botanic Garden; and Danielle Borasky of the University of North Carolina Institute on Aging. Jeffrey Kahan of the University of Michigan provided some important feedback on the first edition that was incorporated into this second edition.

I am especially indebted to Zolna Russell, ASLA, Niall Kirkwood, and George B. L. Gibson for their assistance in developing this project. I am grateful to the many professionals of McGraw-Hill, especially Joy Bramble Oehlkers, and also Michael Mulcahy, David E. Fogarty, Richard Ruzycka, and Jeff Weeks for their skill and effort in bringing this project to fruition. Kay Mikel has my deep appreciation for her able skills and remarkable patience in copyediting this book. I am also indebted to the staff at ITC, particularly Manish Tiwari for proofreading my work and most especially Anupriya Tyagi for her efforts in preparing this book for publication. The combined efforts of all of these people have made this a more pleasant experience and produced a better quality product than I could have hoped for. Please accept my appreciation.

As always, I am grateful for the education, guidance, and experience gained from my association with Robert B. Ludgate Sr. PE, PLS; perhaps the most important of my teachers and mentors. Professor Jack Treadway, PhD. for his encouragement and, George Gibson and William Montley for being influential and valued colleagues. The contributions of these and many other colleagues, clients, and teachers too numerous to name cannot be overstated. The best of my work is a reflection of what they have taught me. Any errors or shortcomings in this project are mine alone.

I appreciate the indulgence of my colleagues at the College of Southern Maryland during the time this book was being prepared, especially Bill Montgomery and Tim Keating. Many thanks to my brother Stephen M. Russ for his effort at producing the many figures and details used in the book, but more important for his good humor and friendship. I am indebted to Tom Mudra for his valuable criticism, support, and friendship. Last, but most of all, I thank Karla, my friend and wife, for her love, patience, company, and enthusiasm for this and all of my projects.

Tom Russ

Site Planning and Design Handbook

CHAPTER 1

Sustainability and Site Design

Humans have a significant impact on the world environment. It has been said that 60 percent of the earth's land surface is under the management of people but that 100 percent of the world is affected by the practices of that management. Whether we are aware of it or not, our activities have an effect on the world. Paul Erhlich and John Holdren (1971) used the formula I = PAT (Impact = Population × Affluence × Technology) to illustrate the relationship of people, per capita rate of consumption, and the economic efficiency of consumption. Although the United States has more efficient and cleaner technologies than some nations, these benefits may be offset by the rate of consumption afforded by its relative affluence. Even though China has many more people, their relative affluence and level of technology were low historically, but China's affluence and technology level have been increasing rapidly in recent years. In either case the environmental footprint is significant.

In 1987 the Brundtland Commission published *Our Common Future*, which recognized that to avoid or at least minimize the environmental impacts of human behavior it is necessary for society to adopt a sustainable approach to development. *Sustainability* was defined as "meeting the needs of the present without compromising the ability of future generations to meet their own needs."

In February of 1996 the President's Council on Sustainable Development (PCSD) published *Sustainable America—A New Consensus for Prosperity, Opportunity and a Healthy Environment for the Future*. The PCSD identified 10 goals, but the first 3 really encompass them all: health and the environment, economic prosperity, and equity. *Equity* refers to social equity (equal opportunity) and intergenerational equity (equity for future generations). To meet the challenges of sustainability we need to change our behaviors—to adapt to a paradigm of economic prosperity, social equity, and environmental sustainability—but these goals have traditionally been viewed as antagonistic or mutually exclusive. We tend to think in extremes: the worst of economic activities compared to the best of the environment, or the most restrictive impact of environmental regulations and resulting dire economic consequences. Economic health and environmental sustainability are not mutually exclusive. The challenge we face is to reconcile our economic interests with our environmental interests.

We have learned that gains or improvements in one area may be offset by increases in another. Between 1980 and 1995 per capita energy consumption in the United States fell, but total energy consumption increased by 10 percent due to a 14 percent increase in population. From 1995 to 2005 the per capita trend in energy has been flat, perhaps even declining a bit, but as the U.S. population increases at a rate of about 3 million people per year, total energy use rises as well. Likewise, although modern cars are 90 percent cleaner than cars built in 1970, there are so many more of them that the efficiency gains are offset to some degree by the increase in the volume of pollution.

The impacts of development and land use patterns were well documented during the last half of the twentieth century. Impacts include a loss of water quality, fragmented and lost wildlife habitat, human health issues, introduction of invasive exotic plants, loss of biodiversity, falling groundwater tables, and more. A 2007 University of Ohio study found that landscape fragmentation—the loss of cohesive patterns of connectedness in a landscape—had increased 60 percent between 1973 and 2000 (Irwin and Bockstael, 2007). Fragmentation is known to be closely associated with a loss of biodiversity and resilience in landscapes. As development proceeds, isolated "islands" of green space and narrow visual buffers give some aesthetic appeal to the finished site, but they are commonly without significant ecological value.

A variety of studies and reports detail the public and personal health impacts of some development patterns. Human health impacts range from obesity, hypertension, and respiratory problems to mental health concerns. The causes are equally diverse and include reduced air quality, traffic noise and vibration, sedentary lifestyles, and a loss of social capital.

Public costs are higher as well. Numerous studies have found that suburban development as it is typically done does not raise sufficient tax revenue to pay for itself and so drives the need for higher taxes for existing communities. Goetz, Shortle, and Bergstrom (2004) summarized more than one hundred studies and found that for every new dollar of revenue raised by development $1.11, on average, was spent providing services to those same developments. A Maryland report found that school bus budgets in that state more than doubled to $492 million from 1992 to 2006, yet the miles driven by buses increased only 25 percent (Sewell, Ahern, and Hartless, 2007). Although some states have laws that allow impact fees, even a quick analysis reveals that these sorts of ancillary costs usually are not captured by them. In addition to these local impacts, human activities are having significant affects on global climate. People around the world have become more aware and concern is being turned into action.

This awareness is made more critical by the population increases expected in the coming decades. The United States currently has a population of more than 300 million people and is expected to grow to between 420 and 438 million by 2050, an increase of nearly 3 million people per year. It is expected that 20 percent of the U.S. population in 2050 will be foreign-born legal residents and that 82 percent of the increase in population will be due to immigrants, their children, and their grandchildren. To respond to this population increase, it is necessary to build the equivalent of a city the size of Chicago every year going forward. What will that development look like?

About 80 percent of the buildings in the United States have been built since 1960. Buildings are responsible for 48 percent of the increase in greenhouse gases produced by the United States since 1990, an increase greater than emissions from either industry or transportation. A building constructed in the European Union typically uses about 25 percent of the energy of a similar building in the United States. The patterns of growth in the United States have changed as well. Sewell, Ahern, and Hartless (2007) found that today most suburban development or sprawl is occurring in bands located 55 to 80 miles from urban centers. This pattern of growth has been underwritten in part by road improvements that enable people to live further from the city centers and encourage more driving and more energy consumption. A study of land development by Woods Hole Research Center (2007) found that development in the study area had increased 39 percent from 1986 to 2000. The center concluded that we should expect a 60 percent increase in total development in metropolitan areas by 2030. The environmental, economic, energy, and public health issues resulting from development as it has been done since 1960 provide a compelling argument that change is required.

Much of the growth in the United States is not a function of population growth, however. Several studies have looked at the trends in growth and found that only about 50 percent of U.S. development can be explained by population growth (Pendall, 2003; Kolankawicz, 2007). What is worse is that states with growth control programs and legislation seem to fare no better than states without such controls when it comes to limiting sprawl (Anthony, 2004). These patterns of development and land use are clearly unsustainable, yet much of existing public policy is focused on encouraging and subsidizing such growth at the expense of existing urban areas. Community leaders are frequently seen in local papers turning over a spade of earth to celebrate new business outside the existing urban center. The new facility, often with tax incentives of one sort or another, will draw employees to it, create traffic, require new infrastructure, and generate housing at the expense of the existing community. New roads must be constructed and sewers and water lines extended, and with new housing come the need for schools and community services. Very often this growth is unaccompanied by real population growth; more land is consumed to support the same number of people. If sustainability is the objective, these events might better be viewed as failures of planning rather than successes.

Generally it takes 20 to 30 years for technology to move from the research and development phase to use in the land development and construction field. Reasons for the lag time vary but include developing the awareness and demand necessary to bring along ordinances; however, a more common reason is the natural and predictable resistance of people to change. The various parties to development all bring their own interests to the process, and, in turn, each stakeholder assesses development differently: how will the site fit into the community, will it be a financial success, does the plan meet code and ordinance?

It is the job of the designer to find the synthesis of all these often adversarial views. The designer also has the greatest opportunity to innovate and introduce alternatives to the planning and design of sites and landscape. With a duty and responsibility for the health and safety of the public, the professional designer has the burden to make the site "work." With the realization of the impacts of site development, introducing alternative, more sustainable practices to site development can best be done by site design professionals. Regulatory agencies may create a framework for more sustainable design practices, but in the final analysis the site design professional must implement these guidelines. Public officials and reviewers, however, share responsibility in educating the public and elected officials regarding the importance and desirability of change.

Our experience with change is largely based on introducing new materials or methods into design and construction. The change required by the introduction of new regulatory or permitting programs is a familiar experience for most of us. Contemporary site planning and design is changing to adopt into practice much of the knowledge and information gained as our awareness of environmental risks has improved (Table 1.1). Sustainability requires a broader and deeper view of site planning. The leadership of this change is coming from many different places, but changing emphasis may require

High-risk problems	Medium-risk problems	Low-risk problems
Habitat alteration and destruction	Herbicides/pesticides Oil spills	Oil spills
Species extinction	Toxins, nutrients	Groundwater pollution
Overall loss of biodiversity	Biochemical oxygen demand and turbidity in surface water	Radionuclides
Stratospheric ozone depletion	Acid deposition	Acid runoff to surface water
Global climate change	Airborne toxins	Thermal pollution

Adapted from *The Report of the Science Advisory Board Relative Risk Reduction Strategies Committee to the EPA* (Washington, D.C.: U.S. Government Printing Office, September 1990).

TABLE 1.1   Relative Environmental Risks as Ranked by Scientists

many of us to reevaluate our past work and assumptions and begin to approach design differently. There can be a great deal of resistance to such change; methods and principles that have been acceptable in the past and that we thought were successful may have to be abandoned for other methods and for new ways of thinking. Some of the logic we have used to plan and design sites will be augmented with new and additional considerations. In some cases it may be replaced entirely. It is difficult to objectively study the impacts of past practices and not recognize that a new paradigm is in order. If we are to build the equivalent of another Chicago every year to respond to our growing population and minimize the impacts of doing so, the practices we follow and the principles we employ must change. During this period of change, the design principles of land development in a sustainable postindustrial society will be determined. It is an exciting time for design professionals.

In the United States site design has always been an issue of local control and practices because, in part, the conditions and needs of local communities and landscapes are too diverse to be addressed in any single ordinance or set of regulations. Nonetheless, common, if not universal, practices and methods have served design professionals and communities well. The increasing awareness of the need for more sustainable land development includes emergent practices that also have broad application and value. In recent years the federal government and many states have passed incentives to encourage green building. Some states offer tax incentives to encourage energy efficiency and the use of green methods and materials. It is a practical certainty that being able to provide such service to clients will be a competitive necessity in only a few short years. It is through the design professions that these changes to land development, site planning, and design will be introduced to most communities. This is the subject of Chap. 2.

Population and Demographics

Trends in population and demographics have important implications for planners, and the U.S. population is projected to increase to at least 420 million by 2050. Much of the population growth in the United States is occurring in the southwest and southeast. Known as the Sun Belt, much of this area is semiarid to arid land where water may be

FIGURE 1.1   Dryscaping for a desert home reduces the need for water and other inputs to maintain a healthy and attractive landscape.

in short supply. Shifts in populations will put increasing pressure on existing supplies and require more conservation. Dryscaping and infiltration of storm water are already becoming standard practices as part of conservation efforts (Fig. 1.1).

The emergence of energy as an issue in California in 2000 and 2001 is an example of the complexity of the problems we face. Consumers are interested in access to affordable power but have been reluctant to authorize construction of new generating plants. Clean alternatives for generating electricity, such as wind generators and large solar installations, often have met with local resistance. Although conservation has not been a significant part of our national strategy, designers might anticipate more opportunities for innovation in site design that contribute to energy efficiency as well as water conservation. Conservation-related design is viable because it pays for itself and contributes to the bottom line of business.

According to the U.S. Census, 77 million people in the United States were over 50 years old in 2000. In the midwestern and northeastern states populations are growing older. In some northern states the number of births per year is less than the replacement level, and these states may experience a decline in population as other parts of the country expand rapidly. Florida is well known as a retirement destination, but populations are growing older in Pennsylvania, West Virginia, Iowa, and North Dakota as well. In part this is because many younger people are moving to the Sun Belt states while older folks tend to remain close to home even in retirement, "aging in place."

Retirees are not evenly distributed across the country (Fig. 1.2). In 2003 Florida had the greatest percentage of residents over age 65 at 17 percent, but California had the largest population of older residents (about 4 million). The next oldest states include

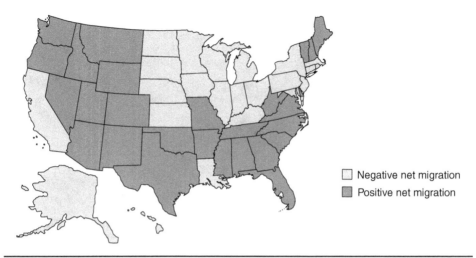

FIGURE **1.2**   Moving to the Sun Belt: net migration of population over 65, 1995–2000. Retirees tend to relocate to a few parts of the United States, concentrating the need for services. (*Source:* U.S. Census Bureau, August 2005. *Internal Migration of Older Population: 1995–2000.* Used with permission of the University of North Carolina Institute on Aging.)

Iowa, North Dakota, Pennsylvania, and West Virginia with about 15 percent each. The states with the fastest growing populations over age 65 were Nevada and Alaska. This distribution seems to demonstrate two general trends in retirement: one group that prefers to stay in their life-long communities and another that uses retirement to move to what they believe to be a more habitable climate or area.

The number of older people is expected to double by 2025 in Montana, Idaho, Wyoming, Colorado, New Mexico, Arizona, Utah, Nevada, Washington, Oregon, the Carolinas, and Texas. Although many Americans are moving away from urban centers, immigrants tend to concentrate in "gateway" cities like Chicago, New York, and other former industrial cities. The number of immigrants to the United States promises to continue to be a factor in overall population growth.

It is expected that by 2030 about 20 percent of the population of the United States will be aged 65 or older. About 78 million people are planning on retiring in the next 20 years. The oldest baby boomers enjoyed their 60th birthday in 2006. Boomer retirements will begin in earnest in 2010 and continue far beyond 20 years. As this is being written, the fastest growing age group in the United States is the 85+ group. The implications of this aging population are significant in many facets of our society and economy. This is true for planners and site designers as well. To appreciate the scope of the impacts and how we might prepare for and respond to them, some introductory discussion is appropriate.

First, it may be necessary to reconsider what our view of aging is (Fig. 1.3). Key among our considerations is that the people who comprise this growing graying demographic are not easily captured by any one set of characteristics. For example, reports often relate how healthy the aging population is, and in fact the relative health of older people has continued to improve; but about 20 percent of them still report some form of disability or chronic illness. This will include more than 14 million people should the

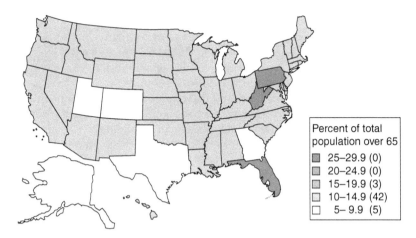

FIGURE 1.3   The graying of America: percent of total U.S. population over 65 in 2000.
(*Source:* U.S. Census Bureau, 2005. *State Interim Projections by Age and Sex: 2004–2030.* Used with permission of the University of North Carolina Institute on Aging.)

rate remain flat through 2030 (Fig. 1.4). It also means that any adult community is likely to be a microcosm of the various characteristics that make up the demographic. Design, therefore, should attempt to accommodate the community as a whole rather than any subset. It is true that as one ages mobility, balance, and perception are all subject to change, but the degree to which that happens to an individual is influenced by many different factors. What this means from a practical standpoint is that there is no average person on which to base a design.

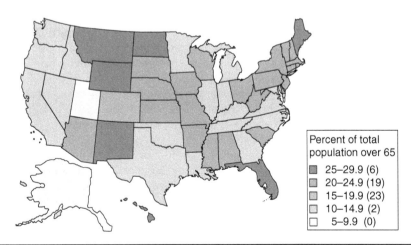

FIGURE 1.4   The graying of America: percent of total U.S. population over 65 in 2030.
(*Source:* U.S. Census Bureau, 2005. *State Interim Projections by Age and Sex: 2004–2030.* Used with permission of the University of North Carolina Institute on Aging.)

The relative wealth of the retiring boomers has also received a good deal of interest. Much of this trend in retiree wealth is due to company-funded retirement, private savings, and Social Security—the often discussed "three-legged stool." DeVaney and Chiremba (2005) found that the degree of preparation for retirement declined as one moved from early boomers (born 1946 to 1954) to the younger boomers (born 1955 to 1964) and on to Generations X and Y. Furthermore, the number of people participating in company retirement plans also has declined significantly, effectively removing one of the three legs from the retirement stool. Butrica and Uccello (2004) found that while early boomers are more likely to enjoy retirement at pretty much preretirement levels, younger or later boomers are less likely to be able to maintain their lifestyles. So it would appear that the earliest retirees from the boomer group are likely to be the best prepared for retirement, and as the retirement boom proceeds, the economic well-being of the group as a whole will decline to some degree. This reality may cause designers and planners to rethink how to accommodate the portion of older citizens without the resources to enjoy the active adult lifestyles and care so often portrayed as retirement in the United States.

Implications

With the anticipated increase in population, the need for water and energy conservation and planned growth becomes even more important and "smart growth" becomes critical. For communities in some parts of the country, development pressure will grow, and local government will have the opportunity to deal with growth-related issues including open space and public facilities before the crush. Community consideration of the standards to be used for that future growth should be undertaken as soon as possible: what is the community's vision for its future?

The growing older population nationwide represents opportunities for design firms but also represents significant challenges in some states where the majority of population growth is among the oldest people. The percentage of older people will continue to increase in the coming years, representing about 1 out of 5 people in the United States by 2050. It is expected that the baby boomers will enjoy a relatively healthy and active retirement that may represent a continuing demand for housing and recreation. The nature of these products should be expected to change, however. Some cultural observers anticipate a return to simpler values and even a growing spirituality in the culture as the boomers reach retirement. These trends may indicate a growing philosophical awareness of the boomers or may simply reflect lower retirement income. Communities that allow for real estate and school tax abatement for older taxpayers may experience shrinkage in local tax revenues at the same time that the population ages in place and demand for services for older citizens rises. This is especially true in those states in which the trend in the average age of the population increases as young people move away and older residents remain.

Early indicators of two seemingly contradictory trends have been observed as retiring baby boomers move back into traditional large urban centers and into small towns. The reasons for these anticipated trends are equally diverse. Some retirees desire the cultural, civic, and social resources provided in large cities; others seek to escape the city for the perceived benefits of small rural towns. Their decisions may in part lie in the costs associated with these choices. Small town life may be less expensive than an active urban lifestyle. In the end these would appear to be quality of life choices by a very diverse demographic group. Both have important implications for communities and for site designers (Table 1.2).

State	Total population			Population age 65 and older		
	2000	2025	% change	2000	2025	% change
Alabama	4,451	5,224	17.4	582	1,069	83.7
Alaska	653	885	35.5	38	92	142.1
Arizona	4,798	6,412	33.6	635	1,368	115.4
Arkansas	2,631	3,065	16.5	377	731	93.9
California	32,521	49,285	51.5	3,387	6,424	89.7
Colorado	4,168	5,188	24.5	452	1,044	131.0
Connecticut	3,284	3,739	13.9	461	671	45.6
Delaware	768	861	12.1	97	92	(5.2)
District of Columbia	523	655	25.2	69	92	33.3
Florida	15,233	20,710	36.0	2,755	5,453	97.9
Georgia	7,875	9,869	25.3	779	1,668	114.1
Hawaii	1,257	1,812	44.2	157	289	84.1
Idaho	1,347	1,739	29.1	157	374	138.2
Illinois	12,051	13,440	11.5	1,484	2,234	50.5
Indiana	6,045	6,215	2.8	763	1,260	65.1
Iowa	2,900	3,040	4.8	442	686	55.2
Kansas	2,668	3,108	16.5	359	605	68.5
Kentucky	3,995	4,314	8.0	509	917	80.2
Louisiana	4,425	5,133	16.0	523	945	18.2
Maine	1,259	1,423	13.0	172	304	76.7
Maryland	5,275	6,274	18.9	589	1,029	74.7
Massachusetts	6,199	6,902	11.3	843	1,252	48.5
Michigan	9,679	10,072	4.1	1,197	1,821	52.1
Minnesota	4,840	5,510	13.8	596	1,099	84.4
Mississippi	2,816	3,142	11.6	344	615	78.8
Missouri	5,540	6,250	12.8	755	1,258	66.6
Montana	950	1,121	18.0	128	274	114.1
Nebraska	1,705	1,930	13.2	239	405	69.5
Nevada	1,871	2,312	23.6	219	486	121.9
New Hampshire	1,224	1,439	17.6	142	273	92.3
New Jersey	8,178	9,558	16.9	1,090	1,654	51.7
New Mexico	1,860	2,612	40.4	206	441	114.1

TABLE 1.2   Population Change from 2000 to 2025

State	Total population			Population age 65 and older		
	2000	2025	% change	2000	2025	% change
New York	18,146	19,830	10.9	2,358	3,263	38.4
North Carolina	7,777	9,349	991	2,004	102.2	20.2
North Dakota	662	729	10.1	99	166	67.7
Ohio	11,319	11,744	3.8	1,525	2,305	51.1
Oklahoma	3,373	4,057	20.3	472	888	88.1
Oregon	3,397	4,349	28.0	471	1,054	123.8
Pennsylvania	12,202	12,683	3.9	1,899	2,659	40.0
Rhode Island	998	1,141	14.3	148	214	44.6
South Carolina	3,858	4,645	20.4	478	963	101.5
South Dakota	777	866	11.5	110	188	70.9
Tennessee	5,657	6,665	17.8	707	1,355	91.7
Texas	20,119	27,183	35.1	2,101	4,364	107.7
Utah	2,207	2,883	30.6	202	495	145.0
Vermont	617	678	9.9	73	138	89.0
Virginia	6,997	8,466	21.0	788	1,515	92.3
Washington	5,858	7,808	33.3	685	1,580	130.7
West Virginia	1,841	1,845	0.2	287	460	60.3
Wisconsin	5,326	5,867	10.2	705	1,200	70.2
Wyoming	525	694	32.2	62	145	133.9

Adapted from U.S. Census Bureau, 2000.

TABLE **1.2**   Population Change from 2000 to 2025 (*Continued*)

Anticipated Effects of Global Climate Change

Global climate change models anticipate a broad range of impacts. These impacts are believed to be under way already and will begin to manifest significant changes on the environment within the next 25 years and beyond. Many of these changes and impacts have direct implications for the development of land.

North America has a largely urban population; 75 percent of the population lives in cities or the suburban fringe of metropolitan areas. Moreover, 75 percent of the population lives in what are termed *coastal communities*, that is, communities influenced or situated by large bodies of water. The United States is the world leader in the production of greenhouse gases, the human-cause of climate change. As governments around the world have recognized the trends indicating climate change is already occurring, international pressure has been increasing for the United States to change its behavior.

Most climate change models are based on a doubling of carbon dioxide in the atmosphere. Carbon dioxide is a minor constituent in the atmosphere, representing only about 0.03 percent in the atmosphere. At the time the industrial revolution began, there were about 280 parts per million (ppm), down from 1600 ppm about 300 million years ago. Much of the carbon dioxide from earlier epochs has been sequestered in deposits of coal and oil, in peat bogs, and in tundra. In 2008 carbon dioxide was about 385 ppm, approximately a 35 percent increase from the preindustrial revolution level. It is estimated that carbon dioxide is increasing by about 2 percent annually and that a doubling of carbon dioxide over preindustrial revolution levels will occur in the second half of the twenty-first century. Current trends indicate the atmosphere will contain about 500 ppm by 2050 if current practices are not changed. It is anticipated that there will be important changes in world climate with such a rapid and dramatic increase in carbon dioxide levels.

The models used to predict climate change trends are projections based on complex sets of factors. Different models give different results, but in general there is valid and significant agreement on global climate trends. There is a great deal of variability in the climate and weather of the United States and Canada. Projections of these models may have limited use on a local level, but it is important to note that observed changes in weather and climate are consistent with the predictions of global climate change. Uncertainty exists in the models partly because of the limitations of data and science's ability to model something as complex as world climate, but also because it is unknown how people and governments will react to the information. If governments and business respond and reduce the emissions or alternatively increase the sequestration of carbon, for example, the impact and degree of change may be less. All of the models presume a doubling of carbon dioxide by 2100; more recent data from the International Panel on Climate Change (2007) indicates the doubling may occur faster than originally expected. Global average temperature increased 1°F in the twentieth century, but most of the increase occurred in the past 30 years, indicating that the rate of warming is increasing (Table 1.3).

The 2007 report from the Intergovernmental Panel on Climate Change (IPCC) was significant for several reasons. First, it acknowledged that the evidence for human-caused global climate change was "unequivocal." This was the strongest language used in any of the four IPCC reports. Second, the fourth assessment report was the first to rely primarily on observed changes in global climate rather than model-based predictions. Even the best-case scenarios of climate change indicate significant effects, but the effects are not expected to be the same everywhere.

The area of greatest temperature change is expected to be in a zone from northwestern Canada, across southern Canada and the northern United States, to southeastern Canada and the northeastern United States. Average temperatures are rising significantly because the lows are not as low as they used to be. Average temperatures are expected to increase as much as 4°F over the next 100 years. This increase in temperature will decrease the area and length of time of annual snow cover and should result in earlier spring melts. The risk of rain-on-snow storms will also increase, and with it the risk of associated floods. Further, the reductions in snowpack have a direct influence on water supply. For most of the western United States, snowpack is the largest reservoir of water storage and directly affects stream flow.

The world's oceans are warming as well. The temperature of the sea is expected to rise and influence the weather. Thermal expansion of the ocean and increases in runoff

State	Temperature change (°F)				Precipitation change (%)			
	Spring	Summer	Fall	Winter	Spring	Summer	Fall	Winter
Alabama	3	2	4	2	10	15	15	No change
Alaska	5	5	5	10	15	10	Slight change	Slight change
Arizona	3–4	5	3–4	5	20	Slight change	30	60
Arkansas	3	2	3	2	15	25	15	No change
California	<5	5	<5	5	20–30	No change	20–30	>20–30
Colorado	3–4	5–6	3–4	5–6	10	Little change	10	20–70
Connecticut	4	4	4	4	<10–20	<10–20	10–20	>10–20
Delaware	3	4	4	4	<15–40	15–40	<15–40	>15–40
Florida	3–4	3–4	3–4	3–4	Little change	Little change	Little change	Little change
Georgia	3	2	4	3	10	15–40	15–40	10
Hawaii	3	3	3	3	Uncertain of changes	Uncertain of changes	Uncertain of changes	Uncertain of changes
Idaho	4	5	4	5	10	Little change	1	20
Illinois	3	2	4	3	10	25–70	15–50	10
Indiana	3	2	4	3	10	10–50	20	10
Iowa	3	2	4	4	10	20	15	10
Kansas	2	3	4	4	15	15	15	Little change
Kentucky	3	<3	>3	3	20	30	20	<10
Louisiana	3	3	>3	<3	Little change	10	10	Little change
Maine	<4	>4	>4	<4	Little change	10	10	30
Maryland	3	4	4	4	<20	20	<20	20
Massachusetts	4	5	5	4	10	10	15	20–60

Michigan	4	4	4	5–15	20	5–15	5–15
Minnesota	4	<4	4	Little change	15	15	15
Mississippi	3	2	4	10	15	15	Little change
Missouri	3	2	3	15	20–60	15	Little change
Montana	4	4	5	10	10	10	15–40
Nebraska	3	3	4	10	10	10	15
Nevada	3–4	5–6	3–4	15	(10)	30	40
New Hampshire	4	5	5	Little change	10	10	25–60
New Jersey	4	>4	>4	<10–20	10–20	10–20	>10–20
New Mexico	3	5	4	15	Slight decrease	Slight increase	30
New York	4	>4	>4	<10–20	10–20	10–20	>10–20
North Carolina	3	3	3	15	>15	>15	15
North Dakota	4	3	4	5	10	20	25
Ohio	3	3	4	5–25	25	20	5–25
Oklahoma	2	3	3	20	20	Slight increase	Little change
Oregon	4	5	5	Slight increase	Slight decrease	15	15
Pennsylvania	<4	>4	>4	10	20	50	20
Rhode Island	4	5	4	10	10	15	25
South Carolina	3	3	3	15	>15	>15	<15
South Dakota	3	3	4	10	10	10	20
Tennessee	2–3	<2–3	2–3	20	30	20	Slight increase

TABLE 1.3 Anticipated Temperature and Precipitation Impacts of Climate Change (*Continued*)

13

State	Temperature change (°F)				Precipitation change (%)			
	Spring	Summer	Fall	Winter	Spring	Summer	Fall	Winter
Texas	3	4	4	4	10	10	10	(5–30)
Utah	3–4	5–6	3–4	5–6	10	(10)	30	40
Vermont	4	4	5	5	Little change	10	10	30
Virginia	3	3	4	3	20	20	20	20
Washington	4	5	4	5	Little change	Little change	Little change	10
West Virginia	3	3	4	3	20	20	20	>20
Wisconsin	4	<4	4	4	Little change	15–20	15–20	15–30
Wyoming	4	5	4	6	10	Slight decrease	10	30

Adapted from the U.S. EPA.

TABLE 1.3 Anticipated Temperature and Precipitation Impacts of Climate Change (*Continued*)

from glaciers and ice fields are expected to continue and result in rising ocean levels. In places such as Texas and Louisiana, rising seas may be made worse by concurrent land subsidence. The world's oceans are expected to rise by 20 inches or more by 2100. Such an increase has significant implications for coastal communities. An increase in the intensity, though not the frequency, of hurricanes has been observed as the world's oceans have warmed.

Perhaps a more troubling issue is the acidification of the world's oceans. In point of fact the world's oceans are slightly alkaline, but there has been a reduction in the alkalinity of the seas as carbon dioxide levels in the atmosphere have increased. The seas absorb carbon dioxide from the atmosphere and in so doing help to mitigate the accumulation of the gas in the atmosphere. As the amount of carbon dioxide dissolved in seawater increases, so do the hydrogen ions and hence the pH is lowered. As the oceans become more acid, it is expected that there will be a negative impact on calcifiers—organisms that use calcium carbonate to construct shells or skeletons—because calcium carbonate readily dissolves in acidic conditions. These organisms represent an important part of the marine food chain. They include corals and shellfish and are widely distributed throughout the seas. The science on this point is not conclusive; some calcifiers actually became slightly more robust under some circumstances of mild acidification.

As sea levels continue to rise, increases in shore and beach erosion should be anticipated along coastlines. Barrier island communities may experience significant losses. Local and state governments will be required to devise strategies for affected communities that may require significant public expense. Insurance for coastal properties can be expected to rise significantly. Reinsurance companies have reported catastrophic insurance losses associated with weather, increasing to $300 billion worldwide through 2007. Several major insurance companies announced in 2007 that they would no longer write new flood insurance policies for properties within 2500 feet of the mean high tide line in states from Delaware to Mississippi, including waterfront along the Chesapeake Bay. This makes publicly funded insurance the only source of support for affected landowners.

Beach replenishment will become an increasingly expensive and perhaps more futile effort (Table 1.4). Barrier islands should be expected to shift landward in response to deepening oceans. Necessary mitigation methods such as the construction or improvement of existing sea walls or bulkheads or installation of revetments or levees on bayside beaches would add costs to the beach replenishment efforts. It is important to note that some of these costs are already being paid. Sea level rise has significant implications for water supply as well. Saltwater encroachment may become a larger problem as coastline communities continue to grow and groundwater use increases. It is expected that as much as 50 percent of the coastal wetlands will be inundated. Louisiana is currently losing 35 square miles of wetland each year due to saltwater intrusion.

Coastal wetlands generally can adapt to nominal sea level rise and fall. As vegetation experiences seasonal diebacks, decaying detritus adds to the wetland soil and allows the wetland to "lift" in response to moderately rising seas. This capacity is believed to be limited to about a 2 millimeter (mm) per year lift. Sea level rise along much of the eastern coast of the United States has exceeded this rate, and the rate of sea level rise appears to be increasing, in effect drowning the wetlands.

Rising sea levels will also complicate floods on tidal influenced rivers and streams. Increased storm surges may back up streams and change flood plain characteristics. It has been calculated that a sea level rise of 40 inches (1 meter) would result in a flood

State	Cumulative costs of shoreline protection (millions of dollars)
Alabama	60–200
California	174–3,500
Connecticut	500–3,000
Delaware	34–147
Florida	1,700–8,800
Georgia	154–1,800
Hawaii	340–6,000
Louisiana	2,600–6,800
Maine	200–900
Maryland	35–200
Massachusetts	490–2,600
Mississippi	70–140
New Hampshire	39–104
New Jersey (Long Beach Island only)	100–500 bulkheads and sea walls
New York (Manhattan Island only)	30–140 bulkheads and sea walls
North Carolina	660–3,600
Oregon	60–920
Rhode Island	90–150
South Carolina	1,200–9,400
Texas	4,200–12,800
Virginia	200–1,200
Washington	143–2,300

Compiled from U.S. EPA information.

TABLE 1.4   Estimated Cost of Sand Replenishment for a 20-inch Rise in Sea Level

with a frequency of 15 years actually inundating the same area a 100-year flood did previously (Table 1.5). FEMA estimated that rises of 12 and 36 inches would increase the area affected by a 100-year flood from 19,500 square miles to 23,000 and 27,000 square miles, respectively. Damage resulting from these floods would be expected to rise 36 to 58 percent for a 12-inch increase and from 102 to 200 percent for a 36-inch increase.

Precipitation patterns along the Gulf Coast, central and northern plains, and parts of the midwestern and northeastern United States may increase as much as 10 to 20 percent annually. More frequent storms of higher intensity may change the distribution of precipitation and result in less infiltration and a greater amount of runoff. The result would be falling groundwater tables and less water in streams and lakes. The shortened

State	Temperature change +/(-) (°F)	Precipitation[a] (% change)	Sea level change[b]	Anticipated sea level change (inches) (2000–2100)
Alabama (Tuscaloosa)	(0.1)	20	9	20
Alaska (Anchorage)	3.9	10	–	10
Arizona (Tucson)		3.6	20[c]	–
Arkansas (Fayetteville)	0.4	20	–	–
California (Fresno)	1.4	20	3–8	13–19
Colorado (Fort Collins)	4.1	20	–	–
Connecticut (Storrs)	3.4	20	8	22
Delaware (Dover)	1.7	10	12	23
Florida (Ocala)	2	[d]	7–9	18–20
Georgia (Albany)	(0.8)	10	13	25
Hawaii (Honolulu)	4.4	20	6–14	17–25
Idaho (Boise)	<1	20[e]	–	–
Illinois (Decatur)	(0.2)	20	–	–
Indiana (Bloomington)	1.8	10	–	–
Iowa (Des Moines)	(0.02)	20	–	–
Kansas (Manhattan)	1.3	<20	–	–
Kentucky (Frankfort)	(1.4)	10	–	–
Louisiana (New Orleans)	No change	5–20		
Maine (Lewiston)	3.4	20	3.9	14
Maryland (College Park)	2.4	10	7	19
Massachusetts (Amherst)	2	20	11	22
Michigan (Ann Arbor)	1.1	20	–	–
Minnesota (Minneapolis)	1	20	–	–
Mississippi (Jackson)	2.1	20	5	15
Missouri (Jefferson City)	(0.5)	10	–	–
Montana (Helena)	1.3	(20)	–	–
Nebraska (Lincoln)	(0.2)	10[f]	–	–
Nevada (Elko)	0.6	20	–	–
New Hampshire (Hanover)	2	20	7	18
New Jersey (New Brunswick)	1.8	5–10	15	27

TABLE **1.5** Climate and Sea Level Change

State	Temperature change +/(-) (°F)	Precipitation[a] (% change)	Sea level change[b]	Anticipated sea level change (inches) (2000–2100)
New Mexico (Albuquerque)	(0.8)	20	–	–
New York (Albany)	>1	20	10	22
North Carolina (Chapel Hill)	1.2	5	2	12
North Dakota (Bismarck)	1.3	(10)[g]	–	–
Ohio (Columbus)	0.3	10[h]	–	–
Oklahoma (Stillwater)	0.6	20	–	–
Oregon (Corvallis)	2.5	20[i]	4	6
Pennsylvania (Harrisburg)	1.2	20	–	–
Rhode Island (Providence)	3.3	20	2	12.4
South Carolina (Columbia)	1.3	20	9	19
South Dakota (Pierre)	1.6	20	–	–
Tennessee (Nashville)	1	10	–	–
Texas (San Antonio)	0.5	(20)	25	38
Utah (Logan)	1.4	20	–	–
Vermont (Burlington)	0.4	5	–	–
Virginia (Richmond)	0.2[j]	10	12	23.3
Washington (Ellensburg)	1	20	8	19
West Virginia (Charleston)	101	10	–	–
Wyoming (Laramie)	1.5	(20)	–	–

[a]Change may not address all parts of a given state
[b]Rate of change historically
[c]Some parts of Arizona have experienced a 20 percent decline in precipitation
[d]Precipitation has decreased in the south and keys and increased in the north and panhandle
[e]Precipitation has decreased as much as 10 percent in some parts of Idaho
[f]Except in western Nebraska, where precipitation has fallen by 20 percent
[g]Except southeastern part of South Dakota, where precipitation has risen slightly
[h]Precipitation has decreased in southern Ohio
[i]Except leeward side of Cascade Mountains, where precipitation has decreased by 20 percent
[j]Other parts of Virginia have shown a decrease in temperature
Compiled from U.S. EPA information and James G. Titus and Vijay Narayanan. 1995. "The Probability of Sea Level Rise." EPA 230-R98-008.

TABLE 1.5   Climate and Sea Level Change (*Continued*)

snow season may result in less snowpack in western states and earlier runoff. Reservoirs built to collect runoff for use throughout the year may begin to have a longer service period and experience shortages earlier in more frequent dry years. Earlier runoff may result in lower stream and river flows later in the summer as well. Reduced flows could affect hydroelectric production in some places. More frequent and intense rains will result in increases in storm runoff, erosion, and slope instability. The increase in runoff may require a rethinking of the *maximum probable storm* event in many places. It may require retrofitting exiting storm water collection and control devices to retain more water and encourage infiltration.

Paradoxically, along with an increase in precipitation there is expected to be an increase in the number and severity of droughts. Increased temperatures will result in an increase in evaporation and a loss of soil moisture. The loss of soil moisture and the increased runoff associated with more intense storm events may result not only in lower streams and rivers but also in warmer streams and rivers. Cold water fisheries may become endangered in the southern-most ranges. Falling levels in the Great Lakes have already been observed, and it is possible that falling levels could limit commercial traffic in the St. Lawrence River at certain times during dry years. This may be offset, however, by a longer ice-free season in the Great Lakes. The causes of the declining levels in the lakes are still being evaluated, but several causes are thought to be at work: reduced snowfall and rain in the contributing watersheds and the combined effects of gravel mining and widening and dredging the St. Clair River to facilitate commercial traffic. In essence the latter activities may have resulted in an unintended draining of the upper Great Lakes.

An increase in carbon dioxide should result in more robust plant growth. Some have observed that this is the "upside" to global climate change and will increase food and fiber production. Other studies have found that as carbon dioxide levels increase, some plants reduce their rate of photosynthesis. Still others observe that the increased production of plant mass results in an increase in plant litter and thereby changes the carbon-nitrogen ratio in the soil, in effect reducing the amount of nitrogen available for plants. The increase in leaf area will also increase the amount of transpiration, contributing to the drying of soils.

Implications

The implications of climate change may be significant. It is possible that most of the United States will experience an increase in the frequency of precipitation, both in terms of the amount of rainfall and its distribution. Increased erosion and perhaps slope destabilization in some places can be expected with such an increase. Coastal communities may experience an increase in flooding and beach erosion. Flood prone areas may increase in size as the sea levels rise. Public health officials and communities may become more sensitive to areas of standing water as subtropical and tropical diseases expand their range. Design strategies in affected coastal communities may provide significant opportunities for innovation and problem solving.

Site planners and designers will have to respond to these trends in both retrofitting existing facilities and designing new projects. While infiltration will continue to be an important element of site planning, perhaps the wet pond will be less desirable with the spread of West Nile Virus or malaria. Clearly site planners will have to account for the life cycle and habitat preferences of the mosquitoes that transmit such diseases in their design and planning.

Anticipated warming in most places will result in increasing cooling costs for buildings and homeowners. Properly locating a building on the site and planning plantings to lower energy costs will become even more important elements of the site plan. As temperatures increase, plants growing at their southern range may be subject to significant heat and increasing drought-related stresses. Some places may see a shift in "native species," particularly those living at the margins of their tolerance.

Land Use

Since World War II the growth of suburban development has been the most important and possibly the most environmentally damaging trend. At the beginning of the twenty-first century more people live in the suburbs than in the former urban centers. There has been a growing awareness that suburbs as they have evolved are unsustainable, but that awareness has done little to slow growth or change consumer preference. There is a general acknowledgment that cities offer a greater cultural experience, but populations have not started to return in significant numbers. People have voted with their feet and their checkbooks and shown their preference for suburban living over city living. Builders respond to market demand; they do not, for the most part, create it. Changing such a trend would require changes to public policy that are politically difficult, if not impossible, to achieve. Local ordinances tend to favor low-density development and highways rather than parks and higher-density development. It is difficult for planners and designers to influence this trend on a site-by-site basis, but planners and designers can address the impacts of suburban development through design. Figure 1.5 illustrates the effect of urban or suburban expansion without population growth. As sprawl continues, we consume more and more land per person, more infrastructure per person, and have a greater environmental impact as well.

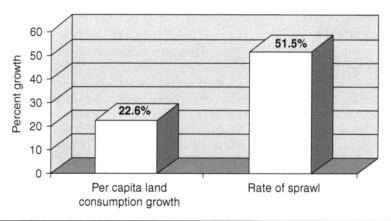

Figure 1.5 Growth in per capita land consumption compared to overall sprawl rate. The overall rate of sprawl was more than double the growth of per capita land consumption (1970–1990) in the average of the one hundred largest U.S. urbanized areas. (*Source:* U.S. Bureau of Census reports on Urbanized Areas, 1970 to 1990.)

Figure 1.6   A traditional street and neighborhood. In surveys people express a preference for neighborhoods with traditional characteristics such as narrower streets and shopping and recreation within walking distance.

Paradoxically, many people living in the suburbs seem to prefer what might be considered urban values and character. The National Association of Home Builders (NAHB) study (Currens, 2004) found that those surveyed would prefer to live within walking distance of schools, shops, and community facilities (Fig. 1.6). The study also found that in spite of the standard practices of most zoning ordinances people would rather live in a place with narrower streets and more public open space (Fig. 1.7). During a time when American families have become smaller by nearly half, new houses have ballooned to more than twice their previous size. As the population has become older, however, there is an increasing interest in smaller homes. In some metropolitan areas most of the homes built and purchased are townhouses and condominiums. Part of this popularity may be due to the cost of housing in urban areas, but many of these units are higher-end dwellings located near shopping or social and cultural features of the city.

The popularity of the southwestern United States has its own significant challenges (Fig. 1.8). The influx of people from more humid parts of the country has brought with it an expectation of life and an aesthetic that often is simply out of place in the desert. The native people of these dry places have long ago found ways to live that recognized the character of their region. Our culture is faced with learning and acting on the lessons already known by so many, but our footprint is so much larger and deeper. It remains to be seen whether we can find ways to live sustainably and successfully in the desert.

FIGURE **1.7**   A contemporary urban neighborhood.

FIGURE **1.8**   Homes should reflect their region and environmental characteristics as does this development in the southwest.

The southeastern United States is also growing and facing problems with water supply as well as significant declines in other environmental indicators such as air quality, biodiversity, and human health. This move to the south and the suburbs leaves many cities with declining populations and tax bases but faced with underutilized infrastructure and the remains of an industrial past that lasted only 50 years in many places. Brownfield opportunities in cities in the last few years have provided designers with unique challenges. This requires a different mind-set and more than a few new skills. Site designers must confront the impacts of industrial contamination; we can no longer assume that a site is healthy. Professional boundaries often blur within the context of these projects, and design professionals may find themselves working on more diverse project teams as they search for innovative solutions to complex problems.

Energy

It is widely believed that the world is facing a time of increasing energy supply issues. The modern global economy and the U.S. economy have grown in part on the foundation of relatively inexpensive energy primarily provide by various forms of fossil fuels. We have leveraged the tremendous concentration of energy found in these fuels to create ever-more productive processes and systems, which in turn enabled the production of lower cost products, faster, cheaper transportation, and new materials. Today the United States is the largest consumer of oil in the world but produces less than 50 percent of its consumption. In 1994 the United States consumed 17.7 million barrels of oil each day (mb/day). By 2007 that amount increased 17 percent to 20.7 mb/day. China's consumption in that time rose 140 percent from 3.16 to 7.58 mb/day. Other Asian nations also increased oil consumption 60 percent in this time as they moved toward ever-more modern economies. Total world oil production of OPEC and non-OPEC producers in 1994 was 75.76 mb/day. By 2007 this had risen to 85.36 mb/day, an increase of 12.6 percent. Total reported global demand for oil in 2007 was 85.36 percent. Even a cursory review of global oil production trends suggests the time of oil surpluses has ended. Ever-growing demand will result in higher energy costs and tighter supply, and energy conservation and efficiency will become more important considerations in development of all forms. Buildings represent a significant source of energy demand associated with land development, and site designers will be called upon to participate more broadly and to contribute to the new principles that are already being used in the marketplace.

Water

Much of the United States enjoys an adequate supply of water although the amount of precipitation and surface water availability declines as we move from east to west (see Table 1.5). Local variability is significant, ranging from 1 inch per year in the southwest to more than 60 inches per year in the southeast. Such variability suggests the difficulty in finding wide-ranging solutions. Although water is a renewable resource, supply issues do exist and promise to become more significant as time passes. Annual natural variations in precipitation can result in local and regional water management issues and conflicts. It is unclear to what degree these natural variations will be exacerbated at the local level by climate change, but most climatologists agree that extreme weather events and patterns will become more frequent and more persistent. This suggests that periods of wet or dry weather patterns may last longer and be more intense. Water policy tends to be a regional concern, but clearly there is a role for the site planner in water management issues.

Water supply is an issue in many localities and efforts at water conservation in communities in the southwestern and western states are notable. In recent years concerns with supply have become greater in the eastern states as well as populations grow and demand rises. Water use on a per capita basis peaked in 1975, but population has increased dramatically since then so total water use continues to rise, albeit more slowly. Planners generally use a figure of 100 gallons per day per person for planning based on historic records, but this figure includes only domestic use by individuals. Most water is used for other purposes including irrigation, power generation, and commercial use. In general as a community grows, water demand increases several times faster than the domestic use alone would indicate. In 1990 water use in the United States was about 1300 gallons per person per day. About 70 percent of this is withdrawn but eventually returned to the source; the remaining water is "consumed."

There are limited practical opportunities to develop or expand new sources of potable water. These include recycling water, desalinization, expanding the use of existing sources, and conservation. Recycling water through gray water systems and other approaches have been successful in many places, but most often they are used in limited applications. The cost of recycling water on a community basis is at least several times more expensive than developing new public or community water. Desalinization is energy intensive, and though technologies in recent decades have reduced the cost of desalinized water, it remains an expensive source of water. As energy costs continue to rise, the cost of desalinized water also may rise unless new advances can keep pace. Desalinization may be affordable in areas where brackish water is to be treated; however, affordability is relative to community resources. Expanding withdrawal from existing sources may be more affordable, but as pressure on these resources increases so does their vulnerability to the effects of drought.

Conservation is the most affordable and practical approach to the water issues facing communities. Designers have an important role to play in water conservation. It is recommended that low-impact design be utilized to reduce the water demand of a site and to maximize the amount of runoff retained on the site. Employing vegetated swales, constructing rain gardens, using permeable paving, and reducing lawn areas are important elements of water conservation in the site design. The use of gray water and recycled water for landscape purposes, selecting native plants, and collecting and storing runoff on site also contribute to reducing the impact of site development. Working with architects to install green roofs and designing on-site sewage collection systems can also be part of the conservation strategy.

Site design and planning today have started to move beyond the practices and paradigm of the past. Designers working in the contemporary marketplace are or soon will be expected to bring solutions to the problems discussed in this chapter for their clients. While many of the professionals' familiar skills will still be needed and valuable, they will undoubtedly be informed by the emerging considerations and concerns of the communities and clients they serve.

CHAPTER 2

Sustainability and the "Green" Site

The site exists as part of a larger landscape and ecosystem, and sustainable site design must include broad considerations of the environmental role of the site as well as the program or intention of the project. Sustainable design must recognize and retain as many of the functional elements of a site as possible but also consider the relationships between the site under consideration and the community at large.

Change tends to come slowly to the land development process, but it does come eventually. In 2008 California became the first state to pass a statewide building code requiring water and energy conservation. A number of large cities have passed ordinances requiring green roofs, and more than 280 local governments in the United States have committed to energy conservation and greenhouse gas reductions. States are committing to green development policies for public construction, and some are offering incentives to the private sector to do the same. Many communities are requiring greener development, better street design, and more sensible use of resources and capital. These development trends embrace a sustainable environment and a robust economy, which are not mutually exclusive concepts as they are often portrayed today. Sustainability is not and cannot be antidevelopment; instead, it is the basis for thoughtful, intelligent, and rational development.

Change brings many challenges. As we begin to think about sustainability and land development, it is important to note the contribution land development and construction make to our economic well-being. Nationwide about 5.5 percent of the workforce is directly employed by the construction industry, approximately 7.7 million jobs in 2005. Residential and commercial construction typically represents about 10 percent of the gross domestic product of the United States. After mortgage debt is removed, the net value of developed real estate in the United States is about $11 trillion. This does not include the value of roads or other civic infrastructure. Real estate represents the largest source of personnel wealth and savings for most Americans. Construction and development represent important economic activities. With the growth in population we can expect demand for more development: more homes and more commercial space. Studies by Woods Hole Research Center (2007) and the University of Ohio (Irwin and Bockstael, 2007) suggest that in parts of the United States development could increase by as much as 60 percent by 2030. In this same time frame, much of the infrastructure and most of the buildings in the United States will reach the end of their initial design life. Retrofitting and updating the existing "pre-green" built environment represents its own challenges and opportunities.

The issue is not whether we will have development but rather what that development will be. What construction methods will we employ? What materials will we use? How will the form of our designs reflect the more thoughtful and less harmful function of our projects? The impacts and issues discussed in Chap. 1 suggest that a move toward sustainable development is not only desirable but quite necessary. A plan that is concerned with sustainability cannot consider the building and the site as separate elements because they interact in important ways. This interaction is the concern of this chapter.

Sustainable Development Principles

Our cultural context for sustainability is in its infancy, but the dialogue is well under way. Important voices are encouraging us not to go back but forward, and to solve problems through design. Although no single set of guidelines has emerged, there is a growing recognition of the principles that lead to sustainable design and development. The groundwork for sustainable design was established by Christopher Alexander and Ian McHarg as early as the 1970s. Today the views of leaders such as William McDonough and Emory Lovins are moving into boardrooms and legislatures and are beginning to change the expectations of design professionals.

This discussion of principles will necessarily be incomplete because so many efforts are occurring on so many fronts that it is impossible to capture the full range of subjects completely. The Sustainable Sites Initiative, a partnership led by the American Society of Landscape Architects, the United States Botanical Garden, and the Lady Bird Johnson Wildflower Center, is collaborating to create voluntary national guidelines and performance benchmarks for sustainable land design, construction, and maintenance practices. The initiative is a dynamic undertaking with the objective of producing a series of reports to serve the practitioner and the concerned public. Among the first of its products is the "Guidelines and Principles of Sustainable Sites." Produced in draft form in 2008, this report provides an excellent overview and specific assessments of what should be considered first principles for site designers. The draft includes numerous case studies, summarizes measurement and analytical tools, and makes the argument for sustainable sites from a number of perspectives. These first principles are summarized in Table 2.1.

The definitions of "sustainable development" are too numerous to count, and the phrase is in danger of becoming another meaningless mantra. But design professionals need to recognize the intellectual and professional challenge of finding a workable balance with nature. This is an important time for design professionals, and architects have made important advances in green buildings, although the practices are not main stream yet. Guidelines for sustainable site development practices are listed in Table 2.2, but most examples of their use are notable because they are still unusual. We must move to a marketplace of ideas and practices that make these examples unremarkable.

Sustainable site planning must include considerations of the impact of development on the local ecosystem, the global ecosystem, and the future. Principles of "green site work" encourage the designer to consider the nature of the building materials, the flows of energy, and materials required for the life of the project. The designer should consider the life cycle costs of the materials being used, the ultimate disposition of the site and the materials, and ways in which these environmental impacts can be reduced or mitigated.

The longer the useful life of a building or a site the longer the environment has to "amortize" the impacts, but designing a site with an extended life span requires the designer to consider future uses and changes and to incorporate that thinking into the

Do no harm

Make no changes to the site that will degrade the surrounding environment. Promote projects on sites where previous disturbance or development presents an opportunity to regenerate ecosystem services through sustainable design.

Precautionary principle

Be cautious in making decisions that could create risk to human and environmental health. Some actions can cause irreversible damage. Examine the full range alternatives—including no action—and be open to contributions from all affected parties.

Design with nature and culture

Create and implant designs that are responsive to economic, environmental, and cultural conditions with respect to the local, regional, and global context.

Use a decision-making hierarchy of preservation, conservation, and regeneration

Maximize and mimic the benefits of ecosystem services by preserving existing environmental features, conserving resources in a sustainable manner, and regenerating lost or damaged ecosystem services.

Provide regenerative systems as intergenerational equity

Provide future generations with a sustainable environment supported by regenerative systems and endowed with regenerative resources.

Support a living process

Continuously reevaluate assumptions and values and adapt to demographic and environmental change.

Use a systems thinking approach

Understand and value the relationships in an ecosystem and use an approach that reflects and sustains ecosystems services; reestablish the integral and essential relationship between natural processes and human activity.

Use a collaborative and ethical approach

Encourage direct and open communication among colleagues, clients, manufacturers, and users to link long-term sustainability with ethical responsibility.

Maintain integrity in leadership and research

Implement transparent and participatory leadership, develop research with technical rigor, and communicate new findings in a clear, consistent, and timely manner.

Foster environmental stewardship

In all aspects of land development and management, foster an ethic of environmental stewardship—an understanding that responsible management of healthy ecosystems improves the quality of life for present and future generations.

Source: "Guidelines and Principles of Sustainable Sites" 2008 draft report. The Sustainable Sites Initiative, U.S. Botanic Garden, Washington, D.C. Reprinted with permission from the *Sustainable Sites Initiative Guidelines and Performance Benchmarks Draft 2008*. The Sustainable Sites Initiative is an interdisciplinary effort by the American Society of Landscape Architects, the Lady Bird Johnson Wildflower Center, and the United States Botanic Garden to create voluntary national guidelines and performance benchmarks for sustainable land design, construction, and maintenance practices.

TABLE 2.1   Guiding Principles of a Sustainable Site

1. Minimize cooling loads through careful building location and landscaping.
2. Utilize renewable energy resources to meet site energy demand for lighting.
3. Install energy-efficient lighting.
4. Use existing buildings and infrastructure instead of developing in "greenfields."
5. Design to create or contribute to a sense of community.
6. Design to reduce dependence on the automobile.
7. Reduce material use or increase the efficiency of material use.
8. Protect and preserve the local ecosystem. Maintain the environmental function of the site.
9. Specify low-impact.
10. Design site and buildings for longevity and to be recycled.
11. Design to minimize the use and runoff of water.
12. Minimize waste.

TABLE 2.2   Guidelines for Green Site Planning and Design

design. The most sustainable development is redevelopment; reuse increases density and eliminates the loss of open space. Materials should be selected on the basis of durability and low environmental impact. Recycled materials are of low impact and efficient. Better than recycling materials is the reuse of entire buildings. Many construction materials have significant environmental impacts either in the manufacturing process or in their final disposition as waste material. Others contain ozone-depleting compounds that continue to volatilize and pollute even after installation.

Reducing the impact of development may be possible by reducing the footprint of a building either by modifying the footprint to the most efficient shape or by building multiple stories. Reducing the surface area of a structure will reduce energy requirements as well.

Sites should be designed to treat storm water as a resource, capturing runoff and encouraging infiltration, and should use water efficiently. Use native plants suited to the local climate and precipitation and practice "dryscaping" techniques where applicable (Figs. 2.1 and 2.2). Site planning should incorporate the existing environmental function of a site to the extent possible. Wetlands and important ecosystem elements such as habitat, tree masses, and stream corridors should be preserved. The ubiquitous lawn has a notoriously high environmental impact because of the requirements for pesticides, fertilizers, need for irrigation, and continual mowing. Lawns should be minimized and replaced with native species of plants selected for their aesthetic quality and drought resistance. Buildings and tree masses can be positioned to minimize cooling costs.

Green development encompasses a range of design, construction, and operational approaches that reduce the environmental impacts of development and promote human health, well-being, and productivity. Variously called sustainable design, green architecture, restorative design, or ecodesign, these approaches share the following elements:

- Use of regionally available, sustainably harvested, low impact, and reused/recycled materials
- Design sensitivity to energy use, the incorporation of energy conservation, and renewable energy generation

FIGURE 2.1   The headquarters of the Chesapeake Bay Foundation is a LEED Platinum Certified building and site. Note the meadow of native plants. (See also color insert.)

FIGURE 2.2   The Chesapeake Bay Foundation site includes a crushed stone parking area and native vegetation. (See also color insert.)

- Water conservation
- Waste minimization
- Incorporation of natural light, appropriate ventilation, and human scales
- Design and construction techniques that evaluate and minimize environmental impacts
- Site development practices that minimize and mitigate impacts

More than 80 percent of all buildings in the United States were built since 1960, and the impacts of development and urbanization are well understood. As the serious environmental effects associated with greenhouse gas emissions have become known, the parts played by buildings and development have been more closely scrutinized. The Department of Energy (Battels and Burns, 2000) reports that 82 percent of the human-caused greenhouse gas emissions are energy-related carbon emissions, and of that 48 percent of the increase in emissions since 1990 is attributable to increasing emissions from the building sector. In fact, buildings (residential and commercial) are responsible for more greenhouse gas emissions than either the industrial or transportation sectors.

Energy efficiency is a central concern of green development, and 50 percent of U.S. electricity is generated by burning coal, the least efficient and dirtiest of the major fuel sources. (Energy efficiency is measured as the amount of energy expended for each unit of gross domestic product.) Since the 1970s, the energy efficiency of U.S. buildings has remained flat, but the number of buildings has grown exponentially. Since the early 1990s, the European Union (EU) has sought to increase energy efficiency across the board, and in 2002 the EU passed rules requiring efficiency in commercial and government buildings. The contemporary office building in the EU is four times more energy efficient than its counterpart in the United States (Fig. 2.3). In addition to these environmental advantages, the EU building is 75 percent less expensive to operate.

Energy efficiency in buildings can be improved through the use of natural light, building orientation, and material selection. Green buildings are healthier and more productive spaces than traditional construction. The increased natural light is among the commonly appreciated features found in green buildings. Careful selection of materials such as floor and wall coverings and the design of a building to passively move air can contribute to cleaner indoor air. As global energy supplies tighten due to increased demand and pressure mounts to respond to global climate change, institutions and business can take a positive step through green building. The costs of green buildings are typically no different or only nominally higher than traditional construction, and the life cycle savings and operation costs are significant. Lower energy costs and reduced water use and waste generation are the most common areas of savings. Green buildings are healthier and constitute a more desirable working and learning space.

Measuring Performance

Some buildings are considered "high performing" because of energy efficiencies, but these buildings are generally not "green" in a strict sense. Green buildings exist on a continuum ranging from fairly straightforward attempts to reduce the environmental footprint of a building to very sophisticated structures. Several guidelines have emerged to guide and measure the process of designing, building, and operating a green building.

FIGURE 2.3 A green roof, which reduces storm water runoff and rooftop albedo and increases energy efficiency. (*Source: Image courtesy of Roofscapes, Inc.* See also color insert.)

The National Institute of Standards and Technology (NIST) developed the Building for Economic and Environmental Sustainability (BEES) model with support from the EPA and HUD. This approach evaluates the life cycle costs and environmental impacts of building materials in 10 areas of concern, which enables designers or builders to determine the environmental loading of a material before they specify its use. The American Society for Testing and Materials (ASTM) has also developed an approach for evaluating the life cycle costs of building materials (Standard Guide for Environmental Life Cycle Assessment of Building Materials/Products, E 1991–98). This is a broad-based approach that includes consideration of embodied energy, raw materials acquisition, and environmental impacts.

The best-known approach is the U.S. Green Building Council's Leadership in Energy and Environmental Design (LEED) program. This comprehensive approach is chief among the reasons LEED-certified buildings have been shown to have significantly lower operating costs and healthier and more productive occupants in addition to protecting the environment. Unlike BEES and the ASTM method, LEED does not certify materials or processes, although these standards might be used by designers specifying for a LEED project.

The U.S. Green Building Council (GBC) created and oversees the LEED program, and in 2009 several notable changes were undertaken. First, the LEED certification process was moved from the GBC to the Green Building Certification Institute, which was created for this purpose and gives the certification process a degree of third-party credibility. The second significant change was adoption of the LEED 2009 update in November 2008, which provides for regional credits that reflect issues that may be of greater concern in a given area. The program provides greater weight for credits that reflect concern with climate change and energy efficiency. The LEED process is a consensus standard, and changes reflect a process of collecting input from across the building industry, reiterative comment periods, and a final vote by about 18,000 member organizations.

LEED certified professionals are employed in the planning, design, and construction processes. Projects are evaluated in five areas of concern:

- Site design and planning
- Energy use
- Water management
- Materials resources and waste
- Indoor environmental quality

Specific guidelines are published for each area, and a Green Building Rating System describes how design choices will be rated in terms of LEED points.

A detailed review of the rating system is beyond the scope of this book, but a LEED certified building generally will utilize the following considerations:

- Consideration of building position for solar access and wind direction, with regard to energy impacts
- Materials selection subject to environmental and life cycle considerations
- Design for energy efficiency and performance
- Design and select materials and equipment with consideration for high-quality indoor air
- Minimize waste in construction and operations
- Weigh capital costs savings against operation cost savings
- Use of published measurement strategies such as LEED

Sustainable site concerns include the following:

- Landscaping for energy efficiency
- Rethinking grounds maintenance to eliminate toxins
- Reducing water consumption through design, plant selection, and maintenance practices
- Being aware of site specific concerns (e.g., soil limitations)
- Accommodating access, possibly including public transportation
- Using site features to contribute to building performance
- Locating buildings with regard to solar and seasonal influence
- Maximizing local energy alternatives

Benefits to green buildings extend beyond the environmental performance of the building. Green buildings have been found to increase worker and student productivity as much as 6 to 12 percent. Such significant improvements have been made in worker productivity in these high-performing buildings that companies almost cannot afford not to build green! Similar improvements have been seen in less worker turnover (Fahet, 2005).

The nature of the activities in buildings is so variable that it is difficult to draw meaning from broad claims. By looking at a narrower type of building, we may be able to cautiously draw some general conclusions regarding some advantages of green buildings and sites. A sufficient number of green school buildings have been constructed to provide a basis of study. Simply put, performance improves in green schools. Studies have found that indoor air quality and classroom lighting have direct effects on both teacher and student performance (Heschong Mahone Group, 1999). Green buildings commonly feature significant day lighting, and the character of day lighting is carefully considered and controlled. The quality of air and the acoustics within the classroom also have a direct influence on student learning. The available studies focused on elementary and secondary schools, and the results are notable. For example, improvements in lighting alone were correlated with 7 to 18 percent higher scores in the end-of-year examinations over classrooms without such improvements. Students in the improved classrooms also did 20 percent better on math exams and 26 percent better on reading tests. This suggests that a deeper understanding of building environments is important.

Capital Cost Implications

The data on the cost of green buildings are difficult to synthesize or reduce to any specific building project. In general, it is more cost-effective to build green ideas into a new building or site, although retrofitting offers advantages in some cases. Cost comparisons are difficult to assess because true or life cycle costs of traditional construction are rarely accounted for. For example, green materials tend to be more durable than traditional construction. This may result in higher construction or development costs but a much longer life cycle and fewer maintenance costs. Since capital costs and operational costs are not usually considered together, the life cycle costs cannot be compared. In general, green construction is cost competitive for capital projects and is more cost-efficient from the operations standpoint. Figures routinely used in the literature suggest that green architecture increases construction costs 2 to 11 percent (Kats et al., 2003).

Among the most comprehensive studies of the cost of green buildings was the 2004 Davis Langdon study, which compared the costs of green architecture to traditional architecture from two perspectives: (1) what would the cost difference be between a traditional building and the same building as a green building, and (2) a direct comparison of 45 buildings seeking LEED certification and 93 buildings not seeking any green certification. LEED uses a point system to guide choices that range from building location and orientation, building materials, landscaping, water and energy conservation, and light pollution to transportation. Eligible buildings may apply for and be recognized as Certified or Silver, Gold, or Platinum Certified, depending on the number of points they achieve (see Fig. 2.1). In general the Davis Langdon study drew the following conclusions:

- Most green buildings can meet the goals of LEED within or nearly within the original program budget.
- Many non-LEED buildings included green elements for purposes of operational efficiency without specific regard to environmental performance or certification.

- The key to the cost performance of green buildings lies in the program planning phase, the expertise of the project team, and project management/oversight (Davis Langdon, 2004).

The costs of green buildings have also been evaluated in a study commissioned by the U.S. General Services Administration (GSA). The 2004 study evaluated the costs for buildings seeking Certified, Silver, and Gold LEED ratings. The study only considered courthouses and building modernization but concluded costs may range widely depending on the rating being sought. In cases where low or no cost features are used, the study found "the overall cost premium [to be] surprisingly limited, even at higher rating levels. Under certain conditions it is possible to show a slight decrease overall" (Steven Winter Associates, 2004).

These and other studies demonstrate that the capital costs of green buildings are often no more or only nominally more than those for traditional buildings. The Davis Langdon (2004) study strongly suggests that cost performance can be related to management of the process from planning through construction. Other studies have indicated that although costs may rise slightly as greater efficiency is designed into buildings, the rate of savings increases more dramatically.

Operating Costs

Operation cost data are highly variable, but green building savings are most often associated with lower energy costs. Electricity cost savings are in the range of 45 to 55 percent. Some sophisticated energy conservation systems have a payback period of 7 to 9 years, but more common energy efficiency features have a payback of less than 2 years. Kats et al. (2003) looked specifically at public buildings and found that the median payback period for increased capital cost was 2.6 years or less. High-performing buildings saved, on average, $0.87 per square foot per year in lower energy costs, and 3 percent of the savings was derived from more efficient lighting and load responsive HVAC equipment. Water use can be reduced by as much as 90 percent, but savings of around 50 percent are more common.

Among the chief advantages to green buildings are the excellent life cycle costs. It is estimated that the life cycle savings of the typical green building is 10 times the initial investment. That is, for every $100,000 in initial capital investment, a savings of $1 million is achieved over the life of the building (Weidt Group, 2005).

Green Building Materials

The choice of building materials is as important as the site design or choice of construction methods. Designers have significant influence over the materials used through the specifications made in the design and planning. Many designers are not aware of the implications of choosing one material over another beyond cost and specific performance criteria. Site designers have fewer material choices than architects, but awareness of site materials is just as important. As a matter of practice, materials should be selected in part because of their durability. The process of manufacturing materials is energy and material intensive, and durable materials usually require less maintenance over a longer service life. Materials that require less maintenance or maintenance that has a lower environmental impact are preferred. Heavily processed or manufactured materials have a higher embodied energy; that is, greater energy inputs are required to manufacture the product than a material with a lower embodied energy. Locally produced products require less transportation energy and produce less pollution. Designers should seek durable, locally produced, low-maintenance products with low embodied energy ratings. For example, local hardwoods are preferable to tropical woods, and local stone to imported stone.

The best choice for materials may be recycled materials. Using recycled materials reduces solid waste, eliminates the energy of manufacturing, and reduces the impact on natural resources. Some ways of using recycled materials in site work include specifying the use of fly ash in concrete, furniture made from recycled plastic, and pavement containing ground tires. Avoid materials with toxins such as pressure treated lumber by specifying alternatives such as recycled plastic lumber.

Choosing a green building material involves consideration of the entire life cycle of the material: the manufacture of the material, the impacts of its use, its distribution and service life, and finally its disposal. Every stage of the material's life involves energy use and environmental impacts. The BEES life cycle assessment model evaluates 10 impacts of building materials:

1. Global warming potential
2. Acidification potential
3. Eutrophication potential
4. Natural resource depletion
5. Indoor air quality impacts
6. Solid waste impacts
7. Smog
8. Ecological toxicity
9. Human toxicity
10. Ozone depletion

Each of the calculations involves converting impacts to a known and given reference point provided in the BEES documentation. The program then calculates the environmental loading of the product to allow designers to compare alternative materials. BEES software is available from the National Institute of Standards and Technology (NIST) along with a manual that describes the use of the software, explains the algorithms, and provides examples of material and product data already evaluated using BEES.

ASTM Standard Guide for Environmental Life Cycle Assessment of Building Materials/Products (E 1991–98) describes a four-step process for conducting a Life Cycle Assessment (LCA): definition of goals, analysis of inventory, impact assessment, and interpretation of findings. The LCA is comprehensive and includes considerations of embodied energy, raw materials acquisition, environmental impacts from cradle to grave, and performance. Other more approachable methods have also emerged through public and private green building initiatives throughout the world. Many of these organizations have established standards or thresholds that products must meet to be listed as "green." Most of the work has been done on materials used in buildings, but materials used in site development are not without their environmental "signature." The general requirements for green building materials are summarized in Table 2.3.

1. Products made from recycled or salvaged materials.
2. Products made from wood harvested from Forest Stewardship Council certified forests.
3. Products made from materials that are renewable in the short term (10 years or less).
4. Products that do not contain toxics or environmentally damaging materials.
5. Products (or methods) that reduce the material volume required.
6. Products that reduce environmental impacts during the manufacturing process, construction, renovation, or demolition.
7. Products (or methods) that are energy efficient or that reduce the heating and cooling loads on a building.
8. Products that are reusable or recyclable.
9. Local products rather than products from far away.

TABLE 2.3   Green Building Material Requirements

The American Society for Testing and Materials (ASTM) Subcommittee on Sustainability has developed a Standard Practice for Data Collection for Sustainability Assessment of Building Products (E-2129). This standard includes a checklist to guide the process of evaluating the environmental character of products. Most of the processed or manufactured materials specified in site work are related to paving, utility, or storm water pipes. Even with these few categories of materials, a wide range of choices is available for designers to consider.

Pipe Materials

Pipes are selected primarily for storm water drainage, sanitary sewage conveyance, or the distribution of water. Water systems commonly required ductile iron or steel pipe, but there are many choices of material for storm water and sewage collection. Selecting pipe materials might be a matter of complying with local ordinance or preference, but selecting materials should also involve an understanding of the costs and benefits of the possible choices.

ABS

ABS (acrylonitrile-butadienne-styrene) is used primarily as waste and storm water pipe. ABS is lighter than PVC but is more than twice as expensive. ABS has almost twice the thermal expansion of PVC, but the resin material from which it is made is expensive to manufacture. ABS manufacturing involves a number of toxic materials and environmental impacts, and instances of off-quality material in the marketplace have resulted in failures in the field.

Cast Iron

Many building codes still require cast iron pipe, but these tend to be more a reflection of political and economic pressures than the value of the material itself. Cast iron is durable and has a low thermal expansion coefficient, but its great weight and associated labor costs would seem to offset those values. Cast iron is no more durable than PVC, for example, and the energy and environmental impacts of cast iron pipe manufacture are quite high.

Concrete Pipe

Although very durable and resistant to wear, concrete pipe is heavy and expensive to install. It is still required in some local and state codes because of its durability. The strength of concrete makes it useful in applications in which there is minimal cover or where significant loads are expected.

HDPE

HDPE (high-density polyethylene) is the lowest cost, lightest, and most flexible of the pipe materials. HDPE is relatively simple to manufacture, and it is the most easily recycled pipe material. It is manufactured in long sections familiar as the coils of pipe material often used to reline old pipelines and sewers. For all of its positive characteristics, HDPE suffers from the greatest expansion coefficient of any of the popular pipe materials—more than twice the thermal expansion of PVC—which limits is usefulness for many applications.

PVC

PVC (polyvinyl chloride) is widely used because it is high strength, lightweight, low cost, easy to work with, and durable. It is used in a wide array of products, but for site concerns it is used primarily as pipe or site furniture. About 60 percent of the PVC in the United States is used in the construction industry. Available pipe diameters in PVC range from 1/8 inch to 36 inch. Nearly all wastewater sewers constructed in the United States today are built of PVC pipe.

Manufacturing PVC has some environmental costs. Vinyl chloride is a carcinogen produced from ethylene and chlorine. PVC manufacturing produces about 4.6 million pounds of vinyl chloride emissions each year. PVC manufacturing has been associated with the presence of dioxin in the environment, but research has not established a clear risk associated with the quantities observed. More dioxin, one of the most toxic substances known, is produced when PVC is burned, however.

Some concerns associated with the decomposition of PVC are associated primarily with architectural or electrical uses of plasticized PVC and do not appear to be relevant to the exterior site applications of the material. PVC is difficult to recycle; a wide range of formulations are used in different products, making it difficult to use the material in the manufacture of postconsumer goods. Incinerating PVC is problematic because it has low fuel value and it turns into hydrochloric acid as it burns, increasing the wear on incinerators.

Many products made of PVC have formulations that include lead and other toxins. Although these products are not usually associated with site development applications, there is noteworthy concern about the environmental costs and impacts of PVC manufacturing, use, and disposal. Calls for stopping the manufacture of PVC because of these concerns have been raised.

Vitrified Clay Pipe

Vitrified clay pipe (VCP) has been largely replaced by the use of PVC, but it still has some applications. Many VCP installations have been in use well over a hundred years. It is durable, resistant to chemical corrosion, and has the lowest thermal expansion coefficient of any pipe material. The weight of VCP (8.9 lbs per ft for a 4-in. VCP versus 2.0 lbs. per ft for a 4-in. Schedule 40 PVC) leads to more handling and greater labor costs for installation. As PVC has become the material of choice, the availability of VCP has dropped in some areas.

Recycled Plastic Pipe

Recycled plastic pipe (RPP) is available as a stock item in Canada, Australia, and Europe but usually requires a custom order in the United States. Early attempts at RPP were reported to suffer from a number of quality issues ranging from variations in material hardness to load bearing capacity. As with many products, quality has improved with experience. RPP offers an opportunity to reuse plastics that might otherwise be dumped in a landfill or burned. The pipe is manufactured in corrugated and smooth surfaces for use as storm water and sewer pipe.

Cement and Concrete

Concrete is widely used in all types of construction because of its ability to be cast in a desired form and its durability once it is cured. Cement manufacturing and concrete mixing is a large business sector involving about 210 cement plants and almost 5000 ready-mix plants in the United States. Most ready-mix concrete for residential purposes is approximately 12 percent cement. The most common cement used is Portland cement.

Manufacturing cement involves mixing a source of calcium (usually limestone) with finely ground additives (such as bauxite or iron ore) in a rotary kiln heated to about 2700°F (1480°C). As the kiln mixes the heated materials, a series of chemical reactions occurs. The materials form a molten mass that is cooled and then ground to a powder, which is mixed with some gypsum to become cement. The cement is mixed with sand, aggregate, water, and possible admixtures specified to control setting time or plasticity of the final material.

Environmental Considerations

The raw materials of cement are common enough. It takes about 3400 pounds of raw material to produce 2000 pounds of finished concrete. The most significant environmental impacts of cement manufacturing and concrete use are the amount of energy consumed, the energy-associated emissions of carbon dioxide and other greenhouse and acid-forming pollutants, the dust that results from the manufacturing process, the pollution impact on surface waters from run-off, and "washout water."

Manufacturing cement is an energy-intensive process involving burning fossil fuels to generate the high temperatures of the rotary kiln. Some cement plants have been converted to burn hazardous wastes or other solid waste to extract the energy value. The high temperature of the kiln provides fairly complete combustion with low levels of residual air pollution. According to the Portland Cement Association, a single cement kiln can consume more than a million tires each year. Other elements of concrete do not require the substantial energy inputs of cement manufacturing, and the use of fly ash in concrete reduces the energy load even more (Cockram, 2006).

In addition to the energy costs, there are environmental impacts associated with fugitive dusts. The EPA estimates that for every ton of cement manufactured 360 pounds of alkaline dust is generated. Much of this dust is generated during the manufacturing process, but some occurs in handling and transporting the cement and in the mixing process. At the cement manufacturing plant, much of the dust is captured in baghouses or by other pollution control equipment. Some of the dust is used for agricultural soil amendments, but much of it is used for landfill. Dust generated at ready-mix facilities and construction sites generally is not controlled.

The alkaline character of cement may result in runoff or washout water with a pH as high as 12. High alkalinity is particularly harmful to aquatic life. Runoff from most concrete and ready-mix sites requires a surface water discharge permit. Washout on construction sites should be properly collected and managed on site.

Fly Ash Concrete

Fly ash is a residual by-product of burning coal that has become a common substitute for Portland cement in concrete. Fly ash is produced in the generation of electricity and industrial processes. In the past, fly ash was used for a variety of purposes but most commonly as landfill. Replacing Portland cement with fly ash, or using the two in combination, reduces the amount of Portland cement required, offsetting the environmental costs to some degree. The advantages of using fly ash are well documented. Fly ash concrete is stronger, although it may take longer for strength to develop. Fly ash concrete tends to increase the time it takes for concrete to set. An advantage in the summer, allowing longer working times, this may be a disadvantage in the winter. Concrete mixes can be adjusted for weather conditions. Local ready-mix plants can provide mixtures that are seasonally adjusted to a given area. The time for strength to develop can be reduced to be comparable to Portland cement if a fly ash/Portland cement mixture is used (15 to 30 percent fly ash). Fly ash concrete requires less water per unit of volume, which reduces shrinking and cracking. Fly ash concrete may not accept color dies or acid finishes with the same results as Portland cement concrete.

Environmental Strategies for Concrete Use

The key to the wise use of concrete begins with proper specification of materials and estimates of volumes. Alternative designs or products that minimize the amount of material necessary may be possible. Precast products, for example, may use less material than cast-in-place alternatives and reduces on-site waste. Specifying fly ash concrete or fly ash/Portland mixtures can improve strength and reduce the amount of material required. Solid waste that may be produced can be crushed and used as fill. Arrangements should be made to collect washout water and to control runoff from such areas.

Recycling Asphalt Paving

Recycling paving involves milling the top surface of a roadway or parking lot and removing as little as three-quarters of an inch to as much as three or four inches of the pavement. There are several methods for recycling the removed material. Recycling may be done in place, crushing the milled materials and mixing them with new asphalt emulsion and perhaps new asphalt materials and repaving the surface. This is often done using a "train" of equipment to mill, crush and mix, and repave the road in a continuous "ribbon." In other cases the material is transported off-site to a plant where remixing occurs. In some cases the pavement is heated during repaving to soften the material and bond the new surface. Recycling paving is a very cost-efficient approach. Other recycled materials may be used as road base material. For more information on paving, see discussions in Chaps. 4 and 6.

Treated Lumber

Wood is widely used in landscaping, and in most contemporary applications treated wood is specified because it lasts up to 30 times longer than untreated lumber. It could be argued that the extended service life helps to save trees that would otherwise be harvested and that this offsets the environmental problems associated with treated wood. In the past wood was treated primarily with creosote, essentially a coal tar distillate, but creosote treated wood is less common today. The remaining wood preservatives fall into two categories: oil-based preservatives and water-based preservatives (Table 2.4).

Some concerns with using treated wood include whether the material will come into contact with people or animals or any water body, including groundwater. Alternative materials should be considered if the treated wood is to come into direct contact with food supplies. Treated lumber should not be used where it will come into direct contact with drinking water, although federal guidelines allow for incidental uses such as for docks and bridges. The type of treated lumber should be carefully considered for use in playground equipment or picnic facilities; creosote and penta should not be used for these purposes.

Disposing of treated wood is difficult; it is, after all, treated to resist decomposition. Ideally waste wood should be recycled, but it should not be composted. Some states prohibit burning treated wood. Ultimately, using treated wood is a commitment to using toxic materials in the site. The belief that pressure treated wood will last a very long time reflects a successful marketing strategy more than a fact. A technical report (McQueen and Stevens, 1998) indicates that the average life of a pressure treated deck is only about 9 years. Treated wood may be insect resistant and perhaps rot resistant, but it is not moisture resistant. Repeated cycles of wetting and drying inevitably begin to warp and split the wood, and the structure slowly tears itself apart. As the structure is replaced or rebuilt, the treated lumber cannot be recycled, composted, or burned. The specifier should be at least as concerned with moisture resistance if durability is a concern. Redwood, cedar, and cypress are commonly

Preservative	Type	Character
Creosote	Oil	Restricted use only
Pentachlorophenol (penta)	Oil	Teratogenic properties; restricted use only
Copper napthenate	Oil	
Chromated copper arsenate (CCA)	Water	Pressure treatment only; contains arsenic and chromium
Ammoniacal copper quaternary compound (ACQ)	water	Pressure treatment only; does not use toxics arsenic and chromium

TABLE 2.4   Types of Common Wood Preservatives

thought of as rot resistant woods, but in fact only the heartwoods of these trees are demonstrably rot and moisture resistant. Even heartwood does not generally outperform treated lumber. If treated wood is to be used, the best option for the environment is ACQ, but consideration should be given to specifying rot resistant species from native trees or recycled plastic lumber.

Deconstruction

With interest in sustainability has come an emerging marketplace for reusable or recycled materials and the infrastructure for finding and selling such materials. This, in turn, has led to a revitalized deconstruction industry. The industry is still at the early stages of developing the methods and practices of building deconstruction, materials salvage, and management of abandoned and vacant property. This may be a natural extension of the 1990s brownfield movement that focused on finding effective uses for abandoned and environmentally unsafe properties, but it points to the potential for a marketplace for recycled materials. Abandoned or condemned homes may contribute to a loss of local property values and reduce the desirability of otherwise strong neighborhoods (Fig. 2.4). In many cities such structures are routinely razed. Removing valuable materials such as flooring, windows, doors, trim, and fixtures allow these items to live again in new or remodeled buildings.

Deconstructing buildings saves useful materials for reuse in new construction and rehabilitation projects and creates more jobs and business opportunities than demolition (Fig. 2.5). Even buildings with minimal potential for rehabilitation may be valuable sources of useful building materials. The process of deconstruction may have more value to architects than to site designers, but many repositories of recovered material include pavers, stone stairs and curbs, planters, exterior lighting, exterior metal work, and other materials that may be useful (Fig. 2.6). The challenge is that the designer must become familiar with the deconstruction practitioners in her marketplace.

Confirming that materials are recycled or contain recycled materials may be a necessary element in establishing a site or building that is sustainably designed. A number of organizations provide certifications of one sort or another. For example, Scientific Certification Systems (SCS) rose out of the need for such a system created by the U.S. Green Building Council's LEED program. The focus is largely on finishes and building elements as opposed to site elements, but SCS does certify wood, cement, rock, and other materials used in site work. Paving operations have been using alternative and recycled materials for years. Specifications for the use of recycled material as aggregate in paving are available from most state highway departments.

The use of recycled materials for LEED certification may require some life cycle information or documentation of origin. SCS does certify manufactured products that contain a minimum percentage of recycled materials to qualify for LEED; however, there is no formal process for documenting or certifying building materials recovered by deconstruction for reuse. As interest in green building grows and more owners become interested in LEED certifications, such a system may be developed. Individuals engaged in deconstruction confirm that no system is currently in place nationwide.

A notable exception to this is "The Reuse People" (TRP), with headquarters in Oakland, California. TRP typically completes an inventory of materials prior to

FIGURE 2.4   The presence of abandoned houses may lead to unwanted activities and reduce both the value and livability of neighborhoods.

deconstruction. To comply with Internal Revenue Service (IRS) regulations, they require an independent appraisal to determine the value of donated materials. On donations of $5,000 or more, their system tracks material from deconstruction to the point of sale or reuse to meet IRS requirements. Items are labeled with a unique job and piece number as the deconstruction proceeds. Materials of many pieces such as bricks or lumber are gathered in lots and inventoried, then given a unique lot number. These identifiers are maintained in an inventory database. Each lot can be traced to a specific project or source, providing a chain of custody and perhaps the needed documentation for certification. The cost of the inventory and tracking system for a typical residential deconstruction is estimated to be $1.25 to $1.50 per square foot of building. As building size increases—for example, in commercial buildings—the cost per foot decreases (Ted Reiff, personal communication). The additional cost of this

FIGURE 2.5   Site deconstruction.

FIGURE 2.6   Workers engaged in the deconstruction of a house. The reuse of valuable building materials is an important aspect of sustainable architecture. (*Source: Image provided by and used with the permission of Second Chance, Inc., Baltimore, MD. See also color insert.*)

inventory may be offset by an increased value for reuse materials whose origin can be documented.

Sustainable Site Planning

Among the first considerations for the site planner is to determine how to minimize the disturbed area necessary for the project. Key aspects of minimizing the disturbed area are the degree to which habitat and open space are preserved and created. Not all open space is equal in this concern: athletic fields, for example, are not considered to be habitat or open space for purposes of sustainability, but a green roof might be. Strategies for minimizing the disturbed area include clustering buildings, increasing density, and encouraging smaller building footprints. Clustering buildings reduces the disturbed area and allows the designer to minimize road length and paving. Recognizing that the disturbance of the site affects the landscape well beyond the property line, the designer looks for ways to maintain or reestablish links to other parts of the landscape ecosystem through the building location decision. Care should be taken to protect stream corridors, wetlands, and other unique or important landscape features. Storm water management is a key component of sustainable site design. This is discussed more fully in Chap. 8.

Building Location

The location of a building on the site is a critical element of site planning. The building should be located to minimize the impact on the site while maximizing the function and quality of the designed space. Selecting a location is a combination of managing the solar influences of the site, balancing the earthwork, and maximizing the utility and aesthetics of the site.

Locating proposed structures offers the designer the first opportunity to focus the design of the site in a sustainable direction. The building location fixes the limits and extent of disturbance. Building location has important implications for the energy costs of heating and cooling. For northern areas, buildings should be located on the portion of the site that receives the most light during the hours of greatest sunshine, particularly in the winter months—about 9:00 a.m. to 3:00 p.m. The building should be located in the northern most part of this area, but allowances should be made for adequate distance from neighboring properties to allow for possible shading due to future development. Open space should be located on the southern side of the building. Open space with a southern exposure is preferred over open space with a northern exposure.

Building shape may be more important than orientation, but site designers may not have influence over the shape of the building. Square buildings are inefficient shapes for heating and cooling, although they tend to be more efficient than a long, narrow building on a north-south axis. The best combination of shape and orientation is an elongated building on an east-west axis. In northern latitudes in winter, buildings oriented on an east-west axis receive almost three times as much solar radiation on the south side of the building as on the east or west. This situation is reversed in the summer.

The location and shape of buildings can be managed to reduce the site albedo and the heat island effect created by development. The use of vegetated roofs can further reduce these effects.

Site Maintenance Considerations

The operating and maintenance costs of a site are a reflection of the design. Reducing the need for additional watering and reducing the chemical inputs needed to maintain a landscape are critical concerns. Site designers are well versed in the elements of design needed to facilitate traffic, pedestrian movement, and the functional and aesthetic aspects of a site; but sustainability adds to these elements. Sustainability may require smaller turf areas and more reliance on native species of plants. The designer should have some local climate knowledge and an understanding of the microclimates that will be created in the site. It is likely that a working knowledge of local soils will need to be supplemented with specific soil tests to ascertain the right plant selection to minimize reoccurring inputs.

The choice of plant species and materials used on the site can make important contributions to the environmental performance of the site. From trees providing cooling shade to buildings and parking lots, reducing site albedo and heat generation and retention help reduce energy demand. Reduced turf area and increased use of meadows and natural vegetation increase biodiversity on the site. Selecting plants that form natural communities and have supporting interactions will reduce the need for fertilizer and pesticides. The use of design to capture and retain precipitation will lower the costs of infrastructure and reduce the need for additional watering. Designers might consider the use of nonpotable water for landscape watering either by using on-site retention ponds or innovative wastewater systems. More information on these issues is provided in subsequent chapters.

Moving to Sustainability

Sustainability concerns go beyond the selection of materials. The layout of a site, the types and character of groundcover, and the management of the various landscape functions are critical issues. All of these issues have implications for site planners and designers. First, what is the role of site development in contributing to these effects, and how might those effects best be mitigated? Second, given that these decisions will influence the use and function of a site, how do we account for these changes in planning and design?

Site planning, design, and development professionals are moving toward including sustainability as a matter of practice. It is up to the planner and the designer to synthesize all of the issues and interests and then educate the parties about the value of the plan and the design. To include issues of sustainability, the planner and designer should become students of those subjects as much as the other subjects that are incorporated in a site plan.

The site planning and design professions are embracing the concerns with sustainability as we grow more aware of issues of climate change, energy, and the anticipated pressures of continued population growth. More to the point, communities and clients are also requiring more sensitive and intelligent design. The opportunities to address these concerns are expected to grow in years to come. Although much has been done to improve our understanding of our relationship with the environment, much more remains to be done; the design paradigms of the future are just now being formed.

Begin to consider issues for site and community design that go beyond mitigating the impacts of site disturbance and the disruption of environmental services. As concern with energy conservation and efficiency grow, transit planning and local sources of energy are likely to become important to communities. Likewise, concern over quality of life issues may lead to a greater premium on communities that provide more manageable commutes or to walkable communities. In addition, access to local food and other resources may become important elements in the sustainable community of the near future.

CHAPTER **3**

Site Data and Analysis

I n many respects site analysis is the most important step in the successful site design process. The purposes of site analysis are to gather data for preliminary planning, evaluate the site for compatibility with the proposed project or use, recognize concerns requiring additional study, and form an understanding of the administrative requirements of the project such as required permits and approvals. The value of the site analysis is in its clear and complete identification of issues and the character of the site as they relate to a proposed use. The site analysis should be as far-reaching and broad in scope as feasible, but it is usually subject to fairly limited resources.

Site analysis is a critical first step in planning and designing a site, but too often the value of a thorough evaluation of the site is discounted for the sake of lower costs or short time frames. Discovering site limitations or issues further into the planning and design process can be an expensive lesson. If such issues are discovered after design or in construction, the costs can be significant in economic terms and devastating to one's professional reputation.

Site Analysis

Very often the initial site assessment is part of the proposal effort and is completed "out-of-pocket," but the work should be thorough regardless of the fee because the professional will be held to account for the oversight. Even more troublesome is that the effectiveness of a particular analysis may be difficult to measure until well into design or even after site work begins. Corners cut or inaccurate assumptions made in the site analysis for expediency or economy may result in expensive rework and change orders during the design process or, worse yet, during construction.

The site designer rarely has the resources or time to complete a comprehensive site investigation on speculation of winning work. Therefore, site analyses are usually conducted in two steps: a proposal phase to facilitate winning the work and a postcontract phase. The proposal phase site analysis is extremely important because the proposal, sometimes even including preliminary design and costs, will be based on its outcome. As in-house resources provided for the assessment are usually limited, it is important that they be used carefully. The costs of collecting physical information at this stage of a project may be problematic, so other sources of information must be found.

Site characterization is a more detailed site investigation that is usually undertaken after some degree of preliminary site planning. Site characterization generally includes a geotechnical analysis of subsurface conditions such as depth to bedrock, depth to groundwater, seasonal high water table, and specific soil tests. The American Society of Testing and Materials (ASTM) has developed a Standard Guide to Site Characterization for Engineering, Design, and Construction Purposes (D-420). This guide provides the site designer with a consensus standard with which to plan and evaluate site characterizations.

Chief among the concerns and underlying the analysis of a site is coming to an understanding of the environmental functions of the site. As site designers become more sensitive to the environmental impacts of their work and strive to offset them, it is important to have a clear understanding of the contribution made by the site.

Location

The first consideration of the site analysis is to locate the site. Site location entails more than simply locating the site on a map. Location, in this sense, refers to the project's relationship to the community. Commercial projects are concerned about visibility, site access, and traffic. Is the traffic past the site adequate, or is it congested? Is the street infrastructure adequate for the anticipated increase? What sort of improvements might be anticipated? Is the site accessible from the street? What sort of on-site improvements might be expected to facilitate access? Is the interior of the site visible from the street? From how far away will drivers be able to see the site? Can traffic access the site from both directions? Is a left-hand turn possible? Are the neighboring sites commercial or residential? Are off-site improvements required? Are the necessary utilities nearby?

Residential projects have different concerns. How far away are schools, government services, and shopping? Are local roads and streets adequate to handle increased traffic? Is the character of the area conducive to the proposed project? Will future residents be able to enter and leave the site without traffic congestion? Are adjacent properties developed? If not, what will zoning allow?

Collecting Site Information

A number of existing sources of site information should be readily available within the office, and the Internet gives the designer access to many other sources. This information is available in fairly specific forms and may contribute to the site analysis effort at little cost.

Site analysis is an interpretive process. A broad array of information is collected from fairly limited individual sets of information, and these data sets are combined to project a future use of the land. In general, preliminary site assessments are based on precious little "new" information; that is, much of the analysis is based on existing sources of information or firsthand observation. It is how the site information is understood and used that makes the difference in site analysis. Site analysis is not done in a vacuum; the context of the proposed use frames the scope and character of the effort. For example, among the most important considerations is the topography of the site. Sites with significant change in elevations are typically difficult and more expensive to develop. Of course, the same steep slopes that are a source of concern for the commercial builder may be the bread and butter of the resort or high-end residential developer.

Topography

The United States Geological Survey (USGS) is a valuable source of topographic information. A local selection of the 7.5 minute quadrangle series of topographic maps is found in every design office. The amount of detail and relative accuracy for the cost is difficult to improve upon. USGS maps are available from a variety of sources, including the Internet (www.usgs.gov). Commercial sources of topographic information are available at

Web sites operated by firms working in partnership with the USGS on a variety of projects. Even more convenient are free sources of topographic information now found on the Internet (see App. C).

The most basic element of site analysis is the lay of the land. The topography of a site may dictate the purposes for which the site may be used and eventually the layout of the proposed project. The location of buildings and roads, pedestrian circulation, and the arrangement of storm water features are all commonly affected by topography. The analyst must consider how the existing topography affects the proposed use. Although the contour intervals are fairly large, the relative accuracy of the quad maps allows for interpolation for general planning purposes but not for design.

The preliminary analysis of the site provides an early look at how the proposed development will fit into the site. Will significant earthwork be necessary? Will retaining walls or other appurtenances be required? Can the site be accessed from adjacent roads? Is there visibility into the site from adjacent roads?

The nature of the material making up the slope is also important. A soil survey may provide important information pertaining to the erodability of soils and the risks associated with cut and fill operations. Removing established vegetation from slopes may create unstable conditions requiring additional engineering and construction costs. Many land development and zoning regulations include restrictions on the development of steep slopes. More detailed information on soils is provided later in the chapter.

A slope analysis is done to identify the areas of steep slopes and the possible location for building sites and access. The slope analysis is usually a graphic representation of slope shown in classes or ranges. The ranges are sometimes established by local ordinances, which describe the parameters to be observed when conducting a slope analysis and steep slope development restrictions. The slope analysis may identify possible routes for on-site traffic circulation as well as drainage patterns. The restrictions imposed by slopes become more apparent when examining a finished slope drawing. Development patterns that are in tune with the site will be clearly evident.

From a hillside the long views are generally considered the most valuable. A site analysis should include identification of the long views and any obstructions or limitations to them. Site development should proceed with the maintenance and optimization of the long views in mind. Undesirable views should also be identified and addressed in the analysis.

The approach to the site and the actual means of access onto the site are key elements. The best paths of circulation, the minimization of impact on the site to develop these networks, and the extent of required cuts and fills all must be considered. Existing design requirements in ordinances may require revision to make the hillside project work. What works on a flat site may not work on the hillside without extensive earthwork and disturbances. Sight distance for egress to public roads should also be considered.

Other elements of the site analysis include the identification of canyons, wetlands, rock outcroppings, existing structures, unique habitats or natural features, neighboring land uses, and utility locations. Flat and low areas present their own concerns. Boggy or wet areas may be wetlands and restrict development. Sites that are low or flat may be difficult to drain and present difficult design challenges of their own. The location of rights of way, easements, and other encroachments is also important.

Findings of the site analysis may indicate that further research or study is required to determine the stability of slopes, hydrologic conditions, or the extent of wetlands.

The site analysis is the foundation of the plan. It will provide the framework from which the planning and design are developed.

The aspect of the site may also be an important factor. Orientation toward the sun may influence how well selected vegetation will perform and will affect the performance of buildings as well. A north-facing slope will be cooler than a south-facing slope; a southwestern exposure may be quite hot in the summer. The implications of aspect can be translated into energy consumption and other features of the development. Building orientation is becoming a more important factor as global climate changes and energy efficiency concerns rise.

In addition to topographic maps, the USGS can provide aerial photographs, digital orthophoto quadrangles, and other high-quality sources of site data, and a number of Web sites offer free aerial photography (see App. C). Through the Center for Integration of Natural Disaster Information (CINDI), the USGS has a greater deal of information about regional and local site hazards such as earthquakes, landslide risks, groundwater conditions, flood risk, and more. The USGS also has information about site geology. A series of geologic maps and information on geologic hazards (sinkholes, slides, earthquakes, faults, etc.) is based on the topographic quadrangle maps. These maps include known paleontological information as well. The USGS completed a survey of the biological status of the United States in 2000, which includes information on endangered as well as exotic invasive species.

USDA Plant Hardiness Zones

The USDA updated the Plant Hardiness Zone Map so familiar to growers and planners in 1990 and reformatted the map in 1998. The new version incorporates new temperature information by using coldest weather data from the years 1970 to 1986. The map introduces a new zone, Zone 11, which is essentially a frost-free zone. Discussion of the Plant Hardiness Zone Map is included in this section on zone analysis to encourage landscape architects and site planners to consider potential impacts of global climate change in their evaluation of a site.

It is estimated that warming trends may have significant impacts over the next hundred years, with notable changes occurring by 2025. These changes may significantly affect the performance of designs under consideration today. Although no broad consensus as to how to address these concerns in design is "on the boards," designers should begin to consider incorporating the most likely scenarios and trends in their work. Trends in climate change raise different concerns for various parts of North America.

FEMA Maps

The Federal Emergency Management Agency (FEMA) is best known for the flood maps it has published over the years. Just as the USGS is more than topographic maps, FEMA provides much more to the site analysis process than flood information. FEMA maintains a Web site that allows the designer to create a fairly site-specific map of hazards related to earthquake, tornadoes, wind, and hail as well as floods.

FEMA's Web site (www.fema.gov) includes a number of valuable links, one specifically for design professionals' questions. Unfortunately, FEMA does not yet provide Flood Insurance Maps online, but maps may be purchased in either paper or digital form through the Web site. FEMA does provide information on changes to the existing maps on its Web site.

Vegetation

An assessment of existing vegetation may tell a designer a great deal about a site. Evidence of second growth vegetation is an indication of past activities that should be reconciled by the analyst with other sources of information. If the site indicates significant disturbance from past activities, there should be a record somewhere of what those activities were. The quality of vegetation is also an important consideration. Quality specimens of trees or a valuable population of another type of plant should be protected or incorporate into a future design. The presence of water tolerant plant species may indicate a high water table or frequent flooding, whereas poor quality or stressed vegetation may indicate problematic soil or subsurface conditions.

Prior to making a site visit, the analyst should consult local or state sources for information pertaining to protected plant species. In many cases, the location of populations of protected species is mapped by these agencies. The discovery of such a plant population or community could have a significant impact on the future use and development of the site.

Trees or tree masses may contribute value to the finished project, and their location must be considered in the assessment. Mature trees are known to increase the market value of property, and a qualified arborist should be asked to assess the condition of specimen trees to determine their relative value. A variety of evaluation methods are available, but they generally have these elements in common: the type of tree and the characteristics of the species as displayed by the specimen such as form, color, shape, and condition.

James Urban (1989) has developed a practical and usable approach to tree evaluation (Table 3.1). This method was specifically developed for city trees, but the fundamental

1	Excellent condition	No noticeable problems, branching is regular and even, normal sized leaves, normal color.
2	Good condition	Full grown with no tip dieback, may minor bark wounds, thinner crowns, slightly smaller leaf size or minor infestations.
3	Fair condition	One or more of the following: (a) minor tip or crown dieback (less than 10 percent), (b) small yellowed or disfigured leaves, thinner crown, (c) significant limb wounds, (d) recent large branch removed that minimally affects shape, (e) large insect infestation, (f) any problem that should be repaired without long-term effect on the plant's health.
4	Poor condition	Any of the following: (a) crown dieback from 10 to 25 percent, (b) significantly smaller, yellowed, or disfigured leaves, (c) branch removal that affects the crown shape in a significant way, (d) wounding to the bark that will affect the trees health.
5	Very poor condition	Any problem that is so significant that it grossly affects the shape or the health of the tree. Tree that has little hope of survival.
6	Replace	Some green may be seen, but the tree is not going to survive.
7	Dead	

Source: Urban, James R. 1989. "Evaluation of Tree Planting Practices in the Urban Environment." *Proceedings of the Fourth Urban Forestry Conference.* Paper presented at the 1991 Annual Meeting of the American Society of Landscape Architects, Kansas City, MO.

TABLE 3.1 Urban's Tree Condition Methodology

approach can serve as a guideline in evaluating the trees on a given site, particularly during the early site analysis stage.

Aerial Photogrammetry

Aerial photogrammetry provides an accurate mapping of topographic and physiographic features using low-level aerial photography. The topography is interpolated from limited topographic data collected on the ground. Properly prepared photogrammetry meets National Map Accuracy Standards and may be significantly less expensive than traditional field topographic methods, especially on large projects or projects with significant topographic variation or many features (Table 3.2).

The ability to collect aerial photography may be hampered by vegetation that obscures the ground and therefore may only be collected during winter months in some areas. The cost of photogrammetry prohibits its use in the preliminary analysis stage, but many municipalities have photogrammetric information available for review.

Historical Aerial Photography

Unlike photogrammetry, existing aerial photography can be a valuable source of information for the site designer at a relatively low price. Private firms may have generations of aerial photography taken on speculation or on contract. Many communities also have collected aerial photography over the years. Some state geological surveys and the USGS also have historic aerial photography available for purchase. The American Society for Testing and Materials (ASTM) has developed a Standard Guide for Acquisition of File Aerial Photography and Imagery for Establishing Historic Site-Use and Surficial Conditions (ASTM D5518-94e1). The guide can assist in identification of public sources of existing aerial photography as well as provide information regarding the specifications of such photography.

Public sources of photography are helpful, but many private sources exist as well. Private firms may be willing to work with the designer to enlarge and prepare special prints of photographs. Photography firms may be reluctant to enlarge photography to the scales useful for site planners because of the inherent distortion and inaccuracy that can be anticipated in the resulting print, but these enlarged photos are a valuable planning and analysis tool. The most accurate part of a photograph is at the center of the lens. The curvature of the lens results in minor distortions toward the edges and corners of the picture that increase as the photograph is enlarged beyond the intended scale. Such enlargements are of limited use but may be adequate for preliminary planning purposes.

Enlarged aerial photographs sometimes reveal site features not clearly visible at ground level such as drainage patterns, sinkholes, and the remains of historic structures. Old aerial photography may reveal features that have been obscured by later site activities or development. An aerial photograph is also helpful in presenting the site analysis data to clients and others who may not be comfortable reading plans. A series of historic aerial photographs show the site conditions at one site at three different times in the past (Figs. 3.1, 3.2, and 3.3).

USDA Soil Survey

Soil surveys have a compendium of valuable information. Soils are classified as "series," and these types are further refined into detailed soil map units. The soil descriptions include information on slope, depth to bedrock, soil texture, erodability, rock, and

With a view to the utmost economy and expedition in producing maps which fulfill not only the broad needs for standard or principal maps but also the reasonable particular needs of individual agencies, standards of accuracy for published maps are defined as follows:

1. Horizontal accuracy. For maps on publication scales larger than 1:20,000, not more than 10 percent of the points tested shall be in error by more than 1/30 in., measured on the publication scale; for maps on publication scales of 1:20,000 or smaller, 1/50 in. These limits of accuracy shall apply in all cases to positions of well-defined points only. Well-defined points are those that are easily visible or recoverable on the ground, such as the following: monuments or markers, such as benchmarks, property boundary monuments; intersections of roads, railroads, etc.; corners of large buildings or structures (or center points of small buildings); etc. In general what is well defined will be determined by what is plottable on the scale of the map within 1/100 in. Thus while the intersection of two roads or property lines meeting at right angles would come within a sensible interpretation, identification of the intersection of such lines meeting at an acute angle would obviously not be practicable within 1/100 in. Similarly, features not identifiable upon the ground within close limits are not to be considered as test points within the limits quoted, even though their positions may be scaled closely upon the map. In this class would come timberlines, soil boundaries, etc.

2. Vertical accuracy, as applied to contour maps on all publication scales, shall be such that not more than 10 percent of the elevations tested shall be in error more than one-half the contour interval. In checking elevations taken from the map, the apparent vertical error may be decreased by assuming a horizontal displacement within the permissible horizontal error for a map of that scale.

3. The accuracy of any map may be tested by comparing the positions of points whose locations or elevations are shown upon it with corresponding positions as determined by surveys of a higher accuracy. Tests shall be made by the producing agency, which shall also determine which of its maps are to be tested, and the extent of the testing.

4. Published maps meeting these accuracy requirements shall note this fact on their legends, as follows: "This map complies with National Map Accuracy Standards."

5. Published maps whose errors exceed those aforestated shall omit from their legends all mention of standard accuracy.

6. When a published map is a considerable enlargement of a map drawing (manuscript) or of a published map, that fact shall be stated in the legend. For example, "This map is an enlargement of a 1:20,000-scale map drawing," or "This map is an enlargement of a 1:24,000-scale published map."

7. To facilitate ready interchange and use of basic information for map construction among all federal map making agencies, manuscript maps and published maps, wherever economically feasible and consistent with the uses to which the map is to be put, shall conform to latitude and longitude boundaries, being 15 minutes of latitude and longitude, or 7.5 minutes, or 3-3/4 minutes in size.

Source: United States Geological Survey, "United States National Map Accuracy Standards," http://rmmcweb.cr.usgs.gov/public/nmpstds/nmas647.html

TABLE 3.2   U.S. National Mapping Program Accuracy Standards

FIGURE 3.1   Aerial photograph of site showing conditions in 1963.

drainage characteristics (Fig. 3.4). Soil maps are generally accurate, but occasionally field observations indicate soil conditions at odds with the survey. In such cases local Natural Resources Conservation Service (NRCS) offices can be helpful in resolving the discrepancy. USGS soil surveys are now available online.

Although soil borings and test pits may be done eventually, the site analysis may use existing sources of information such as the local soil survey or a previous soil analysis. In addition to describing the character of the soil, the soil survey includes information about different management techniques, engineering characteristics, and uses for the land. For site designers, charts describing the engineering and development capabilities of the land are an important part of the soil survey. Each local soil survey includes a description of how the survey was made and how to read the survey.

FIGURE 3.2   Aerial photograph of same site showing conditions in 1970.

Hazardous Soil Conditions   Expansive soils occur in every state, and these soils may cause extensive cracking of sidewalks, foundation failures, retaining wall failure, and so forth. Table 3.3 outlines the characteristics of expansive soils under wet and dry conditions.

Liquefaction, a condition in which solid ground can turn mushy when soils are vibrated, is associated with earthquakes. Under certain conditions soils lose all bearing capacity; buildings or bridges can slip or sink (like quicksand) and buried structures can float to the surface (tanks). These conditions have been associated with fine- to medium-grained sands and silts found in loosely packed layers. In general, the greater the soil density, the lower the liquefaction risk. A clay content of 15 percent or more is adequate protection from liquefaction (Brown et al., 1986).

Another form of liquefaction is found in quick clays, which can become "quick" or liquefy. Confined to the northern states and Canada (New York and Vermont have had quick clay failures), these very fine, flourlike clays are formed as sediments in shallow waters and later raised above sea level. Collapse of quick clays has been associated with high water content: as the material weight exceeds its shear strength, slope failure results.

FIGURE 3.3   Aerial photograph of same site showing conditions in 1988.

Hydrology

The presence of water on the site and the general pattern of drainage are key concerns of the site analysis. Water is often the key feature of a site. Waterfront—the presence of a stream or pond—brings added value, but it also raises concerns for development. The presence of a surface water feature may be coincidental with a fairly high water table or shallow geological features. Drainage patterns should be carefully observed in the field as well as being examined in published sources of information. The presence of associated wetlands and floodplains must be preliminarily located, and the location and extent of riparian zones should be noted. The location of water features and other hydrologically linked features of the site should be carefully observed and evaluated.

It is important to locate and identify springs and seeps in the site analysis process. Very often these features are located on USGS maps or soil surveys, but the analyst should confirm their presence in the field. It may be appropriate to consider local off-site

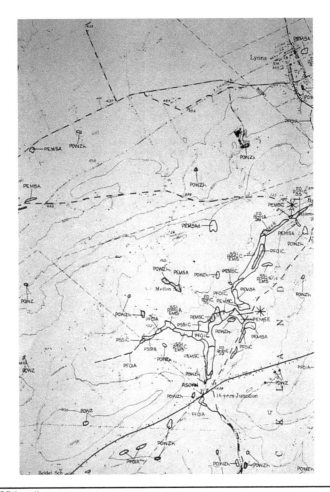

FIGURE 3.4 USDA soil survey map.

hydrology as well. The analyst should consider storm water drainage on the site as well as drainage from other sites onto the subject site. Of particular concern are the volume, concentration, and quality of run-on storm water. Sites located along streams in the lower reaches of a watershed may be affected by conditions higher in the watershed. Begin to identify storm water management strategies in the site analysis. The drainage pattern of the site and the presence of water features will indicate the likely location of storm water collection facilities.

The site analyst should consider the sensitivity of hydrologic features to development. Erosion and sedimentation during and after construction may represent a serious threat to surface water quality and habitat. If significant measures will be required to protect surface waters, these should be discussed in the site analysis. Many states have programs designating streams and lakes of high quality and providing special protection measures for these waters. Determine whether receiving waters are high quality or restricted and how their status might affect the project.

Under dry conditions
• Soil is hard, resists penetration by knife blade, and is difficult to crush by hand.
• A cut from a shovel leaves a shiny surface.
• Surface may display cracks in a more or less regular pattern.
• The width and spacing of cracks indicate the relative expansion potential of the soil when wetted.
• Surface irregularities such as footprints and tire tracks cannot be obliterated by foot pressure.
Under wet conditions
• Soil is very sticky and will accumulate on shoe soles to a thickness of 2 to 4 in. when walked on.
• Soil can be molded into a ball by hand and will leave a nearly invisible powdery residue on hands after they dry.
• A knife or shovel will penetrate the wet soil quite easily, and the cut surface will be smooth and tend to be shiny.
• Freshly machine scraped or cut areas will tend to be smooth and shiny.
• Heavy construction equipment such as bulldozers and compacting rollers will develop a thick soil coating, which may impair their function.

Adapted from Gary B. Griggs, *Geologic Hazards, Resources and Environmental Planning,* 2nd ed. Belmont: CA: Wadsworth, 1983.

TABLE 3.3 Recognition of Expansive Soils in the Field

In addition to sedimentation issues, the non-point-source pollution programs of the National Pollution Discharge Elimination System (NPDES) have required municipalities to reevaluate storm water management schemes. The need to establish total maximum daily loads (TMDLs) for affected waters may result in more stringent design requirements in the coming years.

Local Records and History

Land use planning and development is generally an issue and a concern for local government. Local governments very often have substantial information about a site. As discussed in preceding sections, aerial photography, mapping, and other physiographic information is often available from local governments. The regulation of land use, however, is usually done at the local level.

Zoning

Of all the local sources of information, zoning regulations are probably the most important. Zoning regulations provide a prescription for how development is to be done in a community. The general conditions of development are described in terms of what development is encouraged and where in the community it will be. Zoning maps provide an overview of the community's vision for itself: not only indicating how a site may be developed or used but also how surrounding sites might be used.

Zoning regulations may contain design criteria such as parking configuration, lot sizes, setbacks, road width, road profile restrictions, and sign requirements, to name a few. Local regulations may also include specific performance requirements such as noise, solar access, or pollution loading restrictions. Zoning ordinances restrict development by providing the limits and conditions of development, but they facilitate development by providing developers with a guidance document. A clear evaluation of the zoning particulars of a site is a critical requirement for a complete site analysis.

Occasionally zoning may include overlay zones that have important implications for land use. Overlay zones such as steep slope restrictions, watershed protection, historic preservation, or aquifer protection may severally limit land development activities or require a higher order of performance from the design, construction, and operation of a site.

Land Development Regulations

The scope of land development regulations varies widely from place to place. Very often these regulations reflect an evolution of practices as much as they reflect a cogent regulatory process. Local ordinances are most valuable because they provide a glimpse into the experience of a municipality by reflecting their concerns and bias. Some ordinances are very prescriptive; others are concerned more with performance. In any case, understanding the local land development ordinances is second only to understanding the zoning regulations.

Land development regulations typically include requirements for local street design, open space, lighting, subdivision standards (to be considered in conjunction with the zoning requirements), minimum landscaping, and similar site development parameters. The primary differences between zoning and land development regulations are in the underlying authority. Local officials may have the authority to waive or modify provisions of the land development ordinance on a case-by-case basis, but zoning regulations are enforceable and cannot be waived without justification and a formal hearing process. Although procedures exist to provide for variances and exceptions to zoning ordinances, these procedures are formalized and offer little latitude to zoning hearing boards.

Zoning requirements of initial concern include the permitted uses, density, minimum lot sizes, setbacks, and open space. Care should be taken to consider the effect of wetlands, floodplains, or other site conditions that might influence the useful area in terms of density on the proposed site. Some zoning ordinances require special setbacks between different types of uses, such as a buffer area between residential and commercial land uses. The requirement for buffers, screening, and open space should be noted.

Utility Mapping

Location of utilities is made possible using maps provided by local utility companies. Increased use of geographic information systems has helped to provide reasonably accurate utility data in most places. However, utility maps generally are not considered accurate, and locations should be confirmed in the field for design purposes.

Historical Value

Historical societies and agencies may have important site information. Identification of historic and archaeological elements is very important because most states have regulations protecting historic or archaeological materials and sites. Discovering that a site has a historical feature or value is a critical piece of data in the early analysis. Sources of information regarding these features include local and state historical agencies and societies, local government records, USGS maps, and libraries. Sometimes local names for features such as bridges and roads are indicators of a historical or cultural element of value. Historical sources often have informative value as well. Place and road names can provide insight into former conditions and uses. A site located on Swamp Road, for example, could suggest seasonal flooding or wetland conditions not in evidence at the time of a site visit.

Local historic and cultural values are sometimes hard to discern. Written information may address the physical area of value but not address the community's attachment or less tangible values such as views or local character. These values are often unwritten and informal, but they may represent a significant, albeit unofficial, community interest that should be addressed. Though more difficult to identify, analysts should be sensitive to community values.

Infrastructure

The location of surface and subsurface utilities is part of the site analysis. The analyst should identify the location, capacity, and access for all necessary utilities, as well as the requirements for connections. Of particular importance might be moratoriums on sanitary sewer or water connections or exorbitant connection fees. Equally important is consideration of the interferences between utilities either on the site or in bringing the utilities to the site. Access to public water and sewer should be evaluated. The capacity of existing water and sewer may be of concern in some communities and should be evaluated at an early stage.

The capacity of road networks to accommodate proposed traffic is also a concern. Are local roads of a type and design sufficient for the proposed project? Are turning radii adequate? Will traffic signals and other improvements be necessary? Requirements to upgrade public highways may be prohibitive for some projects.

Assessing "Fit"

Fit is difficult to define, but, like quality, you will recognize it when you see it. In some places fit is as simple as reading the zoning and local development plans; in other communities assessing fit is more difficult. In general fit is determined by how the project design and function fits into local zoning, land development plans, the physical aspects of the site itself, the neighborhood, occasionally the region, and finally with the values and needs of the community itself. It could be argued that these elements are listed in order of increasing difficulty for assessment and accommodation.

Program Requirements

The process of collecting site information is much the same for every project, but the analysis is always performed in the context of a proposed use or project. It is necessary to have an understanding of the proposed project when conducting the site analysis. In most cases the designer must rely on the client and experience to form a working understanding of the proposed project. Projects with a poorly defined program should be addressed cautiously by the professional. Experience suggests that a high risk of failure is often associated with such projects; disappointed clients and unpaid invoices seem to accompany poorly defined or considered projects. Occasionally designers are asked to evaluate a site for its possible uses, in which case a series of analyses are done presuming different uses and parameters, but in most instances the analysis is conducted with an end use in mind. The analysis must consider the fundamental elements of a given project such as the site of proposed buildings, access to and from the site, lot layout, parking requirements, vehicular and pedestrian circulation, and a general strategy for storm water management. Physical development constraints such as slopes, wetlands, and floodplains must be accounted for in a preliminary fashion. Site analysts should extend their efforts to consider the off-site issues as well, which may include traffic issues, local flood or storm water concerns, or infrastructure issues.

Permitting and administrative requirements are particularly important in contemporary site development. Knowing which permits are necessary and the expected lead time required is often a critical element in a project. The professional should attempt to assess the desirability of the project to local government and people as well.

ADA and Pedestrian Access

The Americans with Disabilities Act (ADA) became law in the United States in 1990. Under the act a person with a disability is entitled to the same access and accommodations as the public in general. As a result, building and site owners were required to remove barriers wherever such an accommodation was considered "readily achievable." The readily achievable test can be ambiguous for existing buildings, but for new construction it is clear that all public-accessible designs must incorporate ADA principles and requirements. The "Americans with Disabilities Act Accessibility Guidelines" (ADAAG) were promulgated by the Architectural and Transportation Barriers Compliance Board; these guidelines are available on the ADAAG Web site (see App. C).

Although many of the design conventions of ADA have become commonplace, site designers may want to consider forming a preliminary analysis of the accessibility issues that may be encountered. It is recommended that designers confirm standards with an updated government source. Proposed changes to some of the ADA site standards have been made public for comment but were not yet approved at the time of this writing. Most of the proposed changes are concerned with buildings, but a few changes relate to site work. For the most part, details in this book reflect the proposed changes to the site standards. ADA issues regarding open space, recreational facilities, historic landscapes, or steep sites may present particular design challenges. It is not too early to be thinking about these issues and their impact on the design.

Community Standards and Expectations

Community standards and expectations are usually unwritten and often ambiguous, but they can be very important considerations in the site analysis. Site designers may intuitively be able to assess the expectations of a community by observing what has been accepted in the past; for example, what does the community and neighborhood around the site look like? Standards of plantings, architectural elements, styles, materials, and how pedestrians and vehicles are treated in existing design all comprise standards and expectations that often exceed written ordinances. Loss of locally used open space or of access to other land might engender resistance to a proposal by the community. Anticipating and addressing these expectations in the early phases of design may contribute significantly to the project's acceptance by the community.

Environmental Concerns

In the recent past, site analysis necessarily expanded to include at least a cursory assessment of the environmental conditions evidenced on a site. Environmental, in this sense, refers to the narrow considerations of past industrial or commercial activities and their impact on the site. An analyst should be aware of conditions that may indicate environmental contamination. Another environmental aspect of growing concern to site designers is the impact of environmental trends such as global climate change and its anticipated impacts and the growing demand to incorporate sustainability into site development. In particular, site designers working in coastal areas subject to tidal influence or in areas with important hydrologic characteristics such as wetlands or cold water fisheries may wish to consider the anticipated impacts. Designers may choose to incorporate these impacts into the selection of plant types and design considerations.

Beyond these concerns is a need for a deeper understanding of what the site does systemically in the environment, that is, as part of a larger landscape. Elements of the landscape provide particular environmental services ranging from habitat to temperature modification. The site assessment process must grow to accommodate this sort of ecological services analysis (Table 3.4). The ability to understand the contribution of landscape complexity and to measure these functions of the landscape in terms of environmental quality and economic value has improved dramatically.

Identify vegetative community(s)
Presence of native and nonnative species
Presence of invasive exotic species
Biological diversity
Habitat, seasonal and year around
Presence of colonial birds
Erosion protection services
Stream/wetland protection services
Hydrology
Surface water present
Water purification services
Flood buffers
Seasonal hydrology
Wetlands
Riparian functions
Ground water recharge
Soils
Nutrient transfer
Permeability
Soil structure
Soil productivity (tilth)
Local climate
Wind breaks
Temperature modification

TABLE 3.4   Ecological Services Analysis

There is a corollary to preserving the environmental functions of a site and that is a more complete understanding of the impacts of the proposed change to the site. In most cases the environmental impact of development is not limited to a loss of environmental functions but has a broader impact that is worthy of our attention. Another sort of assessment is necessary in the planning stage if we are to build sustainable sites. The questions raised by these concerns will be discussed throughout this book.

Environmental Site Assessment

The legacy of our past industrial waste disposal practices and experiences like Love Canal prompted lawmakers to pass environmental laws to protect the public and to compel landowners to pay for the cleanup of their property. Today prudent real estate buyers and nearly all lenders require an environmental site assessment (ESA) of a property before committing to a purchase. As with any aspect of real estate development, planning is the key to managing this process. An ESA is a risk assessment used in the planning and feasibility stages of real estate development. Assessments are used to evaluate all types of property—virgin land, recycled land, and renovation properties—for conditions that are indicative of possible environmental contamination. The presence of actual contamination could trigger liability for the costs of site cleanup and restoration for the owners and users of the property. By identifying the conditions prior to purchase, a buyer can avoid or minimize exposure to the costs of remediation. Lenders want to limit their exposure to lawsuits and liability for cleanup responsibilities and will demand full disclosure of any known contaminants or conditions. The information in the site assessment report should identify any recognized environmental contamination and describe what further steps might be required. Environmental site assessments are also performed in conjunction with applications for liability protections or release under various brownfield statutes and regulations. A more detailed discussion of environmental site assessment is provided in App. A.

The most common and widely accepted site assessment protocols are those developed by the American Society for Testing and Materials (ASTM). These consensus standards are developed by practitioners and users of ESAs. The standing ASTM committee meets periodically to consider and occasionally revise the standard guidelines to reflect current practice (see App. B). ASTM has developed a variety of assessment protocols focused on various assessment activities. A partial list of the assessment standards that may have application in site planning and design is provided in Table 3.5.

Why Perform a Site Assessment?

Environmental site assessment has become a common practice because of the risk purchasers assume when they take ownership of a property. Under the federal Comprehensive Environmental Response Compensation and Liability Act (CERCLA), a landowner is liable for the environmental conditions on the site whether the individual or company had any knowledge or involvement in causing the condition. This liability can include the costs of cleanup as well as damages to third parties. The Small Business Revitalization Act has given some important relief for landowners, but caution is still advised when purchasing property.

The law provides buyers with several avenues of defense from this liability. These include acts of God and the "innocent landowner" defense. The innocent landowner defense is available to parties that can demonstrate that prior to acquiring a property they had no knowledge of or reason to know of any adverse environmental conditions. They would demonstrate that they undertook an investigation into the historical use

E-1528	Standard Practice for Environmental Site Assessments: Transaction Screen Process
E-1527	Standard Practice for Environmental Site Assessments: Phase 1 Environmental Site Assessment Process
E-1903	Standard Guide for Environmental Site Assessments: Phase II Environmental Site Assessment Process
D-6235	Standard Practice for Expedited Site Characterization of Vadose Zone and Ground Water Contamination at Hazardous Waste Contaminated Sites
E-1984	Standard Guide for Process of Sustainable Brownfields Redevelopment
E-1861	Standard Guide for Use of Coal Combustion By-Products in Structural Fills
D-5746	Standard Classification of Environmental Condition of Property Area Types for Defense Base Closure and Realignment Facilities
E-2091	Standard Guide for Use of Activity and Use Limitations, Including Institutional and Engineering Controls
D-5730	Standard Guide for Site Characteristics for Environmental Purposes with Emphasis on Soil, Rock, the Vadose Zone, and Groundwater
D-5745	Standard Guide for Developing and Implementing Short-Term Measures or Early Actions for Site Remediation
E-1923	Standard Guide for Sampling Terrestrial and Wetlands Vegetation
E-1912	Standard Guide for Accelerated Site Characterization for Confirmed or Suspected Petroleum Releases
E-1689	Standard Guide for Developing Conceptual Site Models for Contaminated Sites
E-1624	Standard Guide for Chemical Fate in Site Specific Sediment/Water Microcosms
D-6429	Standard Guide for Selecting Surface Geophysical Methods
D-6008	Standard Practice for Conducting Environmental Baseline Surveys
D-5928	Standard Test Method for Screening of Waste for Radioactivity
D-5745	Standard Guide for Developing and Implementing Short-Term Measures of Early Actions for Site Remediation
D-5717	Standard Guide for Design of Ground Water Monitoring Systems in Karst and Fractures Rock Aquifers
D-420	Standard Guide to Site Characterization for Engineering, Design, and Construction Purposes
D5518-94e1	Standard Guide for Acquisition of File Aerial Photography and Imagery for Establishing Historic Site-Use and Surficial Conditions

TABLE 3.5   ASTM Standards for Site Assessment

and current condition of the property and could find no indications of environmental contamination. This investigation would have to meet a standard of due diligence or customary commercial practice. Buyers of commercial property and lenders minimized their risk by engaging an environmental professional to complete an investigation. Eventually the consensus standard emerged as a means of evaluating this good commercial practice. Site professionals may have an additional interest in the ESA because of the potential for a late discovery of an environmental condition to disrupt the design and development process. Further, site design professionals may elect to fold elements of the site assessment, a transaction screening, into their own analysis of the site.

Format of a Site Assessment

Typically a transaction screen and a Phase I Environmental Site Assessment should be conducted before title is transferred. The Phase I Environmental Site Assessment requires the services of an environmental professional. A transaction screen may be performed by a person with knowledge of land and real estate, and a site design professional has adequate knowledge to conduct this analysis. The professional can purchase a preprinted checklist from ASTM that provides the entire Standard Guideline E-1528. Using the checklist, the site professional can walk through a cursory site assessment process as part of the site analysis. Information collected in the screening process could contribute to the site analysis by identifying additional concerns that might affect the proposed use. The outcome of the site assessment may be to recommend that the client conduct a Phase I Environmental Site Assessment.

Very often lenders require a Phase I Environmental Site Assessment as a minimum acceptable level of investigation, and the transaction screen may be used to provide guidance. The screening process is a straightforward evaluation of the property, which is most appropriate for properties where no development has occurred. Despite these limitations, the site professional should consider adding the screening to the typical site analysis process. Some lenders have an in-house screening process, but the ASTM Transaction Screening Guide (E-1528) is the most commonly used format. Table 3.6 describes the level of inquiry common in an environmental screening.

Has the site been filled in the past?
Is there any knowledge that the fill could contain hazardous materials or petroleum waste products?
Is the property in an area currently or historically used for industrial or commercial activities?
Is the property zoned for industrial or commercial uses?
Are adjacent properties used for industrial or commercial activities?
If there are existing or previous commercial or industrial uses, was there any indication hazardous materials may have been used, generated, stored, or disposed of?
Does the site drain into a municipal collection system?
Do adjacent properties drain onto the site?
Are there reasons to suspect the quality of runoff from adjacent parcels?
Are there transformers on the property?
Is an on-site well required for water supply?

TABLE 3.6 Level of Inquiry for an Environmental Screening

The Phase I Environmental Site Assessment

Several factors contribute to deciding to perform a Phase I Environmental Site Assessment. First, if the buyer is a professional developer or a person familiar with real estate, it is likely that the buyer would be held to a higher standard of inquiry than a simple home buyer. This is probably true of site design professionals as well. Second, if a site has been used for industrial or commercial activities, it should be assumed there is a greater chance that hazardous materials may have been used or stored on the property. This increased risk would compel a greater level of inquiry. Finally, many lenders require a Phase I Environmental Site Assessment as a minimum level of inquiry.

The Phase I Environmental Site Assessment process is usually completed by a qualified environmental professional. Although some states have defined the minimum qualifications for performing an ESA, most states have not. To determine if your state has minimum qualifications for environmental professionals, contact your state environmental agency. The ESA process requires interdisciplinary skills, so it is difficult to prescribe a specific set of narrowly defined qualifications. Perhaps the best indicators of an environmental professional's qualifications are the combination of specific experience and education of that individual. Experience that is specific to the type of property or issues to be assessed should weigh more heavily than other experience. When evaluating education and training, consider the academic background of individuals but also review their commitment to continuing education and training. The ESA is a relatively new process that continues to evolve. It is critical that the environmental professional keep up to date with the latest standards and guidelines.

The ASTM Standard Practice for Environmental Site Assessments: Phase I Environmental Site Assessment (E-1527) provides clear guidance with which to undertake an ESA but also allows for the exercise of judgment and discretion by the environmental professional. The purpose of the assessment is to provide a standard that would allow property buyers and developers to meet the requirements established by the laws and courts to minimize the risks of environmental liability associated with buying property. The standard also can be used to evaluate the final work product of the environmental professional. A checklist of the key points of the ASTM standard may be used to measure the completeness of the report and work effort (Table 3.7). It should be noted that this checklist is not a part of the ASTM standard guideline.

The Phase I ESA is designed in principle to be a cost-effective overview of a site that should identify indications of recognized environmental conditions. To keep the cost of the investigation at a reasonable level, the typical Phase I ESA involves no collection or testing of samples and is limited to information already available through public sources, interviews, or firsthand observation. This approach allows a buyer to determine whether there is an indication of a problem or an increased risk with a particular property. By limiting the scope of the ESA the cost is minimized, but the conclusions of the environmental professional are drawn from limited information. The environmental professional may be unable to conclude that contamination is or is not present, stating instead that there are indications of this condition or that circumstance, which could indicate contamination.

The ESA report should include copies of the notes collected during interviews, the database review summaries, maps, aerial photos, and any other reasonable documentation

Site Condition
Developed
Existing buildings or structures
Former uses
Known site conditions
Character/condition of existing roads
Points of access and egress (approximate site distances)
Expected road improvements
Visibility into and out of site
Security considerations
Neighboring property uses
Existing rights of way or easements on property
Other encumbrances (condominium or community association)
Zoning Regulations
Zone identification
Minimum lot size
Front setback
Back setback
Side setback, one side total
Permitted uses by right
Permitted uses by special exception
Maximum coverage
Parking requirements
Overlay zoning
Sign requirements
Right of way width
Cartway width
Curb requirements
Sidewalk requirements
Fence regulations
Storage requirements
Landscape Ordinance
Land Development Regulations
Street profile requirements
Site distance requirements
Slope restrictions
Storm water requirements
Landscaping requirements
Lighting requirements

TABLE 3.7   Site Analysis Checklist: Administrative Issues (*Continued*)

Utilities Access (distance to and connections requirements)
Natural gas
Telephone
Electricity
Cable television
Public water
Sanitary sewage
Traffic
Condition of local roads
Access to site
Internal circulation constraints
Impact on neighborhood
Topography
General topographic character of site
Areas of steep slope
Aspect/orientation of slopes
Site access
Slope stability
Soils/geology
Soil types
Depth to bedrock
Depth to groundwater
Seasonal high water table
Engineering capabilities class of soils (density, Atterberg limits, compressibility)
Existing indication of slope instability/site erosion
Sinkholes
Fault zones
Hydrology
Sketch existing drainage pattern, off-sight and on-site
Presence of surface water features
Quality of surface waters
Floodplains
Wetlands
Riparian zones or floodplains
Springs
Wells
Aquifer
Anticipated drainage pattern
Character and quality of receiving waters

TABLE 3.7   Site Analysis Checklist: Administrative Issues (*Continued*)

Vegetation/Wildlife
General types of existing vegetation
Quality of vegetation
Presence of known protected species
Presence of valuable specimens or communities
Presence of exotic/invasive species
Historic or Cultural Features/Community Interests
Known historical features
Unique natural features or character
Existing Parks or Public Areas
Existing informal public access/use on the site
Community character such as architectural style/conventions
Local landscaping
Local materials
Environmental Concerns
Past site uses
Neighboring site uses
Evidence of fill, dumping, or disposal
Evidence of contamination (stained soils, stressed/dead vegetation, etc.)
On-site storage
Impact of site development on local water and air quality

TABLE 3.7 Site Analysis Checklist: Administrative Issues (*Continued*)

referenced in the report (Table 3.8). The environmental professional is expected to exercise good judgment in the completion of the ESA and in some cases may elect to modify the ESA guidelines. While these changes are to be expected, deviations from the standard should be noted and explained to the buyer's satisfaction.

Brownfields

Brownfields are abandoned or underutilized properties that are environmentally contaminated or are perceived as being contaminated from past industrial or commercial activities. Such sites may present a designer with a wide range of unfamiliar site restrictions and conditions. Site planning on such sites must address the contamination or the mitigation strategy selected to protect the users and the environment. Normal practices of site development and storm water management may be restricted. In the past, site planning proceeded on the assumption that a site was "clean." The designer was usually not involved in the remedial action design; sites were cleaned up and then the redevelopment occurred as if on a clean site. To be effective participants in a brownfield

This Phase I Environmental Site Assessment Guidelines Review checklist is to be completed for the quality assurance purpose of verifying the substantive compliance of an ESA report with the ASTM Standard Practice for Environmental Site Assessments: Phase I Environmental Site Assessment Process, E-1527. Except where otherwise noted, this review is based entirely on the report and does not include an independent confirmation of information.
Records review
Does the report reference ASTM E-1527?
Was the ESA conducted by an environmental professional?
Is a résumé or statement of qualification attached?
Were proper minimum search distances used in the record search?
Federal NPL Site List (1 mi)
Federal CERCLIS list (0.5 mi)
Federal RCRA TSD list (1 mi)
Federal RCRA generators list (property and adjoiners)
Federal ERNS list (property only)
Equivalent state lists
State landfill lists (0.5 mi)
State Leaking Underground Storage Tank (LUST) list (0.5 mi)
State registered underground storage tank (UST) list (property and adjoiners)
If proper minimum search distances were not used, was justification for each reduction and the new minimum distance provided?
Did the environmental professional provide an opinion as to the significance of any listing as a *recognized environmental condition* within the minimum search distances?
Was a current USGS 7.5 minute topographic map used as the source of the physical setting data?
Sources used to determine the history of the site and surrounding areas
Aerial photographs
Local historic maps
Historic USGS topographic maps
Fire insurance maps
Tax files
Local records
Interviews
Fifty-year chain of title

TABLE 3.8   Phase I Environmental Site Assessment Quality Assurance Review (*Continued*)

Site walkover
Did the environmental professional report any obstructions, or obstacles, that would prevent a thorough site reconnaissance?
Was the exterior of the property visually and physically observed and the description included in the report?
Was an inspection of the interior of the buildings conducted, including accessible common areas and a representative sample of occupant areas?
Was information from a prior ESA used in the report?
Were changes between the earlier ESA and current observations noted?
Were the uses and conditions of the site reported?
Was the owner's representative present during the site visit?
Were the interviews conducted?
Did the owner provide any additional documentation regarding the site?
Does the report include references to site conditions not visually and physically observed by the environmental professional?
Does the report include
A description of the current site use and conditions?
A description of the adjoining property uses and conditions?
A description of the topographic and hydrologic conditions?
A general description of the structures?
Is the source of potable water identified?
Are the locations of roads and parking areas described?
Are past uses of the property discernable?
Does the report include a conclusion or recommendations?
Based on this review, does the ESA meet the standard guidelines?

TABLE **3.8**   Phase I Environmental Site Assessment Quality Assurance Review (*Continued*)

project, landscape architects and site engineers should be conversant with the environmental professional and understand the value and limitations of the site assessment process. Further, knowledge of the state of practice in site remediation technologies will increase the opportunity for collaboration and innovative site design, enabling site designers to work closely with environmental professionals in the interests of the client and the environment.

CHAPTER 4
Design for Communities

Design and planning is the process of bringing a vision to the point of implementation. The professional considers a broad range of concerns in the synthesis of a design concept: the physical aspects of the site itself, the vision or program of the client, the designer's own creative inclination, the concerns of the community, and the interests of the end-user. The public's interests are represented by a variety of public authorities who regulate and oversee the development process. Land development ordinances act as a set of minimum standards or guidelines, and few can be applied to a specific site or project without some adjustment or accommodation. These standards represent a local view of the minimum requirements for land development and should not be confused with a measurement of design quality. Quality design and development typically need to go beyond the minimum threshold of the ordinance.

Site design professionals must balance the client's objectives with the community's standards and expectations, which are composed of stated, tangible parameters as well as unstated expectations and intangible elements. In addition, the interests of the end-user of the project must be kept in mind. The end-user usually is not included in the discussions that drive the design process. To arrive at a design solution that will satisfy a client, the various regulatory agencies, and still satisfy a future user, the designer must be a student of design outcomes and performance as well as design synthesis.

Site Layout

The most obvious feature of the site is how the proposed project lays upon the land, that is, how the buildings and facilities are organized. The site design is determined first by the land itself and then, in varying degrees, by the values of the developer, the requirements of local ordinances, community standards, and the nature of the project as these elements are perceived and balanced by the designer. The parameters that go into a site layout are diverse, but some important design practices and standards can guide the professional.

The designer's analysis and sensitivity to the site informs the entire design process. An awareness of the site might include its history, its place in a larger landscape ecosystem, its real estate value, and its local political or economic importance. Redevelopment may be the preferred environmental strategy because it involves the reuse of already disturbed land; in a sense, this option is recycling the site. Redevelopment projects should attempt to restore function wherever possible. Honoring particularly important historical aspects of a site should be considered when appropriate. Defining the role of the site in the larger landscape fabric is critical. In developing a new site, the environmental functions of the site should be preserved, and the design should minimize the impact of development.

Figure 4.1   This storefront conforms to the standards of the community.

Recognition of the impacts of urban sprawl and an increasing awareness of smart growth alternatives are beginning to have an impact on site development practices. There is no simple, one-size-fits-all solution to the problems of urban sprawl or the challenges of smart growth, but the range of solutions available to designers will continue to grow with the sophistication and needs of the marketplace. Much has been said and written about the homogeneity of the modern built landscape: every place looks pretty much like every other place. However, many communities have established an identity, if not clear standards. In these communities even the mundane is made to meet community expectations. Note how a common business has adapted to local standards in Fig. 4.1.

Residential Site Design

The primary objective in residential and community site planning is to provide a desirable place to live for the intended users. Different parameters will be applied and different elements will be selected depending on who the end-user is to be. Developments targeted toward young families with children, for example, include features that would be out of place in a project designed for empty-nesters. House size, lot size, common space, and recreation facilities will be quite different, but some commonalities are found in all quality residential developments.

In *Save Our Lands, Save Our Towns*, Thomas Hylton (1995) describes 10 rules of quality development for communities (Table 4.1). In essence Hylton and others have found

1. A sense of place
2. Human scale
3. Self-contained neighborhoods
4. Diversity
5. Transit-friendly design
6. Trees
7. Alleys and parking lots to the rear
8. Humane architecture
9. Outdoor rooms
10. Maintenance and safety

Adapted from Hylton (1995).

TABLE 4.1   Characteristics of a Quality Community

that quality involves careful adaptation of traditional, even archetypal, forms of community design with important accommodations for modern life.

The most desirable communities allow maximum pedestrian access to schools, work, shops, and the like but also provide easy transit in and out of the neighborhood. The presence of human scale streets and buildings, the softening and tempering effects of trees, and the diversity of social and architectural aspects are commonly considered to be important aspects of a community. Although security and safety are often cited as important, achieving these through hardening of buildings and sites is not desirable.

Suburb and exurb neighborhoods often have little connection except through arterials, which may have provision for pedestrian movement or bicycle traffic. This isolation of neighborhoods can work against development of a sense community. This isolation reflects a process in which discrete parcels of land are developed without regard for adjacent parcels subject to future development or even existing development in many cases. Such an arrangement necessarily increases vehicle use and reduces "walkability"; traffic on arterial roads increases, contributing to local congestion and the attendant issues of longer commutes and reduced air quality.

Local streets should be designed with a coherent pattern of circulation, and the project layout should be sensitive to the land and not require substantial alteration and a loss of character. Houses or residential units should be arranged to provide variation and visual interest. After the style and affordability of houses, lot layout and character is the most important element of the typical residential development project. The number of lots is of critical concern to the developer, and lot size and character are important to buyers. In a competitive residential market, developers may compete on the basis of price, quality, or the character of their units or amenities. Valuable lot amenities include the presence of trees, lot shape and size, views, and access to water (Table 4.2).

It is important to begin to identify home sites early in the site analysis. Generally this is done using topographic mapping of the site and walking the entire site to identify valuable locations or site features. Identification of home sites and related issues

Open space feature	Mean score
Adjacent to wet pond	4.44
Adjacent to natural area	4.27
On a cul-de-sac	3.83
Adjacent to golf course	3.67
Adjacent to public park	3.10
Adjacent to dry pond	2.05

TABLE 4.2 Homeowner Preference for Proximity to Open Space Features

will drive the planning and design of the site. Home sites are identified by determining where it would be nice to live; it is fundamentally a simple process. A good location is a combination of the surroundings, access, amenities, and more subjective concerns such as desire for a sense of neighborhood or security. In the development of sites for more affordable homes, lot size tends to be smaller and the linear feet of road per unit lower.

Hillside lots tend to be irregular in shape, reflecting the physical aspects of the site. The lot configurations are designed to encompass a desirable living space in a more difficult development condition. Lot configurations may range from tight clusters that leave large undeveloped portions of the site as open space to individual lots with dwelling units separated by varying degrees of distance. In either case the sites and layout are designed to minimize impact and maximize site value.

The layout of a residential development is part of an overall community design. Communities are more than a collection of houses; they include recreation facilities, schools, shopping centers, workplaces, and religious institutions. Not all projects include all of these features, but it is appropriate for designers and developers to consider how the proposed project will relate to existing or future features. The next section highlights one successful regional approach to community planning and development.

Emerging Practices

The Connecticut River Valley has been inhabited for thousands of years, and its rich, fertile soils and climate and river aspect have attracted people to the valley. From 1951 to 1972, the land in the Connecticut River Valley converted from farmland to development tripled, and projections indicated that this trend would continue. However, existing ordinances and planning regulations did not provide the protection residents felt they needed.

The river valley area comprises 19 towns in three counties. No coordinated effort existed to direct development or the construction of infrastructure on which future development would be attracted. In addition, the features and attributes considered the most desirable (rural character, views, access to open space, and river front) were the first features to be compromised. In the 1980s the Massachusetts Department of Environmental

Management (DEM) established the Connecticut River Valley Action Program to develop a regional approach to planning and conservation that would preserve the scenic, historic, and environmental qualities of the area and still allow for development.

Among the tools developed by DEM was the Agricultural Preservation Restriction (APR) program, which encouraged rural landowners to sell their development rights to the state. In cooperation with other state agencies, the DEM increased support for agricultural activities by providing training in integrated pest management and intensive farming practices to make the agricultural use of the land more effective, more profitable, and more sustainable. The action program has been most widely recognized, however, for publication of *Dealing with Change in the Connecticut River Valley: A Design Manual for Conservation and Development* (Yaro et al., 1988), which describes plausible and effective rural design parameters and policies that have very broad application.

The Center for Rural Massachusetts, under a grant from the DEM, developed the manual from a concern that the only way to avoid a hodge-podge of low-density suburban development and "islands" of preservation was to develop a comprehensive approach to development and preservation. Complete faith in land preservation efforts will ultimately be unsatisfactory due to the limits of preservation resources. Reliance on unregulated market forces was surely not an acceptable alternative. From the outset the center recognized that the development and design process would have to encompass both concerns in a practical fashion.

Design guidelines based on preserving the character of the region and those elements most prized by its residents also provided for viable residential and commercial development. Much of this process involves turning classic planning tools upside down. For example, it is common for zoning to require a commercial shopping center to be set back 100 or even 200 ft from a public right of way. This arrangement forces the shopping center into the familiar "strip" with a sea of parking and macadam in front of it. The center's recommendations were to require a maximum setback of 25 ft from the public right of way, locating all of the parking behind or alongside the building. It also encourages people to walk from store to store and brings the stores into a more "human" scale, akin to the old downtown area. This arrangement is more in keeping with the character of the existing towns and streetscapes of the valley. Merchants accepted the new design because it gave them two places to advertise (front and back entrances).

Landscape requirements for commercial development eliminated the classic "juniper and bark mulch" plantings in favor of native plants and wildflowers. Residential development is encouraged through density bonuses to form clusters and preserve open space. The developer can use the density bonus to purchase development rights sold to the state by local farmers. As a result, a developer of a residential project might be able to build 15 houses in a cluster on 12 acres of ground rather than being restricted to 10 or 11 units. The density bonus encourages the builder to "cluster" the 15 houses on a small portion of the site, leaving the rest of the site in open space.

Although these ideas were not new or unique, the Connecticut River Valley program was able to develop broad support among residents and landowners. Public meetings were held and ideas from the design manual were discussed. The manual identifies eight different landscape types and illustrates possible development scenarios ranging from development under traditional zoning to development under these rural landscape planning guidelines. Sample ordinances for the municipalities to consider and adopt are also included. The successful effort by DEM has been linked to several factors: (a) the public had a vested interest in preserving the character of the area in which they lived and owned land; (b) the Center for Rural Massachusetts dealt with the municipalities and the residents in developing design guidelines that represented the values and objectives of the residents; (c) the plan was practical, encouraging development consistent with the guidelines and stating performance requirements in a straightforward manner; and (d) the information was communicated in a readable, friendly style, using graphics and photos, easily understood by any interested person rather than the "legalese" and "technobabble" used in most documents of this type. The guidelines suggested by the center have been adopted by most of the municipal governments in the Connecticut River Valley, and the region has become a model of effective rural planning.

Lot Layout Alternatives

The rapid expansion of suburbs and edge cities has had several impacts. The cost of housing has continued to rise in real terms over the last 30 years, and affordability has become a major issue in some communities. Rapid development also has been criticized for consuming agricultural land, reducing environmental quality, and abandoning urban centers to poverty and other social ills. These complaints generally are grouped under the umbrella of urban sprawl. Most of these issues require a shift in public policy and political will that is outside the scope of the site design professionals' immediate influence, but development practices have grown to embrace concerns of environmental quality, density, and affordability. As developers respond to the growth and resettlement patterns of the population, concern over the environment and interest in sustainable development and quality communities will continue to grow.

The key to a successful residential design, regardless of the cost of the housing, lies in how effectively the design creates a sense of place and relates to the end-user. Some sites have natural features that may be worked into the design. Other projects must rely on the combination of housing type and landscape architecture to create a feeling on the site that attracts and holds residents. The familiar grid layout of post–World War II residential development is no longer the preferred approach in most communities. Contemporary site layouts rely on more curvilinear street designs and a greater mix of building styles and types than are found in those early suburban projects. The focus of contemporary residential site design is on balancing the number of dwelling units and the development costs with the interests of the community and the environment. This has been described as a quality-of-life approach. Numerous projects have demonstrated that quality development can be affordable and efficient.

When all costs are considered, large lot developments consume more resources than they contribute to a community. The trend in development is toward higher densities generally consistent with the goals of the various smart growth initiatives around the United States. Varied densities and housing types have replaced the familiar uniform density and housing types of the past in some communities.

Work done by the National Association of Home Builders (1986), Randall Arendt (1991), Andres Duany, and others have all found that smaller lots and cluster type developments have equal or greater initial and resale value than traditional residential development. Small lot development usually refers to projects with 6 to 12 units per acre. Resistance to higher densities is common in communities with the more traditional density of 1 to 4 units per acre, but many buyers find the higher densities attractive as long as amenities and privacy are sufficient. The primary target market includes young professionals, couples without children, and empty-nesters, but there are successful small lot communities for every demographic target. Small lot development tends to work best on relatively flat sites. Small clusters are an ideal way of reaching a gross density while preserving important open space features of a site. Site layout is critical to project success and should be focused on lifestyle amenities, emphasizing outdoor living and privacy. Small lot development, especially lots with unusual configurations, work best in more sophisticated real estate markets (Kreager, 1992).

A recent survey of consumer preferences found that more than half of those who said they expected to build a new home in the next 10 years cited "green" features such as energy efficiency and sustainable materials as very important considerations. This number rose to more the two-thirds among those under 30 years of age (NAHB, 2008).

Grid Layout

The grid layout shown in Fig. 4.2 is an efficient way to subdivide property, but it can be monotonous, especially for residential areas. The key advantage of the grid layout is maximizing lots per linear feet of street. The relative ease in finding one's way provides a certain level of comfort for many people, but the straight streets often invite higher vehicle speeds, especially when wide cartways are used. Curvilinear streets are far more interesting visually and may help to manage vehicle speeds, but they are somewhat less efficient with regard to lot count. In addition, finding your way through some of these communities can be confusing. This may be of concern in particular in communities designed for older residents. Alternatives to the traditional grid layout are shown in Figs. 4.3 and 4.4.

A variety of lot configurations have evolved with higher densities to accommodate the smaller lot size and traditional or familiar housing types. Four configuration types are common. Some projects use a combination of strategies; others design around a single lot and housing type.

Deep, Narrow Lots

The deep, narrow lot configuration allows for a familiar lot and house pattern with the garage and front of the house facing the street (Fig. 4.5). Lots typically range from 3000 to 4800 ft^2, about 6 to 8.5 lots per acre. The typical 40-ft wide lot allows for about

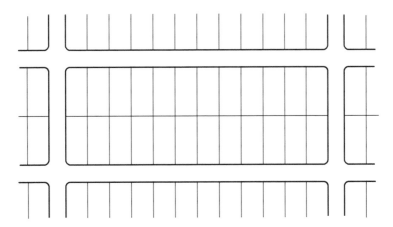

FIGURE 4.2 Grid layout.

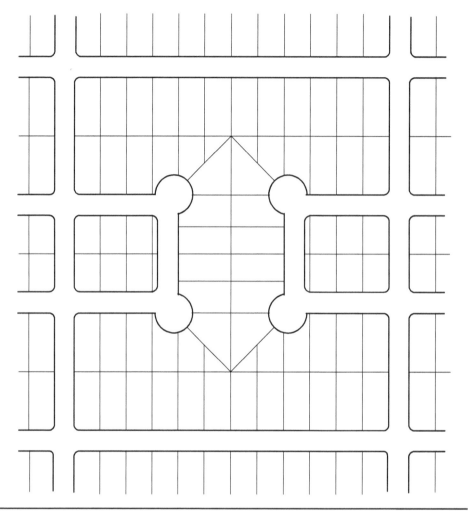

FIGURE 4.3   Alternative grid layout.

10 ft of side yard, which leaves 20 ft for garage and 25 ft for house. Garages are close to the front of the lot, often in front of the house facade to maximize the amount of yard space behind the house. This tends to create an unattractive street view of all garage doors. The deep, narrow lot provides minimal backyard privacy, especially in housing with two or more floors. This may be offset by paying special attention to the location of windows in adjacent units and to visual landscape barriers, but it is difficult to antic-ipate the location of windows and site lines in projects in which different housing mod-els are possible.

Wide, Shallow Lots

The wide, shallow configuration allows for a standard-width house and garage and has the feel of a traditional neighborhood (Fig. 4.6). The wide, shallow lot gives a feeling of a larger lot with more space between units because its longest dimensions are along the

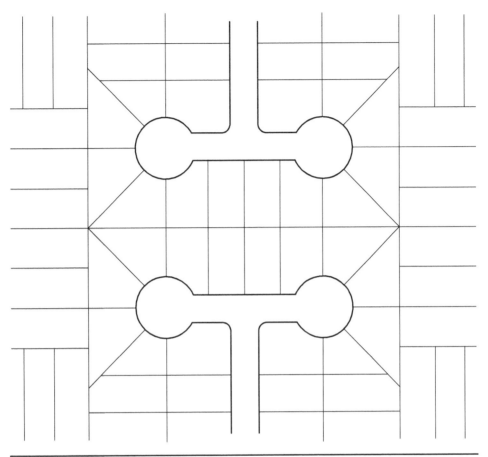

Figure 4.4 Alternative grid layout.

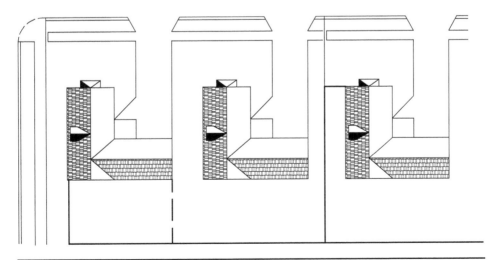

Figure 4.5 Deep, narrow lots.

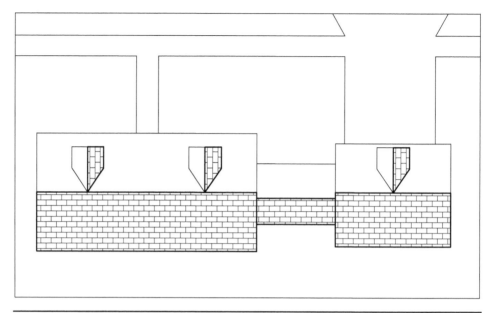

Figure 4.6 Wide, shallow lots.

street frontage. These lots generally yield about 6 to 7 units per acre with lot sizes from 3500 ft². In general, these lots are not as desirable as the deep, narrow lot because of the increased lot costs and lack of useful yard space. Development costs may be higher as well because there are fewer units per linear foot of road and utilities. An increase in lot width of 20 ft will result in almost a 50 percent increase in utility costs per unit over the deep, narrow plan. The backyard of the wide, shallow lot offers little privacy, especially if two-story homes are constructed. Privacy can be increased with the use of fencing and landscaping.

Alley Houses
Another small lot layout alternative is a return to the use of alleys behind the houses, a common configuration in the past (Fig. 4.7). Garages were located in the back of properties and access was over a common alley usually 16 to 18 ft wide. The alley design allows for lots of 3300 to 4500 ft², yielding 4 to 8 units per acre. Many older, desirable neighborhoods using this configuration still exist in cities throughout the United States. By locating the garage in the rear, the streetscape is all house fronts: no driveways and no garage doors. The paved alley increases development costs somewhat, but many traditional neighborhoods using the alley layout have narrower streets and lots that offset the additional cost of the alley. Some municipalities resist the alley arrangement because of increased maintenance; in other cities the alleys are not public rights of way but are held in common by the neighbors through an access easement and maintenance covenant. Projects with alleys provide ideal utility corridors.

Z-Lots
The term *Z-lot* refers to a zero lot line layout in which the house is placed on or very near to one property line (Fig. 4.8). In some configurations the lot lines may jog around

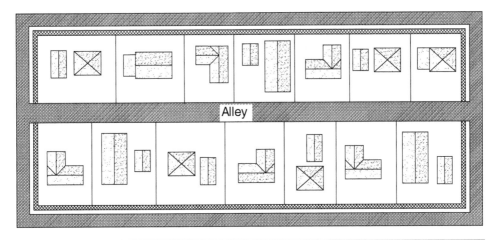

FIGURE 4.7 Alley houses.

FIGURE 4.8 Z-lot configuration.

the building to create a more interesting space. Such lots are said to resemble a "z," hence its name. The z-lot is often slanted relative to the street to increase the appearance of lot width. Houses are designed to increase light and maximize privacy by strategically locating windows and entranceways. Some z-lot developments provide special maintenance easements or even condominium-type arrangements to provide access to buildings for maintenance. Easements along lot lines may be difficult for z-lot configurations.

Connectivity

In traditional urban and early suburban development, neighborhoods were commonly assembled on a pattern determined by preexisting conditions (earlier development, topographic features) and by the local planning authority. As development occurred, it extended the existing pattern of streets and related infrastructure. In recent years residential development has become more cellular in nature, with individual developments commonly located along a road that acts as an arterial collector. This collector is often arterial in function but not design. Isolated groups of homes connected only by arterial roads, often without allowances for pedestrian, bicycle, or other alternative transportation, work against the evolution of neighborhoods and limit access to community amenities to those in automobiles.

Site designers should look for and evaluate ways of connecting to existing neighborhoods and street systems, although resistance to this sort of connectivity has occurred on occasion. The most common concern seems to be that connecting neighborhoods will increase "cut through" traffic. This should be addressed by the use of traffic calming devices and street design to manage vehicle speeds to increase safety, a sense of neighborhood, and reduce the value of connected streets as cut through paths.

Cluster Designs

Cluster designs allow the same number of units on a tract but group the units into clusters of greater density, thereby preserving more open space (Fig. 4.9). A density bonus is sometimes provided to recognize and encourage the preservation of open space. Cluster development can reduce the visual impact of new development on a community as

FIGURE 4.9   This clustered residential development illustrates some of the opportunities for conserving open space.

Allows same number of units in smaller space for more open space
Reduces visual impact on existing community
Allows for open space buffers between incompatible uses
Preserves important natural functions of landscape
Contributes to "rural" character of area
Is sensitive to the character of the site
Establishes a benchmark for future projects

TABLE 4.3 Cluster Design Attributes

well as reduce the environmental effects. Table 4.3 lists some attributes of cluster designs. This configuration allows developers to utilize the land yet preserves valuable natural areas, agricultural land, riparian zones, and so forth. Cluster developments are usually welcomed because they minimize the impact of the development and are sensitive to the rural character, the nature of the site, and the values of the community. Effective and successful cluster developments may also serve to establish a quality threshold for other future projects. Cluster designs have become more common in recent years (Fig. 4.10).

Allowances for Easements and Rights of Way

Allowances for easements and rights of way in higher-density developments may require more planning and thought than for less dense projects. With smaller front and side yards, easements may take a significant portion of the street side of individual lots. Utility easements may restrict planting large trees or building fences. Some utilities prefer that easements be located outside of the cartway to reduce the cost of maintenance and repair. In

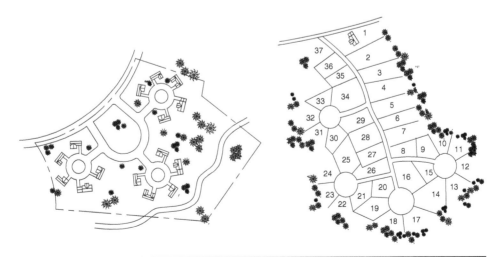

FIGURE 4.10 Examples of possible cluster design layouts.

other cases the proximity of one utility to another may require extraordinary construction methods and increase development costs. Easements along the back of the property are possible for some utilities, but access is required, which may affect the use and enjoyment of the lot. Many small lot projects are designed to allow utilities to be installed within the public right of way of the street, usually between the curb and sidewalk. Still other projects provide a utility corridor easement across front lawns and restrict the amount and type of landscaping that can be used.

Affordable Housing Design

The cost of new development is a concern for many communities. Zoning and land development ordinances are prescriptions for development. Development costs are a function of many factors but among them are the local development standards. Planners and designers know that local development standards can be very prescriptive and can raise the development costs of a project. In turn, these costs are built into the sales price of homes, pricing key people in the community out of the market. Many communities have found that developments produced using their local standards are not consistent with the character of the community and contribute to unwelcome sprawl.

Homes in many older communities continue to command high market prices. Many features that contribute to the continuing attraction and market value of these older homes would not be allowed under current ordinances and practices. Many of the standards for community development today were refined after the Second World War. Street width, lot size, setbacks, and many other aspects of postwar community development were modeled on the grid street pattern and lot layout. Developments with wider streets and larger lots reached their peak in the 1980s, and their popularity has been sustained to this day. The growing awareness of environmental impacts, increased energy costs, cost of the initial development, and life-cycle costs of unnecessary pavement and oversized lots has encouraged a shift toward more affordable and lower impact design without sacrificing public safety or function. Affordable housing remains a concern of many communities. Affordability can be improved dramatically by specific changes in development standards and local practices such as those listed in Table 4.4. Table 4.5 lists some elements of better residential site design.

Urban Infill

Planning and site design is generally focused on new development. With the growing concentration of people living in and moving to cities, it is appropriate that the concern of designers include the sustainable redevelopment of existing neighborhoods. There is a robust but quiet effort in cities to restore, revitalize, and preserve urban neighborhoods everywhere. The deconstruction activities mentioned in Chap. 2 are part of that. Some cities have experienced suburban flight, often leaving urban areas with infrastructure designed for much larger populations than they currently support. Some trends, such as the portion of baby boomers retiring without adequate savings, expected increases in immigration, the cost of suburban housing, and the attraction of urban areas to young professionals and students, suggest renewed interest in an urban lifestyle.

Demolition of vacant or poorly maintained buildings offers opportunities for redevelopment. Attracting retail into cities can be a mixed blessing, but supermarkets and similar stores are commonly seen as desirable and do not always compete directly with

Standard	Single family detached	Single family attached or townhouse
Lot size	4500–5000 ft²	3500–5000 ft²
Lot width (minimum)	No minimum to 50 ft	No minimum to 16 ft
Lot coverage (maximum)	40–50%	50–75%
Setbacks, front	10–20 ft	5–20 ft
Back	5–15 ft	5–10 ft
Side each/total	5/10 ft	0/5 ft
Right of way width	35–40 ft	30–50 ft
Cartway width*	18–28 ft	22–32 ft

*9ft minimum travel lane on low volume local street, 8ft for each parking lane.
Adapted from Welford Sanders, Judith Getzels, David Mosena, and JoAnn Butler, *Affordable Single Family Housing*, Planning Advisory Service Report No. 385 (Washington D.C., American Planning Association, 1984); Welford Sanders and David Mosena, *Changing Development Standards for Affordable Housing*, Planning Advisory Report No. 371 (Washington D.C., The Joint Venture for Affordable Housing, American Planning Association, 1982), and Steven S. Fehr, "Reducing Land Use Barriers to Affordable Housing," *Planning Series No. 10* (Harrisburg, PA, Planning Services Division of the Bureau of Community Planning, Pennsylvania Department of Community Affairs, 1991).

TABLE 4.4   Development Standards for Affordable Residential Design

Narrower, shorter streets
Smaller lots with less restrictive setbacks and lot width requirements
Increase allowable lot coverage
Use effective stream buffers
Increase infiltration of storm water
Use grass lined swales instead of pipes and paved gutters

TABLE 4.5   Elements of Better Residential Site Design

smaller neighborhood stores, especially specialty shops. Vacant lots can be put to use as community gardens, pocket parks, or additional parking (Figs. 4.11 and 4.12). Many older neighborhoods were built before the automobile became the ubiquitous feature that it is today. In such places, narrow streets and the absence of off-street parking make parking and the resulting congestion a particularly unpleasant aspect of urban living. By using vacant lots to provide parking for residents, some congestion can be removed from the residential street and encourage an active pedestrian street life.

Commercial and industrial development can be a bit more problematic. In the past, factories often were constructed within walking distance of housing. This circumstance has resulted in local residents resisting industrial and some commercial redevelopment. Other issues also constrain the redevelopment of urban property for nonresidential

FIGURE 4.11   A neighborhood parking area was created by removing a blighted building. The parking is reserved for residents and authorized visitors using a parking tag system. (See also color insert.)

FIGURE 4.12   A neighborhood park created in the space where a vacant home once stood. (See also color insert.)

uses. Older roads, for example, often have turning radii that are challenging to modern delivery vehicles, and urban sites sometimes have insufficient parking for employees. These situations increase local traffic congestion and increase parking competition. The structure of many older buildings simply is not compatible with modern industrial and commercial uses. Older buildings tend to have lower ceiling heights and smaller rooms than are desired for modern industrial, warehousing, or even commercial uses. These limitations aside, robust and successful redevelopment and revitalization efforts are under way in many cities. Making these efforts sustainable is an important challenge.

Design for Security

In recent years there has been increasing awareness of the role design of public spaces plays in crime prevention and security, particularly as part of efforts to improve distressed communities. Crime prevention through environmental design (CPTED) is most successfully conducted in conjunction with other community efforts, such as community policing and neighborhood awareness. Rob White (1998) of the University of Melbourne observes that there are two schools of thought regarding CPTED. One approach studies how places can be designed and built to be safer simply to create better quality places. The other he describes as "situational prevention," that is, remedial work addressed to specific trouble or hot spots.

Although environmental conditions may encourage or discourage crime, design alone is not the answer. Thefts are higher near schools and rapes are higher near hospitals because of predictable routines that create opportunity. To discourage crime, we must create environments that make it hard for criminals to do their work and that encourage other acceptable or desirable activities. Design is part of a larger strategy that must include management and social and community development.

There is no single formula for the design of defensible space. A thorough understanding of the physical and social environment of a neighborhood is required: What is the physical layout? Who is coming and going? Who belongs and who doesn't? What are the dynamics of the problem? Is it traffic? Automobile or pedestrian? Night or day? What are neighborhood routines?

Design solutions for problems faced by communities range from improving security and safety elements to helping to increase neighborhood identity and pride. Adam Graycar (1998) has observed that crime is not an equal opportunity endeavor; where you live, how you live, and who you are have a great deal to do with your chances of becoming the victim of a crime. Not all crime is considered equal either. Predatory crimes such as homicide or assault are more serious and less common than drug- related crimes and violence and theft. Graycar observes that crime requires three necessary elements: a likely offender, a target, and the absence of a capable guardian. The capable guardian refers to all social, political, and design strategies used to prevent crime (Table 4.6). Situational CPTED focuses on providing physical evidence of the capable guardian by creating spaces that reduce criminal opportunity and increase the risks and effort required.

A community that is aware of what is going on within it and where activities in pubic space are readily observed is less likely to have a crime problem primarily because the community itself, through its interaction and behavior, represents a capable guardian. Much of the CPTED effort is geared toward physically modifying space, but this effort should be a product of community desire and interest. The key to CPTED is the involvement of the community. Designers working with communities become facilitators of the

Provide effective lighting
Design to assure good lines of sight along streets and paths and near buildings
Consider crime prevention when selecting plant materials
Use traffic calming measures and circulation planning to reduce joy-riding
Look for and anticipate escape routes
Encourage people to observe streets and public spaces
Use vandal proof materials and assure quick repair and replacement of damaged materials
Restricting traffic on residential streets (one way streets, traffic calming)
Increased evidence of formal and informal surveillance
Restricting vehicle movement

TABLE 4.6   Site Design Crime Prevention Strategies

community's goals. In most instances the budget for implementing a design is limited, so it is important to have the greatest impact for the resources available. To determine the scope of the problems and to develop a design strategy, the CPTED process usually begins with an assessment of the neighborhood. It may be difficult to determine the boundaries of the neighborhood and the study area, but it is important to have a finite area of consideration.

Working with neighbors and local businesses, the CPTED team identifies the attributes and the problems of the neighborhood. The team looks for positive elements—points of stability such as schools, churches, or long-standing businesses—and locates these places on a map. Next, the problem areas are identified. CPTED teams may elect to map abandoned buildings, vacant lots, high-crime areas, homeownership, parking areas, poorly lit areas, traffic patterns, or anything else that contributes to the character and concerns of the neighborhood. From these maps and the juxtaposition of positive and negative elements, the CPTED team works with neighbors to identify and prioritize steps toward a better community.

In general there are three aspects of defensible space design: territory, access, and surveillance. Territory refers to private and public space. Territory is established by drawing distinctions between spaces (Fig. 4.13). Distinctions can be accomplished by textural changes in pavements or walls, elevation changes (a step up or down), barriers such as walls or fences, visual barriers such as low fences or shrubs (Fig. 4.14), or psychological barriers such as consistent neighborhood organization or themes. When evaluating a space, ask yourself, "What could I get away with here? (Martin, 1997)."

Access refers to providing and restricting access; in short, control. Street blocking is usually not the preferred method. Through streets provide access by pedestrians and vehicles. Some alternatives to blocking streets are intersection narrowing, "s" curves in streets, dual use streets, traffic calming devices, one way streets, turn restrictions, and bollards. Physical access can be restricted. This is known as "target hardening" and

FIGURE 4.13   Fences and outdoor seating in this traditional neighborhood clearly delineate private from public property.

FIGURE 4.14   Bollards and planting used in this city neighborhood separate pubic from private space and signal community activity and surveillance.

involves installing fences and gates or other restrictions. It is sometimes necessary as a preliminary or temporary design element to gain control.

More subtle ways of communicating boundaries and a sense of territory or neighborhood include low fences or walls, colors, or signs that do not actually restrict access but signal to people that this area is set apart. Passing through these barriers signals a transition from one area to another. Such symbolic barriers provide an identity that both residents and visitors can see and that makes a sense of ownership more palpable. Space that does not indicate use or is not controlled within a neighborhood is an invitation to unwanted behavior and is at least an attractive nuisance.

Surveillance refers to seeing and being seen. Windows and doors facing the street allow people to be seen both as observers and the observed. Points of congregation such as playgrounds and porches encourage residents to see and be seen, increasing the degree of visible surveillance in a neighborhood. Lighting is important, but the sense that there are eyes on the street is more likely to be a deterrent to unwanted activity.

With the increased terrorist threat faced today, designers should expect to address security issues beyond crime in the site design plan, especially for public facilities. This may require consultation with a security expert or a design professional with specific security experience. The federal government has developed site security guidelines, but this is an emerging area of practice and the standards are still evolving. The General Services Administration developed a set of security standards in the early 1990s, and every federal facility was assessed and upgraded to minimum standards. More recent studies reported in 2008 by the GAO found that many facilities lacked sufficient security measures. Much of the focus of the standards deals with architectural issues, interior security, and technology, but site planning also plays an important role. Most state and local facilities and many private institutions that might also be targets for terrorists have little or no relevant security. In many cases the short-term answer has been target hardening, which creates a fortresslike feeling to public buildings. Public buildings and public spaces adjoining them are more than the sum of activities that take place within them. They represent the values and the character of the people, so they must remain accessible, attractive, and inviting. Security and safety are important concerns, but it is widely agreed that target hardening is not the first line of defense.

The events of September 11, 2001, in Washington D.C. and New York City caused officials and designers to revisit security as a design element. Security planning and design is completely consistent with the CPTED principles: increased surveillance reduces opportunities to be unobserved and increases the risks of being caught; effective design limits opportunity for access and escape and protects the building and people. There are important differences though. Where crime may be directed to one or a few individuals per incident, terrorism is directed toward the greatest possible number per incident. Criminals look for a means of escape, but we have learned that terrorists may have no thought of escape. The common criminal and the terrorist look for different forms of vulnerability. It is a challenge for the designer to meet these objectives in a fashion that is more than simply hardening the facility.

New facilities that might be the target of such attacks should incorporate security into the most basic design considerations. Redevelopment or retrofitting projects should be aware of the vulnerability of the site and make appropriate recommendations. It is likely that site designers will work in conjunction with security experts, but they should develop an awareness and expertise of their own as well. To not consider these issues in one's design may be seen later, after an incident perhaps, to have constituted a breach in the standard of care expected from a design professional. Many of these concerns are not yet part of building codes or design standards. They may not even be on the client's list of concerns, but they require the attention of the designer nonetheless.

New facilities should ideally incorporate a setback from the street that allows for observation of all approaching vehicles or pedestrians. Federal recommendations for some types of facilities call for a minimum street setback of 100 ft and minimum lot sizes of 15 acres. Clearly this would limit the number of possible urban sites for these facilities. The setback, however, presents an aesthetic concern. Many involved in these decisions agree that it may be a mistake to think of and design for security first. An unadorned open space may facilitate surveillance, but it clearly speaks of a bunker attitude in terms of design. A well-thought-out design would reduce the need for distance as a security strategy by incorporating changes in elevation to make access with a vehicle more difficult and the site more pleasing. Other low barriers, ponds, grading changes, or strategically locating site furniture in the plaza can make a direct path by a vehicle impossible. To protect the building further, the building could be raised above street grade and the plaza used as a transition over the change in grade. The plaza should be designed to function as a public space and should be filled with activities.

The key site design concern is access by pedestrians and vehicles. Security should provide for vehicles and pedestrians to be directed into specific patterns of approach through the site design. The points of access for pedestrians should be limited to provide a maximum amount of surveillance and control. Walkways should be set away from the building, and plant materials and landscape features should not obstruct a clear field of vision around the building. Approaches to entrances should be open but provide controlled access by vehicles. Hardened bollard systems may be used, but other methods such as changes in elevation, raised planting, or water features might produce the same effect without the hardened appearance.

Separate entrance facilities for pedestrians and vehicles might be considered. The separate entrance isolates everyone entering the facility for a security check and could serve as a barrier to vehicles attempting to get to the entrance. The most common method of keeping vehicles away has been to rely on large planters or other heavy items, but large planters or tree masses may create blind spots or hiding places. Landscaping is recommended to be kept below 24 in. in the security surveillance area, but this limits the design's aesthetic value and its potential to contribute to site security. Changes in grade are important design considerations in limiting vehicle access and controlling vehicle and pedestrian circulation. Site lines should be discussed in the planning stage so that tree masses, walls, and other features can be strategically located.

It may be possible to require vehicles to change directions upon entering the site. This will require the vehicle to slow down and reduce the possibility of a ramming or rush to the building using a vehicle. Vehicle access should be on roads that are curvilinear to require vehicles to drive slowly. When barriers are called for that will stop a vehicle, the designer may consult Army TM 5-853-1 and TM 5-853-2/AFMAN 32-1071, Volume 2, for relevant design procedures. Parking should be kept well away from the building, and separate controlled parking may be advisable for key personnel. It is likely that new public facilities will not be built with public parking beneath them. Strict setbacks from the building should be observed for all vehicles. Loading and unloading areas should be large enough for needed queuing but not allow parking. Loading docks should be designed in consultation with the facility management.

Of course, all of this must be accomplished while meeting accessibility requirements and facilitating the smooth operation of the site. The site exterior should be well lit, avoiding dark places near the building. Lighting should be coordinated with exterior closed circuit television systems to keep obtrusive lighting to a minimum but also to avoid "hot" and "cold" spots that may reduce surveillance effectiveness. The combined effect of these measures creates a clear perimeter around the building with an obvious buffer effect to make terrorist or criminal acts more difficult but without the hardening appearance. Design professionals should be cautious, however: security is expensive. One should be careful with site development cost estimates if enhanced security costs are to be included.

Lighting

Lighting serves to improve security and way-finding, but it also provides important visibility to commercial sites and can be used to create special effects and feelings in the nighttime landscape. With the development of specialty lighting products and effects, lighting has become as creative as any aspect of site design and is a specialty of many designers. The design of site lighting is just as often performed by companies selling lighting equipment as by an ancillary service, however. Finding the right combination of products, lighting type, and distribution can be a complex undertaking.

The purpose for the lighting is a critical consideration; for example, lighting for security or surveillance calls for a different strategy than designing for a more intimate space. Lighting is selected on the basis of the type of light, the distance from light source to object, the light of surrounding areas, and the nature of the activity being illuminated (Table 4.7). Many organizations have specific lighting standards or preferences that will influence design. The lighting industry introduces new products and capabilities all the time, and like so many other aspects of site planning, lighting requirements are often a matter of local ordinances.

The distribution and brightness of light are the fundamental elements of lighting design. Distribution of light refers to how much light is cast over an area. Lighting for accent or to create a mood or feeling requires a lighter and more elegant touch. For such applications, the angle and position of the light is determined by the visual or aesthetic effect as opposed to assisting in way-finding or security. By uplighting, moonlighting, or backlighting objects, the designer can create a very different feel from the daylight landscape. Uplighting is most effectively used to feature objects that can be viewed from a limited point of view and is commonly used against walls or fences or in gardens that will be viewed only from one side. The light source is located low and is pointed toward the object and away from the viewer. This orientation lights the object without any glare to the viewer and produces an unusual effect because the eye is not used to seeing things lighted from below in nature. This method is effective at creating dramatic textures and contrasts in the night landscape.

There are several methods for computing the effectiveness of different lighting choices. The point illumination method measures the illumination at a given point and is described as follows:

$$E = \frac{I \cos\theta}{d^2}$$

Area	Activity	Lux (lx)	Footcandles (fc)
Building exterior			
	Entry, active use	50	5.0
	Entry, infrequent use	10	1.0
	Vital location or structures	50	5.0
	Building surrounds	10	1.0
Buildings and monuments			
	Bright surroundings	150–500	15.0–50.0
	Dark surroundings	50–200	5.0–20.0
Bikeways			
	Along roadside	2–10	0.2–1.0
	Away from road	5	0.05
Bulletin boards, kiosks		500–1000	50–100
Major roads		10–20	1.0–2.0
Collector roads		6–13	0.6–1.2
Local roads		4–10	0.4–0.9
Walkways, open air		5–10	0.5–1.0
Walkways, enclosed		6–40	0.6–4.0
Park or garden walkways		20–40	2.0–4.0
Steps in park or garden		10	1.0
Stairways		200–600	20.0–60.0
Gardens		50	5.0
Garden features		200	20.0
Loading areas		200	20.0
Parking areas		10–20	1.0–2.0
Outdoor athletic areas			
	Badminton	200	20.0
	Baseball, infield	110–300	11.0–30.0
	Baseball, outfield	100–200	10.0–20.0
	Basketball	100	10.0
	Football	100–1000	10.0–100
	Field hockey	100–200	10.0–20.0
	Skating	100	10
	Softball, infield	100–500	10.0–50.0
	Softball, outfield	70–200	7.0–20.0
	Tennis	200–500	20.0–50.0
	Volleyball	100–200	10.0–20.0

Source: Harris and Dines, 1998.

TABLE 4.7 Recommended Levels of Illumination

where E = illumination on a horizontal surface, footcandles
   I = lamp intensity in lumens
   θ = angle between the fixture and a point on the ground
   d = distance from the luminaire to the point

The point distribution calculation is useful for determining the constancy of light within its distribution but is a fairly effort-intensive method (Fig. 4.15).

The average illumination method measures a more general distribution of light and can be described as follows:

$$F = \frac{luM}{LM}$$

where F = average illumination, footcandles
   l = lamp intensity in lumens
   u = coefficient of utilization
   M = maintenance factor
   L = horizontal distance between fixtures
   W = width of the area illuminated

To solve for L

$$L = \frac{luM}{FW}$$

Designers should consider changes in the efficiency of the lamp, sometimes referred to as the *maintenance factor*, over its life. Some lamps may vary as much as 75 percent over their operating life. The maintenance factor includes variation as the light source ages as well as the effects of dust or dirt on lamp covers (Table 4.8). Maintenance factors

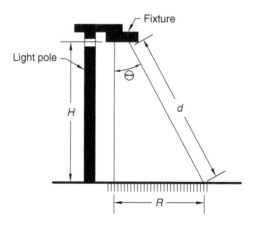

FIGURE 4.15   Point distribution calculation dimensions.

Type of light	Lumens/watt	Life (hours)	Color	Notes
Florescent	70	6000	Good color purity, white	Affected by cold weather
High pressure sodium	130	16,000	Poor color purity, yellow to orange	Washes out colors in landscape
Incandescent	10 to 18	750 to 1000	Very good color purity, yellow	
Low pressure sodium	190	11,000	Poor color purity, pink to orange	Washes out colors in landscape (gray)
Metal halide	90	14,000 cool white	Good color purity	
Mercury vapor	55	24,000	Cool white	Strong in blue-green spectrum
Tungsten-iodine	18 to 20	2000	Good color purity (Deluxe White)	

TABLE 4.8   Performance Characteristics of Different Sources of Light

vary, but 50 percent is a common rule of thumb. Information on illumination and the coefficient of utilization is found in photometric information of the luminaire.

Moonlighting is accomplished by using combinations of light carefully located high up in trees and other low wattage ground level lighting attached to branches and leaves from below. Moonlighting can create very dramatic effects and is especially good for transitions between lighted areas. The filtered light may provide adequate light for walking on a marked path and can be particularly beautiful. These effects can be difficult to achieve if there are more brightly lit areas nearby.

Backlighting is sometimes used to feature a tree or shrub or other element with an unusual or visually pleasing silhouette. Care must be taken to minimize the risk of glare to the viewer, so the height and angle of the lighting is very important. Silhouette lighting can be achieved by uplighting a wall or surface behind an object. Indirect or bounce lighting is achieved by directing light to a surface that reflects the light into or on a desired area. The development of extruded fiber optic lighting and other products has introduced the possibility of drama and beauty into the night landscape.

Commercial Lot Layout

The layout of commercial sites is driven by the nature of the enterprise as well as the local ordinances and community practices and expectations. A key issue for the developer and tenants is location in the community; site selection is extremely important. The ideal commercial site seems to have a somewhat elusive but immutable character. Every community has sites that are successful despite a poor location and others that never succeed regardless of the tenant or business that locates there. A site analysis that studies the development potential or the visibility and traffic past a site often cannot identify the underlying cause of success or failure from the bare facts.

Some of the factors that contribute to the success of a commercial site are related to demographics: is the site located near enough to people with disposable income? Success is also correlated with the type of business or mix of tenants: is the business mix able to draw people either as a destination or on an impulse? Does the mix of tenants support each other and create a draw greater than any one tenant?

Other aspects of site success are well within the scope of the site professional's work. During the site analysis, the site location should be explored. Commercial development with retail shops usually requires a minimum of existing traffic at the proposed location. Very large retail projects may rely on becoming a destination themselves and be less concerned about existing traffic. In either case, existing intersections are prized locations for most commercial projects.

Access to the project site is critical. Accessibility in this sense refers both to the ability of the customer or client to get into the shop or business and to the "visual access" of the site. Although there is not a fixed standard, many retail operations require a minimum number of parking places to be within a given distance from the door. One of the most lamentable aspects of retail development is the visual impact projects have on the community. Even small corner stores can bring a significant change in character to a neighborhood if not designed carefully. The most significant impacts are associated with automobile traffic and parking, but the intrusion of bright lights and noise can also be problematic.

There is a strong preference on the part of retail operations to be able to show the available parking and its proximity to the door to the public. Retail operations often resist attempts to reduce the visual impact of parking (by putting it behind the building or screening it) in the belief that if customers do not see convenient parking they will go somewhere else. Except in smaller projects, in-fill, high-end, or theme-related retail projects, it is difficult to overcome this preference. The designer must also accommodate delivery and distribution traffic on the site. In most projects these activities are located behind the building, further complicating relocating the parking.

The most important part of accessibility is visibility. Customers and clients generally need to see the development. Efforts to mitigate the visual impacts of development are complicated by the need of commercial projects to be seen. In most cases it is necessary for the site professional to find a design that meets both needs, and site screening should be carefully considered (Figs. 4.16 and 4.17). In many cases, no screening is required or expected, but as time passes and the community gains experience with development, these expectations change. Effective signage, distinctive landscaping, and lighting can provide way-finding guides to customers without sacrificing visual or environmental quality.

Alternatives to the traditional strip layout may be used to reduce the amount of impermeable area (Figs. 4.18 and 4.19). Developing commercial sites in a U-shape rather than a strip may increase the number of parking spaces within a given distance from a merchant's door while reducing the coverage of the site. In a strip center, the parking lot is necessarily stretched out before the entire strip, and all stores have an appearance of adequate parking immediately in front of them. By developing in a U-shape, a concentration of parking can be in front of every store when compared to a comparable strip center (stores at the end of the strip or the ends of the U will have fewer spaces than a store in the middle of the strip). The U-shape can be a more efficient arrangement of space and reduce the total coverage on the site.

FIGURE 4.16   Screening at a retail site.

FIGURE 4.17   Screening at a commercial site.

FIGURE **4.18** Screening at a commercial site.

FIGURE **4.19** Screening at a retail site.

Walls and Fences

Fences and walls are common site and landscape features used most often to increase privacy or security, but they also are used to create backgrounds and as features in some applications. Walls are usually freestanding masonry structures with unique design considerations. Wooden fences are more commonly used in residential areas or for aesthetic purposes on commercial sites. The ASTM Specification F 537, Standard Specification for Design, Fabrication and Installation of Fences Constructed of Wood and Related Materials, addresses materials as well as design and construction specifications. Security fences are most often wire or metal and generally are not used for aesthetic purposes although many decorative security fences are available. The range of designs for fences is very wide. Nearly any type of fence is commercially available today, and few fences are specially designed and constructed anymore. Nonetheless, specifying fence materials and construction details are important. Fences should be selected based on the specific objectives for the project. Fences and walls may be important elements in designing for community safety and security as well. As barriers, fences provide guidance to pedestrians, direct traffic, and provide clear demarcation of public and private areas. Even low fences or walls represent a psychological barrier for the casual pedestrian.

Fencing should be of the proper scale and proportion to meet the objective and remain compatible with the design as a whole. Fence or wall textures and design contribute a great deal to its impact. Walls or fences can be made more attractive by introducing elements such as piers or details that break up the monotony of a static unbroken surface (Fig. 4.20). Color also contributes to fence performance. Lighter colored surfaces tend to stand out in the landscape, whereas darker colors tend to recede and blend in. Fences to be installed on slopes present a somewhat greater challenge. As a rule of thumb, fences should ride parallel with the slope rather than stepping down the slope, with each panel horizontal but lower. Solid panel fences usually cannot be installed parallel to the slope and require additional work to fill or enclose the resulting gaps at the downhill end of each section. Care should be taken to be sure the selected fence is consistent with local zoning and association requirements.

The key to fence integrity is the installation of fence posts that anchor and support the fence sections (Figs. 4.21, 4.22, and 4.23). Fence posts may be made of metal pipe, PVC, or wood. Wooden posts should be treated and dry. If treated wood is used, the type of wood treatment should be carefully evaluated (see Chap. 2). The dimension of wooden posts should be selected to provide adequate support for the fence; 4 × 4 is generally considered to be the minimum acceptable fence post size. Posts should be installed to at least the frost depth in places where frost heave occurs and at a depth adequate to resist the anticipated wind loads of a particular area. All corner posts should be set in concrete to add strength to the installation. The construction of arbors and similar structures add visual interest and can be used to incorporate fences into the landscape (Figs. 4.24 and 4.25). Arbors highlight more intimate spaces in the landscape and provide some relief from the sun. Sun filtering fabric can further enhance the value of an arbor. These fabrics are of limited value in areas where one can expect snowfall of any significance because the weight of the snow may damage the fabric. Some people enjoy the arbor as a support for flowering vines.

A less common but elegant method of diversion from the English landscape tradition is the "ha-ha," or sunken fence. This technique of an abrupt change in grade was used to prevent livestock from wandering off without visually cluttering the landscape with walls and fences (Fig. 4.26).

FIGURE 4.20 Picket fence corner detail.

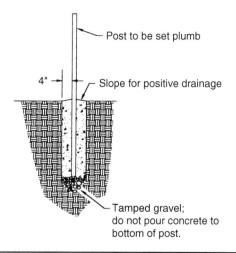

Post to be set plumb

4"

Slope for positive drainage

Tamped gravel; do not pour concrete to bottom of post.

FIGURE 4.21 Wooden post installation, typical.

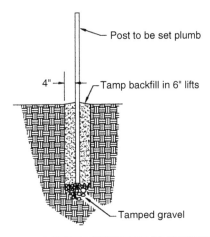

FIGURE 4.22 Fence post set in tamped backfill.

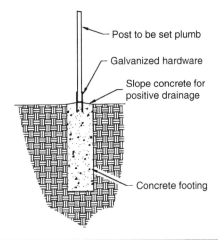

FIGURE 4.23 Wooden fence post anchored in concrete.

Masonry Walls

For more substantial applications, masonry or stone walls may be desirable. These heavy materials require an adequate supporting foundation. All freestanding walls must be designed to resist overtopping due to wind loads and subsurface soil failures. When wind pushes on the solid surface of the wall, it causes the wall to act as a lever, turning on a pivot at ground level. The wall is able to resist overturning by virtue of its weight and by extending the length of the lever by use of a footer. Wind loads vary across the nation and are described or dictated in many local building codes. The weight of masonry materials varies from about 120 lb/ft³ for brick or cement masonry units (CMU) to 145 lb for stone. Concrete mortar typically has a weight of 150 lb/ft³.

To check a wall for overturning, it is necessary to determine the wind load for the area in which the wall will be constructed. Typically loads are determined for a 1-ft

Figure 4.24   An arbor feature.

section of the proposed wall. To determine the wind load pressure, P, multiply the height of the wall by the wind load. The pressure of the wind load, P, is determined at the center of moments of overtopping and righting. The overtopping moment is calculated at half of the wall height above grade plus the depth below grade (Fig. 4.27). For a wall 4 feet above grade, 1 ft below grade, and 0.67 ft thick, P is 3 ft² by 30 lb/ft², or 90 lb. The weight of a 1-ft section of the wall, if made of brick, would be 412.05 lb. Based on this calculation, a wall 0.67 ft thick would be 4.33 ft (height from top of wall to top of footer) × 120 lb/ft³ × 0.67 = 348, plus the weight of the mortar at 0.9 ft × 0.67 ft × 150 lb/ft³ = 90: 348 + 90 yields a weight of 438 lb.

To determine the wall's resistance to wind load, the overturning moment (M_O) and the righting moment (M_R) must be compared. The overturning moment is measured at

FIGURE 4.25 Arbor detail.

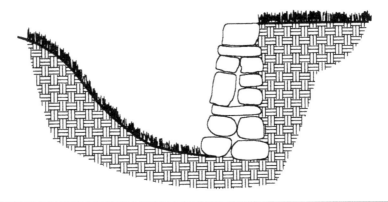

FIGURE 4.26 The sunken fence, or "ha-ha."

half the height of the wall plus the depth below grade, 3 ft in the example; $M_O = 120 \times 3 = 360$ lb. The righting moment is measured as $M_R = 438 \times 0.67 = 293.46$ lb. In this case the righting moment is less than the wind load so additional stabilization is required.

The calculation above is based on a single section of freestanding wall 1 ft long and does not consider other aspects of the wall such as corners, piers, or other support. To prevent overtopping, the wall may also be designed with piers or with sections at right angles to the wall. The lateral support of solid walls is designed using a ratio of the length of the wall between lateral supports to the thickness of the wall: L/T. Table 4.9

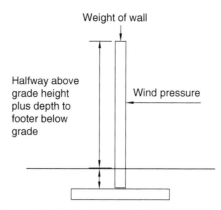

FIGURE 4.27 How to evaluate a freestanding wall for overturning.

FIGURE 4.28 A classic brick entrance.

summarizes the L/T ratio for freestanding walls. The L/T for wind loads for the example is 14. The maximum length of wall between supporting members, therefore, is $14 = L/0.67$ ft, $L = 9.38$ ft. The use of brick to formalize entrance features lends a sense of formality and tradition to the landscape. The brick wall in Fig 4.28 signals the location of this residential entrance but it also provides an introduction to the site in terms of the general period of the site development and architecture.

Eccentric loading on footings may result in footing failure. In most cases it is recommended to keep the weight of the wall in the center third of the footing (Fig. 4.29).

Design wind pressure (lb/in.²)	Maximum *L/T*
5	35
10	25
15	20
20	18
25	16
30	14
35	13
40	12

Source: Harlow C. Landphair and Fred Klatt Jr., *Landscape Architecture Construction*, 2nd ed. New York: Elsevier Science, 1998.

TABLE 4.9 L / T Ratio for Freestanding Walls at a Given Wind Pressure

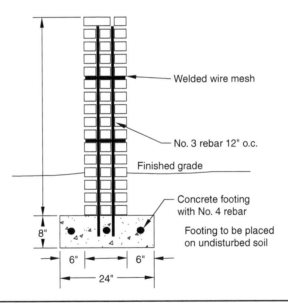

FIGURE 4.29 Brick wall footing detail.

Shifting the wall toward either side of the footing increases the load on that portion of the footing and increases the instability of the wall. In such a condition there is concern with exceeding the strength of the soil because of weight or because of increased pressure as a result of wind load.

Serpentine brick walls have been used in gardens since at least the 1700s and are found in many historic gardens. Besides being decorative, the serpentine wall has additional lateral strength. To keep that strength, it is critical that the wall be carefully designed and constructed. The radius of any curved section should not be greater than twice the above grade height of the wall. The depth of the curve should be at least one half of the

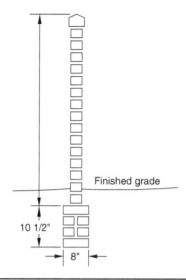

FIGURE 4.30   Serpentine brick wall detail.

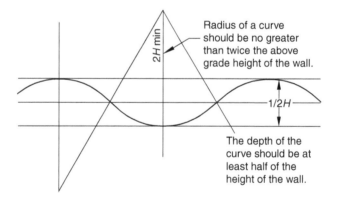

Radius of a curve should be no greater than twice the above grade height of the wall.

1/2H

The depth of the curve should be at least half of the height of the wall.

FIGURE 4.31   Serpentine brick wall detail.

above grade height. Many historic serpentine walls are built using a simple brick foundation (Fig. 4.30). If the wall is in a location where frost heave is a concern, the wall is to bear weight other than its own, or the wall might be bumped by vehicles, a more substantial footing might be in order (Figs. 4.31, 4.32, and 4.33). In the event a more substantial wall is required, an 8-in. wall may be used with a reinforced concrete footing.

Water Features

Ponds and pools have become very popular landscape features in recent years. Successful ponds and pools are always a marriage of design and construction (Fig. 4.34). Even small variances in construction or incomplete details in a design may result in an unsatisfactory pond. A water feature can bring a great deal to a landscape of any size. People are drawn to water perhaps more than to any other single landscape feature; there are

FIGURE 4.32 A serpentine brick wall. (See also color insert.)

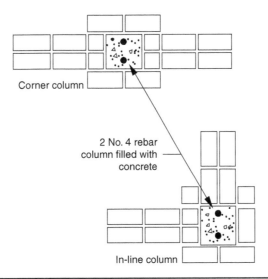

Corner column

2 No. 4 rebar
column filled with
concrete

In-line column

FIGURE 4.33 Pier detail.

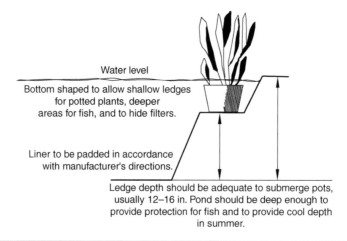

Water level

Bottom shaped to allow shallow ledges
for potted plants, deeper
areas for fish, and to hide filters.

Liner to be padded in accordance
with manufacturer's directions.

Ledge depth should be adequate to submerge pots,
usually 12–16 in. Pond should be deep enough to
provide protection for fish and to provide cool depth
in summer.

FIGURE 4.34 Typical ornamental pond detail.

clearly important psychological or emotional values in well-designed water features. Whether it is the sound of falling water, the turbulence of fountains or falls, or the cooling effect of spray and evaporative cooling, water features are highly valued elements of both the designed and natural landscape.

Water features are a diverse element in the landscape, ranging from natural appearing small ponds to formal precision water veils. The possibilities are limited only by the imagination and the physical characteristics of water. This discussion of water features is limited to small pools and ponds and how these two features differ. Ponds include biotic features such as plants and perhaps fish, whereas pools have no biotic elements. The key to the water feature is the pool or pond: the presence of fountains or falls or other features are framed within the pool or pond (Figs. 4.35 and 4.36).

FIGURE 4.35 A pond with a natural look.

FIGURE **4.36**   A pond with a rustic look.

Concrete had been the most common and popular material for pond or pool construction, but with the development of more sophisticated geotextiles and plastics, fiberglass prefabricated pools and fabric pond liners have become the most common choice. Ponds are constructed using either rigid preformed ponds or liners, most commonly made of fiberglass, EDP, PVC, or similar materials. The pond liner should be selected for durability and ease of installation. Whichever material is chosen, the installed liner should be smooth and curvilinear; sharp corners or abrupt changes in surface aspect should be avoided (Fig. 4.37). Most pond liners are dark colored and tend to produce a reflective surface effect. A light colored pond surface will produce a more transparent effect. In a light colored pond, everything is visible and maintenance becomes a more critical issue.

Pool depth is important. The minimum recommended pool depth is 16 in. in order to operate most submersible pumps. Ponds with fish must provide an adequate depth to allow the fish to over-winter or the fish must be removed each fall. It is important to vary the depth in the pond to allow areas for rooted plant stock as well.

Falls require the addition of a pump. Bazin's formula is used to estimate the flow over the falls:

$$Q = [0.405 + (0.00984/H)] \, [1 + (0.55(H^2/(P+H)^2] \, LH \, (2gH)^{.5}$$

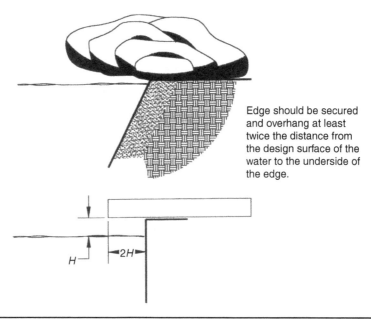

FIGURE 4.37   Pond edges detail.

where Q = volume (cubic feet per second)
  H = head in feet (the height is taken from a position 4 × H from the face of the weir)
  P = height of the water over the weir in feet
  L = length of the weir, in feet
  G = 32.17 (universal gravity constant)

Cubic feet per second can be converted to gallons per minute by multiplying by 448.831.

Pumps

Pond pumps come in two general types: submersible and larger centrifugal pumps located outside the pond. Centrifugal pumps are capable of moving more water, but they generate enough noise that they must be located way from the pond. They must also be protected from the weather, which requires additional plumbing. It may be necessary to use such a system to operate a large water feature. Submersible pumps are more common for smaller ponds. These pumps are located within the pond itself, often in conjunction with a filtration system. Care should be taken to locate the pump out of sight: even though it is located underwater, submersible pumps are often visible and can detract from the overall pond effect.

Specifying Pumps

In sizing pumps for ponds or pools, it is important to remember how water is moved by pumps. The pressure of the atmosphere at sea level in approximately 14.7 pounds per square inch (psi). This pressure is pushing on all surfaces and in all directions all of the time. Water weighs 8.34 pounds per gallon, and there are 7.48 gallons per cubic foot of water, so there are 62.4 pounds of water per cubic foot. One cubic foot of water in a container will exert 0.433 psi pressure at the bottom of the container ($62.4 \text{ lb}/144 \text{ in.}^2 = 0.433$ psi). If the container is filled to 2 ft deep, the pressure increases to 0.866 psi ($2 \times 62.4 = 124.8$ lb, $124.8 \text{ lb}/144 \text{ in.}^2 = 0.866$). If a tube is placed in a container of water and a vacuum of 1 psi is drawn on it, water will rise on the tube 2.31 ft. So, for every foot of rise, the pressure of the water increases 0.433 psi. The pressure caused by the weight of the water is called pressure head, or simply head. Head is measured in feet; every foot of head is equal to 0.433 psi.

If a pond is designed with an above grade wall, the design would have to address the pressure that would be exerted by the water in the filled pond. Pressure on the container wall will range from zero at the water surface to the depth of the water times 0.433 psi, or 62.4 psf (pounds per square foot). The formula for finding the force acting on the wall is as follows:

$$F = 31.2 \times H^2 \times L$$

where F = the force in pounds acting on the wall
H = head in feet
L = the length of the wall

31.2 is the constant in pounds per cubic foot based on the force at the average depth exerted at $H/3$ from the bottom of the container.

Pumps are specified in terms of horsepower and head. The head a pump must overcome is called the *dynamic head* and is measured as the vertical distance the pump must lift the water, the *static head,* and the *friction loss* caused by the roughness of the pipe conveying the water. Charts for various types of pipe and fittings are provided by the manufacturers of those materials. For very short runs of pipes and fitting, friction loss may be nominal. Total dynamic head is the sum of the static head and friction losses.

Horsepower is a unit of power and work. One horsepower is equal to 33,000 ft-lbs per minute, or 746 W. To calculate the necessary horsepower to lift water, the desired flow must be converted from a volume to the weight of the water. This is called the water horsepower:

$$\text{hp} = [(\text{Flow in gpm}) \ (H \text{ in feet})]/3960$$

where hp = horsepower
F = flow in gallons per minute
H = lift in feet

3960 is derived from $(8.34 \text{lb}/\text{gallon}) \times (\text{hp}/3000 \text{ ft-lb per minute}) = 1/3960$

Pumps are unable to operate at perfect efficiency, so more energy must be provided to the pump than is expressed as water horsepower. Motors that drive the pumps are also not 100 percent efficient. To account for the inherent inefficiency of pumps and motors, the formula is modified by an efficiency factor:

$$E_p \text{ and } E_m: \text{hp} = [(\text{Flow in gpm}) \ (H \text{ in feet})]/3960 \times E_p \times E_m$$

In most pumps and motors, efficiency ranges from 50 to 85 percent and 80 to 90 percent, respectively.

Plazas and Patios

The use of plazas or patios in the site plan has become an essential element of most projects. The choices of materials and approaches differ primarily by the type of surface material. All such areas should be designed to be fairly level but with enough pitch to provide adequate drainage. Surfaces should be even and without trip or slip hazards. The base should be substantial enough to resist loads from expected traffic and to resist frost damage. Surface materials can range from poured concrete to pavers to flagstone to brick. The base may be open-graded or impermeable. Bricks and pavers should always conform to the requirements of ASTM C 902, Specification for Pedestrian and Light Traffic Paving Brick, or ASTM C 1272, Specification for Heavy Vehicular Paving Brick, depending on what the expected volume and weight of traffic is. ASTM C 1272 compliant brick is not necessary for most landscape and site planning functions. Although the dimension tolerances and chip resistance are important, the critical elements in selecting brick or pavers for a patio are the durability and abrasion of the material.

Durability is graded as NX, MX, and SX. NX pavers or bricks should be used only for interior applications where wetting and freezing will not be issues. MX and SX pavers are used for exterior applications, but SX is selected where freezing will occur. Abrasion resistance is graded as Type I, II, or III, in decreasing resistance to abrasion. Type III pavers are adequate for residential or light duty patios. Type I pavers are used for heavy traffic areas, including driveways or commercial entrances (Fig. 4.38). Type II pavers might be selected for restaurant entrances or similar uses (Fig. 4.39) (Technical Notes 29).

FIGURE **4.38**   A brick plaza. (See also color insert.)

FIGURE 4.39 Stone walls and arbors.

Although concrete provides a durable and cost-competitive surface, it offers little in the way of aesthetics to the project. Concrete stains and patterning methods may improve the appearance of poured concrete, but the additional steps may reduce or even eliminate the cost savings. The use of color or stains on concrete can be affected by the aggregate used in the mix. If coal ash is used, tests should be done to determine whether there is an effect on the color.

Brick paving is attractive and durable if properly specified materials are used. Brick surfaces may be either rigid or flexible, depending on whether mortar is used to set the brick. Mortarless patios are common, and the brick may be set over a wide range of base materials. This application is at least minimally porous and allows for some infiltration of precipitation. It is recommended that a prepared base (Fig. 4.40) be used to reduce the amount of pumping and movement in mortarless brick systems. Rigid paving systems

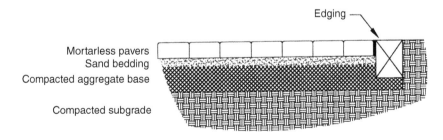

FIGURE 4.40 Flexible mortarless patio detail.

are preferred where steps or exposed edges will be used. Wherever steps, ramps, or exposed edges are used, the brick should be supported by a concrete base. Flexible mortarless systems require support or restraint at the loose edges.

Bed Materials

The bed for bricks and pavers usually consists of a base layer and a setting layer. The setting bed acts as a leveling course between the base and the finished surface. The base provides the strength and resistance to the finished surface. Sand or mortar are the usual setting bed materials although asphalt is also used. Sand represents a very broad range of choices with many regional differences; however, a well-graded (consistent size) washed sand with a maximum particle size of 3/16 of an inch is usually acceptable. Concrete sand that complies with ASTM C 33, Specification for Concrete Aggregates, is acceptable. Sand that meets ASTM C144, Specification for Aggregates for Masonry Mortar, sometimes called mortar sand, is also acceptable. Sand setting beds should be between 1/2 and 2 in.

Mortar setting beds are always used in rigid, mortared surfaces (Figs. 4.41 and 4.42). Mortar should be prepared in accordance with ASTM C 270, Specification for Mortar for Unit Masonry. Type M mortar is preferred in applications where freezing is not expected and consists of 1 part Portland cement, 1/4 part hydrated lime, and 3 3/4 parts sand. Type S mortar may be specified where freezing is an issue. Asphalt setting

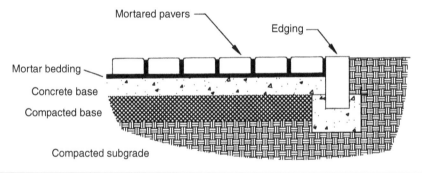

FIGURE 4.41   Rigid mortared paving detail.

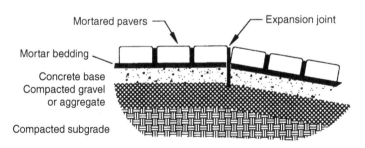

FIGURE 4.42   Ramp detail.

beds are usually only 3/4 in. thick over a concrete or asphalt base and consist of a mixture of about 7 percent asphalt and 93 percent sand.

Base materials are generally aggregates, concrete or asphalt. Aggregates may be crushed stone, gravel, or sand. The use of aggregates may be favored in places where poor drainage or frost damage is a concern. The open-graded base allows water to drain away from the patio. Aggregates should be no larger than 3/4 of an inch, but actual size is selected as a function of the depth of the base and the type of compaction equipment to be used. Sand bases are commonly used for residential projects if the patio is built on undisturbed earth or sufficiently compacted material and frost is not an issue. Sand used for the base should comply with ASTM C 33.

Concrete bases can be either new or existing concrete installed in accordance with the proper methods. If a mortar bed is to be used, the surface should be sufficiently roughened. If a chemical primer is to be used, the manufacturer's directions should be observed. If existing concrete is to be used, it should be carefully inspected for cracks, chips, level, and soundness. Asphalt bases should not be used for rigid paving systems.

CHAPTER 5

Design for People

The human scale of site design is a primary interest for site developers. Site designs reflect the values of the society at that time through the work of designers. The "Ideal City," a painting by Piero della Francesca (Fig. 5.1), reflects the values of the Renaissance: civic order, intellect, and beauty as found in the works of society. "The Ideal City" is presented on a flat plain, its avenues uninterrupted by inconvenient topography or natural features. With the exception of a few clouds in the sky, nature is completely absent. Although the ideal might have been a sterile projection of society over nature, the reality was quite different. Figure 5.2 of an actual village shows its accommodation to the topography, the use of aspect to collect the sun, the use of local materials, and so forth. We have, in other times and places, understood the principles of living with the land.

Modern sensibilities have moved beyond the mythology of Francesca's imaginary city, and we have started to embrace nature in our planning and design. Sites often support multiple uses and users with different needs and expectations, and accommodating those needs and expectations has led to a variety of approaches to design. Early accommodations were usually in the form of some sort of conspicuous add-on, even in new construction. Access ramps, for example, were often reluctantly added to an entrance because the need for accommodation was not addressed early in the design.

Universal design principles have become more widely recognized and accepted in recent years. These principles go beyond site and building concerns to include product and industrial design. In essence the precepts of universal design are intended to provide equity and simplicity in access and use of all products of design. A site designed using these precepts avoids segregating one set of users from another whenever possible. Multiple but equal points of access to accommodate people with accessibility issues are planned to avoid stigmatizing some users. Signage is designed to be useful regardless of one's language. Understanding the limitations of site users who range from toddlers to the elderly requires more than the common human factors and range of motion charts established for the "average person."

General Site Design Guidelines for Pedestrians

There is no shortage of sources for site furnishings today, and the designer can choose from a wide range of well-designed and durable materials in many styles. Virtually all of these furnishings comply with the accepted standards of human dimensions; however, it remains the responsibility of the design professional to select and specify the materials appropriate to the site. A working knowledge of human dimensions and behavior is necessary. Figures 5.3 through 5.8 provide an outline of human dimensions and design conventions.

Figure 5.1   The "Ideal City" by Piero della Francesca.

Figure 5.2   This village illustrates an "organic" form of development that accommodates and uses local conditions to the advantage of residents. (*Photograph by Rebecca Russ.*)

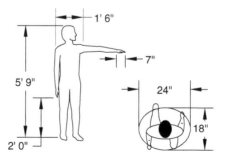

Figure 5.3   Standing and walking dimensions.

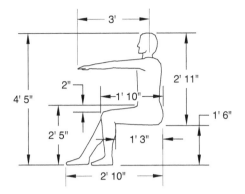

FIGURE 5.4   Chair and table dimensions.

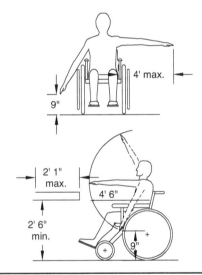

FIGURE 5.5   Wheelchair use dimensions.

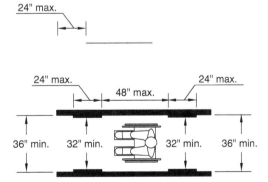

FIGURE 5.6   Wheelchair use dimensions.

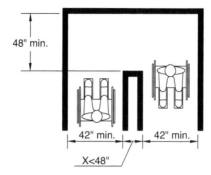

FIGURE 5.7   Wheelchair 180 degree turn.

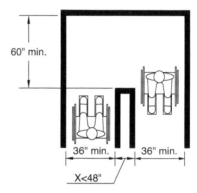

FIGURE 5.8   Wheelchair 180 degree turn alternative.

Pedestrian Walkways

A fundamental element of design for the pedestrian is the pathway or sidewalk (Fig. 5.9). The peak time for walking is midday (countercyclical to vehicle traffic), and sidewalks should be designed to account for this peak time. Many localities have predetermined minimum standards for sidewalk development in residential areas but do not provide

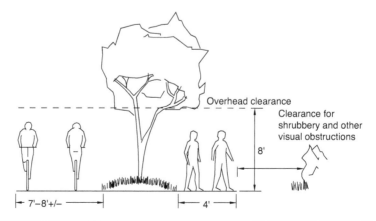

FIGURE 5.9   Pathway design parameters.

guidance for commercial sites or other circumstances where minimums are not adequate. The sidewalk width must provide the level of service suited to the user. The parameters of sidewalk width are the anticipated volume of foot traffic, how quickly pedestrians will be walking, and the desired density of traffic. The width can be determined using the following method:

$$W = V(M)/S$$

where W = the width of the pathway or sidewalk
V = volume in person/minute
M = the space module or square feet allowed per person
S = walking speed in feet per minute

Walking speeds vary greatly among people, but an average walking speed of 4 ft per second is usually assumed. A number of factors influence this speed, and the needs of particular users should be considered. The very young and older people walk slower than the average speed, and people tend to walk faster in the middle of a block and slow down at intersections. The activity people are engaged in affects walking speed as well: for example, shoppers walk slower than commuters, men tend to walk faster than women, and groups of people walk slower than a lone individual. Curbs, islands, circuitous pathways, changes in grade, and even ramps can present barriers of one sort or another to users. Grade changes of more than a few percent should be signaled visually and texturally. To determine the appropriate level of service, designers should weigh the designated site use, the user, and the character of the final design (Table 5.1).

Grades also affect walking speed, level of service, and safety. Sidewalks should be designed with a minimum cross slope of 1 percent to allow for drainage, but the cross slope should not exceed 3 percent. A longitudinal slope of up to 3 percent is desirable, but slopes greater than 5 percent should be avoided in areas where freezing may be an

Level of service	Area per person (ft²)	Interference
A	130	Can walk at desired speed without interference
B	40–130	Must be aware of other pedestrians
C	24–40	Necessary to make minor adjustments to avoid conflicts with other pedestrians
D	1–24	Ability to choose own speed is limited, frequent adjustments necessary
E	6–15	Very crowded, speed is reduced, shuffling pace, occasionally making changes in direction very difficult
F	6	Stationary or shuffling movement only, unavoidable contact with others

Adapted from *A Policy on Geometric Design of Highways and Streets*, 1994, by the American Association of State Highway and Transportation Officials, Washington, D.C. Used with permission.

TABLE 5.1   Levels of Service for Sidewalks

1. Outdoor stairs should be made easier to use than indoor stairways because people tend to be moving faster when outdoors.
2. Avoid the use of a single stair. A minimum of three steps should be used to clearly signal the change in grade.
3. Maintain a minimum tread height of 4.5 in. A maximum tread height of 7 in. should also be observed.
4. Stair treads should be designed with a minimum of 2 percent positive pitch to provide drainage.
5. Vertical distance between landings should be 5 ft or less.
6. Stair design should incorporate visual signals to signal stair treads and edges.

TABLE 5.2   Design Considerations for Outdoor Stairways

issue. Where climate is a consideration, any sidewalk with a slope in excess of 5 percent should be treated as a ramp with associated handrails. Changes in sidewalk width may be appropriate to maintain walking pace where notable changes of grade occur.

When incorporating stairs into an outdoor design, local standards often need to be considered (Table 5.2; Figs. 5.10 and 5.11). When such regulations are not in place, use this equation to determine tread width:

$$2R + T = 26 \text{ to } 27 \text{ in.}$$

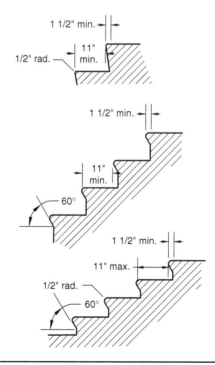

FIGURE 5.10   Usable tread width and acceptable nosing, flush riser.

Figure 5.11 Stair treads with painted nosing.

where *R* = riser height
       T = tread width

Ramps should be designed to meet the following ADA requirements (Figs. 5.12 through 5.26). Ramps with a slope between 1:12 and 1:16 should be designed to not exceed a rise of 30 in. (760 mm) or a run of 30 ft (9 m). Flatter ramps of 1:16 to 1:20 may be designed to a run of 40 ft, but the maximum rise should not exceed 30 in. The minimum clear width of a ramp is 36 in. (915 mm). Ramps shall have level landings at the bottom and top of each ramp and each ramp run. The cross slope of ramp surfaces shall be no greater than 1:50. Outdoor ramps and their approaches shall be designed so that water will not accumulate on walking surfaces. Landings shall be at least as wide as the ramp run leading to it and be a minimum of 60 in. (1525 mm) clear. If the ramp changes direction at landings, the minimum landing size is 60 by 60 in. (1525 by 1525 mm). If a ramp run has a rise greater than 6 in. (150 mm) or a horizontal projection greater than 72 in. (1830 mm), then it shall have

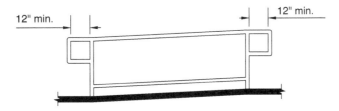

12" min.   12" min.

Figure 5.12 Ramp detail.

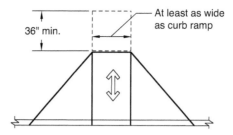

FIGURE 5.13 Curb ramp up detail.

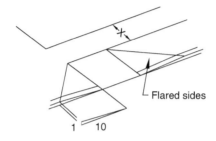

FIGURE 5.14 Curb ramp down detail.

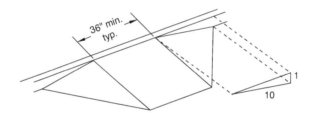

FIGURE 5.15 Built-up curb ramp.

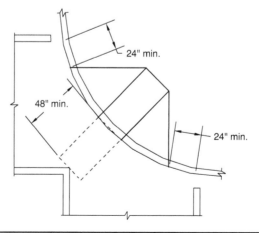

FIGURE 5.16 Accessible corner detail.

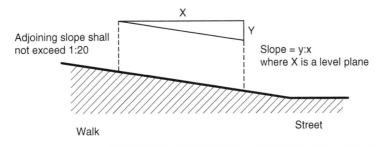

FIGURE 5.17   Measurement of curb ramp slopes.

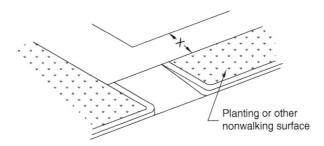

FIGURE 5.18   Sides of curb ramps returned curb.

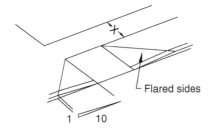

FIGURE 5.19   Sides of curb ramps flared sides.

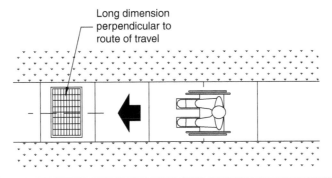

FIGURE 5.20   Gratings orientation.

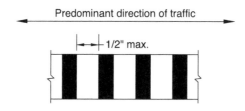

FIGURE 5.21 Gratings.

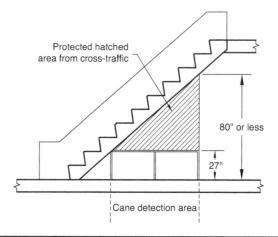

FIGURE 5.22 Protruding objects overhead hazards.

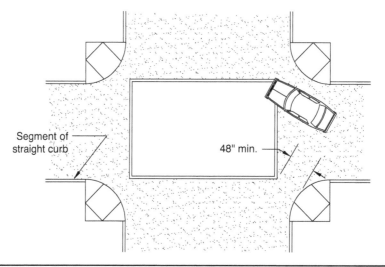

FIGURE 5.23 Curb ramp at marked crossings.

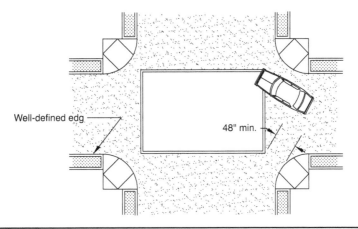

FIGURE 5.24 Curb ramp at marked crossings.

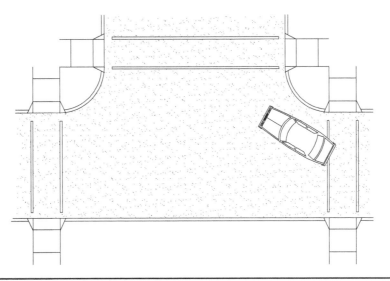

FIGURE 5.25 Curb ramp at marked crossings.

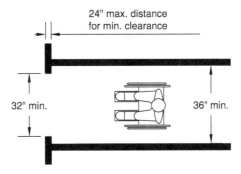

FIGURE 5.26 Minimum clear width for single wheelchair.

handrails on both sides (handrails are not required on curb ramps). Designers may need to consider other factors, such as the number of people using the ramp and the trend toward larger personal mobility vehicles.

Handrails should be continuous along both sides of ramp segments. The inside handrail on switchback on dogleg ramps shall always be continuous. If handrails are not continuous, they shall extend at least 12 in. (305 mm) beyond the top and bottom of the ramp segment and shall be parallel with the floor or ground surface. The clear space between the handrail and the wall shall be 1 1/2 in. (38 mm). Top of handrail gripping surfaces shall be mounted between 34 and 38 in. (865 to 965 mm) above ramp surfaces. Handrails shall not rotate within their fittings.

The Americans with Disabilities Act (ADA) requires that reasonable accommodations be made for those among us with physical limitations or disabilities. Standard practices have been developed to facilitate these accommodations and are broadly followed today. The advent of universal design, in fact, has produced designs that are intended to remove or mitigate the range of challenges "traditional" design presented, which were part of routine design just a few years ago. Redevelopment and revitalization projects, however, often do not meet even these minimum accommodations. Table 5.3 provides a short list of considerations that should be identified in such projects.

In addition to the standards of sidewalk design, we should be aware of the quality of the sidewalk itself. When designing a quality sidewalk, it may be necessary to go beyond the standards and consider how the sidewalk best meets the needs of the various users. Sidewalks are a more intimate space than streets and parking lots where we move enclosed in a vehicle. A high-quality sidewalk creates a human-oriented space for interaction, movement, commerce, relaxation, and perhaps vegetation; and it does this in a manner that is safe. Design will influence how this important public space is used

1. Are an adequate number of accessible parking places designated?
2. Do the designated accessible parking spaces meet design minimums?
3. Is there one van-accessible space for every eight accessible spaces, or are all spaces consistent with the universal parking space design?
4. Are accessible spaces marked using the international symbol of accessibility?
5. Are van spaces marked "Van Accessible"?
6. Is there at least one accessible route allowing access to all public facilities?
7. Are depressed curbs provided on the accessible route?
8. Do ramps meet ADA minimums (1;12 slope or less, 36 in. wide, 30 in. maximum rise, level landing every 30 ft, adequate landing size)?
9. Are overhead and wall clearances adequate?
10. Are surfaces nonslip?
11. Are minor changes in grade beveled to minimize risk of trip or obstruction?
12. Are handrails provided where appropriate?
13. Are textural or audible signals provided where necessary? We should remember that when a site is developed the small, intermittent, and ephemeral streams are replaced by curb and gutter flow.

TABLE 5.3 ADA Site Survey

and contributes to the community. Street furniture and plantings, attractive lighting, appropriate signage, widths sufficient for the level of service, and paving materials all contribute to the quality of a sidewalk.

Paving Materials and Design

The choice of paving materials is broad and generally is determined by the nature of the project and the preferences of the designer and the client (Table 5.4). Areas of concern for paving include installation and lifecycle costs, durability, slip resistance, and appearance. Brick and pavers for pathway and sidewalk paving are described in ASTM C 902 by grades and by type. Type I brick is recommended for high-traffic areas such as driveways or entranceways; Type II is used on walkways and other areas of moderate traffic. Type III is used in areas where low levels of traffic are anticipated such as patios (Figs. 5.27 through 5.30).

Material	Characteristics	Qualifiers
Stone		
Granite	Hard, very dense; difficult to work with, weather resistant; very durable, use in high volume areas	Should have low ferrous or pyrite content to avoid rapid weathering
Limestone	Wide variation in color and durability; susceptible to chemical weathering	Easier to work than granite
Sandstone	Durable, wide range of colors, mostly earth tones	Similar to limestone in workability
Flagstone	Durable; moderate to expensive; may be slippery when wet	
Slate	Durable; expensive; may be slippery when wet	
Brick		
SX grade*	Resistant to frost/freeze and thaw; used as paving material; high installation cost	
MX grade*	Not recommended for use where brick will be saturated with water	Used as a paving material only in dry or well-drained situation
NX grade*	In general not suitable for paving purposes	
Asphalt	Installed in light duty (usually 2 layers) to heavy duty (as many as 5 layers); inexpensive; durability often a function of native soil/subsurface conditions and weather; absorbs heat	Susceptible to damage at edges; susceptible to freeze damage if base becomes saturated; susceptible to damage from petroleum products
Concrete	Versatile, common paving material; durable; good lifecycle costs; multiple surface treatments for texture and color; usually reinforced with wire mesh or reinforcing bar; thickness determined by function and soil conditions	Relatively easy to install

TABLE 5.4 Materials for Pathway and Sidewalk Paving

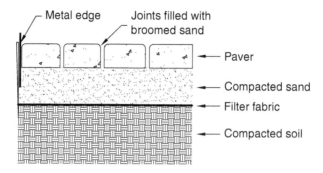

Figure 5.27   Paver installation detail.

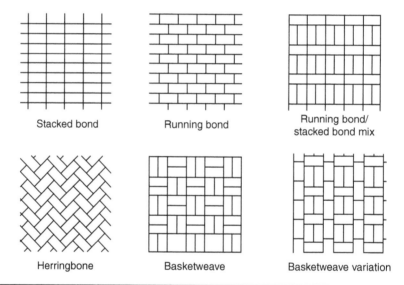

Stacked bond   Running bond   Running bond/
                                            stacked bond mix

Herringbone   Basketweave   Basketweave variation

Figure 5.28   Brick bonds and patterns.

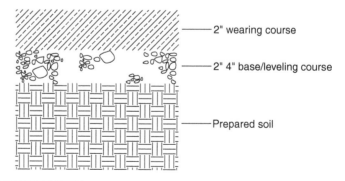

Figure 5.29   Typical asphalt pavement for a pathway, light duty.

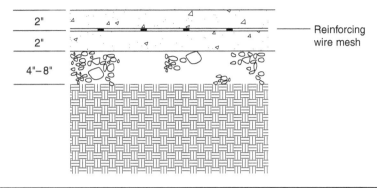

2"

2"

4"–8"

Reinforcing
wire mesh

FIGURE **5.30** Typical concrete pavement for a sidewalk, light duty.

Pervious Paving

Pervious (permeable) paving is an important alternative to traditional paving systems. Pervious paving systems may contribute to the points toward LEED certification. Pervious paving systems have become more widely available and represent an excellent alternative to traditional nonporous paving systems. Pervious paving systems include reinforced turf systems, mortarless pavers, porous paving using concrete or macadam, and gravel and crushed stone. One advantage of porous paving is the ready flow of storm water to the substrate and underlying soil. Care should be taken to be certain the substrate and soil have the capacity to absorb the water they will receive. Roof tops and other impermeable surfaces may increase the amount of storm water flowing to the pervious paving. If the subsurface is unable to absorb the water, unwanted accumulation and saturation of the paving may occur. This can be a particular concern where freeze/thaw cycles occur. It may be necessary to provide a storage volume below the porous paving system, and this could require a designed substrate of 24 to 36 in., perhaps more in areas with high clay content soils.

In general porous paving systems can be designed to handle the light vehicle traffic of driveways and parking areas, but they are not suitable for most roads or areas with heavy vehicle traffic. In a development it might be feasible to use paving of different degrees of porosity so that more heavily traveled areas or areas used by heavier vehicles have less porosity but other areas have more. Porous paving systems are not recommended for areas with slopes greater than 5 percent. Chapter 6 contains more information on porous paving systems.

Signage

Designing signs is a specialty itself, and many types of signs are available commercially. For common signs identifying designated handicapped parking or restroom facilities, it is best to rely on signs that are familiar and in common use. The key elements for signs are readability and effective reading distance. To determine readability, it is necessary to understand the purpose of the sign. Signs providing direction or those meant to draw attention from a distance require larger lettering than signs describing a display or vista immediately before the viewer (Table 5.5). In many communities sign and lettering sizes are regulated in the zoning ordinance. In designing and locating signs, it is

Distance (ft)	Capital letter size (in.)	Symbol size (in.)
30	1.0	3
40	1.0–2.0	4.5
50	1.5–2.0	5
75	2.5–3.0	6.5
100	3.0–4.0	8
150	3.5–4.5	12
200	5.0–6.0	15

Adapted from Charles Harris and Nicholas Dines, *Time-Saver Standards for Landscape Architecture* (New York: McGraw-Hill, 1988).

TABLE **5.5**   Effective Reading Distance and Letter Size

important to remember that the farther away the desired effective reading distance, the larger the letters and the higher the sign must be located. In general a person is less likely to look up more than 10 degrees to view a sign; signs placed above the viewing distance tend not to be seen.

Signs that use symbols to convey information such as warnings or directions are preferred over those that have information in only one language. Likewise, consideration should be given to ADA concerns when designing signage. If the information conveyed on the sign is necessary for access to be provided, textural signals should be installed with the signs. The familiar universal symbols have made sign selection for many purposes much easier. Many standard signs are familiar shapes and colors, and care should be taken not to duplicate these combinations unintentionally. It is easier to read light images on dark colors than the other way around.

Signs directed toward drivers must be visible and readable from quite a distance. Common street and traffic signs have been developed with fairly explicit standards of design and installation; however, drivers have a very short time in which to read and comprehend the information on a specific site sign. In most instances, several signs in a sequence are more effective than providing too much information on a single sign. Information should be organized and presented in a hierarchy of importance from general to more specific rather than a single unweighted set of data.

Open Space Requirements

It is common practice today for developers to provide open space and recreation facilities as part of residential projects. As often as not, these elements are required by local ordinance. However, many communities do not have a coordinated or planned approach to these requirements, and the effect of the ordinance may be to create pockets of playground equipment or open space unrelated and unconnected to the development or to the community at large. Local ordinances may be unclear as to how to evaluate open space: passive open space and active space may not be differentiated, or there may be no qualification or valuation of open space. Without a comprehensive plan, a community may miss opportunities to serve its citizens with the best and most appropriate use and type of open space. Not all open space is of equal value. Sites along busy highways, commercial areas, or industrial zones may not be desirable as open space. Areas of wetland, riparian zones, or flood plains may be desirable for some purposes but not for others. It is just as true, however, that certain active open space features may be desirable for only a very few residents.

Recreation and open space must be planned with regard to the projected users, the physical space, and the capability of a management entity to maintain the facility. These considerations must be measured in the short and long term. New facilities should be planned to work in conjunction with existing facilities. The development of complementing facilities maximizes the recreation/open space dollar, provides a broader choice of activities to the user, and precludes the development of competing and redundant facilities. In developing active or passive open space, developers and communities alike must be concerned about the actual demand, current and future, for those facilities. The demand for a particular type of recreation opportunity or facility should be tied to the target population. If it is to be used exclusively by the new development, then the demographics of the new population should lead the design. If the facility is to have broad-based community use, a different set of considerations is required. The unwanted facility is not an amenity; it does not attract users (or buyers in the case of a new facility). In fact, such underutilized space may be an attractive nuisance that costs more in maintenance and liability risk than it returns.

Active open space must be compatible with the site as well as with the user. An analysis of the site must include existing features such as watercourses, tree masses, topography, adjacent land uses, and areas of historic significance. These concerns, which might otherwise restrict development, may be effectively coordinated with the open space and recreation elements of the design. By first assessing the existing qualities and characteristics of the site, the compatibility of the site and the appropriate open space design can be developed.

Many studies have been done to determine the leisure activities of various age groups and communities. These studies have a shelf life, and they are applicable to a particular population. The studies measure the preferences of a community at a given time; the mix of preferences within a population changes with time. Analyzing the needs of a particular community should include (a) the age group (or expected age group in the case of projections) or the age distribution within the population, (b) the projected number of users within the population, (c) the sources of funding, maintenance, and management and their capacity to maintain the facility, and (d) the availability and accessibility of existing facilities.

The size of facilities is also very important. The proposed active open space must be large enough to serve the user population but remain within the scope of the responsible parties' ability to maintain the facility. An evaluation of the appropriate size or number of facilities should include a projection of the future users. As the population grows older or younger, the demand for facilities will change. Planning the active open space should include not only a demand analysis of today's user but a projected demand of that user in 10 or 20 years.

Active and passive open space should be balanced. All age groups have a desire and an interest in both types of facility. Passive activities include reading, picnicking, sightseeing, photography, people watching, and strolling (as opposed to walking for exercise). Space for passive activities includes unimproved open space, park land, and wildlife habitat, but it can also include space on the fringes of activity areas that allow, or even encourage, people watching and observation. Tables 5.6, 5.7, 5.8, and 5.9 provide an overview of the levels of participation and use of space for various recreational activities.

Activity	Percent participating
Sightseeing/driving for pleasure	72.5
Picnics	70.6
Swimming	66.7
Bicycling	47.5
Hiking/nature walks	40.9
Baseball	32.4
Fishing	31.9
Boating/canoeing	30.7
Golf	29.0
Camping	26.4
Tennis	24.0
Basketball	22.0
Ice skating	21.2
Football	16.5
Hunting/sport shooting	14
Snowmobiling/off-road vehicles	12.0
Horseback riding	11.1
Snow skiing	5.7
Street hockey	5.0

Pennsylvania Department of Environmental Resources, Office of Program Planning and Development. 1986. "Pennsylvania's Recreation Plan 1986–1990."

TABLE 5.6   Percentage of Population Participating in Recreational Activities

Age group	Days per year*
5–9	205
10–19	255
20–29	149
30–44	99
45–64	55
65	15

* Average number of days an individual was engaged in outdoor activities.
Pennsylvania Department of Environmental Resources, Office of Program Planning and Development. 1986. "Pennsylvania's Recreation Plan 1986–1990."

TABLE 5.7   Activity Days by Age Group

Rank	Activity or facility
1	Bicycle paths
2	Tennis courts
3	Swimming pools
4	Ice skating areas
5	Playgrounds
6	Hiking and walking trails
7	Off-road vehicle trails
8	Ball fields
9	Picnic areas
10	Natural swimming areas

Pennsylvania Department of Environmental Resources, Office of Program Planning and Development. 1986. "Pennsylvania's Recreation Plan 1986–1990."

TABLE 5.8 Activities or Facilities in Order of Demand

Activity	Space required	Area required (ft)	Facilities/population
Badminton	1620 ft^2	20 x 44	1/5000
Basketball			
Youth	2400–3036 ft^2	46 x 84	1/5000
High school	5040–7280 ft^2	50 x 84	1/5000
Collegiate	5600–7980 ft^2	50 x 94	1/5000
Tennis	7200 ft^2	36 x 78	1/2000
Handball	800–1000 ft^2	20 x 50	1/10,000
Ice hockey	22,000 ft^2	85 x 200	1/2000
Football	1.5 acre	180 x 300	
Baseball			
Little league	1.2 acre	60 ft baseline	1/5000
Official	3–3.85 acre	90 ft baseline	
Soccer	1.7–2.1 acre	225 x 330	1/5000
Softball	1.5–2.0 acre	60 ft baseline	1/5000
Golf			
Par 3	50–50 acre		1/25,000
9 hole			
18 hole	110 acre min.		1/50,000
Playground/park	1.5 acre		1000
Community park	3.5 acre		1000

Charles Harris and Nicholas Dines, *Time-Saver Standards for Landscape Architecture* (New York: McGraw-Hill, 1988).

TABLE 5.9 Community Open Space Development Standards

The age distribution of a user population is important because the pressure on facilities will vary based on the number of users. The largest proportion of the population uses the more passive open space, but a greater percentage of the age groups that use active recreation facilities actually participate in sports. In a large population with a large number of children, the percentage of individuals that use the available facilities is greater than in an older population group.

Figures 5.31 through 5.36 show the dimensions and layout for various sports activities. Table 5.10 provides detailed field dimensions for various softball and baseball

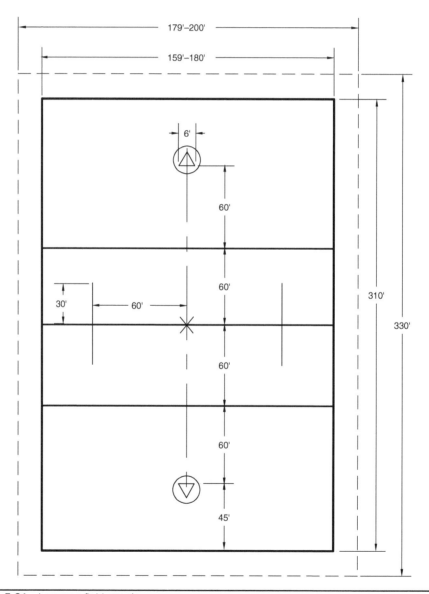

FIGURE 5.31   Lacrosse field, men's.

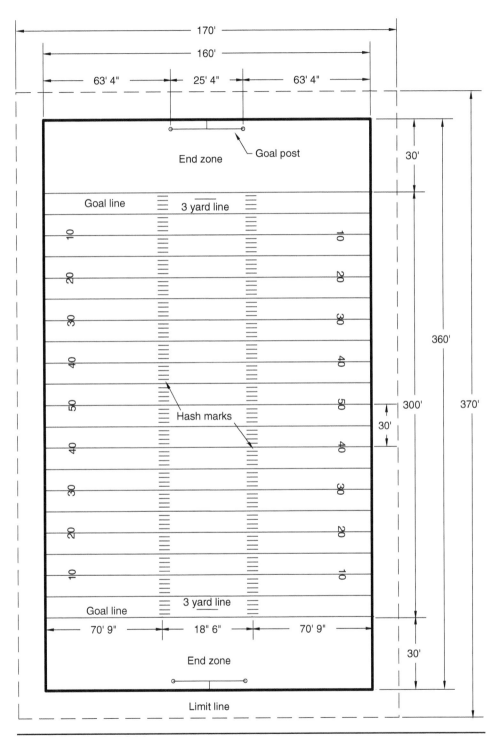

FIGURE 5.32   Football field.

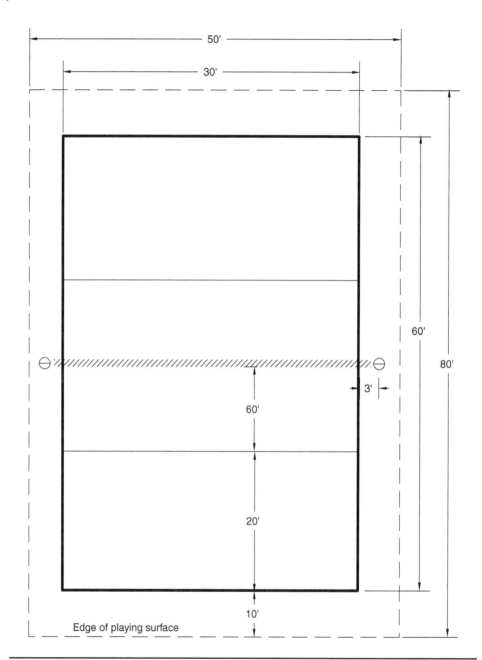

FIGURE 5.33 Volleyball court.

participant groups. Figures 5.37 and 5.38 show subsurface drainage and artificial turf detail. Figure 5.39 provides a reminder that planning for recreational activities in open space must consider cultural as well as athletic activity. Finally, Table 5.11 provides information on area requirements for various community facilities based on the local population.

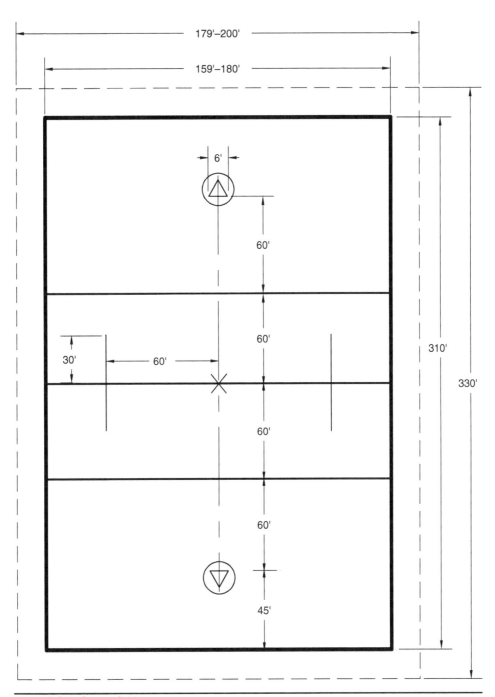

FIGURE 5.34   Soccer field.

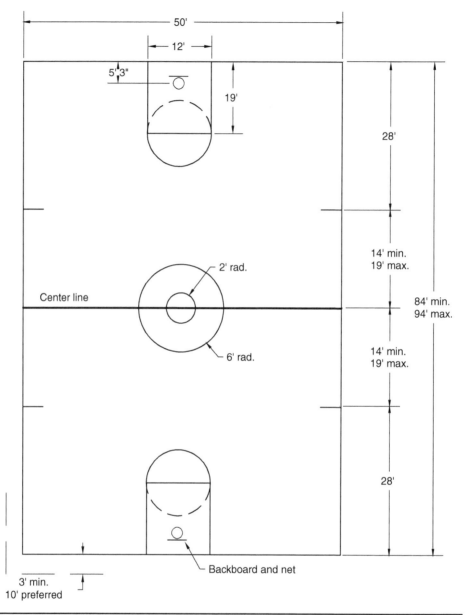

FIGURE 5.35   Outdoor basketball court.

Accessibility and Open Space

The enactment of the Americans with Disabilities Act (ADA) has served to increase our awareness of barriers to access to open space and the need to remove or overcome them. Today plans must accommodate the entire population to a reasonable extent. Parks are specifically identified in the act as a public accommodation that must respond

A) Pitching distance
B) Home plate to backstop
C) Baseline
D) Radius of skinned area
E) Radius of skinned area and bases
F) Foul line
G) Coach box
H) Diameter of pitcher's mound
I) Homeplate to pocket

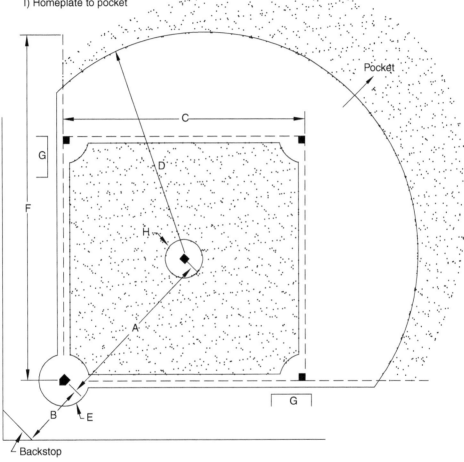

FIGURE **5.36** Baseball diamond.

to the minimum requirements of the ADA, and existing facilities also are subject to the reasonable accommodation test. The act notes the need for attention to the issues of the disabled, including outdoor and recreational design barriers. The design and construction industry have been building new construction with a greater freedom of access for more than 10 years, but the ADA extends the requirement to provide access to existing parks and recreation facilities.

	Softball				Baseball		
	Men's fast pitch (ft)	Men's slow pitch (ft)	Women's fast pitch (ft)	Women's slow pitch (ft)	Little league (ft)	Pony league (ft)	NCAA (ft)
Pitching distance	46	46	46	40	46	54	60.5
Home plate to backstop	25–30	25–30	25–30	25–30	25+/–40	40	60
Baseline	60	60	60	60	60	80	90
Radius of skinned area	60	60	60	60	50	80	95
Radius of base area	30	30	30	30	18	24	26
Foul line	275 min	225 min	225 min	225 min	200	250	350
Coach's box	3 × 15	3 × 15	3 × 1'	3 × 15	4 × 8	8 × 16	5 × 20
Diameter of pitcher's mound	8	8	8	8	10*	15*	10*
Home plate to pocket	275	225	250	225	250	300	400

*The pitcher's mound should be raised 10 in. for little league, 15 in. for pony league, and 10 in. for NCAA.

TABLE 5.10 Baseball Diamond Dimensions

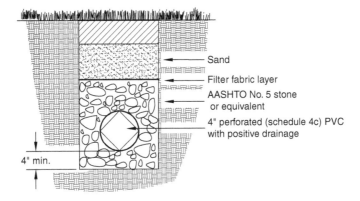

FIGURE 5.37 Subsurface drainage detail.

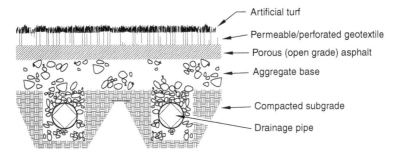

FIGURE 5.38 Artificial turf detail.

FIGURE 5.39 A performance of "Shakespeare in the Park." (See also color insert.)

	Neighborhood population				
	1000 person/ 275 families	**2000 persons/ 550 families**	**3000 persons/ 825 families**	**4000 persons/ 110 families**	**5000/1375 families**
One or Two Family Development					
Acres in school site	1.2	1.2	1.5	1.8	2.2
Acres in playground	2.75	3.25	4.0	5.0	6.0
Acres in park	1.5	2.0	2.5	3.0	3.5
Acres in shopping center	0.8	1.2	2.2	2.6	3.0
Acres in general community facilities	0.38	0.78	1.2	1.5	1.9
Aggregate area					
Acres: total	6.63	8.41	11.40	13.90	16.60
Acres per 1000 persons	6.63	4.20	3.80	3.47	3.32
Square feet per family	1080	670	600	550	530
Multifamily Development					
Acres in school site	1.2	1.2	1.5	1.8	2.2
Acres in playground	2.75	3.25	4.0	5.0	6.0
Acres in park	2.0	3.0	4.0	5.0	6.0
Acres in shopping center	0.8	1.2	2.2	2.6	3.0
Acres in general community facilities	0.38	0.78	1.2	1.5	1.9
Aggregate area					
Acres: total	7.13	9.41	12.90	15.90	19.10
Acres per 1000 persons	7.13	4.70	4.30	3.97	3.82
Square feet per family	1130	745	680	630	610

TABLE 5.11   Area Requirements for Community Facilities

More than 43 million Americans have physical or mental impairments, and as our population grows older, the physiological changes of aging will increase issues and access for even more people. New facilities and major remodeling projects are incorporating at least the minimum standards of access, but it is more difficult to manage the adaptation of existing facilities. Shrinking budgets and the characteristics of older facilities can combine to limit the resources and opportunities to provide access, but access "in the park" may mean more than simply installing a ramp or handrail in the right place. Reducing barriers to parks and open space involves an understanding of users' needs and capabilities, as well the intrinsic value of the site and the desired experiences or program. Standardized solutions or programs that address concerns of access may not be adequate for all projects. Barriers to access in parks and open spaces may be different and affect a broader slice of the population than was originally thought. The physical limits of the site may be inherent to the character of the site. It is important to note that many people with disabilities can satisfactorily access and enjoy a site (independently or with minimum assistance) that is designed for the general public. For a valuable perspective, designers should consult with members of the community with disabilities when working on an open space design.

The physical characteristics of a site also influence the degree of accessibility and the methods of providing accessibility. The quality of facilities and the quality of experience should be considered in any design or evaluation. The National Center for a Barrier Free Environment suggests a systematic or staged approval to maximize the quality of the facility and the program (Table 5.12). A simple system of integrated stages of increasing challenge provides users with the opportunity to determine their own limits. In this way the facility does not act as the limit to participation (Fig. 5.40).

Parks and open spaces that provide varying degrees of access and challenge allow individuals to pursue their own limits of interest and ability. The range of accessibility offers an escalating scale of challenge but provides for a maximum range of access. The details of the mechanics of accessible design have been published and distributed throughout the design and construction industries; the standards for ramp length and height or handrail height are easily obtained (see earlier discussion). Nonstandard concerns should be part of any evaluation; develop a critical eye to assess the facility in terms of users with different capabilities and needs.

For many users, walks and pathways are more than just a means of going from point A to point B; the walk is the experience and the element of interest. Surfaces for stage 1 and 2 walkways should be stable and firm with nonslip textures. Grades for these walks average about 3 percent but should not exceed 5 percent. Depending on the actual grades and length of walks, rest areas with places to sit should be provided at regular intervals. The Minnesota Department of Natural Resources trail planning classification (2007) has been widely distributed and used as a model for designing these elements of walks and pathways (Fig. 5.41).

Stage 1	Provides access to all buildings, secondary facilities, and programs.
Stage 2	In addition to all of stage 1, access is provided to unique opportunities or features.
Stage 3	In addition to stages 1 and 2, various degrees of access and challenge are provided to secondary opportunities or facilities.

Adapted from National Center for a Barrier Free Environment.

TABLE 5.12   Suggested Stages of Accessibility

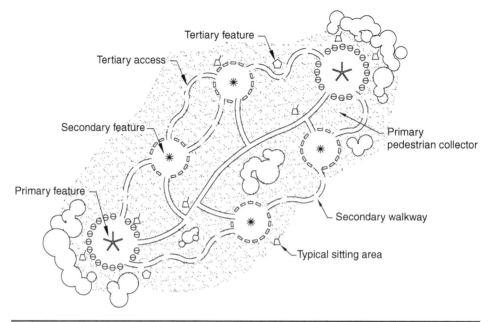

FIGURE 5.40 Phased integrated access.

FIGURE 5.41 This deck is positioned to provide access to the river for those using wheelchairs. The deck design allows for fishing from a sitting position.

Playground Design

Play areas and playgrounds should provide a variety of play equipment, with special areas for different age groups and activities. The design should provide for shade and sunny areas, places for quiet activity and observation, as well as the play facility. The United States Consumer Products Safety Commission estimates 100,000 children are treated at hospital emergency rooms for injuries suffered at playgrounds (private and public). Most of these children are between the ages of 5 and 10 years old. The majority of these injuries are related to design issues rather than supervision issues. The evaluation of existing playground equipment begins with a routine inspection at start-up and throughout the season; loose parts should be tightened and friction points lubricated (Table 5.13).

ASTM has developed three important specifications for playground designers. The Standard Consumer Safety Performance Specification for Playground Equipment for Public Use (F 1487) addresses the safety and performance of equipment; it was revised and updated in 2001. The Surfacing Standard (F 1951) and the Standard Specification for Impact Attenuation of Surface Systems under and around Playground Equipment (F 1292), address surfacing and fall protection. The Americans with Disabilities Act also applies to playgrounds. Selections for playground equipment should be compared to these consensus standards. The U.S. Consumer Product Safety Commission (CPSC) also publishes "Technical Information Guides" to assist in the evaluation and selection of materials and products.

Ideally the playground should not have direct street access and should be located at least several hundred feet from the street. Playgrounds should be sized on the basis of 70 ft² per child or 21 ft² per family. A 2000-ft² playground for small children will serve about 100 families. Approximately 50 to 60 percent of the area should be turf. Equipment should be spaced to provide for safe and comfortable traffic flow; minimum spacing is generally 12 ft between pieces of equipment. Placement and spacing of equipment should avoid overlapping fall zones as well (*The Construction Specifier*, 1985).

Play areas for small children must include benches for parents to sit on and observe their children, and the design should allow for strollers, carriages, and the like. This may require wider sidewalks or paved areas so that standing groups of parents do not

Identify and correct the following potential hazards:
Pinch points or crush points
Sharp edges and catch points
Exposed screws and bolts
Spacing of rings, rungs, rails (choke)
Spacing of equipment
Overlap of fall zones
Hard surfaces
Fall hazards

TABLE 5.13   Evaluation of Playground Equipment

encroach on the traffic pattern. Access to play areas should be limited for security purposes, although care should be taken to avoid an institutional feeling that would discourage use. As a rule of thumb, playground equipment that requires participation should be located toward the entrance of a playground; the presence of groups contributes to the security of the facility.

As the target age group of a playground moves from small children to children between the ages of 5 and 12, there are some additional considerations. It is sometimes true that the play area for these older children includes a "tot lot" facility for younger children. The requirements for older children are developed around or in addition to the tot lot. Older children require larger surfaced or turf areas for participatory games and activities, and the shape and size of these areas deserves particular attention. These types of facilities are often associated with other facilities such as schools or churches. An area of 5 to 8 acres will serve up to 250 families, or about 110 elementary school-age children. For each 50 families, increase the size of the area by 0.2 to 0.4 acres. A maximum population for such a facility is about 1500 families. Above this service level additional facilities should be considered to avoid overcrowding and to reduce the distance to the facility for families (DeChiara, 1984).

Playground Surfacing

The choice of playground surface material is a critical factor in determining the injury impact of a fall. Materials are selected for their shock-absorbing ability. Because head injuries have the greatest life-threatening potential, they are used as the design criteria for surfacing materials. The height of a fall is the next most critical element of playground injury risk. The *critical height* is the approximate maximum height of a fall from which a life-threatening head injury would not be expected (Table 5.14). Critical heights are determined by several different methods, including the Standard Specification for Impact Attenuation of Surface Systems under and around Playground Equipment (ASTM, F 1292). Surface materials should be selected using the critical height of the specified playground apparatus measured from the highest accessible part of the piece of equipment (Figs. 5.42, 5.43, and 5.44).

Equipment	Highest accessible part
Swings	Height of swing at 90° from the at rest position
Slides (including platform)	Top of platform guard rail
Climbers	Maximum height of structure
Horizontal ladders	Maximum height of structure
Merry-go-rounds	Any part at the perimeter on which a child might sit or stand
See-saws	Maximum attainable height of any part
Spring rockers	Any part on which a child might sit or stand

Adapted from U.S. Consumer Product Safety Commission, 1980, *A Handbook for Public Playground Safety.*

TABLE **5.14**   Critical Heights for Selected Playground Equipment

FIGURE 5.42 Playground surface showing a trip hazard.

FIGURE 5.43 A pored-in-place playground surface. (See also color insert.)

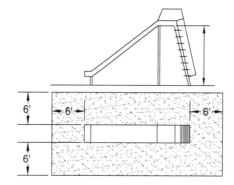

Figure 5.44 Fall zone for a slide.

Many different types of surfacing materials are available commercially. Hard surfaces such as asphalt, packed earth, and turf are not acceptable materials. Available acceptable surfaces are of two types: unitary materials and loose-fill materials. Unitary materials are generally rubber or foamlike materials installed as either interlocking or joined mats, or in some cases poured in place (Figs. 5.45 and 5.46). The performance of these materials varies widely. Specifiers should request current test information for the product to determine its acceptability for a particular application. The disadvantages of unitary materials include its high initial cost (including the cost of base preparation). Some interlocking mats have been observed to curl up at the edges, creating a trip hazard. In addition, unitary materials are subject to damage by vandals in some areas.

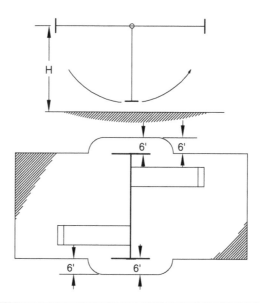

Figure 5.45 Fall zone for a single axis swing.

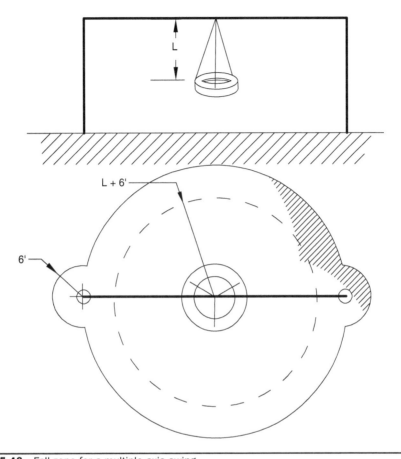

FIGURE 5.46   Fall zone for a multiple axis swing.

The advantages of unitary surfaces are significant. These materials have a consistent performance over their lifecycle. Unitary materials have a low maintenance cost (vandalism costs excepted), and lifecycle costs for unitary materials are often less than for loose-fill materials. The material stays in place: it is not moved during play, and no unwanted objects can be hidden. Unitary materials also provide an accessible surface.

Loose-fill materials include a broad range of products, from sand to shredded bark to shredded foam. The advantages of loose-fill materials are primarily related to cost. Loose-fill materials are relatively inexpensive, readily available, require limited site preparation, and are easy to install. The disadvantages include higher maintenance and life-cycle costs. They are subject to contamination by precipitation, dirt, and other unwanted materials. Their performance may be affected by displacement by children during play and by weather conditions such as high humidity or freezing.

Bicycle and Multiple-Use Paths

According to some reports, more than 30 percent of Americans ride bicycles for pleasure. As interest in bicycling has increased over the past 30 years, interest in bicycle paths and trails has increased as well. Communities across the country have developed or are planning to develop bicycle paths. Bicycle routes are usually one of three types: the dedicated bicycle path system separate from streets and automobile traffic, the designated lane system, and the road sharing system. The dedicated bicycle path system has expanded significantly since the 1980s, with the expanded rails-to-trails network and a number of large residential developments incorporating bicycle paths. The lane system is popular in some suburban areas where wide streets provide adequate room. In other communities, cyclists take to the streets and share the way with automobiles. The Bicycle Institute of America developed a program called Bicycle Friendly Communities to encourage creation and maintenance of bicycle routes (Table 5.15).

Bicycle routes require much the same level of planning and care as street design. Improper planning and installation can result in poor surface conditions and unsafe design. As with streets, an estimate of traffic volume is necessary. Unlike automobiles, however, there is little quantitative information on methods for estimating volume. Recreational cyclists will often drive to a bicycle route many miles from home. Without such supporting data, designers must rely on the experience of others. Fortunately, there is a good deal of experience in the design, construction, and maintenance of bicycle routes in the United States.

In general, bicycle trips are one of three possible types: commuter trip, recreational trip, or neighborhood trip. Commuter trips and neighborhood trips are usually made on public streets, either sharing the travel lanes with motor vehicles or in a designated bike lane. Separate routes are used primarily by recreational cyclists. The design of such routes must consider horizontal and vertical alignment, type of surface material, signage and markings, bicycle and automobile parking, and associated facilities such as

Primary criteria: applicant must meet all four criteria	1. Governing body establishes a written policy designed to develop and maintain "bicycle safe" streets and pathways.
	2. Community budgets and spends $1.00 per capita per year on bicycle facilities and events.
	3. Governing body passes an annual proclamation recognizing May as National Bicycle Month and encouraging citizens to observe Bike to Work Day.
	4. Community establishes a Bicycle Advisory Committee and designates a bicycle issues contact person on government staff.
Secondary criteria: applicant must meet two of the four criteria	1. Community police teach bicycle safety in schools, stressing wearing helmets.
	2. Community sponsors annual cycling event.
	3. Community publishes bicycling information, identifying suggested routes and stressing safety.
	4. Community provides public bicycle parking facilities and encourages private bicycle parking facilities.

From "Bicycle Friendly Communities," *Bicycle USA*, November/December 1994.

TABLE **5.15** Criteria for Bicycle Friendly Communities

FIGURE 5.47 A rest area on a bike trail.

resting places and restrooms. The nature of designated bike routes also varies significantly, from the rails-to-trails route to more strenuous mountain bike routes. The frequency and location of off trail rest areas must be determined according to the use and rigor of a given trail. On a rail-to-trial bike route, where grades do not usually exceed 3 percent, pull-offs and rest facilities should be provided at least every 2 to 3 miles. For trails that are also used by walkers, a rest area should be installed about every mile or so. Rest areas should be set well off the travel lanes of the path and be provided with benches (Fig. 5.47).

Bike trails and pathways are commonly designed to serve pedestrians and other modes of recreation such as roller blades as well (Fig. 5.48). Communicating the rules of the road for these sometimes conflicting uses is best done with clear signage and pavement marking where possible (Fig. 5.49).

Rail-to-trail routes have been so successful and popular because the grades are relatively flat and rarely exceed 3 percent, whereas mountain bike paths may approach 20 percent. In general, bike routes are best limited to a maximum of 4 or 5 percent, with only short sections of steeper grade. The end of an extended steeper section is an ideal place for a wider path surface and perhaps a bench to allow cyclists to pull off the path and rest. At grades over 5 percent, it is difficult to ride without standing. Extended grades of 8 percent or more require most riders to dismount and walk the bike. Consideration should be given to installing wider riding surfaces on the steeper sections of routes with minimum travel lane widths to allow passing. Separating bicycles and

FIGURE **5.48**   A rail-to-trail pathway.

automobiles may be accomplished by providing lanes divided by pavement marking or by constructing lanes separated by barriers (Figs. 5.50 through 5.54).

Drainage is a more important consideration when pathways are paved and drainage is restricted (Figs. 5.55 through 5.59). Provision should be made in the design to assure positive drainage from the path surface. Pooled or standing water represents a danger to cyclists anytime, and especially on curves or turns. Shallow standing water may be a hazard to pedestrians as well if it freezes.

Seating

Commercial sources for seating of all kinds are available, and the design professional's choices will be based on style, materials, durability, and availability of the bench or seating. A key concern is, of course, the comfort of the seat. Designers occasionally elect to design seating also. Figures 5.60 and 5.61 provide common seat and table dimensions.

Site furniture is important for more than the convenience of passers-by. The type of seating helps define the area. Benches facing each other, for example, invite socialization and interaction, bringing more people to the common spaces. Seats near a playground or tot lot encourage adults to bring children and to use the space, in turn this increases surveillance of the play area.

FIGURE 5.49   Rules of the road sign on a bike route.

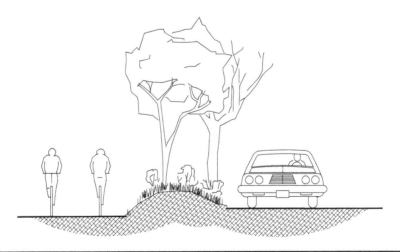

FIGURE 5.50   Design for a bike route separated from automobile traffic.

FIGURE **5.51**   Bike route separated from automobile traffic.

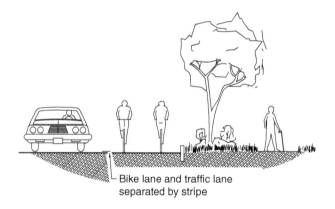

Bike lane and traffic lane
separated by stripe

FIGURE **5.52**   Design with separate travel lanes for motor vehicles, pedestrians, and bicycles.

Accommodating an Older Population

The aging of the U.S. population presents particular opportunities for site designers, and many firms specialize in designing places especially for older folks. Accounting for the interests and needs of the older person in a design requires some understanding of the effects of aging on the individual. Aging occurs and affects individuals at different

FIGURE **5.53**   A bike lane in the street.

FIGURE **5.54**   Multiple users on a pathway.

FIGURE **5.55** Drainage on path surface.

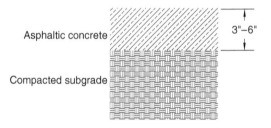

FIGURE **5.56** Asphalt concrete bike route surface (no base).

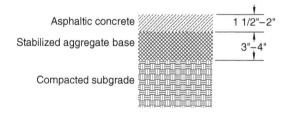

FIGURE **5.57** Asphalt concrete bike route surface (aggregate base).

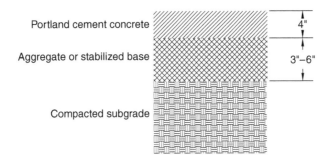

FIGURE 5.58 Portland cement concrete surface.

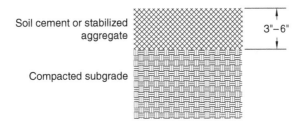

FIGURE 5.59 Soils cement or stabilized aggregate surface.

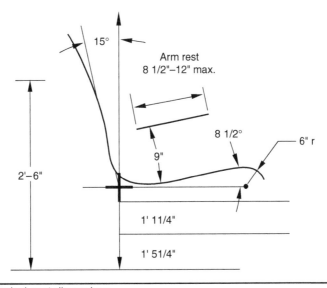

FIGURE 5.60 Typical seat dimensions.

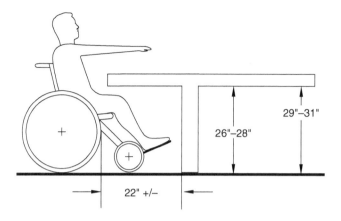

29"–31"

26"–28"

22" +/–

FIGURE 5.61 Typical table dimensions.

rates and in different ways. The effects of aging are functions of genetic predisposition, individual lifestyle choices, and environmental influences.

Aging is natural process that includes a number of physiological changes that influence an individual's ability to perform tasks and limit perception. These effects are present in different degrees in the individuals who make up a community, but site planners and designers should be aware of the range of these normal changes in ability if they are to accommodate them effectively in site development. The physiological changes of aging begin as early as 40 years old when the pupils of our eyes begin to shrink. This change continues for the rest of a person's life, slowly decreasing the amount of light entering the eyes and modifying the ability to see under low-light conditions. A rule of thumb among clinicians is that the functions of systems and organs decline by as much as 50 percent by the time one has reached the age of 70. One perspective is that disease and disability are expected disruptions of life as we age.

The changes in the eye are not limited to a narrowing of the pupil. As we age, the lens of the eye thickens and yellows. The effects of these ocular changes are several. As less light enters the eye, more illumination is needed to see. It has been estimated that a 60-year-old may need three times the amount of light as a 20-year-old in order to see clearly. At the same time, older eyes are frequently more sensitive to intense light and glare. The changes in the lens of the eye reduce the ability to discern between colors, especially greens and blues, and limit depth perception.

Other physiological changes include a loss of elasticity in some tissues, including those of the chest wall. In turn, it requires more energy to breathe and deep inhalation and exhalation are reduced, resulting in lower cardiac function and diminished oxygen levels in the blood. This results in a loss of muscle mass and a relative increase in the percentage of body fat in older people. The loss of visual acuity and muscle mass may lead to decreased mobility, dexterity, and flexibility, and perhaps contribute to a loss of balance. As we age, loss of nerve cells further reduces the amount of sensory information that can be received and processed, and response times and coordination are likely to be slower. For site planners and designers, mobility is a critical concern. There is some experience to suggest that manually operated mobility devices such as walkers and manual wheelchairs are responsible for more injuries than powered or power-assisted devices.

Hearing loss is common in older people. Most hearing loss tends to occur in a limited range of tones or sounds, but some loss can be more pervasive. An individual suffering from hearing loss is often at a distinct disability when interacting with his or her surroundings. Like the loss in visual perception, hearing loss usually occurs gradually, and the individual may not even be aware of the change. Sound provides important information as we move through our daily lives, particularly once we leave our homes and go into the world at large.

Design responses to the aging population are evident all around: tools and utensils with larger handles, changes in the car to increase the elevation of seats and provide easier access and egress, and many other accommodations. Adoption of the Americans with Disabilities Act and the movement toward universal design are largely responsible for these changes, but many also reflect the marketplace of ideas and unmet demand.

These various physiological changes common to aging should be taken into consideration when thinking through design decisions. For example, selecting a street width (see Chap. 6) presents a range of pedestrian safety concerns. Larger turning radii increase cartway width at intersections, which in turn increase the distance a pedestrian must go to cross the street. Larger turning radii may also encourage faster vehicle speeds. An older person with a slower gait may be in the intersection, and at risk, longer than the "typical" person. Traffic signals may need to be timed to accommodate the longer travel time. As the number of personal mobility vehicle (PMV) increases, sidewalk width may have to be increased to accommodate two such vehicles passing one another and to provide sufficient room for walkers and PMVs to comfortably pass.

The changes in visual ability also suggest a number of considerations. The loss of depth perception and vision affect a person's ability to see a small change in grade on a walkway surface. It might be prudent to provide visual signals such as a change in shade or texture at such breaks in grade. The need for greater illumination and careful design for changing light levels is also a concern.

At a community scale, standards may have to adapt to the requirements of a greater population of older residents. Public benches and rest areas may need to be larger or more common. Sidewalk widths and street intersection standards may have to be reconsidered. Allowances for shuttle services to connect older residents with mass transit and other services might be appropriate. Alternative vehicles are likely to become more common in the future, including smaller slower electric or alternative vehicles. Providing a design that can include such elements now or in the future should be considered (Table 5.16).

Walking is the most common exercise activity for older Americans (and for younger ones too), followed by exercising with equipment of some sort, fishing, camping, golf, and swimming. Beyond the obvious design issues, other features can help to make the walkway and park more user-friendly. Visually impaired users may require tactile signals to receive information on their surroundings. Texture changes at breaks in grade or intersections may assist elderly users who have reduced depth perception capabilities. Installing a handrail at a sudden change in grade or a stair on an outdoor walk sends a clear signal to the user and provides the information in a subtle fashion. When possible, both stairs and ramps should be provided; for many people, walking down a ramp is more difficult than using stairs.

In the stage 1 integrated walk network; pavement, color, and texture, as well as signage can be employed to assist users with way-finding and guidance. Construction of barricades to obstruct vehicles must consider the disabled; a cable or chain strung across

Sensory Process and Perception
Age-related sensory losses occur with vision, hearing, taste, touch, and smell. One possible and practical design response to these losses is to load the environment with redundant sensory clues. This includes special attention to
1. the quality and quantity of light.
2. the use of color (brighter colors and those in the orange-yellow-red spectrum are easier to distinguish).
3. contrasts of light and dark shadows and advancing and receding colors as they distort depth perception.
4. the intensity and pitch of sounds (lower-pitched sounds are more easily heard).
5. tactual cues that may be more easily "read."
Central Nervous System and Cognitive Functions
Although many cognitive functions do not change with age, concept formation ability and reaction time may be reduced. To facilitate orientation and promote safety, special attention must be given to
1. decreased concept formation ability affecting orientation or way-finding.
2. slower reaction times.
3. difficulty distinguishing and interpreting background noises from foreground sounds.
Muscular and Skeletal Systems
Muscular strength, agility, and fine motor control may diminish with age. The reduced resiliency of the skeletal system requires attention to safety, security, and environmental negotiability, as injury may be more devastating for older people. These have special implications for the design of
1. ground surfaces and changes in elevation.
2. facilities requiring fine and/or gross muscle movement.
Temperature Adaptation
The reduced ability to adapt to changes in temperature requires amenities and detailing for temperature moderation/control.
Disease
Susceptibility to chronic diseases restrains activity. Special considerations for health-related problems include
1. providing easy access to nearby restrooms.
2. providing options for those with various levels of reserve/energy.
3. limitations on fine motor control and gross movements due to arthritis.

From Diane Y. Carstens, *Site Planning & Design for the Elderly* (New York: John Wiley & Sons, 1985). Copyright John Wiley and Sons. Reprinted by permission of John Wiley & Sons, Inc.

TABLE 5.16 Checklist of Physiological Changes with Age and Some Design Implications

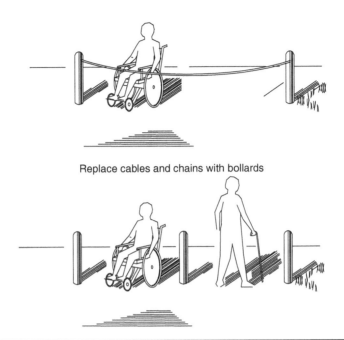

Replace cables and chains with bollards

FIGURE 5.62   Replace cables and chains with bollards.

a pathway can be a significant obstruction. A system of removable bollards might be preferable (Fig. 5.62). By developing clear simple signs with thematic use of color, letter style, or texture as a means of communication, significant information can be provided with a minimum of detail. The use of color to identify a particular degree of accessibility or stage of a facility is simple, direct, and without stigma. In this way, lettering styles and general information can be consistent throughout a facility, conveying a maximum amount of information in a simple useful form.

Walkways should be visually interesting, but encroachment by trees and shrubbery are to be avoided. Lower limbs should be removed to a minimum of 8 ft of overhead clearance at the walkway and no closer than 1 ft to the edge of the walkway (Fig. 5.63). If it is necessary to have a grate in a walkway, the maximum opening in the direction of travel is 3/4 in. Larger openings may catch cane tips or a bicycle tire.

The design of open areas should give particular attention to way-finding. Large undefined areas may be confusing and underused; take advantage of opportunities to view activities in open space. In evaluating open space, the purpose and intent should be identified and evaluation should proceed on the basis of that information. A hierarchy of space is desirable, with smaller private spaces connected to larger public spaces. Areas should have edges or boundaries to reduce ambiguity, provide identity, and assist in way-finding. The facility should be evaluated to remove or mitigate overhead hazards and trip hazards or risks of falls.

The key to the successful redesign or adaptation is to maximize access and maintain the quality of the experience. Barriers that restrict users from general access prevent the maximum use of facilities without a corresponding element of enhancement or need for preservation of quality. The thoughtful evaluation will strike a balance between the

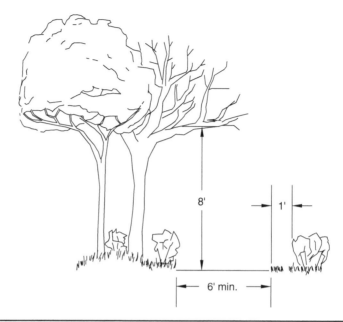

FIGURE 5.63   Minimum path clearances.

removal of borders and the maintenance of the character and fabric of a place or experience. Sensitivity to the special needs of older users may not be intuitive.

Sidewalk Design for Older Adults

Sidewalks take on special significance in the adult community. The basis for sidewalk design in an adult community might not be the standard of walking adults passing each other or walking together. Instead the design should be based on adults seated in personal mobility vehicles (PMVs) or power scooters (Fig. 5.64). These low-cost wheeled

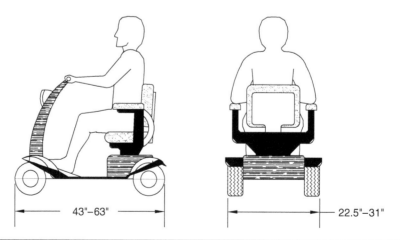

FIGURE 5.64   Personal mobility vehicle dimensions.

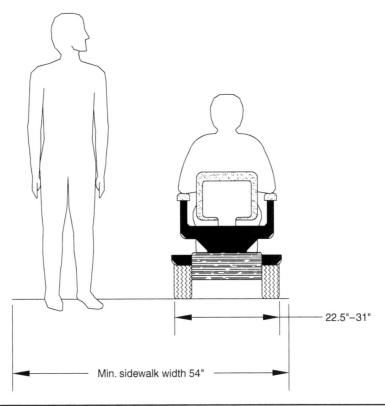

22.5"–31"

Min. sidewalk width 54"

Figure 5.65 Sidewalk dimensions for PMV use.

vehicles are likely to become more common in the future, particularly in communities with a high percentage of adults likely to "age in place." The dimensions for PMVs vary, but the largest tend to be about 26 in. wide and have a turning radius of 50 to 75 in. These dimensions suggest designing wider sidewalks with more generous corners and transitions (Fig. 5.65).

Design for Dogs

As more of our population moves into urban areas and we take our pets with us, dog parks have become a more common feature in existing and developing communities. A dog park is merely open space of some size intended for the use of people with their pets, but, as with most design challenges, there are attributes that make one dog park more desirable than another. Most dog parks are an open area of an acre up to 3 acres in size, surrounded by a fence 4 to 6 ft tall (Fig. 5.66). In general it is considered to be good practice to provide separate areas for small and large dogs. Some parks include a "time out" space for dogs that misbehave or dogs that have not been sufficiently socialized.

Entrances for dog parks should be a double gate system to reduce the chances of escape or unwanted entrance to the park. The entrance should be toward the center of the long dimension of the park. Corner entrances are to be avoided because animals

FIGURE **5.66**   People and pets enjoying a day at the dog park. (See also color insert.)

and owners may be intimidated entering the park from the corner. It is also considered a good practice to locate the entrance as close as possible to the parking area to reduce the amount of time it takes to bring the pet from the car into the enclosure. Water should be provided for pets, and cleanup stations should be located throughout the park.

The dog park must also consider the pet owner. Shade should be provided in the form of gazebos or pavilions, and seating should be provided throughout the park. To reduce congestion and conflict, sitting areas and watering facilities should not be located near entrances. Restrooms should be provided for the human park users.

Ground covers are a challenge in dog parks as dog urine is harmful to grasses. Parks have tried different surfaces including crushed stone and gravel with varying degrees of success. Areas around water fountains tend to become muddy unless care is taken in design to accommodate the traffic and spilled water that should be expected.

CHAPTER 6

Street and Parking Design

Accommodating the automobile presents many challenges and often influences the final design more than most other considerations. This is easily observed in most contemporary developments: making way for the automobile usually takes precedence over all issues of pedestrian access. Much has been written about our dependence on the automobile, and it does not appear that we are going to give up personal transportation in the near term. Recognizing this, site designers should try to mitigate the less desirable impacts of accommodating the automobile.

The impacts of streets and parking lots range from the obvious storm water runoff and localized microclimate issues to isolation of pedestrians and degradation of neighborhoods. Traditional urban neighborhoods were created using a geometry put in place by the municipal authority. Street patterns were established, and development occurred within the bounds of the street and infrastructure layout. Block lengths were often fixed or dictated by local topographic features, and neighborhoods were commonly connected to one another through residential connectors as well as arterial connectors. More recent trends have resulted in wider streets, even in neighborhoods, and in neighborhoods being isolated from one another.

Most city dwellers are familiar with the "heat island" effect: streets absorb solar radiation, and the pavement gets hot during the day and stays warm well into the night. This can result in local temperatures being 10 to 15°F higher than in surrounding areas. One obvious result of the heat island is higher cooling costs. High summer temperatures are stressful, and the environment may be harmful to people sensitive to heat or related conditions aggravated by heat. Warmer summers are expected to increase the health risks and heat-related deaths of residents in several parts of the United States over the next 25 to 50 years. Lighter colored paving materials contribute less to the local heat island effects than dark colored paving material, and incorporating more shade in parking lots could become more common.

In general it is agreed that large areas of paving are necessary accommodations for the automobile but are at best unfriendly. In most cases little effort is made to fit the pedestrian into the design. Applications or designs that must accommodate people and automobiles are faced with a conflict that is generally resolved in favor of the automobile. In the United States since 1940 most designs have favored and even required the use of the automobile. Until recently even suggesting an alternative approach often brought a negative response; the accommodation of the family car at the expense of the family's environment is an accepted practice.

The postwar suburban growth of the 1950s and 1960s gave way to the sprawl of the 1- and 2-acre "estate." These trends reflected the strong, growing economy and a leisure/work ethic that was unprecedented. The environmental costs of the industrial revolution were only beginning to be recognized in the 1950s. By 1970, scientists were turning their attention toward our environment, and much of the news was not good. Now, in the twenty-first century, we understand that we are responsible for the results of our actions, and we are beginning to adapt to the requirements of a sustainable world and economy. We have also learned that workable solutions include development, but that we must do a better job of it.

Parking requirements, for example, are based on a minimum number of required spaces. These design standards have resulted in the huge unused expanses of parking around shopping centers and malls for most of the year. The reserve parking is useful for a few days each year, but the community suffers the impacts of the parking lot every day. Alternatives are rarely considered although a number of them exist. Communities have chosen to subsidize the interests of commercial enterprises and to accept reduced environmental quality. It should not be unreasonable to ask those who benefit from the impact to pay for it. Pervious paving systems, even reinforced turf paving systems for overflow parking areas, may cost more, but the cost could be offset by the reduced impact and preserved environmental quality. In many places neighborhoods are built with streets so wide that pedestrian traffic is discouraged, if not actually dangerous. Pedestrians must cross neighborhood streets more than 30 ft wide that are designed to standards for vehicle speeds in excess of 40 or even 50 miles per hour (mph), even though posted speed limits may be much less. Very few of these standards have been concerned with any aspect of use and function beyond that of the automobile, but street design professionals have begun to move away from some of these standards and toward a more balanced approach.

There have been many attempts to separate traffic from pedestrian activities. One attempt was the "superblock" concept, proposed by architects Clarence Stein and Henry Wright and constructed in 1928 in Radburn, New Jersey. In this design 40-acre superblocks were developed at a density of four units to the acre. Access to the houses was through a cul-de-sac arranged around a central green space and pedestrian network. All of the automobile traffic was kept on the outside of the superblock, and all of the pedestrian activity was focused into the green center. The cul-de-sacs were designed to be only 350 to 450 ft long and had a cartway of only 21 ft. No curbs were used, and the right of way was 35 ft, including a 7-ft-wide utility corridor outside the cartway on both sides of the street. The design resulted in 25 percent less pavement than a common grid street layout and reduced utility infrastructure costs. In practice, however, the superblock was associated with some observed increase in crime.

Since that time, the family car has become an even greater influence on our lives, and we have learned a great deal about how streets work and how drivers behave. The most prominent image of residential streets in contemporary developments is of garage doors with houses attached. Most ordinances require construction of streets that encourage higher speeds, despite the increased risk to pedestrians. Most streets are designed to be conduits or channels; straight and as level as possible. Long straight runs of streets are precisely the conditions that encourage higher speeds and less observant drivers. Experienced drivers react intuitively to the geometry and appearance of the street. Posting speed limits is not an effective means of controlling speeds, especially in residential areas where conflicts between vehicles and people can be anticipated.

Traditional Street Design

Traditional neighborhood streets were narrower and more pedestrian friendly than many modern subdivision ordinances now permit. Many of the most exclusive and desirable communities in the United States feature relatively narrow and curvilinear street networks not found in new developments. The most common reasons given for wide streets are adequate traffic flow, parking, and access for service or emergency vehicles. However, communities with narrower streets have similar service requirements per dwelling unit. Parking presents challenges in communities designed and constructed before the increase in automobile use, but for the most part these problems are solved or at least accommodated by the residents. New projects can easily be designed to address both the use of automobiles and the interests of pedestrians.

Typical streets in recent suburban developments are posted at 25 to 35 mph but are designed for speeds of 45 to 50 mph, and drivers tend to drive faster than the posted speed limit. Research indicates that a pedestrian struck by an automobile traveling 20 mph or less is usually not seriously injured. At 20 to 30 mph injuries are serious, and at vehicle speeds over 30 mph the pedestrian is often killed. Although longer sight distances were designed to increase the safety of the driver, the actual effect has been to encourage speeding, which has put pedestrians in greater danger. An alternative is to design streets that require drivers to be more alert and drive slower and that are friendlier to the pedestrian.

Streets for People

This discussion will include local streets only. Highways, collectors, and high-volume commercial streets must be designed for higher and faster volumes of traffic, and they are clearly not spaces for use by pedestrians. The neighborhood street is a space where automobiles and pedestrians directly compete for use of the space; local streets, shopping centers, office parks, and public places must serve both pedestrians and vehicles. Street designs should address environmental issues such as water and air quality as well as important factors in the quality of a neighborhood.

The typical residential streets in new neighborhoods are often separated by wide, overdesigned cartways that are expensive to build and maintain. These wide streets encourage excessive speed, increase storm water runoff, increase the price of new construction, and have higher ongoing maintenance costs. In return for these overdesigned and underutilized streets, residents are treated to an increased risk of accidents, increased noise levels, reduced neighborhood interaction, and a loss of quality in the appearance of the neighborhood.

Overcoming some of the effects of the typical street or parking lot might include incorporating the methods of storm water management discussed in Chap. 8. By including carefully planned, larger use of infiltration and vegetation, the physical impacts of paving and traffic can be reduced. Well-planned streets go beyond these concerns and also address the integration of pedestrians and vehicles. In an urban neighborhood the streetscape might represent as much as 35 percent of the total neighborhood area, and include all of the public or common space. In urban neighborhoods almost all of this common space is dedicated to the automobile. Residents' use is incidental and at their own risk, but in fact pedestrians do try to use the streets. Neighborhood block parties and street festivals are familiar activities in many cities. Other less obvious but more frequent

Figure 6.1 Children using a basketball hoop on a residential street.

uses are for recreation such as walking, bicycle riding, and playing games. Mitigating the negative environmental impacts of streets should include issues of comfort, safety, access, and traffic control, as well as concerns for the physical impacts (Figs. 6.1 and 6.2).

A movement toward "complete streets" that consider all users in the design and redesign of streets has emerged in recent years in response to these concerns. This idea

Figure 6.2 Pedestrian crossing the street pushing a stroller.

has been endorsed by cycling groups, the American Association of Retired Persons, the American Planning Association, the American Society of Landscape Architects, and the Institute of Traffic Engineers. A Sacramento Transportation and Air Quality Collaborative (2005) report outlines thoughtful street and neighborhood design as a response to public demand for (1) more functional and attractive streets, (2) improved pedestrian and bicycle access, (3) traffic calming without speed bumps, and (4) increased connectivity. The argument for wider streets is commonly that they are safer. The report weighed a number of studies that looked at the relationship between street width and safety and found that wider streets encourage greater vehicle speeds and that "as street widths widen, accidents per mile increase exponentially" (p. 2). Narrower streets may be safer. Many cities and communities across the United States have found that the complete street approach produces safer streets, increases pedestrian and bicycle traffic, and lowers vehicle speeds (Diasa and Peers, 1997; Ridgway, 1997).

The goals of residential street design should be to provide reasonable vehicular and pedestrian access to buildings and residences in a manner that enhances the appearance, security, safety, and enjoyment of the area. Safe vehicle speeds, access for people with mobility restrictions, and a street that is "friendly" encourages interaction, stability, and livability. In addition to increasing the integration of pedestrian and automobile access, design solutions must be developed to overcome the problems streets bring, such as noise, vibration, and air pollution (Table 6.1). Streets may be intimidating to pedestrians and may act as a barrier to a healthy neighborhood if the effort required to safely cross the street is so great it discourages residents from interacting.

In most cases the greatest direct environmental impact of development results from the construction and use of streets, roads, and parking lots. Suburban street width design requirements range from 16 ft to 36 ft (Fig. 6.3). Although some regional differences are appropriate, the typical suburban residential cartway need not be wider than 24 ft. This allows for parking on both sides and one clear traffic lane, or two generous traffic lanes and parking limited to one side. One positive effect of narrower streets is that they slow down vehicular traffic.

Design standards rarely include resident satisfaction among the criteria, and they tend to be prescriptive rather than performance oriented. In a San Francisco study of neighborhood residents, Appelyard and Lintel (1972) found a strong negative correlation between traffic volume and values such as security, safety, neighborhood identity, comfort, privacy, and home—the greater the traffic, the less these values are perceived to be present. Simply put, on streets with large volumes of traffic there is less likely to be a sense of neighborhood and privacy. Interestingly, residents on all streets, regardless of actual traffic volume, are concerned about traffic and safety.

| Traffic accidents |
| Noise, vibration, pollution |
| Traffic speed |
| Nonresident vehicles |
| Appearance |
| Reduction of interaction in neighborhood |
| Storm water runoff |

TABLE 6.1 Problems with Residential Streets

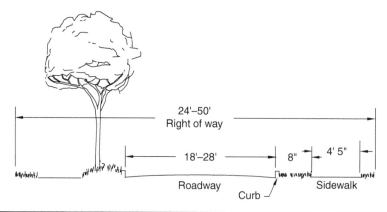

FIGURE 6.3　Typical street cross section.

Institute of Traffic Engineering researchers (Hornberger et al., 1989) found that typical street design standards are made up of width dimensions, grade requirements, and horizontal and vertical curves; but very few, if any, include performance standards. Table 6.2 lists the performance standards suggested by the study. The study points out that street safety problems are a result of conflicting uses in the street space and suggests the solution to these concerns is to further isolate the pedestrian from the street. However, pedestrians constantly use the streetscape for recreation and socializing (Fig. 6.4). Simply imposing design standards that call for segregation of the pedestrian from the street will not solve the problem.

Using the Institute of Traffic Engineering suggestions, one could craft a compelling argument for residential street performance standards. Typically the largest single-body vehicle allowed in most states is the school bus. A residential street designed for a school bus should provide adequate turning radii and lane width. The horizontal and vertical curves should allow for adequate site distances for a school bus at an appropriate design speed. In general it is agreed that an appropriate design speed for a residential neighborhood is about 25 miles an hour. Table 6.3 provides typical street widths, and Table 6.4 lists street width requirements for fire vehicles for a variety of street configurations.

The National Association of Home Builders surveyed 110 communities that allow for narrower residential streets to learn from their experience. The majority of communities surveyed reported that narrower streets performed as well as wider streets with regard to maintenance costs and emergency vehicle access. Parking, traffic, and access problems

1. Adequate maneuvering and access space for the largest vehicle that will use the street
2. Provide for an efficient level of operating speed
3. Adequate parking provisions
4. Standards for lighting, drainage, and separating vehicles from pedestrians

Adapted from Hornberger et al., 1989.

TABLE 6.2　Performance Standards for Residential Streets

FIGURE 6.4   A volleyball net set up on a cul-de-sac.

were rare among the experiences reported. Table 6.5 shows that communities with more pedestrian-friendly streets generally do not feel they have sacrificed vehicular safety or access but instead have found ways to integrate the needs of community and vehicle.

Street width is more than a function of cartway width. Speeds are reduced as drivers perceive the street to be narrower visually; increasing parking densities on wider streets has the effect of slowing traffic. Table 6.6 provides street standards for complete streets.

Type of street	Design speed (mph)	Right of way width (ft)	Traffic lane width (ft)	Parking lane width (ft)
Local, residential	20–25	30–60	9–11	8
Collector, residential	25–30	40–60	12	10
Minor arterial	30–40	100–120	12	10

Adapted from Hornberger et al., 1989; and *A Policy on Geometric Design of Highway and Streets,* 1994, by the American Association of State Highway and Transportation Officials (AASHTO), Washington, D.C.

TABLE 6.3   Typical Street Widths

Width	Source
18–20 ft*	U.S. Fire Administration
24 ft (on street parking)	Baltimore County Fire Department, Baltimore County, Maryland
16 ft (no on street parking)	
18 ft minimum	Virginia State Fire Marshal
24 ft (no parking)	Prince Georges County Department of Environmental Resources, Prince Georges County, Maryland
30 ft (parking one side)	
36 ft (parking both sides)	
20 ft (for fire truck access)	
18 ft (parking on one side)**	Portland Office of Transportation
26 ft (parking both sides)	

*Represents typical "fire lane" width, which is the width necessary to accommodate a fire truck.
**Applicable to grid pattern streets and cul-de-sacs.
Source: Center for Watershed Protection, Site Planning Roundtable, *Better Site Design: A Handbook for Changing Development Rules in Your Community*, 1998 (Center for Watershed Protection, Ellicott City, MD). Used with permission from the Center for Watershed Protection.

TABLE 6.4   Street Width Requirements for Fire Vehicles

Has implementation of reduced street widths created problems for the following?	No (%)	Yes (%)	No answer (%)
Emergency vehicle access	82	8.6	8.6
Traffic congestion	81	14	5
Adequacy of on street parking	63.8	29.3	6.9
Proper functioning of street	63.8	—	19
What specific requirements have been imposed on streets designed with reduced widths?	**No (%)**	**Yes (%)**	**No answer (%)**
Parking on one side	79.3	19	1.7
No parking on street	53.4	44.8	1.7
Additional off street parking	74.1	24.1	1.7

Source: National Association of Home Builders (NAHB), "Street Standards Survey Finds Narrower Streets Perform Well," *Homebuilder*, October 1988.

TABLE 6.5   Responses from NAHB Survey

Item	Low-volume residential	Medium-volume residential	Front-loading residential	Rear-loading residential (no driveways)	Nonresidential	Minor arterial	Major arterial
Daily volume (ADT)	0–750	750–1500	up to 5000	1500–5000	1500–5000	13,000 or less	20,000 or less
Street Characteristics							
Number of travel lanes	2	2	2	2	2	2	4
Width (curb to curb) (ft)	30	32	34–36	41–43	27–30	55–58	64–71
On street parking?	yes	yes	yes	yes	no	yes	no
Parking lane width (ft)	7	7	7	7	n/a	8	n/a
Travel lane (ft)	8	9	10–11	10	10	11	11–14
Left-hand turn lane (ft)	n/a	n/a	n/a	n/a	n/a	10	10–12
Raised median	no	no	no	no	no	no	yes
Maximum block length (ft)	600	800	800	1000	1000	1000	1300
Minimum sidewalk width (ft)	5 (attached) 4.5 (detached)	5 (attached) 4.5 (detached)	5 (attached) 4.5 (detached)	6–8	6–8	6–8	6–8
Bicycle lanes	no	no	no	yes	yes	yes	yes
Landscape strip	yes	yes	optional	yes	yes	yes	yes
Minimum landscape strip width (ft)	6	6	6	8	15 including sidewalk	15 including sidewalk	15 including sidewalk

From Sacramento Transportation and Air Quality Collaborative, *Best Practices for Complete Streets*, 2005. Used with permission from Sacramento Transportation & Air Quality Collaborative.

Table 6.6 Street Standards for Complete Streets

   A survey of the literature and studies associated with pedestrian safety and complete streets strongly suggest that safety is a function of vehicle speed and driver awareness. Residential street design objectives should include reduced vehicle speeds and increased driver awareness. Residential streets should provide enough visual stimulation and variation to generate a sense of prudent caution in drivers (Figs. 6.5 and 6.6). The use of changing lane widths, pedestrian islands, smaller turning radii, and horizontal and vertical curves in street geometry all contribute to increased driver awareness.

   Block length is another important consideration in residential street safety. Studies have found a correlation between block length and vehicle speeds: vehicle speeds increase with block length (Sacramento Transportation and Air Quality Collaborative, 2005). Long stretches of street with no cross streets or traffic controls lead to higher vehicle speeds. The designer should consider block length in the calculus of street design.

   The trend toward isolating suburban developments from one another is discussed in Chap. 4. It is a common practice for new development not to connect to existing neighborhoods or development patterns or provide opportunities for connection to future development. An unintended consequence of this can be an increase in vehicle speeds within the development and traffic volume on arterial collectors. In developments that have only one point of access, all traffic is forced onto arterials. Short trips that might have been restricted to local streets or possibly been pedestrian

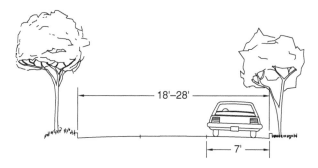

FIGURE 6.5   Residential street design, parking one side.

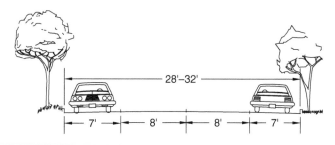

FIGURE 6.6   Residential street design, parking two sides.

1. Provide safe access to residents, including pedestrians, children, and residents with physical restrictions.
2. Reduce traffic speed and volume, and thereby reduce the number and severity of accidents.
3. Contribute as part of the overall design to the character, stability, interaction, and appearance of the neighborhood.
4. Relate to the open space, recreation, and social areas and activities of the neighborhood.
5. Provide access for emergency and delivery vehicles.
6. Provide a reasonable service life.

Adapted from Hornberger et al., 1989.

TABLE 6.7   Goals of Residential Street Design

trips in a more connected arrangement have no alternative but to go to the arterial collector. Likewise, developments with a single entrance/exit frequently employ cul-de-sacs to avoid connecting to adjacent development, forcing all internal traffic onto the one way in or out of the site. Some goals for residential street design are listed in Table 6.7.

Nontraditional Street Design

Streets can be designed to encourage slower and safer vehicle speeds and to enhance the quality of neighborhoods by including planting islands, changes in grade, changes in street width, meandering roads, cul-de-sacs, and rotaries. The Dutch concept of *woonerf* integrates traffic and neighborhoods. This is a distinctly European design that reflects the high density of development and the economy of design found in Europe. We can tap into the vast experience that has been gained by woonerf users and residents in Europe to humanize residential streets in our own projects. The woonerf street is more expensive to build and to maintain, but developers and cities have found that the experience of residents is so positive that they are willing to bear the higher costs (Figs. 6.7 and 6.8). One interesting aspect of the woonerf is the use of pavers instead of poured paving. The paver is used for both its aesthetic value and its role in managing storm water runoff. In some cases the use of pavers to promote infiltration eliminates the need for other storm water management facilities, offsetting the higher cost of the pavers. Some elements of the woonerf that may provide ideas for our own residential street designs are listed in Table 6.8.

Originally the woonerf was developed for use in low-income residential areas, but the idea proved to be so desirable that its use spread to neighborhoods of all types. Many existing streets in European cities have been converted from traditional arrangements to woonerfs. Residents report they find the environment very desirable because of the parklike atmosphere, the character of the neighborhood, and the availability of

FIGURE **6.7** A woonerf. (*Photograph used with permission from Ben Hamilton-Baille.*)

FIGURE **6.8** Another view of a woonerf. (*Photograph courtesy of Ben Hamilton-Baille.* See also color insert.)

1. Rights of way are narrower and completely paved except for planting islands and play areas.
2. Pedestrian walkways are at the same level and grade as the cartway. There is no curb separating them.
3. Vehicle traffic is permitted, but street design and activities require a reduced speed.
4. Areas of potential conflict such as play and social areas are signaled through the use of trees, planted islands, and signs.
5. Travel lanes for vehicles are narrow and change direction often to encourage lower speeds and more awareness on the part of drivers.
6. Two-way streets are encouraged; one-way streets encourage higher speeds.
7. Parking spaces are provided in "clusters" of six or seven and are usually at a right angle to the direction of traffic.
8. The right of way is given to the pedestrian, and traffic speed limits are usually about 15 mph.
9. Signs at the entrance to a woonerf inform drivers that they are entering a residential area and that special conditions prevail.

TABLE **6.8**   Elements of a Woonerf

social opportunities for children and adults. Although the entire woonerf concept is unlikely to be applicable to developing residential projects in the United States, valuable insight can be gained from the woonerf experience.

Traffic Calming

Traffic calming refers to the use of design elements to increase driver awareness and slow vehicle speeds. As previously discussed, street design often encourages driver inattentiveness and increased speed. Traffic calming devices are intended to make the driver more aware of the road and the presence of pedestrians and therefore reduce the number of incidents and accidents. Traffic calming devices should be well thought out and considered before being used in a design.

Complaints about traffic calming are generally of two types: driver exasperation with what is seen as interference with driving and unintended impacts of the traffic calming device. Little can be done about the former, but the latter does require thought on the part of the designer. Most complaints are focused on speed bumps. Speed bump complaints include damage to snow removal equipment, as well as damage to the speed bump, slowed response time of emergency equipment, and accessibility problems for disabled persons.

The speed bump is the least elegant, albeit a very effective, traffic calming tool. Other methods use the natural inclinations and behavior of drivers to reach the designer's objective. It is natural for drivers' attention to increase at changes in the road configuration or layout, and designers can incorporate this tendency into the design to increase driver awareness of pedestrians and slow traffic. Changes in road width, changes in grade, or changes in paving surface texture or color are all effective traffic calming methods that do not share some of the problems of speed bumps (Figs. 6.9 through 6.14).

Traffic calming strategies can be adapted for use on existing streets, which enables them to be employed to address specific issues of traffic or vehicle speed within

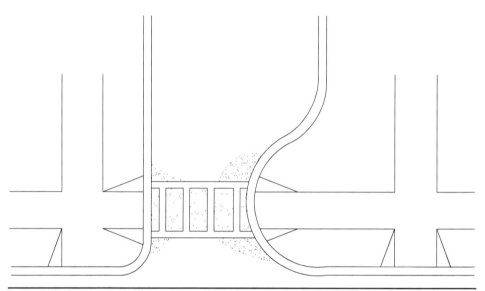

FIGURE 6.9   Design of a traffic calming device called a choker.

FIGURE 6.10   A choker in midblock.

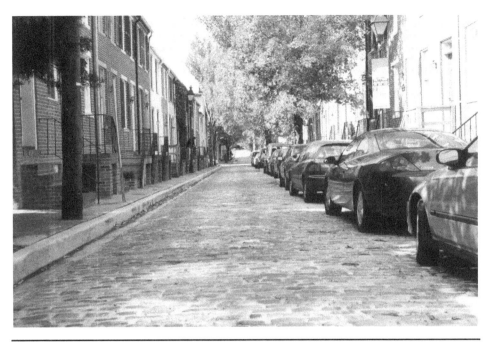

FIGURE 6.11 Narrow streets result in slower vehicle speeds. (See also color insert.)

FIGURE 6.12 Use of visual clues, narrow lanes, and physical barriers protect pedestrians at a busy intersection. (See also color insert.)

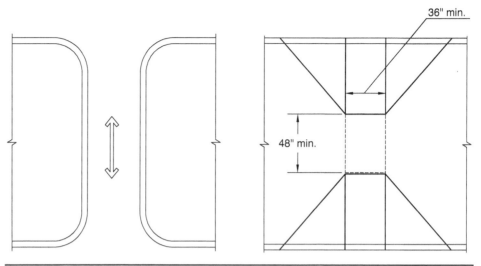

FIGURE 6.13 Pedestrian island detail.

FIGURE 6.14 A pedestrian-friendly street in Asheville, North Carolina. (*Photograph courtesy of the City of Asheville, North Carolina*. See also color insert.)

FIGURE 6.15   Street closures can sometimes be effective as a neighborhood traffic strategy.

neighborhoods. Chokers used at intersections require drivers turning onto a street or in midblock to slow down to negotiate the turn, resulting in increased driver awareness and improved pedestrian safety at crosswalks. If chokers are used at intersections with collectors, thought should be given to a turning lane on the collector to enable slowed traffic to move out of travel lanes. In place of speed bumps, grade changes can be used to slow traffic and reduce the risk of damage to vehicles and allow for snowplowing. Midblock chokers or street closings can also be used to reduce traffic, increase pedestrian use of the street, and foster a greater sense of neighborhood (Fig. 6.15). Neighboring streets may experience an increase in traffic, however.

Roundabouts

Roundabouts have emerged in recent years as a way of improving the safety and performance of intersections. The principle of the roundabout is fairly simple: create a situation that requires drivers to slow down but not stop and allows traffic to move smoothly through the intersection. The modern design is different from the traditional traffic circle in several ways. Cars entering the roundabout must yield to vehicles already in the roundabout, and entering vehicles must slow to give way and merge as opportunities occur. As drivers approach the roundabout, their attentiveness is increased as they observe the change in traffic pattern. Slower speeds and increased driver awareness create a much safer environment for pedestrians. Research shows that roundabouts have reduced fatal and injury accidents by 76 percent in the United States (Baranowski, 2009).

FIGURE **6.16**   A roundabout. (See also color insert.)

The design of the roundabout also decreases the length of time a pedestrian must spend in the traffic lane and offers multiple opportunities for pedestrian islands. In addition to the increased safety of the intersection, the costs to local government may be reduced. The typical intersection with a traffic light costs about $3500 in maintenance and $1500 in electricity annually (Baranowski, 2009). These expenses are eliminated or avoided altogether with a roundabout. The roundabout conveys traffic through the intersection more quickly and more safely than an intersection with a traffic signal, so less time is spent idling through signal phases, and there is less risk of accidents. Finally, roundabouts may be designed to contribute to the beauty of the community by including areas for low plantings or perhaps even a rain garden in the circle (Fig. 6.16).

Cul-de-Sac Design

The cul-de-sac, developed out of necessity, has become a preferred feature for many projects. Originally "dead ends" were seen as necessary evils or the result of poor design, necessary only to accommodate difficult topography or property shapes. As residential development has evolved, planners, developers, real estate professionals, and, most important, home buyers have recognized the desirability of the cul-de-sac location. The cul-de-sac provides privacy, the absence of through traffic, and a sense of inclusivity and neighborhood among the residents.

The cul-de-sac provides a sense of a more secure environment for residents, but more tangible benefits to the properly designed cul-de-sac are also found. The well-designed cul-de-sac uses less pavement for each housing unit than its equivalent in a street might require. This is achieved through the use of narrower cartway widths and landscaped

Topography
Number of units on the cul-de-sac
Cartway and right of way requirements
Parking requirements
Cul-de-sac dimensional requirements
Drainage
Landscape and lighting requirements
Site amenities such as signage, views, and open space access

TABLE 6.9   Factors Affecting Cul-de-Sac Design

islands. The reduced pavement coverage has less impermeable surface area, which results in less runoff and lower street maintenance costs. The narrower cartway width is a practical response to the fact that no through traffic will occur. The limited number of residences on the cul-de-sac should be the primary guideline in determining the cartway width.

The objective of residential cul-de-sac design is to develop an environment that is a pleasant place to live, safe, attractive, and desirable from the day construction is finished through to its maturity. Table 6.9 lists some of the factors that must be considered in cul-de-sac design.

Administrative constraints in the form of local design ordinances and requirements should serve as guidelines for the early design. These guidelines often do not account for the conditions found on a specific site or the requirements of a particular product. Generally design requirements for cul-de-sacs revolve around the number of units allowed, the length of the cul-de-sac, and the radius of the turnaround. The design of the cul-de-sac should be based on its intended use rather than prescriptive standards. A cul-de-sac designed for multifamily units should be different from one trying to create a small separate community feeling. The ideal number of families on a cul-de-sac is difficult to determine. Beyond a single family, the next most basic social unit is a group of 3 to 12 families. This is consistent with the reaction from informal discussions with residents of cul-de-sacs who have indicated that with more than 10 to 12 families there is no special identity among the residents. Most ordinances reviewed limit the number of units to between 21 and 28, but there are few empirical arguments to support such numbers.

The cul-de-sac forms a "cluster" of residences, providing a sense of privacy or exclusivity that many buyers desire. It is possible to arrange several clusters along a single cul-de-sac. In cases such as this, a waiver from a local guideline may be necessary. The requirement to limit cul-de-sac length seems to have developed out of a concern for traffic congestion. If these issues are adequately addressed in the design, a waiver of the requirement would seem appropriate. Cul-de-sac lengths are commonly limited to 1000 to 1500 ft. Figure 6.17 illustrates a number of cul-de-sac configurations. In completing the research for this work, no empirical basis was found for determining a limit to the number of units or the length of a cul-de-sac based solely on the number of dwelling units. The most logical argument for limiting cul-de-sac length is the amount of traffic that might be generated from the single point of ingress and egress during peak traffic times. If lot sizes are an acre or more, the guideline should be adapted appropriately. The distance

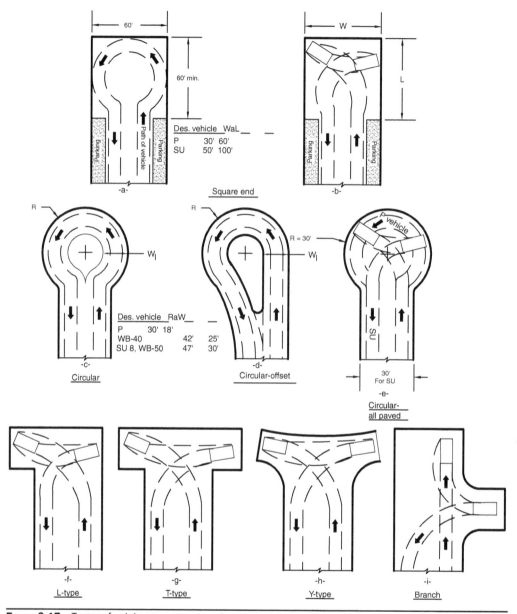

FIGURE 6.17   Types of cul-de-sac arrangements.

between houses can create the same effect as too many units; the sense of place and neighborhood does not develop as it would in a higher-density neighborhood. In a cul-de-sac that exceeds 1000 ft in length, an interim turnaround might be considered.

The design of the terminal end of a cul-de-sac is the source of most discussion and concern. The choice of the design vehicle is fundamental to the design of the turnaround. The design vehicle is the type of vehicle used to determine the radius and cartway width

Vehicle type	Turning radius* (ft)
Small car	19.5
Standard car	22.5
Large car	23
School bus	43.5
Ambulance	30
Trash truck	32
Fire truck	48

*The outer limits of a circular cul-de-sac.

TABLE 6.10   Turning Radii of Selected Types of Vehicles

of the turnaround. Each type of vehicle has its own characteristic turning radius, which can be used to model the most desirable arrangement on a cul-de-sac (Table 6.10). The cul-de-sac is laid out so that the design vehicle can move through the turnaround without backing up.

The design concern on residential cul-de-sacs is how to balance free movement of vehicles and minimize paved surface. The recommended design vehicle for a cul-de-sac should be determined by the project. An industrial park would use a large commercial vehicle as a design vehicle; a project designed to attract families might use a school bus; and a project in an area that receives significant snowfall might design around snow removal equipment. In projects designed for adult residents, the choice of design vehicle might be the family car or a delivery truck. A full-sized family car allows room for small delivery vehicles and trucks to also move through the turnaround without backing up.

Designing for infrequent or occasional use by larger vehicles is an unnecessary commitment of resources and money, which will have an impact on the quality of the residential environment. Limited access by the infrequent larger vehicle must be accounted for in the design, however, such as adding a stabilized turf "shoulder" immediately outside the cartway (Figs. 6.18 and 6.19). Burley et al. (1993) found that stabilized turf works better if it is depressed about an inch from the edge of the road surface. Since only local traffic will utilize the cul-de-sac cartway, width can be reduced to about 20 ft and provide year-round utility and convenience. On a short cul-de-sac, or those serving only 4 to 6 families, the cartway can be reduced to 16 ft. In these cases parking should be evaluated carefully because on street parking is limited.

Ordinances often require a minimum turnaround radius of 50 ft for the infrequent use of fire trucks and tractor trailers. Most vehicles require much less space, and the result is a large, underutilized turnaround. A full-sized car has a minimum outside turning radius of 23 ft, and this design would require larger vehicles to use at least one backing motion to move through the turnaround. A slightly larger vehicle, such as a delivery van, requires a 30-ft outside radius. This radius would provide for free movement by most vehicles but would require a fire engine to make a least one backing motion.

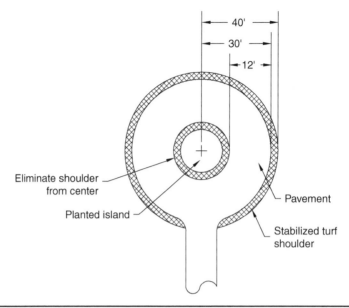

FIGURE 6.18 Cul-de-sac design using stabilized turf shoulder.

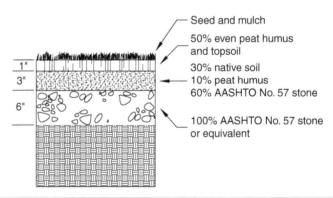

FIGURE 6.19 Stabilized turf shoulder detail.

Although access for emergency vehicles is often cited as the justification for the very large turning radius requirements, in practice this concern does not hold up. Fire equipment is more constrained by the presence and location of fire hydrants than by a restrictive turn. More important, when an emergency vehicle is responding, it is acceptable for the vehicle to steer onto a stabilized shoulder or lawn or enter the cul-de-sac from the left; that is, to go the wrong way around the turn. The backing motion can be made later when the emergency is over.

Another concern in designing the turnaround is snow removal. An outside turning diameter of 32 ft is adequate for most snow removal equipment without backing up except in areas with particularly heavy snowfalls (>150 in./y). In these areas, the additional turnaround width may be used for storage of snow and maneuvering of larger equipment. In areas where snow storage is needed, a center island is often used. In these cases turnarounds of up to 85 ft have been used and a larger center island built. The larger radius may allow for additional or larger lots as well.

As in any choice in a design, there are positive and negative aspects to a cul-de-sac. Some positive aspects, such as security and attractiveness, are difficult to quantify, unless the popularity of homes located on "courts" is any measure. In some areas, homes on cul-de-sacs are valued higher and increase in value faster than similar homes on adjacent streets. The other positive aspects of the cul-de-sac include less pavement per unit, more groundwater recharge, and usually more open space. The criticisms of cul-de-sacs are primarily related to providing for access by larger vehicles, which can be accounted for in a well-thought-out design.

Street Layout and Engineering

Street layout and design must consider the vehicle, visual range or limitations of the operator, safety for vehicle operators and pedestrians, the climate, the geometric configuration, and the character of the overall area. These factors are interrelated. Most municipalities and states have welldefined design criteria for collector roads and highways but have only general criteria for local, smaller volume roads. In many cases, the local road criteria are based on the worst case scenario—the largest anticipated vehicle. This approach has little regard for the behavior of drivers or the quality of the neighborhood. Table 6.11 provides standards for residential street design in low- and high-density environments.

The nature of hillside development generally constrains the standards of classic grid development. Forcing unrealistic standards on an environment that requires special consideration will result in problematic projects. The increased costs of development do not

	Low-density, ordinary hilly terrain	High-density, ordinary hilly terrain
Right-of-way width	40 ft	60 ft
Cartway width	22 ft	36 ft
Sidewalk width	0–6 ft	5 ft
Sidewalk distance from curb	0–6 ft	6 ft
Sight distance	20–100 ft	110–200 ft
Maximum grade	4–8%	4–15%
Maximum cul-de-sac length	1000 ft	500 ft
Design speed	30 mph	20 mph
Minimum centerline radius	250 ft	110 ft

TABLE **6.11**   Residential Street Design Standards

result in an improved living environment but a loss of site character and destruction of the elements that made the site attractive in the first place.

Hillside streets generally are narrower and steeper, mimicking the existing terrain and minimizing the impact of cuts and fills. A rule of thumb is to use the passage of emergency vehicles, such as fire engines, as a test of design fitness. Most design standards reflect the overblown requirements of vehicles built decades ago rather than today's vehicles. Cartway widths as low as 18 to 20 ft should be considered with no parking allowed. If parking is to be allowed, add a lane width of 8 ft for each side on which parking is allowed. Designers might consider varying cartway widths—narrower on slopes, wider on flat areas—to provide parking opportunities. Steep roads can be split, a single lane in each direction separated by a wide area of steep slope. Shoulder widths can be reduced or eliminated in difficult areas. In most cases the split roadway may not provide a substantial savings in cost or in the amount of disturbed area because of the necessary slope lengths. As it is with all elements, this must be evaluated on a case-by-case basis.

Estimating Traffic Flow

A working estimate of traffic flow is necessary to design local roads, internal circulation, and the interface with local collectors. The importance of the estimate of trip generation increases with the size of the project. Traffic flow is affected by a number of factors, but some aspects are fairly intuitive. The nature of the development under consideration is important. A regional shopping center, a retirement community, a development directed toward young families, or an entertainment complex each has different traffic characteristics. In most residential developments, peak flows occur during the rush hours from 6:00 a.m. to 9:00 a.m. and from 4:00 p.m. to 6:00 p.m. Estimating peak time traffic flows from a single family home, for example, is based on 0.8 trips per single family dwelling unit during peak hours. For townhouses or multifamily units, a trip generation of 0.6 trips per unit is used. A single family unit is expected to generate at least 5 round trips (leaving and returning) each day, but the trips are not evenly spaced throughout the day (Table 6.12). In general, there is more traffic in morning peak hours than in afternoon peak hours. Table 6.13 lists minimum design speeds based on average daily traffic (ADT) and design hourly volume (DHV).

Dwelling type	Average	Range
Single family detached	10.1	4.3–21.9
Apartments	6.1	0.5–11.8
Condominiums	5.9	0.6–11.8
Mobile homes	4.8	2.3–10.4

Adapted from Hornberger et al., 1989.

TABLE 6.12   Vehicle Trip Generation in Residential Areas

Terrain	ADT <400	ADT >400	DHV 100–200	DHV 200–400	DHV >400
Level	40	50	50	60	60
Rolling	30	40	40	50	50
Mountainous	20	30	30	40	40

From *A Policy on Geometric Design of Highway and Streets*, 1994, by the American Association of State Highway and Transportation Officials (AASHTO), Washington, D.C. Used by permission.

TABLE 6.13   Minimum Design Speeds Based on Average Daily Traffic (ADT) and Design Hourly Volume (DHV)

Vehicle Dimensions and Turning Radii

Using performance criteria, site designers elect a design vehicle that represents the largest vehicle that frequently uses the street. Different design vehicles are selected for different hierarchies of street design and for the nature of the area in which the street is situated. Collector streets are designed for larger vehicles such as buses and tractor trailers, and residential streets use a smaller design vehicle (Table 6.14). See the section on cul-de-sac design in this chapter for a discussion on design vehicle selection.

Pedestrian safety may influence the design of turning radii. Wide radii allow larger vehicles to turn more easily, in essence turning at a higher rate of speed. Wide turning radii necessitate wider street widths and very wide cartways at intersections. These wider cartways increase the length of the transit a pedestrian must make to travel from

Vehicle	Length	Width	Wheel base	R*	R1	D
Small car	15'6"	5'10"	9'2"	20'	10'11"	10'
Compact car	16'11"	6'3"	10'	21'6"	12'	11'
Standard car	18'	6'10"	10'8"	22'6"	12'8"	11'6"
Large car	19'	6'10"	11'	23'	13'	12'
City bus	40'	8'6"	—	53'6"	33'	22'6"
School bus	40'	8'	—	43'6"	26'	19'6"
Ambulance	20'11"	7'	—	30'	18'9"	13'3"
Limousine	22'6"	6'6"	—	29'	16'	16'
Trash truck	29'	8'	—	32'	18'	16'
UPS truck	23'2"	7'7"	—	28'	16'	14'
Fire truck	31'6"	8'4"	—	48'	34'6"	15'6"

*The R value of the vehicle selected as the design vehicle should not exceed the radii of a paved circle.
From *A Policy on Geometric Design of Highway and Streets*, 1994, by the American Association of State Highway and Transportation Officials (AASHTO) , Washington, D.C. Used by permission.

TABLE 6.14   Vehicle Dimensions and Turning Radii

one corner to another. In addition, vehicles smaller than the selected design vehicle will make turns at higher rates of speed and increase the risk of more serious pedestrian injuries. Smaller radii require slower turning speeds and provide increased pedestrian safety (Figs. 6.20 through 6.26).

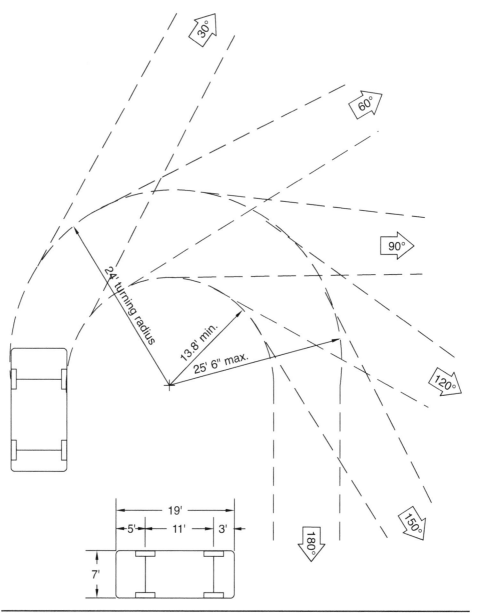

Figure 6.20 Minimum turning path for passenger car (P). [*Source: From A Policy on Geometric Design of Highways and Streets*, Copyright 1994, by the American Association of State Highway and Transportation Officials (AASHTO), Washington, D.C. Used by permission.]

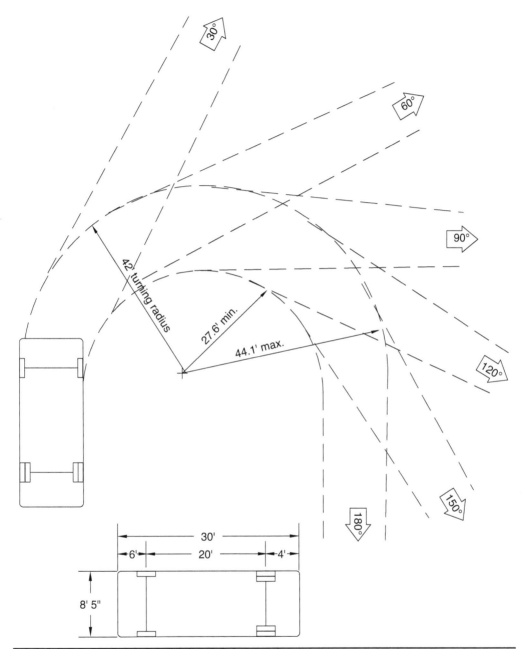

FIGURE **6.21**   Minimum turning path for single unit truck (SU). [*Source:* From *A Policy on Geometric Design of Highways and Streets*, Copyright 1994, by the American Association of State Highway and Transportation Officials (AASHTO), Washington, D.C. Used by permission.]

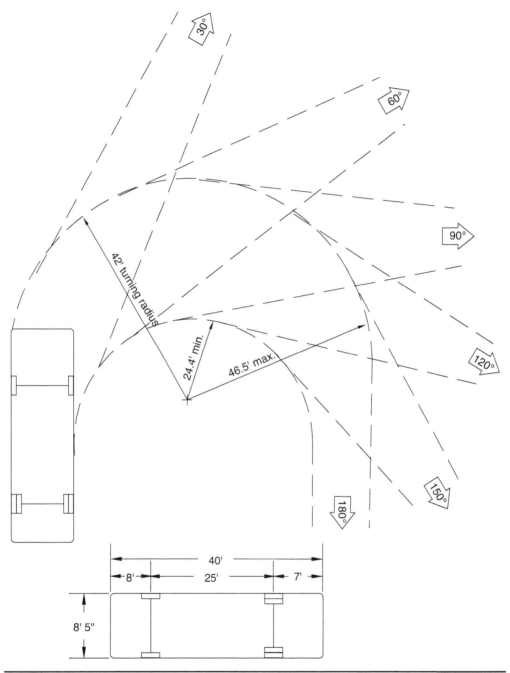

Figure 6.22 Minimum turning path for single unit bus (BUS). [*Source:* From *A Policy on Geometric Design of Highways and Streets*, Copyright 1994, by the American Association of State Highway and Transportation Officials (AASHTO), Washington, D.C. Used by permission.]

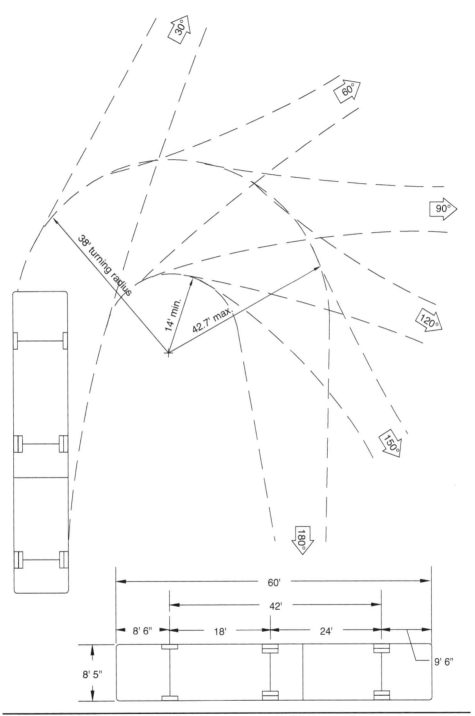

Figure 6.23 Minimum turning path for articulate bus (A-BUS). [*Source:* From *A Policy on Geometric Design of Highways and Streets*, Copyright 1994, by the American Association of State Highway and Transportation Officials (AASHTO), Washington, D.C. Used by permission.]

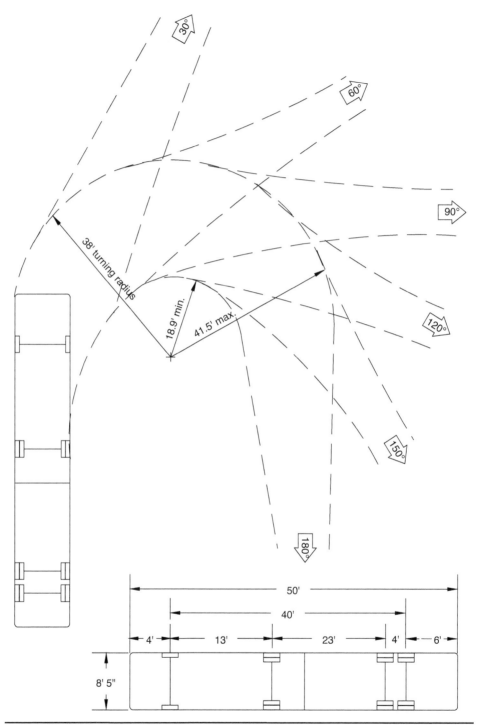

Figure 6.24 Minimum turning path for semi-trailer intermediate (WB-40). [*Source:* From *A Policy on Geometric Design of Highways and Streets*, Copyright 1994, by the American Association of State Highway and Transportation Officials (AASHTO), Washington, D.C. Used by permission.]

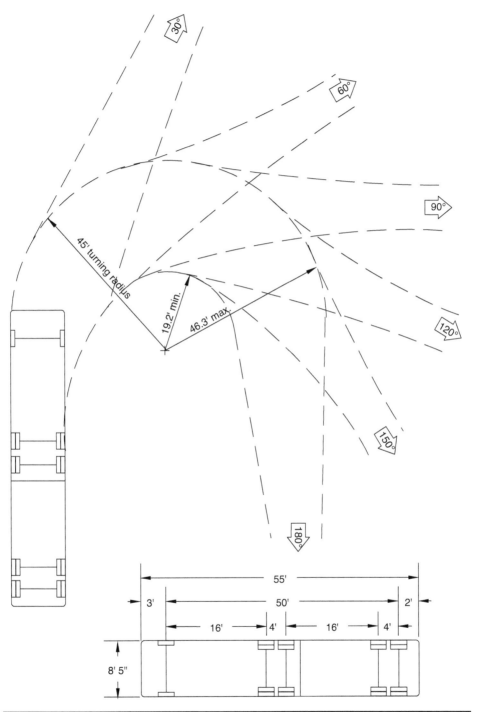

FIGURE 6.25 Minimum turning path for semi-trailer combination large (WB-50). [*Source: From A Policy on Geometric Design of Highways and Streets*, Copyright 1994, by the American Association of State Highway and Transportation Officials (AASHTO), Washington, D.C. Used by permission.]

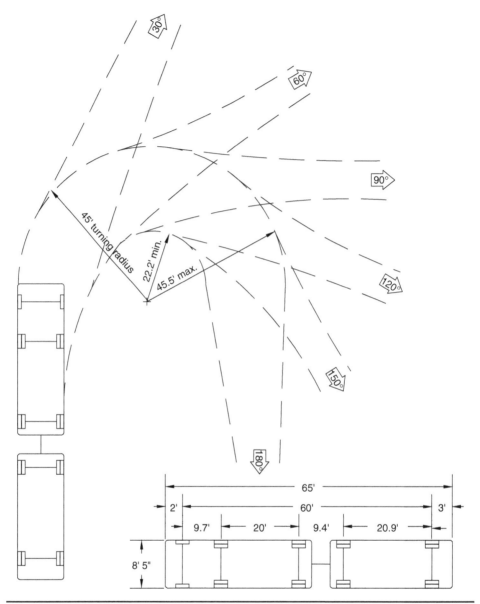

Figure 6.26 Minimum turning path for semi-trailer full trailer combination (WB-60). [*Source:* From *A Policy on Geometric Design of Highways and Streets*, Copyright 1994, by the American Association of State Highway and Transportation Officials (AASHTO), Washington, D.C. Used by permission.]

It may be possible to influence driver perception by installing pedestrian islands (Fig. 6.27) in the intersection that can be mounted and crossed by larger vehicles or to immediately narrow cartway width beyond the radius. These features of a design provide visual "interference" information to drivers, which in turn results in slower speeds. The pedestrian island signals to pedestrians and drivers alike that the intersection is subject to multiple uses.

Figure 6.27   Pedestrian islands provide safety for pedestrians and visual signals suggesting caution for drivers.

Site Distance Calculation

Site distance design is concerned with providing the operator of a vehicle with safe and adequate forward visual access. Site distance is the distance forward that a driver has an unobstructed view of the road. Minimum site distances are determined based on the assumed length of time between the driver recognizing an object in the road and being able to come to a complete stop from the design speed of the road. The factors affecting site distance are the horizontal and vertical arrangement of the road, the height of the operator's eye, and the height of the object to be seen.

Stopping distance is a combination of the time and distance required from the moment of perception to reaction (PR) until the vehicle stops (Fig. 6.28). PR can be expressed as follows:

$$PR = 1.47(t)(V)$$

where PR = stopping distance at a given speed
   t = total of the perception time and length of time braking
   V = the speed of the vehicle

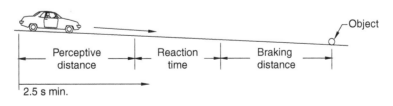

Figure 6.28   Safe sight to stopping distance calculations.

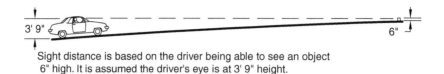

Sight distance is based on the driver being able to see an object
6" high. It is assumed the driver's eye is at 3' 9" height.

FIGURE 6.29   Sight distance parameters.

Braking distance is calculated as follows:

$$d = V^2/30F$$

where d = braking distance
       V = velocity of the vehicle when braking begins
       F = coefficient of friction between the tires and pavement

It is accepted practice to assume for design purposes that the driver's eye height is 3 ft 9 in. above the road surface (Fig. 6.29). In general, an object 6 inches high is assumed to be adequate for measuring sight and stopping distance on vertical curves.

Table 6.15 provides information on the coefficient of friction (F) between the tire and the road. Table 6.16 lists sight to stopping distances when traveling at various speeds.

The weight of a specific vehicle and the grade will affect stopping distance. The weight of larger vehicles is difficult to account for in a design concept; however, it is generally accepted that the heavier weight is offset by the increased height, which allows the operator greater sight distance. Grades can be accounted for in the design. Uphill grades tend to decrease stopping distance, and downhill grades tend to increase it (Table 6.17). These differences are accounted for by applying the percent of grade to the coefficient of friction as a decimal. Uphill grades are added (increasing the coefficient of friction), and downhill grades are subtracted (decreasing the coefficient of friction).

Sight distance on horizontal curves must also be considered. Locating visual obstructions out of the line of sight is necessary to provide safe site distance even on relatively flat surfaces. Intersection and horizontal curves should be designed to

Design speed mph	F*
30	0.36
40	0.33
50	0.31
60	0.30
70	0.29

*Pavement assumed to be under wet conditions.
Adapted from *A Policy on Geometric Design of Highway and Streets*, 1994, by the American Association of State Highway and Transportation Officials (AASHTO), Washington, D.C.

TABLE 6.15   Coefficient of Friction (*F*) Between Tire and Road

Design speed (mph)	Assumed speed for condition (mph)	Reaction time* (s)	Reaction distance (ft)	Coefficient of friction (F)	Braking distance on level**	Sight to stopping distance (computed)	Stopping distance rounded for design
20	20–20	2.5	73.3–73.3	0.40	333.3–33.3	106.7–106.7	125–125
25	24–25	2.5	88.0–91.7	0.38	50.5–54.8	138.5–146.5	150–150
30	28–30	2.5	102.7–110.0	0.36	74.7–85.7	177.3–195.7	200–200
35	32–35	2.5	117.3–128.3	0.34	100.4–120.1	217.7–248.4	225–250
40	36–40	2.5	132–146.7	0.32	135.0–166.7	267.0–313.3	275–325
45	40–45	2.5	146.7–165.0	0.31	172.0–217.7	318.7–382.7	325–400
50	44–50	2.5	161.3–183.3	0.30	215.1–277.8	376.4–461.1	400–475
55	48–55	2.5	176.0–201.7	0.30	256.0–336.1	432.0–537.8	450–550
60	52–60	2.5	190.7–220.0	0.29	310.8–413.8	501.5–633.8	525–650
65	55–65	2.5	201.7–238.3	0.29	347.7–485.6	549.4–724.0	550–725
70	58–70	2.5	212.7–256.7	0.28	400.5–583.3	613.1–840.0	625–850

*PR = $1.47(t)(V)$; in the table t is assumed to be 2.5 s. AASHTO recommends 2.5 s as the minimum reaction time.

**$d = V^2/30F$

From *A Policy on Geometric Design of Highways and Streets*, Copyright 1994, by the American Association of State Highway and Transportation Officials (AASHTO), Washington, D.C. Used by permission.

TABLE 6.16   Sight to Stopping Distances

Design speed	Increase for downgrade (ft)			Assumed speed	Decrease for upgrade (ft)		
	3%	6%	9%		3%	6%	9%
30	10	20	30	28	—	10	20
40	20	40	70	36	10	20	30
50	30	70	—	44	30	50	—
70	70	160	—	58	40	70	—

Adapted from From *A Policy on Geometric Design of Highway and Streets*, 1994, by the American Association of State Highway and Transportation Officials (AASHTO), Washington, D.C.

TABLE 6.17   Effect of Grade on Stopping Sight Distance

provide drivers with clear vision of oncoming traffic and pedestrian activity. The sight triangle is used to determine the clear, obstruction-free area required at an intersection. Many local ordinances include sight triangle design requirements. Figure 6.30 illustrates the sight triangle parameters recommended by the American Association of State Highway and Transportation Officials. In the figure, *d* is the distance traveled by a

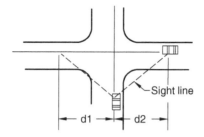

FIGURE 6.30   Sight triangle.

vehicle moving at the design speed during the time required for a stopped vehicle to get under way and cross the intersection or make a turn.

Vertical Curves

The vertical curve of a cartway is actually a parabola as opposed to a circular curve. The basic parabolic equation is as follows:

$$y = ax^2$$

where y = vertical distance from the tangent to the curve
a = a constant
x = the vertical distance from the PVI to the vertical curve, ym

In most instances the vertical curve is designed at the centerline of the cartway. The following formula presumes the vertical curve is symmetrical. Designing a vertical curve begins with selecting the point of vertical intersection (PVI) by extending the opposing slopes to a point of intersection. The PVI is identified as a particular station along the centerline and the grades. Once the PVI and the grades for the proposed curve are known, the designer can set the curve length (Fig. 6.31). The length of the

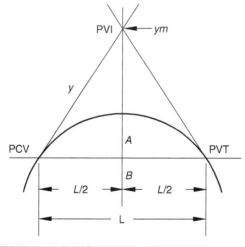

FIGURE 6.31   Vertical curve calculation.

FIGURE 2.1 The headquarters of the Chesapeake Bay Foundation is a LEED Platinum Certified building and site. Note the meadow of native plants.

FIGURE 2.2 The Chesapeake Bay Foundation site includes a crushed stone parking area and native vegetation.

FIGURE 2.3 A green roof, which reduces storm water runoff and rooftop albedo and increases energy efficiency. (*Source: Image courtesy of Roofscapes, Inc.*)

FIGURE 2.6 Workers engaged in the deconstruction of a house. The reuse of valuable building materials is an important aspect of sustainable architecture. (*Source: Image provided by and used with the permission of Second Chance, Inc., Baltimore, Md.*)

FIGURE 4.11 A neighborhood parking area was created by removing a blighted building. The parking is reserved for residents and authorized visitors using a parking tag system.

FIGURE 4.12 A neighborhood park created in the space where a vacant home once stood.

FIGURE 4.32 A serpentine brick wall.

FIGURE 4.38 A brick plaza.

FIGURE **5.39** A performance of "Shakespeare in the Park."

FIGURE **5.66** People and pets enjoying a day at the dog park.

FIGURE **5.43** A pored-in-place playground surface.

FIGURE **6.8** Another view of a woonerf. (*Photograph courtesy of Ben Hamilton-Baille.*)

FIGURE **6.11** Narrow streets result in slower vehicle speeds.

FIGURE **6.14** A pedestrian-friendly street in Asheville, North Carolina. (*Photograph courtesy of the City of Asheville, North Carolina.*)

FIGURE **6.12** Use of visual clues, narrow lanes, and physical barriers protect pedestrians at a busy intersection.

FIGURE **6.16** A roundabout.

Figure 6.50 Cement concrete porous paving installed in a residential driveway. (*Photograph courtesy of Portland Cement Association.*)

Figure 7.9 Slope failure.

Figure 7.11 Slope failure.

Figure 6.54 Cobblestone street installation. The joint spaces between the cobbles allow for drainage to the sand bed.

Figure 8.18 A residential rain garden.

Figure 9.33 A fully revitalized brownfield site, which can be both a source of tax revenues and an economic engine in a neighborhood.

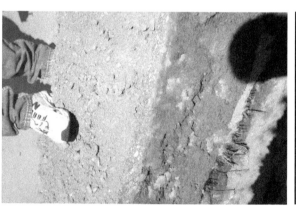

Figure 9.29 Note the unconsolidated fill and stained soil condition.

FIGURE **10.21** People have long known the advantages of strategically planting trees around their homes. These deciduous trees allow the winter sun in but provide cooling shade in the summer.

FIGURE **10.36** A rooftop meadow. (*Photograph courtesy of Roofscapes, Inc.*)

FIGURE **10.8** This strong edge provides clear guidance and direction to visitors to the National Zoo in Washington, D.C. Note the use of textures and colors. This restoration remains faithful to the original Olmstead design but serves the contemporary zoo visitor well.

FIGURE 10.38 A rooftop landscape. (*Photograph courtesy of Roofscapes, Inc.*)

FIGURE 10.39 A meadow designed for a highway right of way.

FIGURE 11.2 A formal hedge and garden.

FIGURE 11.3 A formal public garden, Longwood Gardens, Brandywine, Pennsylvania.

vertical curve is the distance of the tangent from the point of vertical curve (PVC) to the point of vertical tangent (PCT). Elevations are taken from the profile sheet. With this information the vertical curve can be calculated as follows:

(1) Determine the slopes for the respective tangents:

$$(\text{Elevation of PVI} - \text{elevation of PVC})/(L/2) \times 100 = \% \text{ slope}$$

$$(\text{Elevation of PVT} - \text{elevation of PVI})/(L/2) \times 100 = \% \text{ slope}$$

Note that positive and negative values indicate the rise (+) or fall (–) of the slope.

(2) Determine B, the elevation of the intersection of the PVI and the tangent between the PVC and PVT by adding the elevation of the PVC and the elevation of the PVT and dividing by 2.

(3) This is used to calculate the vertical distance from the PVI to the vertical curve, the ym value, by subtracting the elevation of B from the PVI and dividing by 2. This ym value can be used to calculate all other elevations on the curve.

Horizontal Alignment

The design of horizontal curves is concerned with both sight distance and the appropriate radius for the design speed and conditions. The horizontal curve is simply an arc of a circle connecting two tangents. For most local street designs, the centerline of the proposed street is used. When the horizontal direction of the street changes, a horizontal curve is used to make the transition. For most purposes, horizontal alignment should be as direct as possible, but longer transitions may be appropriate under some conditions to minimize the amount of grading or impact on the site. In general abrupt or sharp curves are to be avoided as are multiple compound curves. Exceptions to these guidelines are common, however, when dealing with very low-volume local roads in difficult terrain. Many local land development ordinances require specific minimum horizontal curves.

Figure 6.32 illustrates the relationships used to calculate horizontal curves. The point of curvature (PC) is the point where the curve begins, and the point of tangency

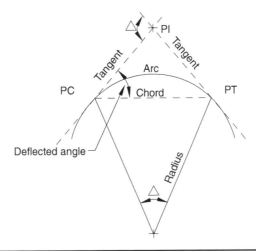

FIGURE 6.32   Horizontal curve calculation.

$T = R\ TAN\ \Delta/2$
$C = 2R\ SIH\ \Delta/2$
$R = 573.L/\Delta$
$L = \Delta R/57.3$
$\Delta = 57.3\ L/R$

TABLE 6.18   The Circular Curve Formulae

(PT) is where the curve ends. Points along the curve are usually given in terms of the stationing on a given road. Arc or arc length (*L*) refers to the length of the curve between the PC and PT. The point of intersection (PI) is the point where both tangents intersect. The Greek symbol delta is commonly used to represent the internal angle. Table 6.18 illustrated the circular curve formulae. The chord is a straight line drawn from the PC to the PT. The deflection angle is the angle between the chord and the tangent. The deflection angle is always one-half of the angle subtended by the arc.

Intersections

Intersections of two or more streets should be carefully designed to provide adequate sight distance as well as a smooth traffic flow. Grades at intersections should be kept to 3 percent or less. On local streets a clear site triangle of no less than 50 ft is required. When local roads dictate an offset intersection, at least 100 ft should be provided between intersections. Streets should intersect at 90° whenever possible (Fig. 6.33).

Parking Area Design

Parking lots can be massive seas of asphalt, contributing to the degradation of local water quality and to increases in urban heat. In addition to the environmental consequences, parking lots are, by function if not design, a place where people and vehicles mix fairly freely, a contest to which the vehicle is better suited. Despite the problems

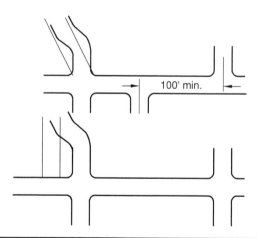

FIGURE 6.33   Street intersections.

with parking lots, we will continue to build and use them in the foreseeable future. As we move toward incorporating principles of sustainability into site design, the options for parking lots are an important consideration.

How Much Parking Is Enough?

Parking requirements are usually set by local municipalities as a ratio of so many spaces per dwelling unit, or square feet of retail space, or seats in a theater. This ratio is based on what is thought to be the minimum number of spaces needed to accommodate a maximum amount of parking demand. This method of calculating parking requirements creates conditions, in some instances, in which most of the parking is rarely used. Table 6.19 shows the range of minimum requirements compared to the actual demand. It is clear that in many cases parking requirements far exceed actual average demand. Parking demand for homes and industrial applications are more easily calculated than the ephemeral demands for a shopping center. The response to uncertainty has usually been to presume the worst case and plan accordingly.

Planning for an average condition may have unacceptable repercussions in some cases. The risk of lost sales because of insufficient customer parking is the most common criticism. Retail businesses make most of their money on the weeks preceding the end of the year holidays, and limited parking is seen as having a cost in the form of lost sales. In addition to the retailers' interests, commercial loans for retail development often include parking requirements that exceed those of the already substantial local ordinance. This approach has worked well for retailers, but the undesirable environmental impacts also have costs, which continue every day regardless of whether the parking is used. If the shopping center is unsuccessful, the impacts continue even after it is closed.

Some strategies have emerged to address the impacts and concerns associated with parking lots. Parking lots contribute significantly to the development cost of a site. Increased runoff from additional spaces affects the size of storm water management facilities. The additional spaces and storm water management facilities require the use of expensive commercially zoned land. Parking space costs range from $1200 to $1500 per space, further increasing the cost of development (Markowitz, 1995). Some communities have looked to their ordinances to find a solution. Instead of requiring a minimum of spaces, these ordinances have a requirement for a maximum number of spaces. Developers wishing to have more space must demonstrate a need during the land

Use	Typical minimum requirements	Actual average demand
Industrial	0.5–2.0/1000 ft^2	1.48/1000 ft^2
Single family homes	1.5–2.5 ft^2	1.11 ft^2
Convenience store	2–10 ft^2	—
Shopping center	4.0–6.5/1000 ft^2	3.97/1000 ft^2
Medical/dental office	4.5–10.0/1000 ft^2	4.11/1000 ft^2

TABLE 6.19   Minimum Parking Requirements and Average Use

development approval process and address how to offset the expected impacts. In this way, parking is developed that will meet the needs of the store operator and the expectations of the community as well.

Shared parking arrangements have become more widely used and accepted. In shared parking arrangements, land uses with complementary parking demands cooperate to lower costs and derive the maximum use from a facility. A business with daytime peak demand may cooperate with a business that has nighttime peak demand. Communities seeking to reduce the impacts of parking may elect to provide incentives in the ordinance for such arrangements.

Design strategies are directed toward minimizing the amount of impervious surface and maintaining the predeveloped rate of infiltration. These objectives are most often accomplished in three ways: (1) reducing parking space size, (2) requiring smaller spaces dedicated to compact cars, and (3) designing spillover parking with pervious surfaces (Fig. 6.34 through 6.44). Arguments against smaller spaces are centered around the recent trend toward larger cars, minivans, and sport utility vehicles. In fact, only the largest SUVs have a larger footprint than a car. These vehicles are not more than 7 ft wide, and many are smaller than a full-sized car. As SUVs and light trucks are required to meet the same fuel efficiency and pollution requirements of automobiles over the next few years, we may see some moderation in their size.

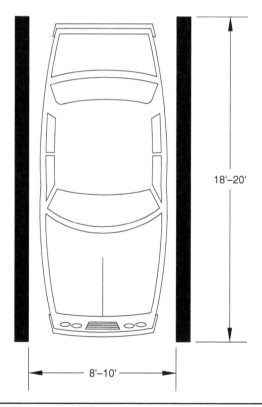

FIGURE 6.34 Typical parking space detail.

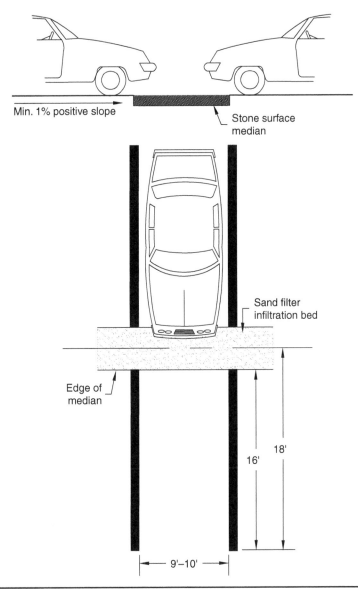

Min. 1% positive slope

Stone surface median

Sand filter infiltration bed

Edge of median

18'

16'

9'–10'

FIGURE 6.35   Revised parking space detail.

Accessible parking space for people with disabilities must be included in the parking site design. Table 6.20 lists these requirements for various sized parking lots. Access aisles adjacent to accessible spaces must be a minimum of 60 in. wide, and at least one of every eight accessible spaces must be served by an access aisle at least 96 in. wide and designated "van accessible." This is not necessary if all required accessible parking spaces conform to "universal parking design" criteria. Table 6.21 lists parking requirements for various land uses.

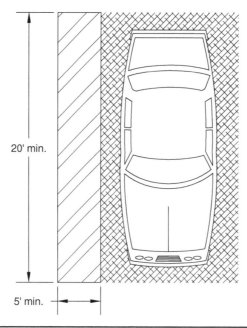

Figure 6.36   Accessible parking space detail 1.

Way-Finding

Finding your way through a parking lot can be a challenge. Designs should include subtle way-finding aids to assist users (Figs. 6.45 through 6.48). This may be of particular importance in very large parking areas or in areas that are often used at night. Parking areas, especially those with unique or torturous layouts dictated by site constraints, may need to include signage or pavement marking to assist drivers and pedestrians.

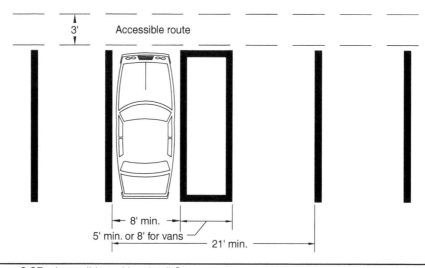

Figure 6.37   Accessible parking detail 2.

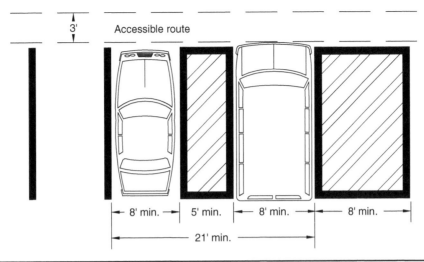

FIGURE 6.38 Accessible parking detail 3.

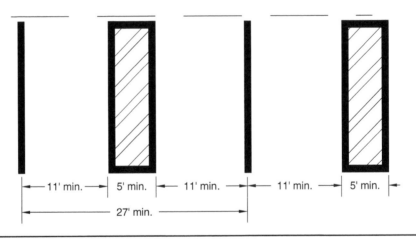

FIGURE 6.39 Universal parking detail.

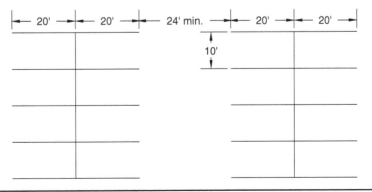

FIGURE 6.40 Ninety degree parking, two-way aisles detail.

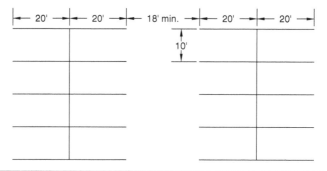

FIGURE 6.41   Ninety degree parking detail, one-way aisle.

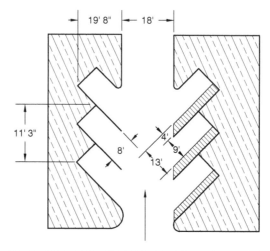

FIGURE 6.42   Forty-five degree parking detail, one-way aisle.

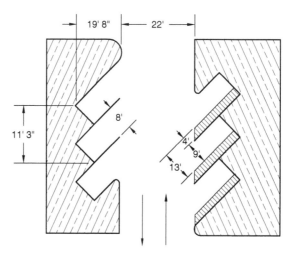

FIGURE 6.43   Forty-five degree parking detail, two-way aisle.

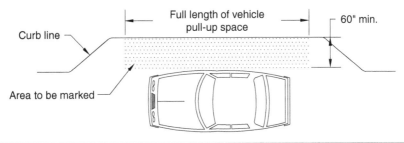

FIGURE 6.44   Vehicle pull-up, drop-off detail.

Total parking in lot	Required accessible spaces
1 to 25	1
26 to 50	2
51 to 75	3
76 to 100	4
101 to 150	5
151 to 200	6
201 to 300	7
301 to 400	8
401 to 500	9
501 to 1000	2% of total
1001 and over	20 plus 1 for each 100 over 1000

TABLE 6.20   Accessible Parking Space Requirements

Pavement Design

Pavement materials are usually dictated by local ordinance and are one of two types: asphalt or bituminous concrete or Portland cement concrete. The functional difference between the choices lies in how load is transferred through the material to the subbase. The design of pavement for most streets is also prescribed by local ordinance and includes required pavement thickness, materials, and cross section (Table 6.22). Designers should review local standards prior to incorporating them into a design. Pavement thickness should be based on or consistent with AASHTO or appropriate ASTM standards.

Porous Paving to Reduce Runoff

The increase in runoff from paved surfaces, and the necessary construction costs and land used for detention basins to offset the increase, can be influenced through the use of porous paving. Porous paving allows runoff to pass through the paved surface and infiltrate back into the soil and groundwater. The permeability of some pavements is as high as 56 in./h (Metropolitan Area Planning Council, 2009). A great deal of work and study has gone into porous paving systems and methods, but their use is still very

Residential	
Single family home	2.0/dwelling unit
Multifamily units	
Efficiency	1.0/dwelling unit
1–2 bedrooms	1.5/dwelling unit
3 or more apartments	2.0/dwelling unit
Dormitories	0.5/unit
Hotels or motels	1.0/dwelling unit
Commercial	
Offices, banks	3.0/1000 ft² GFA*
Businesses and professionals services	3.3/1000 ft² GFA*
Commercial recreational facilities	8.0/1000 ft² GFA*
Bowling alley	4.0/lane
Regional shopping center	4.5/1000 ft² GFA*
Community shopping center	5.0/1000 ft² GFA*
Neighborhood center	6.0/1000 ft² GFA*
Restaurants	0.3/seat
Educational	
Elementary and junior high school	1.0/teacher and staff
High schools and colleges	1.0/2–5 students
Medical	
Medical and dental offices	1.0/200 ft² GFA*
Hospitals	1.0/2–3 beds
Convalescent and nursing homes	1.0/3 beds
Public buildings	
Auditoriums, theaters, stadiums	1.0/4 seats
Museums and libraries	1.0/300 ft² GFA*
Public utilities and offices	1.0/2 employees
Recreation	
Beaches	1.0/100 ft²
Swimming pools	1.0/30 ft²
Athletic fields and courts	1/3000 ft²
Golf course	1/acre
Industrial	
Industrial manufacturing	1.0/2–5 employees
Churches	
Church	1.0/4 seats

*GFA = gross floor area

Source: Charles W. Harris and Nicholas T. Dines, *Time-Saver Standards for Landscape Architecture* (New York: McGraw-Hill, 1988), copyright by The McGraw-Hill Companies, Inc. Used with permission.

TABLE 6.21   Required Parking for Various Land Uses

FIGURE 6.45 Signs can provide direction to special parking areas.

FIGURE 6.46 Paving details in a parking lot are used to guide pedestrians and drivers.

FIGURE 6.47 Striping guides pedestrian access across a parking lot.

localized. Objections to porous paving are often unfounded; but the "facts" can be hard to find, and the objections go unchallenged.

A variety of products on the market consist of an open volume that is to be filled with either soil or aggregate. These cells may be interlocking concrete forms or geotechnical material. The materials are laid in place and backfilled with the media of choice. Grass can be planted in the soil-filled forms to form a turf that has the structural integrity to support even large vehicles.

Porous paving uses a cement paste to coat aggregate, which is poured in place. The absence of sand in the mixture allows for 20 to 35 percent void space in the material. The Portland Cement Association reports that this allows for a permeability of three to eight gallons per minute. Porous cement has been used in the southeastern United States for about 20 years, and it has started to be used in the north and west in recent years. Like other pervious paving systems, porous cement concrete allows storm water to pass directly to the substrate, reducing runoff from the finished site.

FIGURE 6.48 Signs to help drivers find appropriate parking areas and to find their way back to their cars are helpful features.

Subgrade	Bituminous surface (in.)	Base course* (in.)	Subbase** (in.)
Gravelly or sandy soils, well-drained	1–3	4	—
Fine-grained soils, slight to nonplastic	2–3	4	—
Fine-grained soils, plastic	2–3	4	4

*Base course is assumed to have a CBR of at least 70.

**Subbase or bank run aggregate is assumed to have a CBR of 40–60. Also note that a 5-inch concrete slab would accommodate up to a 6000 lb. wheel load on all three soils. In fine-grained plastic soils subject to frost, a granular base of 4 inches would be required for drainage. In addition note that a 4-inch concrete slab would accommodate up to a 4000 lb. wheel load on all three soils and would require a granular base in plastic soils.

Source: Charles W. Harris and Nicholas T. Dines, *Time-Saver Standards for Landscape Architecture* (New York: McGraw-Hill, 1988), copyright by The McGraw-Hill Companies, Inc. Used with permission.

TABLE 6.22 Asphalt Pavement Thickness for Parking Areas, Passenger Cars

A 5-in. pavement with 20 percent voids can store about 1 in. of rain. Typically, porous paving is installed over an open graded stone or gravel base. Depending on the porosity of the base material, a 6-in. base may store up to 3 ft of water. The resistance of porous concrete to damage from freeze/thaw cycles appears to be related to the degree

FIGURE 6.49 Cement concrete porous paving installation. Photograph provided by the Portland Cement Association.

of saturation at the time of freezing. Maintaining high permeability rates is important. Anecdotal evidence suggests that porous concrete clears snow quicker than impermeable pavements. In places where pervious concrete has been in use for 10 years or more, little freeze/thaw damage has been reported.

Critical elements involved in the installation of porous cement concrete include control of the cement-water mixture and compaction. The system works by utilizing a paste of cement and water to bind the aggregate together. If the paste is too wet, it will not have the strength necessary to withstand traffic. If it is not compacted correctly, the aggregate will not bind together properly. Porous cement concrete should be installed by properly trained contractors (Figs. 6.49 and 6.50). Routine maintenance, including vacuuming, should be performed to reduce sediment and debris from accumulating in the concrete-aggregate matrix.

Asphalt cement porous paving is similar to cement concrete porous paving. Asphalt cement porous paving should have a pore space of about 20 percent. It has similar maintenance requirements but requires less skill to install. Asphalt porous paving, even nearly fully clogged, has an infiltration rate greater than most soils. Saturation and freeze/thaw cycles are a concern. Asphalt cement porous paving is installed and constructed using the same equipment as typical bituminous concrete paving. As a result of the studies and the experience of the pioneers in this field, only a practiced eye would be able to detect the difference between porous paving and typical impervious paving. The concern that porous paving requires voids that could catch a narrow heel or cane is unfounded; the voids are too small.

Figure 6.50 Cement concrete porous paving installed in a residential driveway. (*Photograph courtesy of Portland Cement Association*. See also color insert.)

The advantages to using porous paving designs include the recharge of groundwater, a reduction in the amount of particulate from runoff into streams and ponds, preservation of open space, improved site appearance, and reduction or elimination of land dedicated to surface storm water facilities. Objections to the porous paving approach usually include a concern that the pavement will become clogged and no longer function. Studies show that properly constructed surfaces do not clog. Early experience with clogged surfaces was traced to improper design and construction. Some designs incorporate an edge drain system in case clogging occurs many years in the future.

The structural integrity of porous paving is often criticized, and it must be acknowledged that the approach does have limitations. Porous paving designs do not hold up well under truck traffic or heavy loads. These concerns can be addressed by limiting the use of the porous paving to parking areas or roads designated for automobile and light truck traffic only.

Maintenance of the porous surface is limited. Some experience with porous systems has shown that the use of ice melting chemicals and snowplowing can be reduced because the underlying stone retains heat and ice and snow melt away.

The cost of porous paving varies by project, with the most significant factor being the cost of aggregate. Any increase in cost should be balanced against the costs reduced or eliminated by not having to buy additional land and construct a basin. The higher the land cost the greater the feasibility of a porous paving alternative. Table 6.23 compares

Material	Initial cost	Maintenance cost	Water quality effectiveness*
Conventional asphalt/ concrete	medium	low	low
Pervious concrete	high	high	high
Porous asphalt	high	high	high
Turf block	medium	high	high
Brick	high	medium	medium
Natural stone	high	medium	medium
Concrete unit pavers	medium	medium	medium
Gravel	low	medium	high
Wood mulch	low	medium	high
Cobbles	low	medium	medium

*Relative effectiveness in meeting storm water quality goals.

From *Better Site Design: A Handbook for Changing Development Rules in Your Community.* 1998. Center for Watershed Protection. Prepared for the Site Planning Roundtable.

TABLE 6.23   Summary of Issues Related to Various Types of Alternative Pavements

various types of paving materials for initial cost, maintenance, and water quality effectiveness. Figures 6.51 through 6.56 detail alternative paving options.

Reducing the Impacts of Parking Lots

The most effective means of reducing the impacts of parking lots is to limit their size and number. Some of the approaches necessary to accomplish this are beyond the influence of most individual projects and commonly lie in the public policy area. It is within the scope of designers and planners, though, to recommend and influence public policy. Several approaches to minimizing parking have been used.

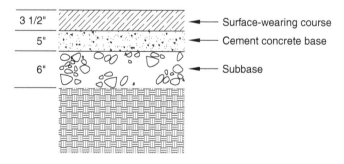

FIGURE 6.51   Typical parking lot paving detail A.

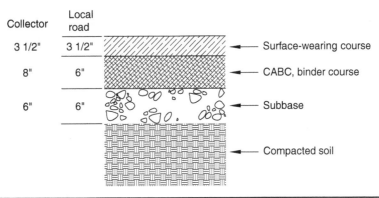

Collector   Local
             road

3 1/2"   3 1/2"   ← Surface-wearing course

8"   6"   ← CABC, binder course

6"   6"   ← Subbase

                        ← Compacted soil

FIGURE 6.52 Typical parking lot paving detail B.

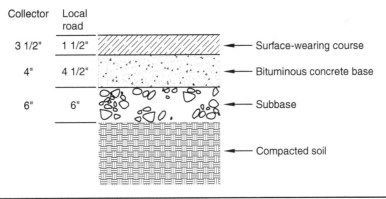

Collector   Local
             road

3 1/2"   1 1/2"   ← Surface-wearing course

4"   4 1/2"   ← Bituminous concrete base

6"   6"   ← Subbase

                        ← Compacted soil

FIGURE 6.53 Typical parking lot paving detail C.

Most zoning ordinances require a minimum number of parking places based on the proposed use of a development. In commercial projects developers routinely want more parking than the minimum, so there is little conflict. If a community is interested in maintaining or improving its local water quality, it might consider allowing a maximum of parking instead as mentioned previously. This coupled with other engineering elements could significantly reduce the "footprint" of development. Performance zoning can provide incentives for minimizing parking, placing parking under buildings, or building parking garages.

The environmental impact of paved parking areas can be substantial. Generally speaking, the impacts are similar to those of streets. Increased storm water runoff, excessive heat retention, and high risks to pedestrians are found in degrees at least equal to, if not greater than, those on streets. A number of elements, such as shading the parking lot, intercepting runoff, and breaking up the long expanses of pavement, can reduce these impacts when incorporated in the design (Figs. 6.57 and 6.58).

By building islands across the slope (parallel to the contours), storm water can be intercepted into the soil of the island. Planting the islands with trees and groundcover

Figure 6.54 Cobblestone street installation. The joint spaces between the cobbles allow for drainage to the sand bed. (See also color insert.)

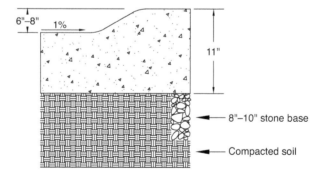

Figure 6.55 Mountable curb detail.

helps to shade and cool parking lots and reduce maintenance costs (Figs. 6.59 and 6.60). The planted island also helps break up the paving visually, making a more appealing site. A minimum amount of planting surface area for a parking lot is about 5 percent of the parking area.

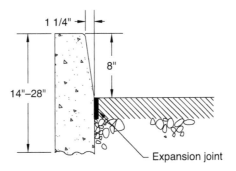

1 1/4"

8"

14"–28"

Expansion joint

FIGURE 6.56   Curb detail.

FIGURE 6.57   A planted landscaped buffer between a residential area and a shopping center.

In areas where deicing chemicals are used, a stone mulch or other material may be more appropriate as deicing materials will harm plants. The use of landscape fabric will contribute to keeping maintenance costs down where stone or other mulches are used. Landscape fabrics are woven and allow water and air to pass through but block light, reducing weed growth. Islands should be designed for snow storage in those areas where large snowfalls are common. In these areas it may be appropriate to space the islands out and to make them deeper or wider to allow for greater efficiency in plowing and snow removal.

FIGURE **6.58** A planted island in a parking lot.

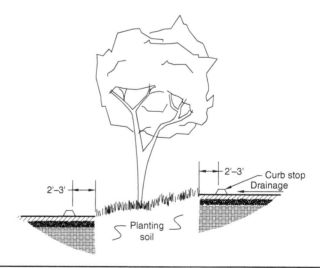

FIGURE **6.59** Detail of planted islands in parking lot.

FIGURE 6.60   A berm and trees are used to buffer the shopping center from an established residential area.

The use of pervious paving in parking for commercial development presents some challenges that must be addressed. Pervious parking generally does not perform well under heavy loads, such as large delivery vehicles or buses. Large snow removal or maintenance vehicles might also prove problematic. In such cases, restrict pervious paving to areas with light traffic such as parking bays, and use a more substantive paving profile in heavy use areas. Most heavy vehicles are also higher than automobiles, and height barriers can be used to restrict entrance to the pervious parking area. Such a barrier would prevent use by recreational vehicles and some heavier SUVs as well. Signs can be used to educate the public.

CHAPTER 7
Site Grading

L and development involves disturbing the existing condition of a site in favor of a different condition, usually directed by a design. A good design considers the character of the site being developed. Sustainable site development requires that design professionals consider the predevelopment environmental function of a site and seek ways to retain that function to the degree it is possible. Minimizing the disturbed area of a site is a critical consideration. Undisturbed and pristine sites may have a higher functional quality than severely compromised former industrial sites, but it is not unusual to find existing important functional elements even on these compromised urban sites.

The National Pollutant Discharge Elimination System (NPDES) was introduced in 1972 as part of the Clean Water Act to control the discharge of pollutants into waters in the United States. Initially the program was focused on "point sources"; that is, industrial or municipal waste sources where the source and the owner could be identified. In the late 1980s the program was expanded to include "nonpoint sources" (NPS); these sources were more ubiquitous and less easily identified. Under the new regulations, all nonpoint sources, including storm water, were to be identified. The program was designed to be implemented in phases. Phase I was put in place in October 1992 and included major construction activities that disturbed 5 or more acres. A proposed Phase II rule was published in 1998, which became effective in 2001. Under the Phase II rule, construction sites of 1 to 5 acres would require a permit. Two permits are available under the NPS rules: an individual permit for specific facilities and a general permit. Most construction sites fall under the general permit program. The general permit has requirements for erosion and sediment control, storm water management, and other controls. General permits are designed to minimize the administrative burden of acquiring the permit and are issued to anyone who needs one. The permit holder is required to give notice of intent (NOI) to use the general permit, which is done by filing a fairly simply form.

More than one party may have to submit an NOI for a given project, and notice must be given at least two days in advance of starting construction. The NOI identifies the permit holder and the location of the activity; it also states the conditions of the general permit, which include a Storm Water Pollution Prevention Plan (SWPPP). In addition to the familiar erosion, sediment, and storm water management requirements, the SWPPP requires identification of any proposed activity or sources of water pollution associated with development and the plan to identify the steps put in place to prevent and respond to any spills or releases. By filing the NOI, the permit holder agrees to these terms. Appendix B includes an outline for a Preparedness, Prevention, and Contingency (PPC) Plan for construction sites. Failure to meet the requirement of the permit can involve delays, fines, and even criminal charges. Under the regulations, states are permitted to take over administration of the program with EPA approval. To date, 42 states have such programs.

The layout and grading scheme of a site should address the physical characteristics of a site, including the functional aspects of the landscape. Ideally the new features such as roads or buildings will fit onto the site with minimal need for large cuts and fills. By minimizing the disturbance and the excavated area at the design level, the designer begins to mitigate the impact of the development. The design should retain as much of the original terrain and character of the site as is feasible: roads should be parallel to contours as much as possible and buildings should be located on flatter areas to minimize grading. Disturbed areas should be kept as small as possible, and strips of existing vegetation should be left in place between disturbed areas. By grading smaller areas individually, the time and area of exposure and disturbance are minimized. The time of disturbance should be managed to minimize the risk of erosion and to maximize conditions to stabilize the site.

Engineering Properties of Soil

The soil survey provides general information relating to topography, depth to bedrock, and hydrologic character of soils, but it is primarily used as part of the site analysis to determine the development capabilities of the soil. Grain size distribution is an important factor in how a soil will behave under different conditions. The variations caused by grain size distribution, clay mineralogy, and organic content in the presence of water are identified by geologists and engineers. The Unified Soil Classification System provides a relatively simple and reasonably accurate description of physical characteristics of soil important to site development. The classification is based on grain sizes from coarse to fine, or on the amount of organic matter in the soil. The classification system includes 12 types of soil: four coarse-grained soils, four fine-grained soils, and four combinations of fine and coarse grains. The classification also includes three organic soils. A coarse-grained soil is one in which over half of the soil is sand sized or larger. A fine-grained soil means half of the soil is silt or clay. Within these categories are subcategories based on the distribution of soil particle size. Table 7.1 lists the symbols use to identify soils, and Table 7.2 provides the Unified Soil Classification System categories and characteristics.

Soils are assessed under the Unified Soil Classification System using a series of sieves. Classification is done in accordance with ASTM 2488 Standard Practice for Description and Identification of Soils (Visual-Manual Procedure) and ASTM 2487 Standard Test Method for Classification of Soils for Engineering Purposes. In general, coarse-grained soils (GW) are preferred for subgrade and base materials, although poorly graded gravels (GP) and silty gravels (GMd) may be used under some circumstances. Soils designated SM or SC are preferred for athletic surfaces and playing fields. Table 7.3 lists the particle size and the proper name for soil fractions of various sizes.

Porosity is the amount of pore space in a soil and is related to grain size distribution and consolidation. Permeability refers to the rate at which water will freely drain through a soil. Clay soils usually have high porosity but low permeability and may settle considerably when loaded with a foundation, but they have lower compressibility and higher strength.

Soil strength refers to a soil's ability to resist deformation, and it is a function of the friction and cohesion of grain-to-grain contact in a soil. Sand dunes are able to stand at the

Soil type	Symbol	Characteristics
Clay soils	C	—
Silts	M	—
Sands	S	—
Gravels	G	—
Organic soils	O	—
High liquid limit	H	Water content >50%, high plasticity (very cohesive or sticky clay)
Low liquid limit	L	Water content <50%, low plasticity
Well-graded soils	W	Particles of all sizes
Poorly graded soils	P	Grain distribution affects consolidation and settlement

TABLE 7.1   Unified Soil Classification System Symbols

Unified soil classes	Shear strength	Compressibility	Workability	Permeability when compacted
GW	Excellent	Negligible	Excellent	Pervious
GP	Good	Negligible	Good	Very pervious
GM	Good to fair	Negligible	Good	Semipervious to impervious
GC	Good	Very low	Good	Impervious
SW	Excellent	Negligible	Excellent	Pervious
SP	Good	Very low	Fair	Pervious
SM	Good to fair	Low fair	To impervious	Semipervious
SC	Good to fair	Low	Good	Impervious
ML	Fair	Medium to high	Fair	Semipervious to impervious
CL	Fair	Medium	Good to fair	Impervious
OL	Poor	Medium	Fair	Semipervious to impervious
MH	Fair to poor	High	Poor	Semipervious to impervious
CH	Poor	High to very high	Poor	Impervious
OH	Poor	High	Poor	Impervious
Pt	Highly organic soils, not suitable for construction			

TABLE 7.2   Unified Soil Classification System

Soil	Particle size
Fines (silt, clay)	No. 200 sieve
Fine sand	No. 40 to No. 200 sieve
Medium sand	No. 10 to No. 40 sieve
Coarse sand	No. 4 to No. 10 sieve
Sand	No. 4 to No. 200 sieve
Fine gravel	3/4 in. to No. 4 sieve
Gravel	3 in. to No. 4 sieve
Cobbles	3 in. to 12 in.

TABLE 7.3 Soil Fraction Distribution

angle of repose because of the grain-to-grain friction. Cohesion is the measure of how soil particles stick together and is most associated with clays. Shear strength is the measure of the frictional resistance and cohesion of a soil. To test shear strength, a four-bladed vane is driven into the soil and turned using a wrench, which measures the force (torque) necessary to turn the vane. The shear strength of the soil is the force applied at the time of failure. In situ field tests are preferred because soil is in its natural condition.

Bulk density refers to the weight per volume of any unit of soil. As a rule of thumb, the higher the bulk density of a soil, the greater the support it can provide for a foundation. Materials with low bulk densities do not provide a solid foundation for construction.

Other tests such as the Atterberg Limits also contribute to understanding and classifying the soil. The Atterberg Limits and Soil Classification quantifies the variations caused by grain size distribution, clay mineralogy, and organic content. The Atterberg Limits are actually two measures: the liquid limit and the plastic limit. These procedures measure the water in a soil at a point where the soil begins to act as a liquid, or begins plastic flow. Water is measured as a percentage of the weight of the soil when dry.

The liquid limit (LL) is the moisture content at which a soil tends to flow and will not retain its shape. A molded wet soil patty is placed in a liquid limit cup, and a V-groove is cut through the patty with a tool designed for the purpose. Using a hand crank, the cup is repeatedly lifted and dropped until the soil flows to close the groove. When the moisture content is sufficient to close the groove (at up to 25 drops), the soil "flows" and the liquid limit of the soil has been reached.

The plastic limit (PL) is the moisture content at which a soil deforms plastically. The soil is rolled into long threads until they just begin to crumble at a diameter of about 3 mm. If a soil can be rolled into finer threads without cracking, it contains more moisture than its plastic limits; if it cracks before 3 mm is reached, it has less.

The numerical difference between the LL and the PL is called the plasticity index (PI). This is the range of moisture in which a soil behaves as a plastic material. Some clays can absorb water several times their own weight; these clays behave plastically over a broad range of moisture content before they start to flow. A PI over 15 is a good indicator of an expansive soil.

The Balanced Site

The most economical grading plan includes a minimum of earthwork with cut and fill in balance. Several factors influence the balance. For example, sites with soils with a high plasticity index or with high organic content may have to be removed and replaced under building pads or where other site structures are planned. Another factor is the tendency of some soils to expand when excavated; some soils "bulk" significantly when disturbed. To design a balanced site, the professional needs geotechnical information regarding the soils' character, the bearing capacity of the soil, its bulking factor, and the depth and character of the bedrock. Traditionally, volumes were calculated using the average-end method; however, most designers today use a computer to determine volumes.

Site grading proceeds from a conceptual grading plan that attempts to balance the site and locate the structures or program elements to maximize the site. From concept the grading plan undergoes a series of iterations, each bringing a greater level of detail to the design until a final grading plan is developed. Final grades are in accordance with appropriate grading standards (Table 7.4). In many places grading standards are included in local ordinances and development regulations. Some government agencies and large development companies may have their own standards to guide the design. Grades are established with concerns for safety, comfort, and access as well as for drainage and local concerns such as ice.

Hillside Developments

Each hillside is unique. The combination of slope, soil, hydrology, geology, vegetation, aspect, and proposed use determine the physical constraints and opportunities for development. In general, it is more expensive to develop on a hilly or steep site due to

Element	Minimum (%)	Preferred (%)	Maximum (%)
Lawns	1	2–8	10
Athletic fields	1	1	2
Mowed slopes	5	10	25
Unmowed slopes	—	25	Angle of repose
Planted slopes	1	5	10
Berms	5	10	25
Crown of unpaved street	1	2	3
Crown of paved street	2	2.5	3
Crown of road shoulders	1	2–3	10
Longitudinal slope of local streets	0.5	1–10	20
Longitudinal slope of driveways	0.5	1–10	20
Longitudinal slope of parking lots	0.5	2–3	20

TABLE 7.4   Typical Grading Standards

higher costs of grading, although higher costs may also be a reflection of a lower density necessary compared to similar flat sites. In spite of the higher costs of hillside development, buyers are attracted to such sites because of the long views and terrain.

Some fundamental elements are found in successful hillside developments. It is often necessary to have flexibility in the design of streets to minimize site development costs and to maintain the character of the site. Finished grading tends to mimic the natural condition as much as possible, and building sites are selected more on the basis of physical conditions. The methods of optimizing the site begin with a careful analysis of the site as discussed in Chap. 3. Hillsides are unique, and the analysis must address and identify those aspects of a specific site that lend it to successful development. Views, slopes, soil conditions, access, utilities, and individual home sites must be evaluated in terms of development costs and market value.

The finished grading of the site should mimic the original terrain. This is especially true if the original character of the site was considered an important element of the project. If the views and terrain are features that prospective buyers would be attracted to, it is important to maintain the sense that they are undisturbed and the site is as natural as possible. The most fundamental aspect of this is the quality of the grading. Figure 7.1 shows a successfully developed fairly high-density residential project on a steep site that retained the site's character. The extra effort is translated into greater market value. New slopes should be graded to appear natural by being uneven, irregular, rounded, undulating surfaces. The regular crisp, straight slope and grading of the typical site is inappropriate for this type of project. Detailed grading work is often overlooked, but it is the

FIGURE 7.1 A hillside development.

foundation for the appearance and character of the entire site. It is this particular aspect of site development that underscores the importance of talented, able professional contractors. Slopes with irregular inclinations rather than a single grade across the entire face of a slope appear more natural. To increase the natural appearance of a slope, the distance between the top and the toe of the slope should vary, providing for different slope lengths.

Minimizing the Impact of Site Grading

The most important element in minimizing the disturbed area is the design itself. Site layout and design should provide an effective synthesis of the development program or objective with minimum disturbance. As the site is graded to provide the necessary shape and surfaces on which to construct the proposed site elements, the impacts of the earthwork increase. Among the most significant is the increased risk of erosion and sediment pollution to streams and lakes, as well as the problem of blowing dust. The grading changes made to the site can result in redirecting site drainage away from existing drainage patterns and into new paths. A temporary construction drainage pattern often is not considered in project planning, and drainage can become a serious problem if not managed properly. The impact could result in off-site damage to habitat and surface water quality, which in turn could lead to fines and increased project costs. Public relations problems and damage to the credibility of those involved often result.

The simplest construction project fosters a wide range of emotional reactions from the community. For example, the loss of wildlife habitat or tree masses can cause an emotional reaction. The loss of open space and green areas may be met with resistance and misunderstanding. This reaction can occur regardless of the real habitat value of these areas; the change and construction activity alone attract attention. Early identification of these habitat areas and drainage patterns must be completed in the planning stages and carried through to the construction phases of the project. If a habitat to be saved is identified in early work, it is important to identify and isolate that area in the field when site work begins.

Critical habitat or areas that are to serve as buffers to such areas should be clearly marked in the field, and operators need to be instructed regarding the purpose of the marks. Tree masses to be saved should be identified and protected by fences or barriers to isolate them from the busy construction activities. The most common environmental impact of disturbed sites is the temporary influence of storm water runoff in the forms of erosion, sedimentation, loss of soil, and degradation of downstream water. Clearing vegetation disturbs the relationship between the vegetative cover and the soil. In the absence of vegetation, the soil is more prone to erosion, water is unable to soak in as easily, and it is more difficult to reestablish vegetation. The loss of cover means the loss of plant surfaces that intercept and deflect the energy of the falling rain before it contacts the soil. Plant protection helps the soil structure to remain intact, allowing for gradual infiltration of water through the soil and resistance to the erosive forces of wind and rain.

The design and management of sites commonly address long-term protection of sites from erosion and storm water damage, but temporary construction conditions often are forgotten. In such cases, the site contractor must deal with the dynamic, often complex storm water runoff conditions that exist as a result of interim conditions during construction. This can be an expensive experience, requiring time and money to repair and maintain temporary features. The designer of the site grading scheme should consider the various interim conditions that will exist during construction and formulate general strategies for how these conditions will be managed.

Another aspect of grading is related to the form, not the function, of the new grades. Grading is often completed without considering the long-term visual impact and appearance of the new shape of the land. Equipment operators may have the final say in how a site will look and how people will appreciate the design. Grading is the foundation for the appearance of a site and is the basis for how the site is seen and appreciated by the ultimate users. A poorly conceived grading plan of a site's final form will have a great impact on the success of the site, physically and emotionally. Final elements that are out of scale or uninteresting may be rejected by people in favor of spaces that are inviting, comfortable, and interesting. The appearance of the final form of grading is as important as the function. Most people find natural outdoor spaces more visually interesting and appealing.

Slopes that are to be mowed should not exceed a 3:1 slope although 4:1 is preferred. New cut or fill slopes should not exceed 2:1. On steeper slopes that exceed 15 ft in height, it may be necessary to include a reverse bench or runoff diversion to convey runoff away. The reverse bench is designed and built to collect runoff and convey it to a stabilized outlet. Benches are designed with a reverse slope of 5:1 and must be wide enough for construction and maintenance equipment. Figures 7.2 and 7.3 provide greater detail of reverse bench construction.

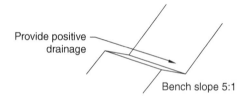

Provide positive drainage

Bench slope 5:1

FIGURE 7.2   Reverse bench detail.

FIGURE 7.3   A reverse bench.

FIGURE 7.4   A partially roughened finished slope.

New slopes that are to be reseeded should be graded in a manner conducive to establishment of new plants. The surface must be roughened to create the microsites necessary for seeds to take root and establish themselves. Slopes are sometimes roughened or "tracked" using construction equipment. Figure 7.4 shows a slope partially roughened using tracked equipment. Chapter 10 addresses revegetation in greater detail.

Minimizing the Disturbed Area

The new features such as roads or buildings must fit into the physical characteristics of the site and minimize the need for large cuts and fills. By minimizing the disturbance and the excavated area at the design level, the designer begins to mitigate the impact of development. The design should retain as much of the original terrain and character of the site as is feasible. To achieve this, roads should be parallel to contours as much as possible and buildings should be located to minimize grading. If such flattened places are in short supply, perhaps the buildings could be clustered and designed to take advantage of the site relief. Keep disturbed areas small and leave strips of existing vegetation in place between disturbed areas. Grading should be timed to minimize time of exposure and scheduled to minimize risk of erosion and maximize growth conditions to restore the site.

By minimizing the area that is to be disturbed, runoff increases and the facilities necessary to handle it can be reduced. The reduced runoff translates immediately to a reduced risk of erosion but also to a smaller requirement for storm water facilities. The areas of preserved vegetation may act as adequate buffers between disturbed areas, reducing the amount of active erosion and sediment protection required. Likewise less clearing and grubbing translates to a greater degree of infiltration capacity. Although some inconveniences may occur during construction, substantial cost savings are involved with the reduction of disturbed area.

Many successful projects throughout the country have adopted this approach to development. Restricting the amount of land to be disturbed to barely more than the footprint of the building can contribute a great deal to the character and value of a site. Such projects generally include a requirement to use native material and natural exterior finishes to enhance the sense of minimal site disturbance and natural appearance. These principles can be extended to nearly any project, but buyers interested in a special living environment are most attracted to this sort of project. Equally important are the environmental services and ecological values these projects retain.

Using Grade Change Effectively

Variations in grade can serve many purposes in site design. Beyond providing well-thought-out transitions from one elevation to another, grading may be used to reduce noise and to provide a visual separation between features or adjacent properties. The separation provided by a change in grade gives the illusion of a greater distance between objects than may exist. Designers can use this perception of distance to increase visual interest and to create a feeling of expansiveness.

A low planted berm between buildings, for example, tends to give a feeling of greater distance when viewed from inside either of the buildings. The berm shown in Fig. 7.5 has effectively screened the residential area from an adjacent highway. Even in areas with little natural relief, subtle combinations of graded berms and vegetation can effectively separate incompatible uses or undesirable views.

Taller berms or changes of grade are useful in sound control (Fig. 7.6). When considering earth berms or grade changes for purposes of sound control, the most effective location for the berm is generally closer to the source of the noise. Berms should be designed so that the source of the noise is visually isolated from the receiver, and

FIGURE 7.5 A berm between the highway and a residential area.

FIGURE 7.6 A grade variation used for sound control.

the berm should be continuous. Although a series of hummocks might be more interesting to see, they will not be as effective as a sound barrier for noise reduction. The length of the barrier should be at least as long, but preferably twice as long, as the distance from the source to the barrier. Planted berms should use plant materials of varying heights to create a dense buffer. Simple screening plantings may visually screen the source but are not as effective as a densely mixed planting. The effectiveness of the mixed planting is a function of its depth and the various textures and surfaces that act to deflect and absorb sound. Vegetated screens are discussed more fully in Chap. 10.

The location of proposed buildings and other site features can be designed to effectively screen sound or create distance from sources of sound. Locate buildings so they back up to the sources of sound and act as a sound barrier or use parking areas to increase the distance from sound sources. Some communities have noise ordinances that specifically deal with construction noise, but for the most part these are not specifically design issues. The most common postconstruction noise complaints are associated with highway or traffic noise. Numerous things can be done to influence traffic noise, but only a few of them are under the control of site designers. Highway noise can be influenced by lower speed limits, reduced starting and stopping, and minimizing grades. Vegetation makes a fairly poor noise screen. The best practice is to use grading to raise or lower the road surface (Fig. 7.7). Sound barriers have had success but may create problems such as sound "reflecting" off the wall, or "valleys" of poor air quality (Fig. 7.8). Perhaps the best approach is a vegetated slope that provides numerous absorbing surfaces and the mass to screen noise, but such screens require space. When there is inadequate space or distance between the source and the affected site, it may be necessary to use structural sound barriers.

FIGURE 7.7   Grading for sound control.

FIGURE 7.8   A sound barrier between a highway and a residential area.

When berms are used to screen a view, careful planning and field measurements must be undertaken to ensure that the area is effectively obstructed. Although screening an unwanted view may be easily accomplished using berms and plant materials, an effective buffer requires some planning and evaluation. Often greater effectiveness can be achieved for a lower cost by staggering the islands and mixing the plant materials by size and species. This approach is generally more attractive and appears more natural. A well-planned mixture of plants, staggered islands, and undulating berms is nearly always a site-enhancing feature.

Site Stabilization

There are two distinct types of stabilization on disturbed sites: temporary stabilization and permanent stabilization. Temporary stabilization is used on a portion of a site that has been disturbed and is to be left in a disturbed state for some time prior to final grading and stabilization, such as soil stockpiles or temporary access points. Temporary stabilization could include vegetation, geotextile fabrics, and stone. These materials are generally inexpensive to purchase, install, and remove. If an area is to remain in a disturbed condition but with no further activity for more than 20 days, temporary stabilization is called for. This guideline must be tempered by local conditions, time of the year, and other relative information.

Permanent stabilization refers to the finished surface of the developed site and may include vegetation, paving, geotextiles, stone, or any combination of these. Vegetation or paving of some type is most often used for permanent stabilization of a site. Vegetation is the least expensive cover material for most applications; however, in areas of high-traffic (pedestrian or vehicular) paving is the obvious choice. In areas with occasional traffic, such as maintenance roads or emergency access ways, a combination of vegetation and paving is desirable. A number of products are available for use in turf as vehicle support systems. The advantage of minimizing paving to reduce runoff and the need for a supporting network of pipes and detention basins justifies using this approach for infrequently used driveways.

Paving is required for general or heavy use parking lots and cartways. The traditional impervious paving of concrete or asphalt concrete is giving way to wider applications of pavers, permeable paving systems, and even stabilized soil for minimal use areas. These alternatives provide the opportunity to collect more runoff for recharge of aquifers and to reduce the amount of runoff from a site.

In areas outside of parking and cartways, vegetative cover is usually used. As previously discussed, one effect of construction activities is the destruction of soil structure. The loss of soil structure increases erosion and reduces permeability of the soil. Before vegetation can be expected to grow and become established in this difficult environment, the soil and the site must be properly prepared. Although preparation does not immediately restore the soil structure, it does provide the elements necessary for the soil to "heal" itself over time.

Mulches

Mulches are recommended for all revegetation efforts. The choice of materials is so broad and with various characteristics that some careful thought and consideration should be given to the selection of a mulch. The complexity of the choice aside, the role of mulch in the vegetation plan should not be overlooked. Each mulch material provides the

Material	Advantages	Disadvantages
Straw	Low cost, available, absorbent, light color	Must be anchored in place 3000–8000 lb/acre, biodegradable, add cost of nets or tackifier, weed growth, short application distance, can be a fire hazard
Wood fiber mulch	Holds seeds/plants in place, can be hydroseeded, inexpensive, stays on slopes, available, 1000 lb/acre	Does not resist erosion or protect from rainfall
Netting/fiber	Resists rain/erosion, absorbs water, holds moisture, good slope protection	Expensive, installation must be in contact with soil

TABLE 7.5 Comparison of Mulch Materials

following attributes: insulates soil to affect temperature, provides runoff protection, reduces evaporation, encourages infiltration, and holds seed in place. Different materials perform these tasks with different degrees of success (Table 7.5). Additional considerations include the means of application and the availability of the material. Cost varies widely: some materials can be purchased and installed for as little as $1800/acre (wood fiber), whereas other materials may cost $18,000/acre (jute matting).

Slope Stability

Constructing new slopes presents a series of issues during and after construction. The stability of slopes is of paramount concern. Slope design begins with understanding the character of the soil and subsurface conditions. The shear strength of slope materials provides a guide to how steep a designed slope may be without additional structural support. Shear strength is a combination of the grain-to-grain friction between soil particles and the cohesive forces that act to hold soil particles together. Shear stress increases as the slope is made steeper, essentially as the ability of the soil to resist gravity decreases. Graded slopes that do not exceed the angle of repose of a dry frictional soil are generally stable.

The grading operation usually involves removing the vegetative cover, the roots of which may serve to mechanically stabilize the slope. Any change in a slope that increases the slope angle destabilizes the slope as it increases the slope loading without increasing the strength of the slope. The weight of the soil and the added weight of water increase the stress by increasing the load on soil particles farther down the slope and, perhaps, compressing the lower soils until failure occurs (Figs. 7.9 through 7.12). On projects requiring the creation of steep slopes, a stability analysis should be performed by a soil scientist or soil engineer. Slope failures can occur for a variety of reasons—both natural and human (Table 7.6). Natural causes of failure include slippage along existing soil transitions or failures associated with structural weaknesses.

Instability in slopes can be addressed by increasing the resistance of the slope to failure or by minimizing the causes of failure. The causes of failure can be addressed by

FIGURE **7.9**   Slope failure. (See also color insert.)

FIGURE **7.10**   Slope failure.

FIGURE 7.11   Slope failure. (See also color insert.)

avoidance or by modifying the design. Changes in surface conditions will alter drainage conditions on the surface and subsurface. These changes may affect the stability of the slope by increasing the amount of water in the slope material or by erosion of the surface. Providing adequate surface and subsurface drainage may be required. In many cases slope failure caused by changes in subsurface drainage is difficult to predict without fairly intensive study; these problems may emerge and must be dealt with after the site is developed. The location of facilities or appurtenances on fill or in the zone of influence for a slope should be carefully evaluated.

Retaining Walls

It is often not practical to reduce the weight or location of features, so increasing the slope's resistance to failure may be necessary. Methods of increasing slope resistance vary from building retaining walls to stabilization by thermal treatment (heating the soil to

FIGURE 7.12 Slope failure.

1. Overloading slope (weight of buildings or roads)
2. Increasing fill on slope without adequate drainage
3. Removing vegetation
4. Increasing the slope grade
5. Increasing slope length by cutting at bottom of slope
6. Changing surface drainage
7. Changing subsurface drainage

TABLE 7.6 Common Causes of Slope Failure

the melting point). Although new methods of chemical and thermal treatment have emerged, these methods are generally considered to be experimental and have not been widely used. The most widely used methods are variations on retaining walls or pilings such as the method shown in Fig. 7.13 or the cantilevered reinforced retaining wall shown in Fig. 7.14. New methods include slope stabilization using anchors, interlocking concrete block walls (Figs. 7.15 and 7.16), and stabilization using three-dimensional geosynthetic materials (Figs. 7.17 and 7.18). Buttresses are sometimes used as an alternative to these methods (Fig. 7.19).

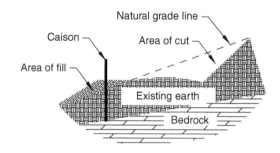

FIGURE 7.13   Caisson and soil buttress for destabilized slope detail.

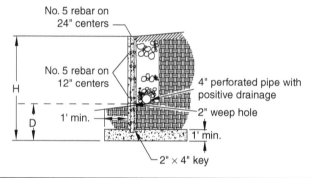

FIGURE 7.14   A cantilevered reinforced concrete retaining wall.

FIGURE 7.15   A large retaining wall using interlocking blocks and tension strips.

FIGURE **7.16** A small retaining wall using interlocking blocks.

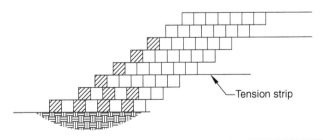

FIGURE **7.17** Slope stabilization using three-dimensional geosynthetics.

Figure 7.18 Slope stabilization using three-dimensional geosynthetics.

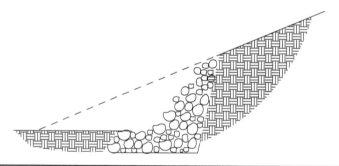

Figure 7.19 Slope stabilization using rock buttress.

For retention of smaller changes in grade, timber and dry-laid stone retaining walls have been used successfully. Proper installation is the key to all of these methods. Small retaining walls are often built incorrectly, without regard to proper stabilization, footing, soil bearing, batter, and so forth. Timber and dry-laid stone walls depend on the depth below grade to resist overtopping by the retained earth. Retaining walls may be of either flexible or rigid construction. For purposes of this discussion, retaining walls are no more than 8 to10 ft in height with a maximum surcharge of 2 ft. Taller walls have more complex influences than those discussed here and should be designed by a structural engineer.

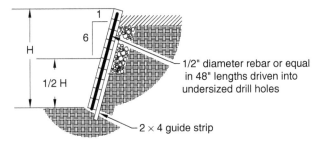

FIGURE 7.20 Horizontal timber wall detail.

Retaining walls are often designed with a batter; that is, they recede away from vertical by a specified amount. Batter is useful to offset the feeling of overtopping from tall, vertical retaining walls, and it helps to hide small imperfections and variation in the wall. In smaller flexible walls, the batter helps to hide and absorb seasonal bulges and movement that might occur and contributes to wall stability. Although it is determined on a case-by-case basis, a batter of 6:1 is commonly used for flexible walls; somewhat less is required for rigid walls.

All retaining walls require a suitable foundation (Figs. 7.20 through 7.23). Flexible retaining walls are usually fairly low and, given a suitable compacted base, may not require footers to extend below the frost line. Retaining walls generally should extend a minimum of 2 ft below grade, or half the above grade height or to the frost line, whichever is greatest. A certain amount of settlement and perhaps seasonal movement can be tolerated in flexible walls. Rigid walls of concrete or masonry construction are used where greater changes in elevation are necessary, where flexibility cannot be tolerated, or where the mass of the wall is used to retain the earth.

Using gabions to stabilize slopes is a common and cost-effective solution. Gabions are manufactured wire mesh baskets that are assembled on the construction site and filled with stone. The gabion is a flexible and permeable structure that can be used to construct retaining walls, toe of slope buttresses, stream bank protection revetments,

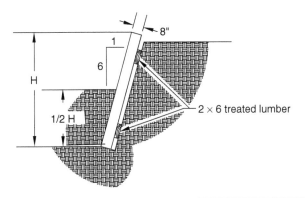

FIGURE 7.21 Vertical timber wall detail.

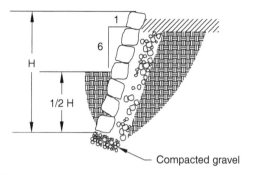

Compacted gravel

FIGURE 7.22   Dry-laid stone wall detail.

FIGURE 7.23   A dry-laid stone wall.

and weirs for storm water and erosion control (Figs. 7.24 and 7.25). Gabions are installed on a surface that has been leveled and compacted. Except for revetments, in most application the gabions are constructed and filled with stone in place. Individual gabion baskets are connected to each other, using lacing wire or ring fasteners. The minimum standards for lacing wire and ring fasteners are detailed in ASTM A975. Gabion wall design is often conducted with the assistance of the manufacturer of the baskets.

All retaining wall designs must address drainage. Crib wall, gabions, and dry-laid stone walls are by definition porous, but masonry and concrete walls must be designed with the means to drain water away from the wall to avoid damage or failure. Water should be directed away from both the top and the bottom of the structure through the

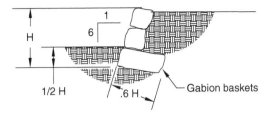

FIGURE 7.24   Gabion retaining wall detail.

FIGURE 7.25   A retaining wall using gabions.

use of positive drainage. Weep holes of sufficient diameter should be installed to relieve hydrostatic pressure from behind the wall.

Erosion and Sediment Control

Erosion is the uncontrolled transportation of soil either by wind or water. The primary short-term concern at most construction sites is erosion due to an unstabilized soil surface and the impact of precipitation and runoff. How erosion works is generally understood; the focus of erosion control is on mitigating these mechanisms. In general, erosion begins with the loosening of soil particles through freeze/thaw or wet/dry cycles or through the impact of falling rain. Erosion is separated into different types by the manner in which soil is moved rather than by the cause.

Splash erosion is simply the result of raindrop impact on unprotected soils. Through the repetitious hammering of raindrops, soil particles are gradually moved down hill. This process is of concern on sites that have unprotected soils exposed to the weather. The larger the raindrops and the greater the slope, the farther down hill the soil particle will move and the greater the risk of erosion. As this process develops, soil is broken up and the process of erosion is accelerated. Even on flat slopes, the destruction of the soil structure is detrimental, resulting in a hard soil crust when it dries. The crust limits infiltration and increases runoff and further erosion. It is difficult to establish vegetation in soils without structure, exacerbating the erosion cycle.

Sheet erosion occurs where there is a uniform slope and surface and runoff flows in a sheet. Erosion in these instances is limited to the loose soil particles. Sheet erosion only occurs in a limited form in the field. Sheet flow tends to concentrate into more defined flows as it is channeled by the irregularities of a site.

Channelized flow results in the types of erosion most of us think of when the subject comes up: rill and gully erosion. Rill erosion is characterized by small, even tiny channels that abrade and intertwine; gully erosion is identified by large channels that are obviously damaging. Where a rill is at worst only a few inches deep, a gully can be 10 or more feet deep.

The impacts of erosion and sediment extend from the aesthetic impacts to the easily quantified cost of dredging reservoirs to recover lost capacity. The U.S. Army Corps of Engineers spend an estimated $350 million annually to dredge rivers and harbors in the United States. Sediment-filled rivers, reservoirs, and harbors cannot be used for shipping or recreation. The loss of soil as an agricultural resource can have a direct impact on the productivity and feasibility of that operation. To replace topsoil with commercially available topsoil would cost at least $40/yd³ ($52/m³), or about $9.2 billion each year in the United States. Adding replacement and dredging costs together makes a compelling economic argument for erosion and sediment control (Table 7.7). The federal government regulates discharges from most construction sites through the National

1. Develop design to fit the site and the terrain.
2. Protect and retain existing vegetation to the extent possible.
3. Protect/revegetate and mulch exposed areas.
4. Minimize steepness of slopes to manage both velocity and flow of runoff.
5. Schedule earthwork and construction to minimize soil exposure and enhance stabilization.
6. Protect new swales and drainage paths. Improve stabilization of existing channels for increased flows and velocities.
7. Trap the sediment on the site.
8. Maintain site controls.
9. Develop contingency plans before they are needed.

Adapted from S. J. Goldman, K. Jackson, and T. A. Bursetynsky, *Erosion and Sediment Control Handbook*, New York: McGraw-Hill, 1986.

TABLE 7.7 Principles of Erosion and Sediment Control

Pollution Discharge Elimination System. Most states have their own version of these regulations and require builders to meet a minimum set of performance standards.

Erosion prevention and sediment control are both proactive strategies. It is not possible to have site development without some earth disturbance, but the amount of disturbance often is well beyond the area required. The less that the area is disturbed, the fewer the controls that are necessary, and the lower the cost of site control. Sediment control is, in effect, planned damage control. These efforts are geared entirely toward collecting, directing, capturing, filtering, and releasing sediment laden runoff after erosion has occurred. Sediment control features, such as a filter fence, sediment traps, stone filters, check dams, and sediment basins are designed according to the requirements in the disturbed area.

Initial erosion and sediment control operations consist of the construction of ingress/egress controls such as tire scrubbers or a stabilized construction entrance that remains in place and working order until earthmoving activities are completed and a driveway or entrance is stabilized. Erosion and sediment controls should be constructed and stabilized and functional before general site disturbance begins. Only limited disturbance is permitted, so allow for the proper function of sediment basins, sediment traps, diversion terraces, interceptor channels, and channels of conveyance.

After completion of the site work and grading, all disturbed banks and open areas are seeded, fertilized, and prepared in accordance with specifications and cultural requirements of the site. Temporary erosion and sediment pollution controls should be maintained throughout the duration of the work until the site is stabilized. After a rain, the devices should be checked and inspected for condition and integrity. Devices that require maintenance, repair, cleanout, or replacement should be addressed.

Silt fencing must be installed parallel to existing contours or constructed level alignments. Ends of the fence must be extended 10 ft, traveling up slope at 45 degrees to the alignment of the main fencing section. Sediment must be removed where accumulations reach one-half the distance above the ground height of silt fencing. Any silt fence that has been undermined or topped must be replaced with rock filter outlets immediately. In long sections of fence, stone filter outlets might be used where water collects or flows behind the filter fence. Storm water inlets must be protected until the tributary areas are stabilized. Sediment must be removed from inlet protection after each storm event.

Sediment must be removed from traps when storage capacities are reduced to 1334 ft^3/acre. Most regulations require that sediment be removed from the basins when storage capacities are reduced to 5000 ft^3 per tributary acre. Stakes located in the trap and marked with the cleanout elevation are required in some jurisdictions. The stakes should be placed about halfway between points of concentrated inflows to the basin risers or outlet. When sediment has accumulated to the cleanout elevations on half the stakes, it must be removed to restore basin capacity.

Any disturbed area on which activity has ceased for more than 20 days must be seeded and mulched immediately. During nongerminating periods, mulch should be applied at the recommended rates. Disturbed areas not at finished grade that will be disturbed again within one year may be seeded and mulched with a quick-growing temporary seed mixture. Disturbed areas that are either at finished grade or will be disturbed again beyond one year must be seeded and mulched with a permanent seed mixture. Diversions, interceptors, swale, channels, sediment basins, and sediment traps are seeded immediately upon the completion of construction. Seeding specifications are best tailored to regional and site requirements.

When applying straw as mulch, the straw should be dry and free from undesirable seeds and coarse material; apply straw at a rate of 115 to 150 lb/1000 ft² or 2.5 to 3 tons/ acre. Mulched areas should be checked periodically and immediately after storms and wind. Damaged or missing mulch must be replaced. A tackifier of asphalt or polymer spray is recommended for application over straw. Apply at a rate recommended by the manufacturer with suitable equipment; in lieu of manufacturers' recommendations apply at a rate of 0.04 to 0.06 gal/yd². Install and use erosion control blankets or netting in accordance with the manufacturers' specifications, and select products for the proper application and conditions.

Sediment basins and traps are used to capture sediment on the disturbed site. In general a sediment basin, or a silt basin as it is sometimes called, is a larger control device used for drainage areas in excess of five acres. The size of the contributing area and specific design parameters are sometimes dictated by local or state regulations. Sediment basins are often large enough that they require substantial space on the construction site. They are usually constructed very early in the construction process and remain until nearly the end of the project. The basin should be located so that it will not capture clean runoff as well as the runoff from the disturbed area: if at all possible, clean runoff should not be mixed with the sediment-bearing runoff. Typical erosion and sediment control design details are shown in Figs. 7.26 through 7.33. Local jurisdictions may have requirements that differ slightly from these suggestions.

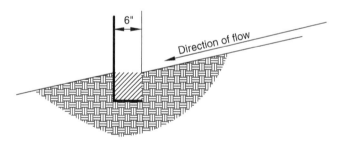

FIGURE 7.26   Filter fabric fence detail.

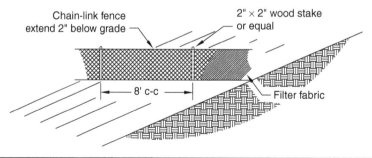

FIGURE 7.27   Reinforced filter fabric fence detail.

FIGURE 7.28 A reinforced filter fabric fence.

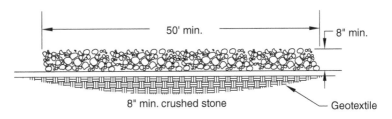

FIGURE 7.29 Site entrance control detail.

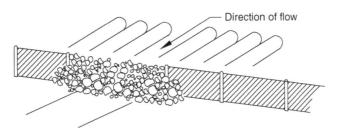

FIGURE 7.30 Stone filter detail.

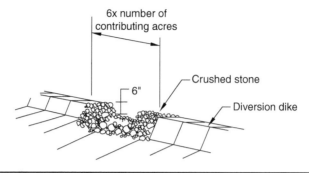

FIGURE 7.31   Diversion dike detail.

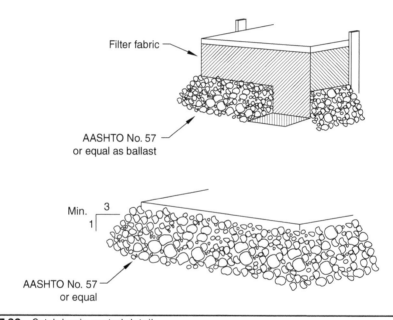

FIGURE 7.32   Catch basin control detail.

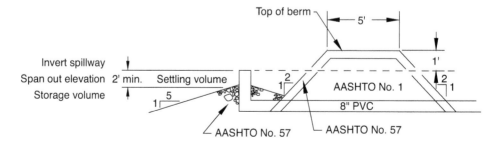

FIGURE 7.33   Sediment trap detail.

Basins are typically designed to contain a 10-year storm, but local and state regulations may differ. Sediment basin outlets are designed to allow the basin to dewater at a rate slow enough to provide for settlement and fast enough to remain in service and reduce the risk of insect infestation. The typical principal spillway is designed with a minimum flow of 0.2 cubic feet per second (cfs), which is equivalent to runoff of 5 in. in 24 hours. Antiseep collars are used in larger basins where berm height exceeds 10 ft or the local soil has a very low clay/silt content (unified soil class SM or GM). Settling and sediment storage requirements for basins differ from state to state. Sediment traps are smaller versions of the sediment basin and are used for drainage areas of less than 5 acres (Figs. 7.34 and 7.35).

FIGURE 7.34   A sediment trap.

Figure 7.35   A sediment trap.

Dewatering outlets are designed using the formula for flow through an orifice:

$$Q = CA\sqrt{2gh}$$

where Q = flow, cfs
C = coefficient of contraction for an orifice, usually 0.6 (sharp edged orifice)
A = area of the orifice in square feet
g = acceleration of gravity, 32.2 /s²
h = head above orifice in feet

The equation can be used to determine the length of time necessary to dewater a basin:

$$T = \frac{A\sqrt{2h}}{3600TC\sqrt{g}}$$

where T = time, hours
A = surface area of the basin in square feet

The formula can also be used to determine the orifice size required to dewater a basin within a required time:

$$A_x = \frac{A\sqrt{2h}}{3600TC\sqrt{g}}$$

Site Management
Construction site managers are faced with regulations for erosion and sediment, but plans require more than rules and guidelines to succeed in the field. Unfortunately erosion and

Figure 7.36   Filter fabric fence failure from poor maintenance.

sediment controls are often the last thing designed and the first thing installed. Installation may be haphazard or incomplete, and maintenance may be limited to responding to complaints and inspections. With increases in local enforcement, a greater emphasis on the performance of grading and erosion and sediment control plans is necessary.

Although the landowner ultimately is responsible for the proper management and control of the construction site, the site manager has day-to-day control. The design professional is often called upon to modify the erosion and sediment control plan to fit site conditions or to address failures (Figs. 7.36 and 7.37). The erosion and sediment control plan should include management of these facilities through the entire project, not simply instructions for how to start and end the project. As with any element of a project, erosion and sediment control should be planned, responsibility and resources assigned, performance expectations communicated, and performance monitored and confirmed from time to time.

Table 7.8 lists some common causes of erosion and sediment control failure. Of these seven causes of failure, the site manager only has control over three: compensating for seasonal differences, installation, and maintenance of facilities. Most of the causes of failure are related to design. Even the best management plan cannot overcome a design problem or extreme weather conditions.

Erosion and sediment controls are often designed without regard for the dynamics of a construction site. Designs tend to address specific moments in the course of the site work and not the constantly changing site conditions. The contractor should review the erosion and sediment control plan to be sure that there is adequate room to store topsoil or excess material. If storage is required, is there a practical pattern for the use of heavy equipment?

FIGURE 7.37   Filter fabric fence failure from poor maintenance.

1. Poor site analysis
2. Design and the site are incompatible
3. Inadequately sized facilities
4. Wrong materials specified or used
5. Poor installation
6. Poor maintenance
7. Failure to compensate for seasonal differences or extreme weather conditions

TABLE 7.8   Common Causes of Erosion and Sediment Control Failure

Temporary drainage conditions may also present a problem if not planned for. The installation of sediment traps and basins may have to consider an interim step or two if significant changes in grade are proposed. Are these interim steps provided for in the plan?

Most important to the contractor: does the plan make sense? A dialogue between the designer and the contractor to exchange ideas and solutions can be an important step in the successful erosion and sediment control plan. The designer is in the best position to initiate this meeting. If a contractor for the project has not yet been chosen, meeting with a qualified contractor may be just as valuable. The closer this working relationship, the better the site controls work. The site manager has an interest in these early stages because eventually he or she is responsible for its implementation. The entire thrust of the management plan is aimed at controlling the causes of failure and maintaining the integrity of the site controls. The site manager must understand the plan before he or she begins. Implementing the plan without comment or revision may be seen as tacit acceptance and approval.

The installation of control features requires adequate information and detailing in the plan. The plan should include construction details for the various facilities to be installed. This would include the routine details but also more specific information such as staple patterns on erosion control fabrics or inverted elevations on sediment trap dewatering outlets. Adequate installation of controls begins with understanding the construction details.

The typical erosion and sediment control plan includes a construction sequence and, when appropriate, phase lines. The designer often is required to make assumptions about the project that may not be true later on. The construction sequence should be reviewed and understood. Items that cause conflicts or are no longer accurate should be addressed to the designer so that a revision can be made to the report. Too often these details are overlooked or discounted as unimportant until there is a problem later in the project and the contractor is found to be "out of sequence." Then this small detail is suddenly disproportionately important.

A project directory is a simple tool, listing the phone numbers, addresses, and FAX numbers of the various people involved in the project. The list normally includes the owner, the project engineer, the project surveyor, the municipal engineer, the site managers (and an alternate or two), as well as any subcontractors or others who might be important. The list should also include names and information about the regulatory and enforcement personnel. The directory should identify what each person listed is responsible for or why the name is listed. Such a directory will help when responding to emergencies and will enable you to solve problems more quickly and smoothly. This preparation is a key means of avoiding fines and enforcement actions.

Start-Up Meeting

The project start-up meeting is a fundamental element of the management plan. It is the site manager's responsibility to organize the start-up meeting. The meeting should be attended by the site designer, erosion and sediment control plan designer, local enforcement personnel, and supervision and staff from the project. It may be appropriate for others such as municipal representatives or environmental regulators to attend as well.

The agenda for the start-up meeting should include introductions of the attendees (a sign-in sheet is recommended to collect phone numbers), review of the scope of the project, and what is to be done in the course of developing the site. A site plan acts as a discussion guide. If phases are involved, the delineation and field recognition of phase lines should be discussed. The construction sequence should be reviewed. A review of the grading operations should include identification of areas of significant cuts and fills and sensitive areas such as wetlands or floodplains. Erosion and sediment controls that will be used throughout the project, maintenance schedules, and repair plans must be discussed. Identify contact people for emergency response. A site walkover should be conducted to familiarize everyone with the start-up condition of the site and areas of concern. This is particularly important if there is existing erosion or sedimentation. Minutes should be taken during the meeting and distributed afterward to all attendees. A copy of these minutes should be kept in the project log.

Once the earthwork has begun and the project is up and running, the site manager will be diverted from the erosion and sediment control plan. A schedule of routine maintenance, developed prior to start-up, is a helpful prompt for the manager to keep the commitment to the plan. By assigning a staff person to follow up on the schedule, the manager can be sure routine inspections and maintenance items are being addressed.

Routine inspections are scheduled at frequencies that reflect the site characteristics, the time of the year, and the condition of the site. A hilly site that is fully disturbed during the rainy part of the year will justify more frequent inspection than the same site partially stabilized during a dry season. Inspections themselves are relatively inexpensive, requiring only a visual check in most cases to ascertain the condition and any corrective action that might be required. A small tape recorder makes note-taking almost effortless.

It is unreasonable to assume that the schedule set out in the beginning of a project will be met perfectly throughout the project. Some flexibility is appropriate in the system. In most cases, slipping the schedule two or three days is not a problem. Inspections should be made after every significant rain or melt event without exception, and the routine inspection schedule can be slipped to reflect these events.

From the start-up meeting and throughout the project until final stabilization is confirmed, a logbook should be maintained by the person assigned responsibility to oversee the erosion and sediment control plan. The purpose of the logbook is to record routine inspections and maintenance as well as the general progress and activity on the site. A well-maintained logbook is a record of performance and compliance with the plan. Records of routine inspections, including corrective actions taken and photographs, are of particular importance. Copies of inspections by regulatory or enforcement personnel and notes and photographs taken during the inspection should also be included in the log. Information regarding precipitation or weather that is pertinent to actions and decisions taken and the required inspections after storm events should be included.

It is not unusual during the course of a construction project to have changes made. The changes may occur because of a change in the project or a change in site conditions encountered during the construction process. It is common to have changes in the erosion and sediment control plan as well. These changes are often a response to an unforeseen condition such as a concentrated flow of runoff where one was not anticipated. The site manager must have the flexibility to respond to the problem quickly. In fact, anything but a quick response would be inconsistent with the objectives of the plan. Once the response is made, a note should be made in the logbook and the owner, site engineer, and regulator should be notified. A copy of the notice should be kept in the logbook.

In addition to the concerns of erosion and sedimentation are concerns over the potential for spills and releases of chemicals or contaminants from the construction site. Quantities of toxic chemicals and potential harmful waste materials are present on construction sites. The nonpoint source program of the Clean Water Act requires construction sites over one acre to operate under a general permit for discharges to water. Larger construction sites may be required to have a Preparedness, Prevention, and Contingency (PPC) Plan. In most states the PPC plan is not reviewed or approved, but construction firms are supposed to have one and are accountable for spills and releases on the site. Spills and releases are common on construction sites but are rarely reported and even more infrequently cleaned up. Most construction personnel may not even be aware of the potential for liability. A sample PPC plan is included in App. B.

CHAPTER 8

Infrastructure

Much of the impact of site development is associated with the installation of necessary infrastructure. To the degree that it is possible, measures should be taken to minimize this impact during construction but also in the design and operation of the infrastructure.

Low-Impact Design

The storm water management and sewage disposal methods selected for a site are where the design intersects directly with the hydrologic cycle. In the past, most infrastructure strategies involved collecting the storm water or sewage, concentrating the various flows, and removing them from the site in the most expedient and cost-effective way possible. Due to a growing appreciation for the true costs of that approach, a general rethinking has developed and a move toward green infrastructure is well under way. The combined strategies being employed in this approach are called by various names but, in general, are referred to as low-impact design or green infrastructure.

The critical elements are that water is considered a resource rather than a problem and that interaction with the environment is carefully weighed to maximize total benefits and minimize costs (Fahet, 2005). Strategies discussed in this chapter include the design of vegetated swales, infiltration structures, rain gardens, and green roofs. Green infrastructure integrates natural services such as infiltration, microbiotic activity in soils, the diversity of stable ecosystems, and the implications of site development to create a win-win situation. The benefits of a green infrastructure are increased infiltration and groundwater recharge, decreased pollution loads on surface water, increased biodiversity, reduction in the heat island effects of development, and improved air quality. Greener sites also bring with them particular emotional benefits ranging from a better learning environment to a heightened sense of personal happiness.

Although not traditionally considered part of infrastructure, green infrastructure designs minimize the disturbed area and maximize retention of native plant communities. Lawn areas are minimized if they are used at all, and landscape areas employ means for capturing storm water to increase infiltration and groundwater recharge. Use of native plants reduces the need for irrigation and toxic landscape supplements.

Storm Water Management

As site work progresses and the natural characteristics and irregularities of the site are graded and removed, the volume and velocity of storm water runoff is increased. Rainfall and runoff are no longer deflected off the surfaces of the vegetation and cannot infiltrate into the compacted soil, so water runs off the surface to lower areas. In the recent past the solution for this change in runoff has been to concentrate the runoff into pipes and convey it to the most convenient point of discharge.

The increase in impervious area as a result of development has important consequences for environmental quality. Habitat quality in streams drops significantly once a watershed reaches 10 to 15 percent imperviousness, and stream habitat is consistently found to be poor (Booth and Reinelt, 1993). As the impacts of site development are better understood, the methods and practices of design and construction must evolve to address these impacts. Storm water management is a critical element in this evolution toward a sustainable site design practice.

In the past storm water has been viewed primarily as a problem, to be collected and disposed of as quickly and as efficiently as possible. With growing concern for our environment and recognition of the need for more sustainable development methods, simple collection, conveyance, and discharge strategies have become less acceptable. Falling groundwater tables, dry streams, and degraded surface quality have convinced us that storm water must be treated differently. As our understanding of the environment and sustainability improves, we have realized that storm water is an important resource.

As runoff moves across the developed surfaces of lawn and pavement, it washes particles and pollutants into the system and ultimately into the stream. Pollutants from such sites include nutrients, sediment, bacteria, oil and grease, heavy metals, chemicals, and pesticides. These are known as nonpoint source pollutants (NPS) because they do not originate from a single pipe or discharge point. Construction sites over an acre in size must address discharge from a site, and large developments and municipalities must acquire an NPDES permit to discharge storm water. For the most part these regulations are enforced by the individual states.

In many urban environments the pollution from storm water runoff from parking lots and streets is much greater than the pollution from factories and sewage treatment plants (Table 8.1). Storm water that is directed across paved surfaces and collected into gutters and pipes convey runoff at a velocity that scours the surface and washes the pollutants along in the runoff. The methods for reducing the impact of development on water quality are straightforward. If the amount of paving and roof surface is reduced,

Storm water management practices	Pollutant removal effectiveness				
	Total suspended solids	Total phosphorus	Total nitrogen	Metals	Hydrocarbons
Dry swales*	91%	67%	92%	80–90%	
Grass channel	65%	25%	15%	20–50%	65%
Roadside ditch	30%	10%	0		
Sand filters	85%	55%	35%	lead 60%	
Filter strips	70%	10%	30%	40–50%	

*Bioretention facilities are assumed to be the same as a dry swale.
Adapted from *Better Site Design: A Handbook for Changing Development Rules in Your Community*, 1998, prepared for the Site Planning Roundtable (Ellicott City, MD).

TABLE 8.1   Pollutant Removal Effectiveness of Storm Water Management Practices for Parking Lots

Practice	Construction cost	Annual operating and maintenance costs	Useful life (years)
Infiltration trench	$0.20–$2.20/ft³	3–13% of capital cost	25
Vegetated swale	From seed $6.50–$9.50/linear foot	$0.50–$1.0/ linear foot	50
Vegetative filter strip	Established with existing vegetation $0	$150–$300/acre	50
	From seed $200–$1000/acre	$800 acre	50
	From seed with mulch $800–$3500/acre	—	50
	From sod $8500–$48,000/acre	—	50
Sand filter	$3–$18/ft³	Probable 7% of construction cost	25
Wet pond	$0.25–$3.00/ft³	0.1–1% of capital cost	50
Bioswale	n.a.	n.a.	n.a.

Adapted from U.S. Environmental Protection Agency (EPPA), EPA-840-B-92-002, January 1993.

TABLE 8.2 Comparison of Costs for Storm Water Management Facilities

the amount of runoff increase can be reduced. The problems are obvious; without paving and roof, and if retaining all of the storm water was required, there probably would be no project. In this case the environment is preserved but there is no construction or building. Development and water quality solutions are a matter of effective design. New development can be designed and existing development can be refitted to slow runoff velocities and volumes and to encourage infiltration. Development and environmental protection can coexist. In light of the recognition of the environmental impacts, sites designs must use more effective and sustainable strategies. Instead of addressing storm water as a problem, designers must see it as a resource. Many effective strategies are familiar and cost effective (Table 8.2).

Estimating Peak Runoff with the Rational Method

The rational method is often used to calculate peak discharge. The primary strengths of the rational method lie in its simplicity and accuracy when applied to watersheds or basins of relatively small size. It can easily be adapted for watersheds that must be divided into smaller subsheds with different surface characteristics. The rational method uses the area of the basin, a runoff coefficient, and the intensity of a selected design storm to determine peak discharge:

$$Q = CiA$$

where Q = peak discharge in cfs
C = runoff coefficient (a ratio of the amount of surface runoff to rainfall)
i = rainfall intensity for a storm duration equal to the time of concentration
A = area of the basin (or subshed)

In general, the rational method proceeds in the following order. First, determine the time of concentration (TC) in order to determine the rainfall intensity (I). Then determine a runoff coefficient and the drainage area. TC is the length of time required for a drop of water to travel from the furthest hydrologic point through a completely saturated drainage area to a point of discharge. The TC is a function of the slope of the land, surface roughness, and type of flow (sheet or concentrated). Find the longest hydrologic flow path—if appropriate, subdivide the path into sections of different conditions (forest, paved surfaces, lawns, etc.)—and calculate the velocity along the path using this formula:

$$t = L/v$$

where t = travel time
   L = length of the flow path
   v = velocity from Manning's formula or from a prepared chart

Travel time for sheet flow is calculated as follows:

$$t = 0.007(nL)0.8/(P)0.5s0.4$$

where t = travel time, hours
   n = Manning's coefficient of roughness
   L = flow length, feet
   P = design storm 24-hour rainfall, in inches
   s = average slope of surface

Design storms are selected on a project-by-project basis, and the 24-hour storm rainfall will differ from place to place. Rainfall charts for specific locations are available from state transportation agencies and local planning agencies. It is always best to use recent local rainfall charts. Agencies may provide rainfall intensity charts as well. It should be noted that rainfall intensity charts are not the same as total precipitation or duration charts. Rainfall intensity specifically refers to a storm with duration equal to the rational method time of concentration. Rainfall intensity is at least a regional calculation determined using the Steel formula:

$$i = k/(t + b)$$

where i = rainfall intensity
   k = rainfall coefficient
   b = rainfall coefficient
   t = travel time

The rainfall coefficients k and b are statistical constants developed for regions for storms of different frequencies (Table 8.3). In recent years the Steel formula rainfall coefficients have been shown to be somewhat less reliable in western states (Fig. 8.1).

Runoff coefficients (C) are selected from charts like the one shown for the rational method in Table 8.4 and are based on the conditions found at the site. Composite or weighted C values are calculated by multiplying the area of each type of ground cover by the appropriate C factor, adding the results, and dividing the sum by the total land area (A).

In general, the design of open channels and pipes are similar in that both may be determined using Manning's formula:

$$Q = [(1.49/n)(a/p)^{2/3}(s)^{1/2}]/a$$

Design storm	Rainfall constants	Region						
		1	**2**	**3**	**4**	**5**	**6**	**7**
2	k	206	140	106	70	70	68	32
	b	30	21	17	13	16	14	11
5	k	247	190	131	97	81	75	48
	b	29	25	19	16	13	12	12
10	k	300	230	170	111	111	122	60
	b	36	29	23	16	17	23	13
25	k	327	260	230	170	130	155	67
	b	33	32	30	27	17	26	10
50	k	315	350	250	187	187	160	65
	b	28	38	27	24	25	21	8
100	k	367	375	290	220	240	210	77
	b	33	36	31	28	29	26	10

From Harlow C. Landphair and Fred Klatt Jr., *Landscape Architecture Construction*, 2nd ed. (New York: Elsevier Science, 1988).

TABLE 8.3   Values of k and b for the Steel Formula

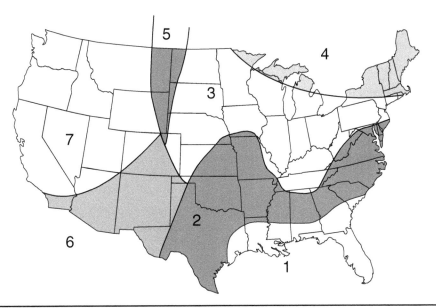

FIGURE 8.1   Rainfall regions for Steel formula.

Type of terrain		Steep >7%	Rolling 2–7%	Flat 2% or less
Wooded				
	Heavily	.21	.18	.15
	Moderately	.25	.21	.18
	Lightly	.29	.25	.21
Lawns		.35	.30	.26
Uncompacted bare soil		.60	.60	.50
Impervious		.98	.95	.95
Residential				
	25,000 ft² lots	.40	.36	.32
	15,000 ft² lots	.50	.45	.40
	12,000 ft² lots	.50	.45	.40
	Townhomes (45% impervious)	.65	.60	.55
	Apartments (75% impervious)	.82	.79	.74
Pasture				
	Good condition	.25	.21	.18
	Average condition	.45	.40	.36
	Poor condition	.55	.50	.45
Farmland	Nongrowing season	.50	.46	.42

TABLE 8.4   Rational Method Runoff Coefficients

The essential difference between them is that while open the hydraulic properties of open channels continue to increase as the channel fills whereas pipes reach their greatest discharge at about 93 percent of total depth (Figs. 8.2 and 8.3).

Strategies in Arid Areas

Much of the United States receives less than 35 in. of rain each year, some areas even less than 15 in. Strategies for storm water management are appreciably different for these dry areas. Even though rainfall depths are much less, arid (less than 15 in. of rain) and semiarid (15 to 35 in. of rain) areas have a much greater pollutant load for each

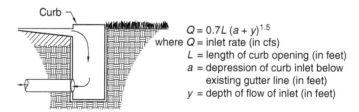

$$Q = 0.7L\,(a + y)^{1.5}$$

where Q = inlet rate (in cfs)
L = length of curb opening (in feet)
a = depression of curb inlet below existing gutter line (in feet)
y = depth of flow of inlet (in feet)

FIGURE 8.2   Calculating curb inlet flow.

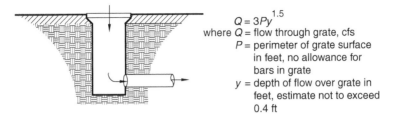

$$Q = 3Py^{1.5}$$

where Q = flow through grate, cfs
P = perimeter of grate surface in feet, no allowance for bars in grate
y = depth of flow over grate in feet, estimate not to exceed 0.4 ft

FIGURE 8.3   Grate inlet flow calculation.

storm event and may experience substantially greater sediment loads due to the lack of stabilizing vegetation. The drier areas also are more concerned with groundwater quality due to the high pollution loads and permeability of some western soils. Pollution prevention is a critical part of storm water strategies in these areas, and street sweeping and drain cleaning are important activities.

Many of the strategies and practices recommended for areas where precipitation exceeds evaporation rates are not practical for these drier regions where dry ponds are favored. For example, wet ponds are desirable in areas with surplus moisture but are impractical in drier climates. However, sand filters, filter strips, and bioretention are still important tools. Key elements in storm water design in these areas minimize ground water pollution, channel erosion, and encourage infiltration (Fig. 8.4).

FIGURE 8.4   An infiltration bed in an arid area.

Swales

Vegetated swales are important tools in implementing a sustainable storm water strategy. Unlike pipes, vegetated swales encourage infiltration, filter water by providing many surfaces for deposition, and reduce the velocity of water. The swale infiltration system increases the capacity of the typical swale to allow infiltration of low flow, frequent storm events. At the same time, it can convey the flow of large infrequent storms, which could not be easily infiltrated through the soil. Swales remain the choice of conveyance systems because of their many positive aspects over pipes (Table 8.5). By using grass-lined swales instead of pipes, site costs can be reduced by as much as $12.00 a linear foot. Adding the swale infiltration trap increases the cost by about $2.30 a linear foot, but because downstream piping and swale systems are smaller, a net savings is possible. Swales are generally calculated to function with at least 20 percent of the depth as freeboard (Fig. 8.5). This allows for some retardance in the design flow due to vegetation or debris.

The design of vegetated swales usually assumes an acceptable velocity of water for a turf channel from 2 to 4 feet per second (fps). The design of channels is accomplished using Manning's formula (Table 8.6). The choice of the coefficient of roughness is the critical step in using the equation (Table 8.7).

Generally a freeboard of at least 20 percent of the design depth, or 6 in. (15 cm), is used to protect against underestimates of the n value and roughening of the channel by vegetative growth and incidental obstruction or debris. Designs for unlined channels are usually limited by either the velocity a channel will allow without suffering damage or the tractive force (Table 8.8). Trials of channel design should be tested using the formula $V = Q/a$, where velocity is a function of the quantity in cubic feet per second over the wetted area.

Economical, cost less than pipes
Increased infiltration/recharge
Provides surfaces for deposition of particulate
Reduces runoff velocity
Easy to maintain
More natural appearance than curbs

TABLE 8.5   Advantages of Swales

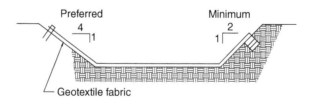

FIGURE 8.5   Trapezoidal swale detail.

Manning's formula
$V = (1.49/n)(a/p)^{2/3}(s)^{1/2}$ where n = coefficient of roughness a = area cross section (in ft^2) p = wetted perimeter s = slope (%) V = velocity
Flow through a grate can be calculated using this formula:
$Q = 0.66CA(64.4h)0.5$ where Q = discharge, cfs C = orifice coefficient (0.06 of square edge opening, 0.8 for round edge opening) A = area of opening in square feet h = depth of flow over opening in feet
Volume of flow in a channel can be calculated using this formula:
$Q = V/a$ where V = velocity, fps Q = discharge rate, cfs a = cross sectional area of the channel, square feet
Emergency spillway
$Q = CLH3/2$ where Q = discharge over spillway, cfs C = coefficient for spillway surface (3.1 for grass) H = height over invert of spillway L = length of spillway
Control of the water through stone media is a function of slope and media size. The rate of travel through the media may be determined by
$Q = 0.4(h1.57/L.57)W$ where Q = volume of water h = depth of water L = flow path length W = width of channel   0.4 = hydraulic conductivity (K)

Source: Gert Aron and Charles McIntyre, "Permeability of Gabions Used as Outlet Control Structures in the Design of Detention Basins." Pennsylvania State University, 1990.

TABLE 8.6   Formulas for Storm Water Calculations

Very smooth like glass or plastic	.010
Smooth pipe (PVC, concrete, vit. clay, etc.)	.013–.015
Concrete pipe 24 in. and under	.013
Concrete pipe over 24 in.	.012
Galvanized corrugated pipe	.024
Straight unlined earth channels in good condition	.020
Open channels lined w/asphalt	.013–.017
Open channels lined w/brick	.012–.018
Open channels lined w/concrete	.011–.02
Open channels lined w/rip rap	.02–.035
Channels lined w/vegetation 11–12 in.	.09–.15
Channels lined w/vegetation 6–10 in.	.055–.08
Channels lined w/vegetation 2–3 in.	.045–.06
Natural channels,* regular section	.03–.5
Natural channels with dense vegetation	.05–.7
Natural channels, irregular w/pools	.04–.10
Rivers, some growth	.025
Winding natural streams in poor** condition	.035
Mountain streams with rocky beds, some vegetation along banks	.040–.050

*Minor streams with a top width of less than 100 ft at flood stage. **Very rough condition, erosion etc.

Source: Data from Ven Te Chow, *Open Channel Hydraulics,* 2nd ed. (New York: McGraw-Hill, 1988); William E. Brewer and Charles P. Alter, *The Complete Manual of Land Planning and Development* (Englewood Cliffs, NJ: Prentice-Hall, 1988); B. Ferguson and T. N. Debo, *On-Site Stormwater Management: Applications for Landscape and Engineering* (New York: Van Nostrand Reinhold, 1990).

TABLE 8.7   Coefficient of Roughness

Material	n	Velocity (fps) for clear water	Velocity (fps) for water with sediment
Fine sand	0.02	1.5	2.5
Sandy loam	0.02	1.75	2.5
Silt loam	0.02	2.0	3.0
Firm loam	0.02	2.5	3.5
Stiff clay	0.025	3.75	5.0
Shales, hardpan	0.025	3.75	5.0
Fine gravel	0.02	2.5	5
Coarse gravel	0.025	4.0	6.0

TABLE 8.8   Limiting Velocities for Channel Design

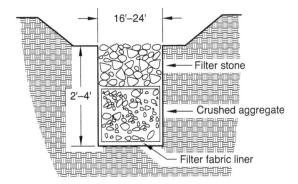

FIGURE 8.6 Swale infiltrator detail.

In cases where velocity may exceed the recommended rate, it may be necessary to reinforce the channel using geotextile fabric. A variety of companies manufacture geotextile fabrics for an even greater variety of applications. Permanent fabrics designed to reinforce vegetated channels extend the designers' choices significantly. Some geotextiles can maintain the channel integrity and hold the vegetation in place even at velocities as great as 13 fps. ASTM has developed standards for testing geotextiles to provide users with a greater degree of certainty when specifying materials.

Geotextiles should be selected on the basis of their ability to resist the flow of moving water, to protect the channel surface, and to hold the vegetation in place. Some geotextiles are designed to act as "armor"; that is, they cover the channel surface and protect it from the erosive force of flowing water much in the same way a concrete lining might be used (Fig. 8.6). Other materials are three dimensional and are incorporated into the soil to act in concert with the roots of plants to mechanically resist erosion. The permanence of the geotextile material is very important. Some materials are designed to bio- or photodegrade; others are intended to remain in place permanently. In most cases swales must be installed to be in service immediately, even before the vegetation is established. This may require the use of temporary geotextiles until the vegetation can stabilize the channel. Proper installation of the appropriate geotextile is critical. Many failures of installed swales occur because the geotextile was not installed properly.

Shape and sinuosity are critical factors in the hydraulic and environmental functions of a channel. Shape refers to the cross-sectional configuration of the channel, and sinuosity refers to the length of a channel over a given distance. Increasing the length of a channel within a given distance requires increasing the number and amplitude of curves within the distance. This increase in length allows a flatter slope over the same distance, which in turn results in slower velocities, less erosive capacity, and more infiltration. The channel can be designed to contain more water in high flow conditions and incorporate special high flow channels that operate in flood conditions. The natural capacity for retention and treatment of water-borne contaminants can be increased by incorporating vegetation and pools in the channels. Careful selection of channel bottom

FIGURE **8.7** A parking lot island infiltrator.

media and plants will further enhance the environmental functions of storm water channels. Figures 8.7 and 8.8 show two types of infiltrators.

The swale infiltrator may be used to introduce a biological treatment to the storm water when this is desirable. The media for the swale may serve as a surface for bacteria

FIGURE **8.8** A swale infiltrator.

and other microorganisms to attach to and may act as a biofilter for the storm water as it passes through. The velocity of water through the media must be controlled to ensure sufficient contact time between the biological agents and the water. The actual time required is a function of the toxins and the ability of the specific biological agents to consume or act on them. Determination of this will require some bench testing by a microbiologist. Once provided with the requirements, the site designer can design the swale accordingly.

Infiltration and Recharge

The preferred method of storm water quality management is to reintroduce the runoff into the soil as quickly as possible to provide the opportunity for groundwater recharge. Infiltration can be used for pollutant removal, but infiltration systems provide only limited cleansing. Infiltration removes particulates and pollutants that might attach to soil particles, but water soluble pollutants such as nutrients, pesticides, or salts travel through the soil medium dissolved in the water. When water soluble pollutants are a particular risk, the design must provide for a biological treatment such as algae in wet ponds or microorganisms in wetlands or in bioretention beds or rain gardens.

Another good reason to consider infiltration is the loss of ground water recharge that accompanies a typical detention basin development. The Chester County Planning Commission in Pennsylvania developed some conceptual models of development for planning purposes and found that the typical developed square mile lost about 10 in. of recharge water (storm water runoff) each year, which represents 40,785,879 gal of water each year! By using infiltration systems where it is possible, this kind of loss can be significantly reduced. About 70 percent of the homes in the United States use groundwater, so protecting and managing our groundwater resources are important and necessary undertakings.

Professionals have significant experience and knowledge using soils as a filter medium, for example, in ground sewage disposal systems. The Environmental Protection Agency (EPA) recommends a 2- to 4-ft vertical separation from the bottom of the infiltration facility to the seasonal top of the water table or bedrock. The feasibility of infiltration is determined using a four-point test:

1. The soil texture is in a class with an infiltration rate that permits adequate percolation of collected water through the soil.

2. Ponding or dewatering time is at least three but no more than seven days.

3. A minimum vertical depth of 2 to 4 ft is available between the infiltration bed and bedrock or the seasonal high water table.

4. The site topography (slope) and the nature of the soil (fill, stability) will permit the location of foundations, utilities, wells, and similar site features.

Soil texture is an important element in determining infiltration rates. Infiltration rates that are too slow will not allow the ponded water to drain within the desired time. Soils with an infiltration rate of 0.17 in/h or less, or with a clay content of 30 percent or more, may be unsuitable for infiltration (Table 8.9). Infiltration feasibility may be determined based on the allowable ponding time (Tp) or storage time (Ts). Ponding and

Texture class	Effective water capacity (Cw)	Minimum infiltration rate (f) (in/h)	Hydrologic soil group sand
Sand	0.35	8.27	A
Loamy sand	0.31	2.41	A
Sandy loam	0.25	1.02	B
Loam	0.19	0.52	B
Silt loam	0.17	0.27	C
Sandy clay loam	0.14	0.17	C
Clay loam	0.14	0.09	D
Silty clay loam	0.11	0.06	D
Sandy clay	0.09	0.05	D
Silty clay	0.09	0.04	D
Clay	0.08	0.02	D

TABLE 8.9   General Infiltration Properties of Soils by Texture

storage times should be kept to a reasonable minimum: 72 hours is a reasonable period to drain an infiltration structure.

The depth of an infiltration structure can be determined using the ponding time and the infiltration rate of a soil:

$$d = f\,\text{Tp}$$

where d = maximum allowable design depth
f = minimum infiltration rate
Tp = maximum allowable ponding time (surface storage)

The maximum depth of an infiltration trench or dry well in which the storage is within a porous media such as stone ballast can be calculated as follows:

$$d = f\,\text{Ts}/\text{Vr}$$

where d = maximum allowable design depth
f = minimum infiltration rate
Ts = maximum allowable storage within subsurface storage
Vr = void ratio of aggregate reservoir

Construction of the infiltration system requires special care. The weight and motion of construction vehicles compresses the soil, closing pores and limiting the infiltration capacity of the soil. The infiltration surface must be protected, and heavy equipment should not be driven over the bottom of the system. Once the site is located, the infiltration area should be staked out and identified. Equipment should work from the side of the area while excavating the trench.

Methods adapted for infiltration include dry wells, swale traps, catch basin traps, infiltration trenches and basins, and rain gardens. These facilities are designed to collect and trap the storm water in the earliest stages of the runoff process. Typically these types of facilities are small in size and located throughout a site. The increase in runoff due to development is offset through the cumulative effect of these small collection facilities.

Dry Wells

Dry wells are small excavated pits backfilled with aggregate in the same manner as an infiltration trench. The primary difference between the dry well and an infiltration trench is in how the water is collected into the system. Trenches are located parallel to the contours and extend along a certain point in the site to intercept runoff. The dry well is designed to collect runoff directly from a roof drain or outfall.

Dry wells are used primarily to collect runoff from small areas such as roofs or section of roofs. In design, the dry well must meet the same tests as the infiltration basin or trench. In most applications the dry well is visible and is near a structure, so the appearance of the dry well at the surface is important. A soil filter may be used to make the dry well disappear from view. The soil filter consists of the top 1 ft of the dry well being backfilled with top soil (Fig. 8.9).

In some cases the dry well concept can be incorporated into a catch basin (Fig. 8.10) that provides infiltration for more frequent storms. This may allow the rest of the conveyance system to be sized differently and result in reduced construction costs. For example, if a 1-year storm can be retained and infiltrated, downstream conveyances may be designed for storms less than 1-year storm.

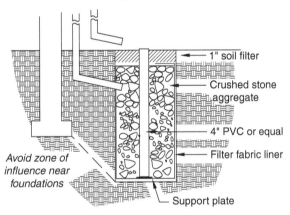

FIGURE 8.9   Roof drop dry well detail.

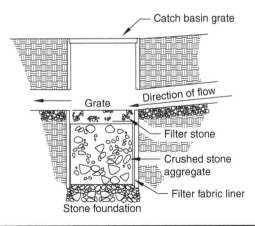

FIGURE 8.10   Catch basin infiltrator detail.

Filter Strips

Vegetated filter strips remove particulates such as metals and phosphorus by filtration through the surfaces of the vegetation and promote some infiltration because runoff is slowed. The surfaces of the plants also act as surfaces for the deposition of contaminants that might exist as films in the runoff, such as hydrocarbons. The presence of a healthy soil medium and plant community provides some inherent microbial action on the contaminants present in the runoff. The microbial action will continue even after the surge of storm water has passed. Properly designed and constructed filter strips may have a particulate trapping efficiency of up to 95 percent (Tourbier and Westmacott, 1981). Contact time—the time the water is in contact with the vegetation—should be maximized by slowing the velocity of the runoff and by designing the strip to be as wide as possible. Velocities should be no more than 1 foot per second (fps) (0.3 m).

Filter strips should be designed with a minimum of 2 percent slope and should not exceed 4 percent. If the slope of the filter strip is less than 2 percent, an infiltration underdrain may be required. The vegetation selected for filter strips is usually grass, and sod may be required to give the strip an opportunity to secure and establish itself. The filter should be a minimum of 15 ft (4.4 m) wide. Native sod forming grasses are recommended; tall fescue, western wheatgrass, ryegrass, and Kentucky bluegrass are all recommended for filter strips. The filter strip should be designed to receive a perpendicular sheet of runoff (Fig. 8.11); a concentrated flow will limit the effectiveness of the filter strip and may damage it.

Sand Filters

Sand filters were among the first water treatment systems devised, and they are still used in many systems today. The sand filter is an effective method for removing suspended solids, but it has no designed biological treatment capacity and cannot remove soluble pollutants. In general, the sand filter is at least 1.5 ft deep and should be used in conjunction with other media or systems to address soluble contaminants. Sand filters have been designed using a layer of peat to increase the efficiency to 90 percent of suspended solids, 70 percent of total phosphorus, 50 percent of total nitrogen, and 80 percent of trace metals (Schueler, 2000). The peat and sand filter is usually planted with a cover of grass to increase the removal of nutrients and provide filter surfaces for the deposition of films. The combination of peat and sand is a very effective filter (Fig. 8.12); effectiveness can be increased still further when the filter is used in conjunction with a presettling facility.

Filters of peat or composted materials are a relatively new technology and have much greater removal efficiency than sand alone: up to 90 percent removal of soluble metals, 95 percent of suspended solids, and 87 percent hydrocarbon capture, as well as

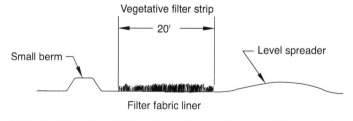

FIGURE 8.11   Filter strip detail.

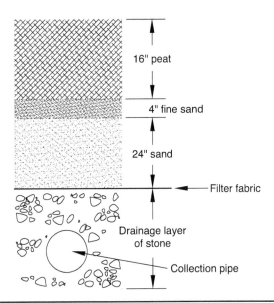

FIGURE 8.12   Peat and sand filter detail.

high rates of removal for other materials. The peat compost filter has only moderate rates of nutrient removal: 40 percent of total phosphorus and 56 percent of Kjeldahl nitrogen (Scheuler, 2000). Using peat alone is an effective filter material but releases an effluent with a greater turbidity. The compost used in such filters should be of deciduous leaves. The peat compost filter requires maintenance and a change of filter material approximately once every 2 years, depending on loading.

The principles of the sand filter may be applied to parking lots. The quality of infiltrating runoff can be improved by designing parking lot edges with a sand filter (Fig. 8.13).

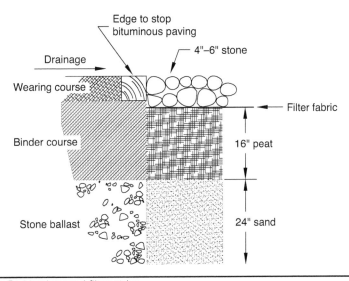

FIGURE 8.13   Parking lot sand filter strips.

Infiltration Trench

An infiltration trench is another method of capturing water and allowing for recharge (Fig. 8.14). The infiltration trench is generally 2 to 10 ft deep (0.6 to 3 m). The depth is constrained by the same criteria as for the basin (i.e., depth to bedrock or the seasonal high water table). The trench is lined with filter fabric and filled with stone. The spaces between the stones provide the storage area for the runoff. The void space of backfill is assumed to be in the range of 30 to 40 percent for aggregate of 1.5 to 3 in. (4 to 8 cm). Void space refers to the spaces between the solid particles of the fill. Although an emerging spillway is usually not designed for an infiltration trench, the design and construction should consider and address the circumstance of an overflow. An observation well (Fig. 8.15) should be installed in the infiltration trench to monitor the sediment level in

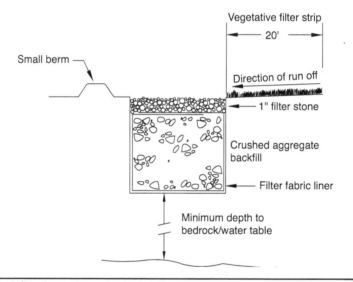

FIGURE 8.14   Infiltration recharge basin detail.

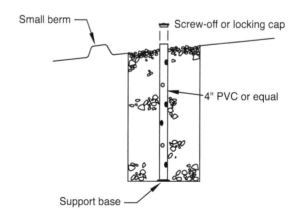

FIGURE 8.15   Inspection pipe detail.

FIGURE 8.16   An infiltration trench in a median.

the trench and the dewatering time (Maryland State Department of Education, 1999). Figure 8.16 shows an infiltration trench in a median.

The amount of void space, referred to in most standards as the percentage of voids, is variable by the type of material. The National Stone Foundation suggests that 35 percent voids is a good rule of thumb, and trenches following this rule have functioned well within expected performance guidelines. A more accurate percentage of voids can be calculated using the following formula:

$$n = 1 - (d/G \times 62.4)$$

where n = percent of voids
$\quad\quad d$ = dry density of stone
$\quad\quad G$ = specific gravity of stone

The dry density of a particular stone is usually available from the quarry where the stone is graded to specifications (Table 8.10). If more specific data are not available, the mean specific gravity of 2.6 is used. The cubic feet of stone necessary to store a given volume of water can be determined using this formula:

$$k = (1/n) \text{ storage volume required in cubic feet}$$

where k = volume of stone required
$\quad\quad n$ = porosity of stone

Stone size	d/cf	n	e
2A modified	108.92	0.328	0.489
2B	96.08	0.408	0.688
3A	96.00	0.408	0.69
3a modified	112.0	0.320	0.448

TABLE 8.10   Dry Density per Cubic Foot of Typical Stone

In study at Pennsylvania State University I determined a formula for the rate at which water will move through a gabion. This same formula has been used to determine the rate at which water will move through the stone ballast of the infiltration trench, or to design an outlet structure of stone. The formula is as follows:

$$Q = 0.40 \ (h1.57/L0.57) \ W$$

where h = the ponding depth or head in feet
L = flow path length in feet
W = width of the structure in feet
0.40 = hydraulic conductivity (a constant)

This formula also can be used to determine the control of an infiltration/detention system with an outlet structure, whether the outlet structure will control the peak flow or the time through the ballast.

Infiltration Basin

For the purposes of design, the infiltration basin serves the same function as the detention basin; that is, it offsets the increase in runoff from the developed site. It is designed according to the parameters described for an infiltration trench. The infiltration basin outlets through the pore space in the soil rather than through a surface outlet structure. This allows for some recharge of the aquifer and minimizes the pollutant impact on the receiving surface water. In general, infiltration basins have a large surface area to provide the maximum possible soil surface contact for the collected runoff; the greater the surface area, the faster the volume can infiltrate into the soil. It is important to remember that oil and grease, floating organic material, and fast settling solids need to be filtered from the infiltration basin. This may be accomplished through the use of a vegetative filter strip, which acts as a filter by slowing surface runoff velocity and providing many surfaces that act as filters for the deposition of grease and oil.

Construction inspection should pay particular attention to the level of the infiltration system. It is important that water enters the infiltration system as a sheet flow. Concentrated flows should be spread out using a level spreader or other device. It is also important that sediment-laden runoff be diverted away from the infiltration trench during construction.

Rain Gardens

Rain gardens, also called bioretention basins, are shallow areas designed to collect storm water (Figs. 8.17 and 8.18). They are usually designed to drain fairly quickly to

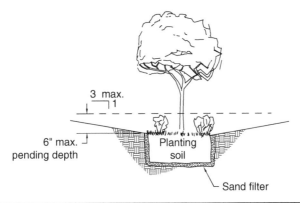

3 max.
1

6" max.
pending depth

Planting
soil

Sand filter

FIGURE **8.17**   Rain garden detail.

FIGURE **8.18**   A residential rain garden. (See also color insert.)

allow typical landscape plants to be used. Rain gardens have become common features in landscapes, and their hydrologic role is not usually highlighted. Rain gardens provide an elegant opportunity for designers to incorporate the aesthetic and functional elements of a landscape into a single feature. Rain gardens have excellent pollution removal capabilities, removing 60 to 80 percent of nutrients and as much as 99 percent of heavy metals.

Rain gardens are designed after natural upland areas. The use of native plants reduces the maintenance costs and the need for supplementary water supplies in most cases. The rain garden is sized to the area contributing runoff and is designed to serve drainage areas up to one acre. The volume of the rain garden is based on the level of control desired: for example, if the first half-inch of rainfall is to be controlled, the rain garden must be designed to collect the desired volume and allow the excess to drain away or bypass the rain garden. Multiple small rain gardens generally operate better than a single very large garden. Larger rain gardens tend to become and remain saturated. Rain gardens are ideal for use in planted islands in parking lots and as planted features within a landscape.

Maximum ponding depth in the rain garden should be limited to about 6 in., and the design should allow the pond to drain away within 3 days to protect the native plants and to discourage insects from breeding. A minimum of 2 ft of planting medium is required. To assure appropriate permeability, the clay content of the soil should be no greater than 10 percent. Studies have found that a soil pH of between 5.5 and 6.5 is ideal for maximum absorption of pollutants and associated microbial activity (Schueler, 2000).

Rain gardens increase the treatment capability of retention by adding the biological elements of the filter strip to the infiltration trench. Quite a lot of work has been done with bioretention strips and basins. In spite of a good deal of variability, all of these systems are a combination of filtration and biological action by soil/plant communities and infiltration. Effective innovations for the treatment of urban runoff can be adapted to some brownfield sites.

The bioretention swale has received high marks for treatment of the first flush of runoff. The bioswale uses a grass strip as a filter to reduce runoff velocity and to remove particulates. The swale employs a media of sand or other material with a topsoil cover to further filter the runoff and as a media for microbial growth and rooting media for swale plantings. Hydrocarbons are degraded and metals are bound to organic constituents in the topsoil layer. As a system, the bioswale has very high removal efficiencies: up to 92 percent of total suspended solids, 67 percent of lead, 30 to 80 percent of total phosphorus, and 75 percent of total petroleum hydrocarbons, as well as other materials.

Detention and Retention Basins

Although detention basins are designed to mimic the storm water flow that existed before development, they do not account for the many other aspects and functions of the natural drainage basin. As a result, the downstream water bodies may suffer degraded water quality, loss of habitat, and reduced recreation value. Before development the site provided a buffer for flows, retaining water and detaining runoff, so that flooding was delayed and reduced. Other incidental values included filtering fine particles and increased infiltration and diversion created by the vegetated and irregular natural surfaces. Comprehensive design can identify and imitate some of the characteristics of the natural storm water management system, but the natural system is nearly always superior to the designed system. Efforts should be made to retain and enhance the existing drainage system whenever possible.

The most familiar methods of managing storm water runoff are detention or retention basins. Detention basins are usually dry basins that only fill with water during a rain. They work by delaying the storm water so that it is released at a rate that mimics the predevelopment flow. A retention basin holds the water in a pool. The only outlet is through emergency spillways that allow the basin to overflow in a controlled manner if it should become too full. The retention basin loses water through infiltration and evaporation. These basins are often part of a larger plan that incorporates storm water management into water features.

Detention basin effectiveness is a function of the drainage area in which it operates and the location of the basin in the watershed. The lower the basin is in a watershed, the less effective it is in providing a positive or beneficial effect. It is possible that a properly constructed basin could actually make a downstream flooding problem worse. The basin functions by detaining the water it collects and releasing it at a rate calculated to be equal to the predevelopment rate. However, the development of a site results in more runoff, so a rate of discharge equal to the predevelopment rate means it will take longer for the runoff to be discharged.

When it rains, it takes a period of time for the runoff to collect and run to the low points. In a watershed this "lag time" can be hours or days, depending on the size of the drainage area. Before a site is developed, areas low in the watershed may collect and runoff before the main portion of the flood travels down to that point in the watershed. The runoff from the lower end is discharged before the "flood" arrives. After development and installation of the detention basin, this increased runoff is stored and its discharge is delayed. In some cases the delay may be long enough to coincide with the "flood," and the basin may make the flood worse by contributing more water to the peak flow. In such a case, the project and certainly the downstream landowners may be better off without the basin. The impact of a basin can be determined quantitatively but not without some expense.

In terms of storm water management, not all sites are created equally. If a project site is high in the drainage area, it can be difficult to collect enough water in the basin to offset the increase in runoff due to development, and detaining floods nearer the bottom of a watershed may create more problems than it solves. Clearly the best design solution locates the basin so that it serves its purpose within a watershed. However, the site designer is constrained by the limits of a given site and the local design parameters.

Detention basins may be designed to meet a predevelopment storm rate of discharge, but the nature of a basin is to concentrate the flow, usually from a single outlet, and to extend the time of discharge to account for the increased volume from the developed site. Site designers must study existing drainage patterns and pathways to identify opportunities that exist on the site. Much consideration should be given to using existing drainage paths. Where increase in flows and velocities will occur, it may be appropriate to enhance existing drainage ways to account for the increase rather than obliterating them in favor of a new path. The drainage patterns on a site that have developed as part of natural landscape processes can often be converted into effective drainage ways for the new development. In some cases these drainage pathways, left in place through the site, may double as a greenway and walkway for pedestrians, combining the necessities for drainage and open space.

Existing channels may require some attention to stabilization and alignment because of the change to the hydrologic and hydraulic character of the project site, but these should be undertaken with care to imitate the natural appearance and function of drainage ways. Changes in the volume and concentration of runoff will have an impact on streams. Consideration should be given to creating pools and ponding areas to collect and trap water in high flows. The creation of flat areas to intercept runoff and encourage infiltration might be developed to function as wetlands. The development of wetland pockets could prove to be an important storm water quality feature, as well as adding visual interest and habitat areas.

Designers and developers should encourage local governments to create storm water authorities that encompass the entire watershed. Although watersheds may include any number of municipalities, the watershed-based approach is a more accurate and effective means of managing storm water runoff. Watershed authorities have been created in a number of places, most notably in Florida. In principle the storm water authority is able to develop a more efficient and less expensive management approach. Public facilities are more likely to be located where they will provide the greatest benefit, and the expense of many uncoordinated and often poorly maintained private facilities can be avoided. Developers can contribute to the authority based on runoff quantities and avoid the expense of dealing with storm water on a site-by-site basis.

Designers must find ways to put the landscape to work. Storm water detention basins should be used to improve a site by finding new ways to offset the storm water increase and provide benefits the simple detention basin does not offer. These benefits might include recreation or aesthetic qualities, perhaps even wildlife habitat, or a water quality-enhancing design. With careful design and consideration, perhaps all of these goals can be met.

An alternative to the infiltration and recharge methods is the development of a wet pond or a retention basin. The design of wet ponds should be left to design professionals trained and experienced in balancing the site constraints with a pond. It is generally a balancing act between cost, site issues (such as slope or drainage area), appearance, and pond function. The advantages of a wet pond include an effective process for the removal of certain urban pollutants through settling in the permanent pool. The geometry of the pool is an important aspect of the pond's capability to remove or reduce pollutants. Ponds are sized with regard to the flow of water through the pond, pond volume, depth, and the expected particle sizes to be encountered in order to allow for the necessary settling time. The activity of plants and microorganisms necessary for the reduction of pollutants occurs primarily at the bottom of the basin. The shape of the basin (geometry) must minimize currents and maximize the travel time from the point where storm water enters the pond to any point of outlet or overflow (Metropolitan Washington Council of Governments, 1992).

The surface area and depth of the pond should be designed to avoid "dead" storage or areas that do not get mixed into the rest of the pond. Pond depths will vary according to the purpose. The marsh or littoral zone is usually 6 in. to 2 ft deep and provides the most effective removal of nutrients and some other pollutants. The basin should include an area equal to 33 percent of the pond surface area that is from 3 to 6 ft deep for fish. An additional 25 percent of the pond should be at least 3 ft deep and within 6 ft of the shore. These shallow and deep areas provide a combination of the effects and uses of the pond.

The minimum drainage area for a wet pond is 10 acres. The drainage area should be adjusted according to the rainfall characteristics of the area, the amount of anticipated runoff, the type of land use, pond geometry and depth, and the settling rate of the expected particulates. The drainage area should be large enough to contribute adequate supplies of water to the pond. The first parameter to consider is the ratio between the drainage area and the pond surface area. The recommended range of the ratio is from 10 to 50. This range could represent a 1-acre pond in a 10-acre watershed or a 10-acre pond in a 500-acre watershed.

If the volume of a pond is much greater than the volume of runoff coming into the pond, the result will be a longer residence time. The residence time is important because

FIGURE 8.19   A wet pond.

the settlement of pollutants occurs primarily when the water is not moving in the pond. Studies have shown that two-thirds of the incoming sediments settle out in the first 20 hours (Metropolitan Washington Council of Governments, 1992). However, significant phosphorus reduction takes up to 2 weeks. Phosphorus is a pollutant with serious water quality consequences. The volume of water required for storage of 2 weeks is very large. Volumes this large will affect the pond's ability to function as a detention basin and meet peak discharge control requirements. The combination of purposes— storm water detention and water quality—must be carefully balanced.

The ratio of the wet pond volume to the mean runoff volume is another key guide to pond design. In general, the larger the surface area of a pond, the greater its pollution removal efficiency. The smaller the area ratio (larger pond surface), the greater the efficiency of the pond in removing pollutants. A pond can be made deeper to achieve water quality, but increased depth is not as effective as a larger surface area. A volume ratio of 2.5 is suggested to achieve 70 percent removal of sediment loads, or a residence time of about 9 days. The 9-day residence time is generally recognized as a middle ground, providing water quality improvements but avoiding the large volume required for the 2-week residence time (Fig. 8.19).

Other Considerations

Other ways of dealing with storm water might be described as avoidance strategies; by simply not creating runoff, the need to deal with it is eliminated or at least reduced. Runoff can be minimized by reducing paved surfaces or by using more permeable

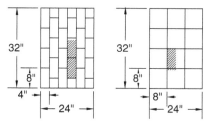

In 4" × 8" paver pattern the joint opening is equal to 60.8 in.² In the 8" × 8" pattern the joint is equal to only 33.4" of opening.

FIGURE **8.20**   Open joint paver detail.

surface materials. Increased permeability of paving surfaces offers the greatest opportunities. By minimizing runoff, water quality objectives are also usually met.

A key concern of the development community is that these strategies will severely reduce the amount of allowed coverage on a parcel. To zone for such a low density, however, would probably cause development to sprawl even more, increasing the roads and infrastructure necessary and resulting in other undesirable impacts. In fact, watershed managers have come to realize that the best way to reduce the unwanted stream impacts of development are to concentrate development in areas with 80 or even 100 percent impervious coverage. Such dense development has a negative impact on some streams or portions of streams, but the impact on others is avoided or minimized.

Using open joint pavers instead of other impermeable paving can provide some infiltration through the joints. Figure 8.20 illustrates the effect of an open joint paver design utilizing quarter-inch joints filled with sharp sand. The 4-in. by 8-in. design with a quarter-inch open joint provides the equivalent of a 60.8 in² opening in an area of 32 by 24 in.

Reducing cartway widths where possible, as discussed in Chap. 6, may contribute to the quality of development in a variety of ways. Using smaller paved areas in cul-de-sacs, by using smaller radii and designing centers with rain gardens or other infiltration features, reduces impermeable areas. By reducing parking lot size and space size requirements or encouraging shared parking arrangements, the amount of area required for parking can be reduced. Figure 8.21 shows a grass paver installation. Figure 8.22 provides details of installation. Table 8.11 lists the cost of various types of permeable pavements.

When a site is developed, the small, intermittent, and ephemeral streams are replaced by curb and gutter flow, but these replace only the conveyance of runoff and none of the filtering and delay of natural channels. Lawns can be graded to include subtle channels or collection areas that will delay runoff and increase infiltration. Likewise, the edges of parking lots or driveways can be designed to collect runoff and encourage infiltration. Where swales are used, choose vegetation that will provide a relatively high Manning's coefficient of roughness and delay runoff. By increasing the travel distance and decreasing the rate of runoff, more water is retained and may infiltrate into the soil.

FIGURE 8.21   Grass pavers.

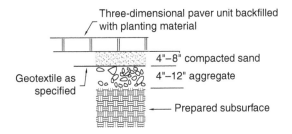

FIGURE 8.22   A typical section of grass paver installation.

Green Roofs

Rooftop rain storage installations have been used for some time in Europe and were successfully introduced to the United States in recent years. Even common flat roofs can be designed to reduce runoff by increasing the roughness of the roof surface or by restricting roof drains. Such installations can significantly reduce runoff volumes and in turn reduce development costs. In older cities the installation of roof top systems can contribute to reducing the costs of rehabilitating infrastructure (Miller, 1998).

Vegetated roof covers, or "green roofs," provide an important strategy for the management of storm water. Although not common in the United States yet, they are included among the best management practices already adopted or under consideration by local governments across the country. Research in Europe found that green

Product	Manufacturer	Cost/ft²*
Asphalt	Various	$1.00–$2.00
Geoweb	Presto Products, Inc.	$2.00–$3.00
Grasspave2TM, Gravelpave2TM	Invisible Structures, Inc.	$1.50–$2.50
GrassyTM pavers	RK Manufacturing	$1.50–$3.00
Geoblock	Presto Products	$2.50–$4.00
Checkerblock	Hastings Pavement	$4.00–$4.50
Grasscrete	Bomanite Co.	$4.00–$4.50
Turfstone	Westcon Pavers	$2.00–$3.00
UNI Eco-stone	Concrete Paving Stones	$2.50–$4.00

*Includes material cost, typical shipping and installation on a fully prepared base course. Does not include cost of gravel or soil and grass fill or labor. These costs are approximately $0.10 to $0.25/ft². Adapted and updated from Dereck Booth and Jennifer Levitt, "Field Evaluation of Permeable Pavement Systems for Improved Stormwater Management." *Journal of the American Planning Association,* 1999, 65(3).

TABLE 8.11   Cost of Various Types of Permeable Pavements

roofs can reduce runoff on a site in a temperate climate by 50 percent, sometimes more (Miller, 1998). The green roof employs a relatively thin layer that acts as the root zone for the plants as well as the collection media for storm water and the means of conveying excess water from the roof. Roofs and media must be designed to perform these several functions and consider local precipitation intensities, the needed storage capacity, media porosity, the cultural requirements of selected plants, and the roof load of the fully vegetated and saturated material.

A green roof straddles the line between architecture and traditional site design, but it is worthy of mention here because of its important role in storm water management and the sustainable site. The structural support of the roof must be designed for the soil medium and nature of the green roof. Green roofs may be fairly thin soil media or up to a depth of several feet. The thicker soil layer may require structural support for 50 to 100 lb/ft², perhaps more in some situations. The thinner layer might only require structural support of 15 to 50 lb. The nature of the landscape selected will determine the amount of maintenance and upkeep.

Some green roofs have the soil medium and vegetation placed directly on the roof. This approach requires a drainage system and a barrier layer to contain roots. Another approach is to use containers placed on the roof. The container approach provides for flexibility and limits power costs but may not provide the same advantages of energy conservation and the collection of runoff.

Gray Water Systems

Gray water is wastewater from washing operations but does not include sanitary (toilet) or food wastes. In general, most wastewater from residences and many commercial enterprises would be classified as gray water. Gray water contains fewer pathogens and

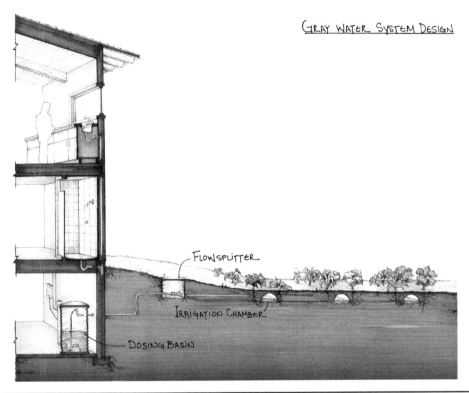

FIGURE 8.23 A diagram of a gray water collection and distribution system. (*Courtesy of Clivus Miltrum, Inc.*)

nutrients than black water (toilet and food wastes). The pollutants in gray water tend to decompose more quickly than those in black water. It should be noted that some local regulations may discourage use of gray water systems whereas others encourage them.

The basic gray water system includes the collection of water from showers, sinks, and washing machines. The water is filtered using a typical primary treatment methodology to remove particles: solids are allowed to settle, floating materials are removed. The water is sent to a sand or soil filter that acts like a traditional leach field to remove and treat pollutants (Fig. 8.23). Since the gray water is much cleaner to begin with, the output is much cleaner as well.

Sanitary Sewer

The most common sanitary sewer collection systems are gravity flow systems. Gravity collection systems are designed to use as few pumps as possible by taking advantage of the natural lay of the land and by careful design and construction. Gravity systems in areas with little topographic relief are limited by the practical depth limits of installation. Infiltration and sedimentation problems associated with low velocity may occur. In places with very steep topography, high-flow velocities may result in problems of odors (caused by turbulence) or separation of liquids and solids.

Minimum daily flow = 0.66 average daily flow	
Minimum hourly flow = 0.5 minimum daily flow or 0.33 average daily flow	
Maximum daily flow = 2 × average daily flow	
Maximum hourly flow = 1.5 maximum daily flow or 3 × average daily flow	

TABLE 8.12   Dry Weather Domestic Wastewater Flows

Most municipalities establish fairly explicit design standards for sanitary sewer design and construction. Sewer flows are generally calculated using a peak hourly flow rather than an average flow because the distribution of flow is not constant (Table 8.12). Peak flow times tend to be about 1.5 times greater than the maximum daily flow, or about 3 times the average flow. Peak periods of flow are coincidental, with some lag time, with peak water demand. Flows are lowest in the early morning hours and increase as people rise and prepare for their day. After a midday dip, flows increase again in the evening hours. Table 8.13 lists typical daily wastewater flows for a variety of buildings and uses.

Source	Gallons/person/day
Airport	5 per passenger
Apartments	75 per resident
Bathhouses and swimming pools	10
Camps	
With central comfort stations	35
With flush toilets, no showers	25
Construction camps, semipermanent	50
Day camps (no meals)	35
Resort camps (day and night)	100
Seasonal cottage	50
Country club (per resident member)	100
Country club (per nonresident member present)	25
Church (per seat)	6
Dwellings	
Boarding house	50
Luxury residence	150
Multiple family	60
Single family	75
Factories (gal/person/shift)	35
Hospitals (per bed space)	250

TABLE 8.13   Typical Daily Wastewater Flows

Source	Gallons/person/day
Hotels (2 persons/room)	80
Hotels w/o private bath	50
Institutions (other than hospitals)	125
Laundry, self-service, per machine	300
Mobile home parks (per space)	250
Motels (per bed, with kitchen)	50
Motels(per bed, no kitchen)	40
Picnic parks (per visitor)	5
Restaurants(toilet and kitchen waste, per patron)	10
Restaurant (per meal served)	3
Restaurant (additional for bar/lounge)	2
Schools	
Boarding	100
Day (no gym, or showers or cafeteria)	15
Day (with gym, showers and cafeteria)	25
Day (with cafeteria only)	20
Service station (per vehicle served)	10
Theaters (per seat)	5
Travel trailer or RV park with hookups (per space)	100
Office workers (worker per shift)	25

Source: Compiled from *Manual of Septic Tank Practice, Operation and Maintenance of Wastewater Collection Systems* (U.S. EPA Number 430975009, January 1967).

TABLE 8.13   Typical Daily Wastewater Flows (*Continued*)

Gravity sewers are designed to provide a minimum flow velocity of at least 2 fps, known as the scouring velocity. At velocities less than 2 fps, solids may settle out of the flow and result in sedimentation in the pipe, reducing the capacity of the pipe and eventually causing a blocked pipe. Velocities are also best kept below 10 fps to minimize turbulence and splashing. Higher velocities may increase the wear and decrease the life of concrete pipes and facilities. Municipal design standards may require the use of abrasion resistant pipe materials when velocities exceed 10 fps. As a rule of thumb, scouring velocity should be reached and exceeded during peak flow periods but not necessarily during low flow periods.

In general, gravity sewers are not constructed with pipe diameters less than 8 in. and have manholes at regular distances (Table 8.14). Manholes should be placed to provide future access to maintenance workers and equipment and are used at all changes in grade, pipe size, and direction.

Pipe size (in.)	Minimum spacing (ft)	Maximum spacing (ft)
8–15	400	600
18–30	600	800
36–60	800	1200
>60	1200	1300

TABLE 8.14   Suggested Manhole Spacing

Depth of utility trenches is a concern for several reasons. The safety of workers is the first concern. Designers should be aware of the risks involved in working in deep trenches, particularly in unconsolidated or unstable soils. Whether working drawings include shoring instructions or warnings is a practice that varies from location to location and even from firm to firm. Including safety instructions on working drawings may increase the designer's liability for construction conditions; on the other hand, noting the installation should be in compliance with federal or state safety standards and regulations may serve to protect the designer from liability. Trench depth also influences the costs of installation and maintenance.

From a performance standpoint, trench depth is a concern in terms of the earth loads on the pipe. The ability of a pipe to resist deformation under a load is a function of the depth and the width of the trench. As trenches are dug wider, the sides of the trench offer less and less support to the pipe. As the depth of the trench increases, the backfill and surface load increases. The selection of pipe should include consideration of the loads that will be developed in buried pipes. Most pipe manufacturers provide tables for the designer to determine loads on pipes under various field conditions.

Bedding materials also contribute to the performance of pipes by assisting the pipe in handling the backfill and surface loads. Pipes are tested in laboratories for their ability to support loads and are given a strength rating usually expressed in pounds per foot. Since bedding materials vary from place to place and will perform under field rather than laboratory conditions, they are identified by standard class designations. The standard class designation refers to a bedding material's ability to support the "load factor" and is based on a "three-edge" bearing test. The ability to support the pipe to the three-edge bearing load is rated as 1. The most common bedding materials are concrete, crushed stone, or suitable local materials.

Relatively low strength Portland cement concrete (2000 lb/in.^{2}) is used to support sewer pipe in class A bedding and will develop a load factor of 2 to more than 3, depending on the degree of steel or wire reinforcement used. Class A beddings is expensive and is usually used only in very deep trenches or where there are anticipated high surface loads (Fig. 8.24). When Class A bedding is used, pipes are blocked in place and grade while the concrete is poured in place. Class B and C beddings are commonly constructed of crushed stone ranging in size from one-quarter to three-quarters inch (Figs. 8.25 and 8.26). In most cases, stone bedding is superior to compacted sand or gravel, except for some plastic pipes. Class B and C beddings are the most common types used due to their fairly high load factors, ranging from 1.5 to 1.9, and their reasonable cost. Class D and sometimes class C beddings may be constructed from local or native materials by carefully excavating a trench bed and using the compacted native material as bedding. Class D bedding is usually not recommended.

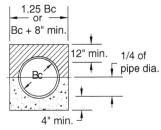

Concrete cradle load factor 2.8

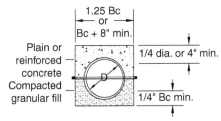

Concrete arch load factor 2.8

FIGURE **8.24** Class A pipe beddings.

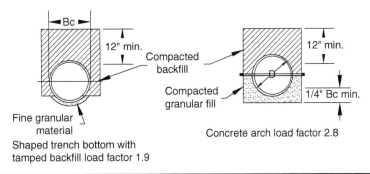

Shaped trench bottom with
tamped backfill load factor 1.9

Concrete arch load factor 2.8

FIGURE **8.25** Class B pipe bedding.

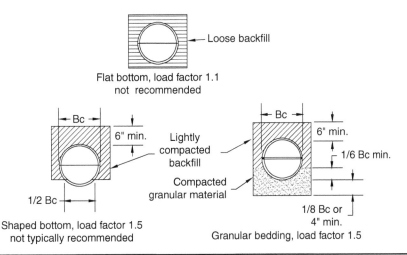

Flat bottom, load factor 1.1
not recommended

Shaped bottom, load factor 1.5
not typically recommended

Granular bedding, load factor 1.5

FIGURE **8.26** Class C pipe bedding.

On-Site Sewage Disposal

On-site sewage disposal systems, also called soil absorption systems, are commonly used in areas where public sewage collection and disposal are not available. In general these systems are comprised of a holding tank and a drain field. The tank provides for settlement and some digestion of the solids. Liquids rise to the surface and are conducted either by gravity or by a pump to a drain field. The drain field is essentially a manifold system of perforated pipe that distributes the effluent from the tank to a prescribed area. The design of on-site sewage disposal systems must conform to state or local guidelines and requirements, but there are similarities found in these regulations.

On-site sewage disposal utilizes the ability of soil to absorb and treat the effluent as it percolates through the soil matrix. The soil must have a fairly high degree of permeability but not so high as to present a danger of contamination to groundwater supplies. On-site design proceeds on the basis of field tests that measure the permeability of soil, or the rate at which waste will percolate through the undisturbed soil. The "perc" rate is determined by filling a series of small holes or pits. After the hole has drained thoroughly once, the hole is refilled and the rate at which the water drains is recorded. An acceptable perc rate is neither too fast nor too slow, based on local regulations. Other design concerns include the slope of the proposed drain field and the distance to the water table and bedrock. The actual size of the drain field is calculated as a function of the perc rate and the volume of loading (see Table 8.13). There must be sufficient drain field area to allow for complete absorption of the effluent.

On-site system failures are common. The proper installation of the distribution manifold is critical. The pipe system must be installed flat to provide for even distribution over the entire drain field. If low spots should occur, the waste effluent will tend to collect in the low spot and overload that portion of the drain field. Likewise, if the holding tank becomes filled with solids, the quality of the effluent will degrade and solids may block the distribution system causing overloading.

In areas where perc rates or soil depth are inadequate for on-site disposal, sand mound systems are sometimes used. Sand mounds are raised areas constructed of sandy soils that are designated by local authorities as having acceptable percolation rates. The sand mound is designed to meet the percolation and loading requirements in much the same way as a typical in-ground system except that the mound is raised and installed above grade, usually on top of the native soils. In some applications the sand mound system is coupled with a small aerobic treatment system. The sand mound is always loaded under pressure using a pump to ensure even distribution of the effluent throughout the drain field.

Constructed Wetlands for Sewage Treatment

There is a growing interest and experience in using constructed wetlands as an integral part of on-site and community sewage disposal systems. Large systems require careful consideration of volume and effluent quality and are usually designed by a qualified engineer. Smaller systems for individual residences or a few residences may be designed and built without an engineer's seal in some states. These systems are generally subject to seasonal effects and so are more common in southern states. The approach to these systems varies from state to state and among municipalities within states, but a general overview is possible here.

Constructed wetlands are used as a treatment system for on-site sewage disposal systems that have physical limitations or in cases where an existing system is failing.

Properly constructed and operating systems have no odor and are quite flexible in terms of design form; they may be long and narrow or compact and rectilinear. They do take up space on a site but provide attractive landscapes when carefully designed and located. Depending on soil conditions, a typical constructed wetland for a residential system will probably be 300 ft^2 or more. Traffic of all sorts should be routed away from the wetland, and surface drainage should be diverted.

The systems do require a functioning septic tank. Solids are removed by the tank, and only liquid effluent flows to the wetland. Typical constructed wetlands have a limited capacity to treat solids. The tank effluent is subject to action by plant roots and microflora and fauna in the wetland. The high-quality wetland effluent flows through the gravel and is then discharged to the drain field. These systems most commonly are constructed of a shallow depression (+/− 18 in.) lined with an impermeable liner and filled with clean washed gravel or crushed stone (do not use limestone). Septic tank effluent is introduced through a manifold to ensure a fairly even distribution across the wetland bed. Selected plants are planted directly in the gravel; additional soil is not used. The effluent is collected in a discharge manifold at the far end of the wetland and conveyed to the leach field.

Plants species frequently recommended for these systems include iris (Iris), canna lilies (Canna), calla lilies (Zantedeschia), bulrushes (Scirpus), cattails (Typha), rushes (Juncus), and sedges (Carex). Care should be taken to remove and wash soil from the roots before planting. These systems do require some maintenance. Plant debris and unwanted vegetation should be removed. Care should be taken to avoid introducing harsh chemicals to the septic system. Large volumes of water (e.g., draining a pool) should not be discharged to the septic system. Also, plans should be made to water the system if residents are away for more than a few days.

CHAPTER **9**

Landscape Restoration

Site Planning and Landscape Ecology

Landscape ecology focuses on cause-and-effect relationships and has made important contributions to our understanding of how development affects the environment. Major areas of concern include the fragmentation of habitat, biological diversity, the design and management of land resources, and sustainable development. Emerging as a distinct science in the 1960s and 1970s, landscape ecology is still a young science. It embraces the concept of the "total human ecosystem"; that is, that humans, along with all of our activities and cultural complexities, are part of the landscape. To attempt to describe or study the landscape without considering the influence of human activity would be a pointless exercise, and landscape ecologists have recognized that a reductionist approach to science is inadequate to wholly describe the complexities of landscape ecosystems.

Landscape ecology is a broadly interdisciplinary science. Ecologists, physicists, biologists, and geographers are as concerned with values and ethics as they are with the systems approach of this new science. A new language, a new means of describing the ecosystem, is beginning to emerge from their work. For example, there is a recognition that order, as it is commonly understood to exist in nature, probably does not exist at all. Instead we look for order and select those things that best support our understanding of it. In fact, order is probably more complex and is better studied and expressed through fuzzy set theory or fuzzy logic. Using the fuzzy approach, qualitative elements of the landscape can be described mathematically and quantitative values can be expressed in words.

Landscape ecology offers important information for those engaged in site planning and design. By understanding the principles of landscape integrity, the site planner can incorporate these elements into the site design. Landscapes can be described in terms of four general elements of vegetative mass and form: patches, edges, connecting corridors, and mosaic (Dramstad et al., 1996).

Patches are concentrations of habitat type, most commonly visualized as a woodland patch in the midst of farmland or an urban area in the middle of a national forest. Patches may be small, such as an undeveloped city lot, or large such as a park. Patches can arise from human activities such as farming or urbanization, from natural resource distribution such as a desert spring or emerging wetland, from natural succession or homeorhesis (Naveh and Lieberman, 1994), or from some intervening disturbance. Not long ago patches were considered less than optimal. They were often described as degraded islands, disconnected areas isolated from the rest of the ecosystem. It has been found, however, that patches can be beneficial, depending on their character, size, and location. A patch contaminated with industrial wastes is a degraded site with little redeeming value, but relatively small patches of woodland adjacent to farm fields or suburban or urban areas may be very productive. Diversity declines and extirpation increases as patch sizes decrease and isolation, or the distance between patches, increases. The quality of the habitat is also a function of size; the smaller the patch size, the less diverse it is because the number of possible habitat types is reduced. There is no simple minimum patch size recommendation; some small patches can preserve specialized or unusual habitats like wetlands. Careful assessment is necessary to be sure small patches are sustainable.

The *edges* or boundaries between different habitat types are blurred. There is no bright line between the meadow and the deep woods, or between upland and open water. These zones of transition are called ecotones, which contain aspects of both areas and are often the most productive parts of a landscape. The littoral zones that are the transition from upland to open water are usually more productive than either the upland or the open water. Both terrestrial and aquatic animals use the littoral zone to feed and to mate. Likewise the transition from deep woods to meadow is more productive than either of the habitats connected by it. Edges act as buffers and filters. Natural ecotones tend to be curvilinear and provide soft transitions full of the complexity of the areas they border. By contrast, the boundaries of human activity tend to be straight and abrupt, providing little buffer or transition.

The value of *connecting corridors* increases with the fragmentation associated with human activity. With the encroachment of development and farmland, natural habitat has routinely been cut up into patches and isolated. Even patches located near one another can be isolated by barriers such as major highways, railroads, or fences. Linear developments like electric transmission corridors or pipelines prevent the movement of wildlife, but connecting corridors such as floodplains may serve as pathways from one patch to another. The key is to recognize these elements and to provide connections between them. To be effective, the planner must understand what animals or plants are expected to use the corridor. For example, some species require a visual connection, so corridors must be visible from one patch to another.

Mosaic refers to the overall form of a landscape: the pattern of patches, edges, and connectivity. Even though the landscape mosaic itself is usually beyond the scope of a given land development project, the site planner must understand how a site fits into the landscape mosaic to incorporate the principles of patches, edges, and connections into the plan.

Restoring Landscape

Landscape restoration encompasses a broad range of activities and concerns, including rehabilitation, reclamation, and remediation efforts. Rehabilitation refers to actions taken to restore environmental functions and the vitality of a landscape. In some rehabilitation projects, the salient underlying features of the landscape are still present but because of urbanization or other landscape disturbances the quality and functions of the landscape have been degraded. Stream and wetland restoration and revegetation projects are examples of rehabilitation.

Reclamation projects are usually undertaken on landscapes in which features have been obliterated by development, agriculture, or mining operations. Reclamation projects usually require construction of new landscape features to replace what has been lost. Reclamation projects might include constructed wetlands, infiltration features such as rain gardens, or eliminating invasive exotic vegetation and encouraging the return of native species.

Remediation activities are concerned with mitigating a condition that has resulted in a degraded landscape. Dealing with acid mine drainage or contaminated runoff from a brownfield site are examples of landscapes in need of remediation. A given landscape restoration project may involve all three activities.

Landscape restoration as an area of professional practice is not new, but it has grown dramatically in recent years to become a major area of practice and innovation. As site development practices expand to include concerns about environmental impacts and sustainability, many of the practices used in landscape restoration will become more common.

Restoring Vegetative Cover

Soil structure is the arrangement of soil particles into aggregates of mineral soil material, organic material, and microorganisms. The agglomeration of soil into aggregates is an important element of a healthy soil ecosystem, but it cannot be accomplished within the time frame allowed for revegetating a disturbed site. On the disturbed site, the structure of the soil is destroyed through the operations of grading and compaction. The loss of soil structure results in a decrease in soil permeability and an increase in erodability. Soils with a granular structure naturally allow for infiltration and resist erosion. Increased runoff and erodability results from the earthmoving activities, and timely planned attention to stabilizing the site is critical to a successful project (Darmer, 1992).

In addition, the graded and compacted surface is generally not ideal for establishing vegetation without specific steps to prepare the soil, an appropriate selection of materials, and a plan for maintenance. Vegetation is cost-effective and generally considered an attractive method of preventing erosion.

Site Preparation

In most circumstances, allowances should be made for a soil analysis. Although there is no typical site, restoration soil conditions are often dry, compacted, and infertile with little resemblance to the original native soils. On many sites fill has been brought from off-site, even from myriad sources, and on others unpredictable "made-land" conditions exist. The results are unpredictable, if not unproductive, soils. In some cases it is necessary to rework the soil for up to 30 in. in depth. Establishing plant growth without characterizing the soil will yield uneven results.

Collection of the soil sample is a function of the homogeneity of the soil, the ease of collection, and the construction of the sampling equipment. When contamination might be an issue, the required decontamination procedures may affect the collection of soil samples. Sample planning can be done, using aerial photography, USGS, or site maps. The character of the sample is a function of the objective. Different types of samples are required for different analyses: bulk densities require an intact core; nutrient analysis requires a well-balanced composite sample. When collecting samples for nutrient analysis, each soil sample should consist of 5 to 20 cores taken at random locations throughout one field or area. The area should be no more than about 20 acres. Keep in mind that each sample should represent only one general soil type or condition. When sampling for engineering classification, sample areas that are clearly unique separately.

Sampling for nutrient analyses is usually done with clean stainless steel, chrome, or plastic buckets and tools. Brass, bronze, or galvanized tools should be avoided. Engineering analysis samples are usually collected as intact cores taken with split spoons on drilling rigs or direct push machines. Hand samples are taken with hand augers or coring equipment. Samples collected for chemical analysis might require special nonreactive equipment and special sample preservation.

Soil sampling may also be done for other purposes. Geophysical techniques use profiling or sounding methods to identify the presence of buried metal objects or to map the subsurface features. Profiling is used to define the lateral extent of a feature such as an area of buried wastes. The result is a contour map of the area or object. Sounding is a radar technique used to determine the depth of an object at a specific location. Soundings are taken on a grid pattern to allow interpolation of the depth and area of objects. Methods of geophysical testing include ground penetrating radar, electromagnetic exploration, seismic refraction, and magnetometer surveys.

Ground penetrating radar (GPR) provides a shallow cross section of subsurface objects. GPR can penetrate up to 40 ft in sandy soils but is limited to the first 4 ft in clay soils or soils containing conductive wastes. Data from GPR must be used in conjunction with supporting data from bore hole logs and resistivity or conductivity tests. The GPR coverage is affected by terrain and site vegetation. The GPR antenna is dragged along behind a vehicle along a cleared path 3 to 4 ft wide. The distance between paths varies by the type of equipment used. A typical day's survey costs $5000 to $20,000, including interpretation of the data and preparation of a report.

Electromagnetic (EM) exploration includes several techniques that contrast the conductivity of materials being screened. These techniques are useful for mapping metallic plumes and locating buried objects such as tanks, pipes, utilities, or drums. Magnetometer surveys determine magnetic anomalies and are used like EM surveys.

Seismic refraction is a geologic investigation tool with only limited application in environmental site assessment work. It is used for mapping bedrock surface areas and may be useful in groundwater or environmental pathway studies where influences over contamination plumes are being sought.

Other soil testing methods include soil gas studies, which identify the presence of volatile organic compounds (VOCs) such as solvents, oils, gas, and cleaning fluids. Samples of the air in the soil are collected at known depths and locations and analyzed. Samples are mapped to illustrate the area of contamination and the mobility of the contaminant. Study areas are usually selected because of known or suspected dumping or disposal. The presence of VOCs in the soil indicates contamination near the monitor point and possibly in the groundwater. Soil gas surveys are used to determine the placement of borings, to monitor points or wells, and to more precisely define the area of contamination. In grab samples a probe is inserted into the vadose zone and air is drawn into a sample container with a vacuum pump. Static samples are taken using a tube-containing activated charcoal, which absorbs the gases. A third method does not involve collecting samples but rather takes a reading on a photo ionization detector (PID) or on a flame ionization detector (FID). Table 9.1 lists some things to consider when collecting soil samples.

These tests will provide the fundamental data for determining the characteristics of the soil and the cultural requirement and amendments necessary for a successful revegetation effort (Sobek et al., 1976). In addition to examining the soil, a visit to the area surrounding the site to identify local vegetation can provide important information on native plants and the climate and precipitation requirements for the proposed vegetation. It is important to

| 1. Subdivide the area into homogenous units and, if necessary, subdivide these into areas of uniform size. |
| 2. Establish a grid to locate sampling points. Composite samples of each area should be comprised of 10 to 20 samples. Care must be taken to use uniform size cores/ slices of equal volume and equal depth to develop the composite. |
| 3. Test for:
standard water pH and/or buffer pH
percent of organic matter
cation exchange capacity
particle size distribution
salinity
available nutrients |

Adapted from the U.S. Environmental Protection Agency, *Process Design Manual for Land Treatment*, Section III (1977).

TABLE 9.1   Planning and Collecting Soil Samples

notice differences that occur at various elevations, slopes, exposures, and aspects to design a revegetation plan that can be sustained through the seasons and through climate extremes such as drought or wet years, or heavy winds or snows (Brown et al., 1986).

The plant material selected to stabilize and revegetate the site must be able to establish quickly in this harsh environment. In general, native species are a good choice as they have predictable performance and growth habits in the geographic area. They are adapted to the general soils and climatic conditions and are best suited to the extremes as well as the average conditions that could be expected.

The introduction of acrylic polymers in recent years has improved the success of stabilization and revegetation projects, particularly in droughty soils. Acrylic polymers are added and mixed with soils to create a film that allows air and water to penetrate but still binds the soil particles together. It is nontoxic, and runoff does not stain concrete.

The disturbed, barren, and compacted soil surface of an impacted site is a difficult place to reestablish plants. There is little protection for seedlings and young plants, and mulches only protect the earliest stages of growth. Young seedlings are particularly susceptible to damage from wind and rain and heat and cold stress. In areas where summer temperatures may reach 37°C (100°F), the hard surface could result in 55°C (130°F) temperatures at the soil surface. Climatic extremes are often even worse on a disturbed site. Without cover, the wind will dry the unprotected surface more quickly and erode the unprotected soils. Rainfall on unprotected soils may result in significant erosion and downstream sedimentation.

Throughout the United States, the regional offices of the Natural Resources Conservation Service (NRCS) and the various state universities and agricultural colleges provide recommendations for seed mixtures for effective erosion control. These offices are an excellent source of information; however, the designer/developer should consider the various mixtures in light of the specific application. Certain plant materials chosen for a commercial or industrial application may not be appropriate or desirable in a residential application. The designer must have accurate topography for the site as well as climactic information and data about site hydrology to complete a successful revegetation plan.

Cultural Operations

Seed bed preparation generally occurs after "finish grading" is completed; however, the surfaces to be seeded are hard and smooth and not ready to be seeded by any means. Graded slopes to be seeded should be 2:1 or flatter. Steeper slopes may require special treatment if vegetation alone is used to stabilize the slope. The interim condition between finish grading and stable vegetated slope is a fragile one. On slopes steeper than 3:1, stepping the slope can help vegetation become established (Fig. 9.1). Slopes should be left in a rough condition. A smooth slope is a more difficult surface on which to establish vegetation than a slope left with clods and imperfections. Another version of the stair-stepped slope is the grade left with a serrated blade drawn across the slope, parallel with the contours. The surface is left with many locations for seed to become established. Seeds blown or washed from one location are likely to be deposited in microsites created by the steps in the slopes (Fig. 9.2). Over time the edges of the stairs are worn down and debris from above fills in the trough, leaving a smooth desirable surface (Rogoshewski et al., 1983).

Compaction can extend deep into the soil, and simply "scratching up" the seed bed will not provide for infiltration of air and water to plant roots. The soils may require deeper conditioning prior to seeding using equipment that is able to plow to the necessary depth. Although an initial stand of vegetation may germinate and appear vigorous, the compacted subsoil restricts root growth and infiltration of water and will eventually result in the concentration of salts in the topsoil, limiting successful plant growth. In addition, slower growing deeper rooted plants will not establish on the site (Brown et al., 1986). Once these cultural operations are complete, final seed bed preparation can begin. Fertilizer, pH, and organic additives should be determined by the soil tests.

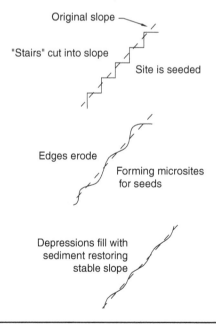

FIGURE 9.1   Stair-stepping detail.

FIGURE **9.2** Tracking on a slope.

Blending soils to create a soil medium with a greater absorption capacity may be part of the plan. Combining soils of different particle size increases the permeability or moisture retaining capabilities of a soil. Layering different soil materials over a barrier to encourage root growth and aeration and allow drainage away from the impermeable cap materials is another means of preparing the soil for planting.

Seeding should be performed as quickly as possible after final grading. Hydroseeding—applying seed, fertilizer, mulch, and lime in a single operation—is the most efficient seeding method for large areas. For level areas, seed drills are often used, but this requires several passes to apply all of the constituents. All cultural seeding operations should be performed at right angles to the slope (parallel to the contours). If the plan includes shrubbery, trees, or seedlings, these must be planted by hand (Darmer, 1992).

Mulches are generally recommended for all revegetation projects, and mulch comes in a wide variety of materials with various characteristics. The role of mulch is important and should not be overlooked. Mulch is an insulator that affects soil temperatures as well as providing protection from runoff and precipitation, which reduces erosion and evaporation, encourages infiltration, and holds seed in place. Different mulch materials perform these tasks to different degrees.

Selecting Plant Materials

Plant materials selected to revegetate a site must be able to establish quickly in a harsh environment. In general, native species are a good choice because they have predictable performance and growth habits in the general soils of the area and in the climatic conditions. Plan for the success of revegetation in the extremes of the environment, not only for average conditions; the droughty summer and especially harsh winter are to be expected in the plan. Native species may be best suited to respond to these variations, and introduced species should be carefully evaluated before they are used. The EPA has established criteria for selecting plant materials, differentiated for grasses and forbs and for shrubs and trees (Table 9.2).

Plant selection must consider the growth habits, rooting depth, and rate of establishment of specific plants. The time of year for seeding is also an important consideration; the rate of maturation from germination and the expected temperature and precipitation must be appropriate. Some cool season grasses will not germinate in high temperatures or, once germinated, will suffer from the extreme temperatures whereas warm season grasses may require higher temperatures to germinate. The plants selected for the revegetation plan must be compatible with each other as well as resistant to insect damage and diseases. The long-term permanent

Grasses and Forbs
Availability of seed
Resistance to erosion and traffic stresses at the site
Adaptability to critical conditions such as pH, soil texture, drainage, salinity, and wind erosion
Adaptability to climate of site such as sunlight, exposure, temperatures, wind, and rainfall
Resistance to insects, diseases, and other pests
Compatibility with other plants selected
Ability to propagate
Consistent with long-term maintenance plans and succession plan
Shrubs and Trees
Availability in required quantity
Capability to produce root systems as required by the site characteristics
Ability to become established quickly
Tolerance of site conditions, acid, saline, wet, droughty, or compacted soils
Compatible with principles of secondary succession
Ability for vigorous growth after relief of moisture stress; regrowth after damage
Ability to reproduce
Value to wildlife
Ability to create islands of fertility by creating a point of accumulation for organic matter, detritus, and nutrients
Ability to withstand traffic stresses
Resistance to insects, diseases, and other pests
Compatible with other plants selected for the project
Relative maintenance requirements and cost
Tolerance for site-specific stresses

From A. Sobek, W. A. Sknuller, J. R. Freeman, and R. M. Smith, *Field and Laboratory Methods: Applications to Overburden and Minesites* (Industrial Environmental Research Laboratory, 1976).

TABLE 9.2   Criteria for Selecting Plants for Restoration Projects

stabilization plan should include grasses, legumes, shrubs, and trees. Generally speaking, perennials are best planted in the fall, and annuals should be seeded in the spring.

Using Sod

Although sod materials can be expensive and require additional installation efforts, sod is appropriate for certain locations and applications. The range of plant materials available in sod has grown appreciably and includes wildflowers and special order mixtures in addition to the familiar fine turf sods. When using sod, it is important to confirm that the material conforms to the requirements set forth by the governing certification agency; usually the state department of agriculture. Sods are generally qualified by the quality of the root development as compared to the top growth.

In addition to their immediate visual impact, sodded areas resist erosion and quickly cover areas in the summer when cool season grasses will not grow. The preparation of the site to be sodded is similar to the process already described for seeding. The surface is graded to reflect the final grade and cultivated to a depth of at least 3 in. (7.5 cm). Soil amendments and fertilizers may be place in the soil before cultivation. The sod is placed by hand so that the edges abut; open joints and gaps should be filled with sod cut and shaped to fill the opening. After placing the sod, the area is rolled or lightly tamped to "seat" the sod onto the prepared surface. The key to establishing a healthy sod area on the site is preparation and follow-up, including regular watering and care until the sod is established.

When using sod in swales or on slopes, some extra precautions are necessary. The pieces should be installed from the bottom up toward the top in horizontal strips with the long edges of the sod running parallel to the contours. Individual pieces should be staggered to offset the vertical joints. On steep slopes greater than 5:1, it may be appropriate to anchor the sod in place using wood stakes driven flush with the surface of the sod.

Enhancing Slope Stabilization with Trees

Although the grasses and forbs used to stabilize a slope immediately after the disturbance may become established and even thrive, long-term success of the stabilization can be improved by incorporating trees into the stabilization plan. The deeper root penetration serves to bind the slope together and to provide additional cover and slope protection from precipitation (Figs. 9.3 and 9.4). Nitrogen fixing "nurse trees" (Table 9.3) should be included and represent approximately 25 percent of the tree/shrub component (Vogel, 1987). The use of selected trees and shrubs also gives the designer some control over the slope as it matures. Trees and shrubs are a natural and perhaps even necessary element for the long-term stabilization of disturbed slopes.

Although the tree has very little value in protecting the slope from erosion initially, it does have a role to play over time. The canopy provides protection for the soil from the sun and rain and shade to the understory. The leaves from deciduous trees contribute to the ground litter, which helps stabilize the surface and contributes to the evolving soil structure (Vogel, 1987, p. 67).

The expense of tree planting on very large sites can be offset by planting seedlings. Individual seedlings and installation costs are relatively low when compared to larger trees, but some investigation into mortality rates, species, and long-term costs is justified. The solution may be in planting a combination of sizes and species. The mix can take advantage of cost advantages of younger trees and the greater vigor and success rate of larger trees. The actual plan will reflect budget consideration, site characteristics, and available plant species.

Figure 9.3   Trees planted on a slope as part of a stabilization plan.

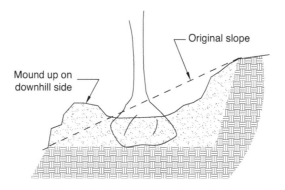

Figure 9.4   Tree planting on a slope detail.

Indigobush (Amorpha fruticosa)
Lespedeza (Lespedeza spp.)
Bristly Locust (Robinia fertilis)
Rose Acacia (Robinia hispida)
Autumn Olive (Eleagnus umbellata)
European Black Alder (Alnus glutinosa)
Black Locust (Robinia pseudoacacia)

Table 9.3   Nitrogen Fixing Trees and Shrubs

The competition between herbaceous plants and trees/shrubs may be a matter of concern. Allelopathy—the chemical competition between plants—or even shading young trees and shrubs with a vigorous herbaceous layer may require steps to reduce the competitive stress on the slower growing woody components of the planting plan. The use of larger trees/shrubs to overcome the influence of the herbaceous layer is cost prohibitive. Another approach is to plant the site in alternating strips (Table 9.4). The "herbaceous" strip would be fertilized, the alternating strip containing shrubs/trees would be fertilized for the woody plants and planted with an unfertilized herbaceous layer (Vogel, 1987, p. 37).

Eastern Region of the United States	
Plant type	**Characteristics**
Washington hawthorne (Crataegnus phaenophrum), tree	Deciduous. Medium growth rate to 30 ft (9 m). Dense twiggy upright growth. Use 5–9 ft (1.5–3 m) spacing on well-drained to moderately well-drained soils.
Scotch pine (Pinus sylvestria), tree	Evergreen. Rapid growth rate to 50 ft (15 m). Dry to somewhat poor-drained soils. Very rugged tree. Lower pH limit is 4.0. Throughout most of eastern United States.
Common juniper (Juniperus communis), tree	Evergreen. Slow growth. Use 4–6 ft (1.5–2 m) spacing, prefers limestone soils. Dry to moderately well-drained soil.
Black locust (Robinia pseudoacacia), tree	Deciduous. Rapid growth to 50 ft (15 m). Can be direst seeded. Widely adapted to different soils. Good leaf litter, use in planting mixes. Nitrogen fixing. Lower pH limit is 4.0.
White pine (Pinus strobus), tree	Evergreen. Rapid growth. Prefers rich, moist especially heavy soils. Used for screens. Lower pH limit is 4.0.
Hackberry (Celtis occidentalis), tree	Deciduous. Moderate rate of growth to 25 ft (8 m). Tolerates acid soils to pH 5.0. Tolerates poorly drained soils to excessively drained soils.
Thornless honeylocust (Gleditsia triacanthos enermis), tree	Deciduous. Moderate growth rate to 35 ft (11 m). Moderately drained soils. pH 6.5 lower limit.
Red oak (Quercus rubra), tree	Deciduous. Moderate rate of growth in acid soils.
Gray dogwood (Cornus racemosa), shrub	Deciduous. Rapid growing shrub. Prefers sunny location, but will tolerate shade. Will grow in wide range of soils. Forms colonies. Lower pH limit is 5.0.
Red chickberry (Aronia arbutfolia), shrub	Deciduous. Moderate growth rate. Tolerates dry to somewhat poorly drained soils.
Tartarian honeysuckle (Lonicera tatarica), shrub	Deciduous. Rapid growing in well-drained sunny location. Lower pH limit is 5.0.
Arrowwood (Viburnum dentatum), shrub	Deciduous. Rapid growth. Prefers well-drained to moist soils. Sunny location. Lower pH limit is 4.0.

TABLE 9.4 Characteristics of Selected Trees and Shrubs for Use in Restoration (*Continued*)

Eastern Region of the United States	
Plant type	**Characteristics**
Red osier dogwood (Cornus stolonifera), shrub	Deciduous. Rapid growth in well-drained soils, sunny location. Forms thickets. Lower pH limit 4.5.
Forsythia (Forsythia intermedia), shrub	Deciduous. Rapid growth in well-drained soils, sunny location, tolerates stony rough slopes. Vigorous growth.
Japanese juniper (Juniperus procumbens), shrub	Evergreen. Rapid growth. Sandy and loamy moderately moist soil. Prefers sun. Hardy, low-spreading shrub.
Sargent juniper (Juniperus chinensis sargentis), shrub	Evergreen. Moderate rate of growth. Prefers moist, slightly acid sandy soils. Tolerates droughty banks. Low creeping shrub.
Indigobush (Amorpha fruticosa), shrub	Deciduous. Adapted to wide conditions, fairly slow growth rate. Can be seeded. Lower pH limit is 4.0.
Autumn olive (Elaeagnus umbellata)	Deciduous. Competes well with established herbaceous layer. Used as a nurse plant. Lower pH limit is 4.0. Growth to 20 ft (6 m).
Western Region of the United States (less than 80 in. of rain)	
Plant type	**Characteristics**
Arizona cypress (Cupressus Arizonica Greene), tree	Evergreen. May be established from direct seeding. Persistent once established, but as a seedling only poor tolerance for drought. Prefers gravelly northern or cut slopes. Tolerates high temperatures. Precipitation range from 16–20 in. From southern Texas to Arizona.
Big tooth maple (Acer grandidentatum Nutt.), tree	Deciduous. May be established by seeding, but slow rate of growth for seedlings. Has a moderate rate of spread once established. Prefers well-drained soils of porous sandy to gravelly loams. Will grow on steep slopes. Tolerates moderately acidic to slightly basic soils. From Utah and western Wyoming to southeastern Arizona and New Mexico.
Bur oak (Quercus macrocarpa), tree	Deciduous. May be established by seed or by container stock on difficult sites. Adapted to a wide range of soils, will tolerate soils from a pH of 4.0 to moderately basic. Drought resistant but intolerant of floods, precipitation range from 15–40 in. From the Dakotas and northeast Wyoming to midwest and south to Texas.
Green ashe (Fraxinus pennsylvanica), tree	Deciduous. Slow to establish and may need protection from competition initially; it is tolerant of moderately basic to strongly acid (pH 4.0) soils. Prefers alluvial soils, tolerant of periodic flooding and drought. Precipitation range 15–45 in. From central Montana and Wyoming to Dakotas, throughout eastern United States.
New Mexico locust (Robinia neomexicana A. Grey), tree	Deciduous. Fair rate of success from seed, seedlings drought resistant. Good spread particularly on harsh sites, thicket forming. Prefers moist soils on canyon bottoms, bottom of north slopes. From west Texas to Arizona through Utah and Colorado.

TABLE **9.4**   Characteristics of Selected Trees and Shrubs for Use in Restoration (*Continued*)

| Western Region of the United States (less than 80 in. of rain) ||
Plant type	Characteristics
Pinyon pine (Pinus edulis), tree	Evergreen. Best results with nursery stock. Very long lived, good rates of natural spread, can become a pest once established. Adapted to calcerous caliche soils. Good on harsh eroded sites. Tolerant of drought and heat. Precipitation range 12–18 in.
Ponderosa pine (Pinus ponderosa), tree	Evergreen. Best results with nursery stock. Good drought and fire tolerance. Not tolerant of shade or saline and sodic soils. Precipitation range from 15–25 in. but can survive on as little as 7 in. From western Dakotas to Montana to Arizona and Texas.
Quaking aspen (Popolus tremoloides), tree	Deciduous. From container or nursery stock. Short-lived but forms thickets or colonies with extensive shallow root system. Prefers deep sandy to silty loam soils ranging from moderately basic to moderately acidic. Widely adapted to western United States. Precipitation from 15–30 in.
Antelope bitterbush (Purshia tridentata), shrub	Evergreen. Persistent on a range of soil pH, good for stabilization, useful as browse. Resists drought and moderate salt. Intolerant of high water table, flooding. New Mexico to California, north to British Columbia. 10–25 in. of precipitation.
Apache-plume (Fallugia paradoxa), shrub	Semi-evergreen. Weak competitive ability but establishes quickly on disturbed slopes, prefers full sun, moderately basic, well-drained soil. Tolerates drought and salt. West Texas through Arizona.
Big sagebrush (Artemsia tridentata), shrub	Deciduous. Long lived, persistent competitor, prefers well-drained, deep, fertile soils, will tolerate a range of pH conditions, Tolerant of drought and salt, intolerant of high water table. From Arizona and New Mexico to Nebraska. Precipitation range from 7.5–17 in.
Chokecherry (Prunus virginiana), shrub	Deciduous. Fair to poor germination when seeded but spreads quickly from roots to form thickets, does well with grasses and forbs. Prefers well-drained, moderately acidic to moderately basic, silty to sand soils. Intolerant of clayey or poorly drained soils. From 12–30 in. of precipitation. Widely distributed in cooler areas of northern and western United States.
Curlleaf mountain mahogany (Cercocarpus ledifolius), shrub	Evergreen. May be difficult to establish from seed but persistent once established. Prefers basic, well-drained clayey soils. Tolerant of drought and salt. New Mexico and Arizona to Montana to 10,000 ft. Precipitation 6–20 in.
Desert bitterbush (Pursha glandosa), shrub	Evergreen. Establishes well from seed, tolerant of drought. Persistent and spreading. Prefers well-drained sandy to clayey soils. Southwestern Utah to southeastern Nevada and California.
Douglas rabbitbush (Chrysothamnus viscidiflorus), shrub	Deciduous. Persistent and excellent spreader, may compete with grasses and forbs. Prefers basic, well-drained clayey to coarse textured soils, broad range of adaptability, weak growth in acid soils. Precipitation range from 6–20 in. From New Mexico and Arizona to Montana.

TABLE **9.4**   Characteristics of Selected Trees and Shrubs for Use in Restoration (*Continued*)

Western Region of the United States (less than 80 in. of rain)	
Plant type	**Characteristics**
Fringed sagebrush (Artemisia frigida), shrub	Evergreen. Fair competitor but may be slow to establish from seed. Prefers well-drained neutral to slightly basic soils. Tolerant of drought. Fair salt tolerance. Precipitation range 8–20 in.
Gambel oak (Quercus gambelii), shrub	Deciduous. Persistent once established but spreads slowly. Prefers sandy and gravelly loams on slopes. From west Texas to Arizona to Utah and Colorado, southern Wyoming. Precipitation range 16–20 in.
Golden current (Ribes aureum), shrub	Deciduous. Persistent spreader, good compatibility with grasses and forbs. Adapted to well-drained alkaline soils on shallow slopes. From Utah to eastern California. Precipitation range 8–14 in.
Gray molly summer cypress (Kochia americana var.), shrub	Evergreen. Prefers alkaline or saline clay soils. Excellent drought and salt tolerance. Precipitation range 6–10 in. From New Mexico and Arizona to Montana and Idaho.
Green ephedra (Ephreda viridis Coville), shrub	Deciduous. May be established by prepared direct seeding, poor rate of spread. Prefers well-drained alkaline soils, adapted to dry shallow soils on slopes. Tolerant of salt, excellent drought resistance. Intolerant of high water table or floods. Precipitation range from 8–14 in. from Utah and northern Arizona to eastern California.
Longleaf snowberry (Symphoricarpos longiflorus gray), shrub	Deciduous. May be difficult to establish by seed but good persistence and compatibility. Prefers well-drained to dry soils, will tolerate acid and basic conditions. Fair drought tolerance. Intolerant of salt. Oregon south to Texas and California.
Saskatoon serviceberry (Amelanchier alnifolia), shrub	Deciduous. Persistent with fair spread after only fair establishment by either seed or cutting. Prefers medium texture, well-drained soils. Fairly resistant to drought but intolerant of flooding or salt. Precipitation from 14–20 in. Western Texas and New Mexico to Montana to west coast.
Shadscale (Atriplex confertifolia), shrub	Deciduous. Establish from cuttings, good rate of spread after established. Prefers alkaline soils. Adapted to a range of soil textures. Excellent tolerance of salt and drought. From New Mexico to Canada, west to eastern California, Oregon, and Washington. Precipitation range from 4–8 in.
Siberian pea shrub (Carangana arborescans), shrub	Deciduous. May be established by seeding. Persistent with fair rate of spread once established. Fair compatibility with grasses and forbs. Will tolerate soil pH across broad range (pH 4.0–12.0). Prefers well-drained soils; adapted to shallow, infertile, and rocky soils. From northern great plains to central Utah and Colorado. Introduced from Siberia and Manchuria.

Source: Adapted from Willis G. Vogel, *A Manual for Training Reclamation Inspectors in the Fundamentals of Soils and Revegetation,* prepared for the Office of Surface Mining and Enforcement by the U.S. Department of Agriculture (Berea, KY, 1987); D. Brown, C. L. Hallman, J. Skogerbee, K. Eskern, and R. Price, *Reclamation and Vegetative Restoration of Problem Soils and Disturbed Lands* (Park Ridge, NJ: Noyes Data Corp. 1986); and P. Rogoshewski, H. Bryson, and R. Wagner, *Remediation Action Technology for Waste Disposal Sites* (Park Ridge, NJ: Noyes Data Corp., 1983).

TABLE **9.4**   Characteristics of Selected Trees and Shrubs for Use in Restoration (*Continued*)

Trees and shrubs do better in a soil that is about 30 in. thick as opposed to thinner soils that are adequate for grasses and legumes. Compacted soils act to resist root growth, and routine root ball planting methods may be inadequate in disturbed soils. The heavily compacted soils do not provide an opportunity for root penetration; the excavation process smoothes the soil surfaces in the excavated planting pit, which further reduces the already limited pore space and transmission of air and water. The "teacup" effect occurs when the backfilled soils in the planting pit become saturated with water that cannot drain away in the compacted surrounding soil. Ultimately the plant will die in this circumstance.

Contemporary recommendations for planting trees discourage the "pot" even in native soils. The new understanding of plant growth recommends the planting pit be five times the width of the root ball, but only deep enough to situate the root ball at the proper depth. Organic matter can be added to the soil. The root should sit on undisturbed soil to reduce settling. The root area should be carefully backfilled to eliminate large voids, but do not compact the backfilled pit too much. Water can be used to settle the ground naturally.

Where slope stabilization by tree planting is required, the slope should be mulched with woodchips to a depth of 4 to 6 in. on the slope immediately upon completion of grading. Woodchips should be approximately 2 in. square, and the mulch should be applied uniformly over the planting area.

Trees should be of a species that is adapted to growing on slopes. Seedlings should have had two full growing seasons in nursery beds prior to planting. Seedlings should be set vertically and roots spread carefully in a natural position in the planting hole. All trees must be thoroughly watered the day they are planted (Fig. 9.5). Use excess excavated material to provide a curb for water retention. The area should be fertilized with approximately 500 lb of 10-10-10 fertilizer per acre, worked into the slope prior to application of the woodchips.

Streams

In most urban and suburban areas, stream buffers are routinely removed or severely minimized as part of the development process. The developed landscape quickly concentrates and quickly conveys runoff to streams. Most of the runoff that reaches stream buffers is in the form of concentrated flow rather than the sheet flow that might occur in an undeveloped drainage condition. In this concentrated form, the runoff crosses the area that would have been the stream buffer in a pipe or channel. The concentrated runoff also conveys the particulates and pollutants that would have been filtered and trapped by the buffer directly into the stream.

Protecting existing stream buffers and banks is far preferable to having to work on restoration and try to mimic what nature had already established. Stream buffers should be designed to provide at least a minimum width indicated by the specific site and stream conditions. Effective stream buffers in developed or urbanized areas may range from as little as 20 ft to more than 200 ft as a function of topography, the amount of impermeable area, and the degree to which runoff is concentrated. Most local ordinances and standards are amalgamations of experience and liberal borrowing from other standards. Most communities with stream buffer standards require a minimum total width of at least 100 ft or that the buffer meets the 100 year floodplain standards.

Figure 9.5   Tree watering.

Stream buffers are usually designed to incorporate three distinct zones or functions (Fig. 9.6). The zone nearest the stream usually extends a minimum of 25 ft from the stream bank, and improvements are significantly restricted to such minimal encroachments as unpaved foot paths and swales. Utilities and paved crossings are kept to a minimum, and the stream zone remains in mature and dense vegetative cover. Beyond the stream zone, the middle zone is often used for complementary purposes such as bike paths or storm water appurtenances. The middle zone contains the 100 year floodplain, seasonal wetlands, and other habitat features. The middle zone is usually a minimum of 50 ft, but its width in practice is a function of the floodplain width, the presence of critical habitat or wetlands, and topography. The outermost zone is an area of initial transition from the more developed landscape to the stream. It may be a lawn with shrubs and trees in which a variety of activities may be conducted. Gardens and recreational activities are completely compatible with the transition zone.

The goal of the stream buffer is to re-create or maintain to the extent possible the predeveloped conditions of overland sheet flow, infiltration, and the process of filtration and

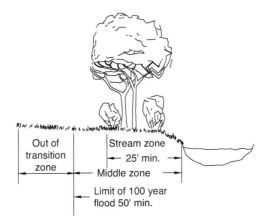

Out of transition zone

Stream zone
◄─ 25' min. ─►

Middle zone

Limit of 100 year flood 50' min.

FIGURE 9.6   Stream buffer design considerations.

deposition provided by vegetation. In general, native species of vegetation should be encouraged and invasive exotics removed. The shape of the stream buffer may be fairly irregular if it is properly designed to account for the floodplain, important habitat, and topographic features. The development planning can accommodate the variations in the buffer by varying lot width and depth or by modifying the site layout. Stream crossings should be kept to a necessary minimum. Table 9.5 lists some of the benefits of urban stream buffers.

1. Reduces small drainage problems and complaints
2. Allows for lateral movement of the stream
3. Provides flood control
4. Protects from stream bank erosion*
5. Increases property values*
6. Enhances pollutant removal
7. Provides food and habitat for wildlife*
8. Protects associated wetlands
9. Prevents disturbances to steep slopes*
10. Mitigates stream warming*
11. Preserves important terrestrial habitat*
12. Supplies corridors for conservation*
13. Provides essential habitat for amphibians
14. Fewer barriers to fish migration
15. Discourages excessive storm drain enclosures/channel hardening
16. Provides space for storm water ponds
17. Allows for future restoration

*Benefit amplified by or requires forest cover.
From Center for Watershed Protection, *Better Site Design: A Handbook for Changing Development Rules in Your Community*, 1998, prepared for the Site Planning Roundtable (Ellicott City, MD). Used with permission from The Center for Watershed Protection.

TABLE 9.5   Benefits of Urban Stream Buffers

Streams are formed by water and gravity and influenced by geology and climate. Less obvious are the biological elements of a stream, which contribute to its function. Climate dictates the amount of water through precipitation and evaporation and influences the vegetation and the richness and texture of the soil. Geology affects the character of the soil and the slope of the land. The amount of water and the distribution of water ultimately affect the character of a stream. Climate also dictates the biological character of a watershed, which has important influences. The amount of rain is important, but the distribution of rain over time and geography is also important. The richness and texture of soils (which are functions of climate and geology) and the interactions of soil with plants and animals determine the rate of infiltration, but also the amount of sediment that is washed into a stream, the amount of water supplied to the stream in summer or dry months, and to some degree the temperature of surface water.

In humid climates the action of precipitation and running water coupled with the biologic activity weathers rock into soil quickly. The presence of decaying vegetation contributes an important organic element, creating a rich complex soil texture that results in limited overland flow, high infiltration rates, and ultimately the slow passage of water through the soil to streams. Arid climates have less precipitation, less vegetation, and infiltration rates are slower; there is more runoff, and the landscape reveals the erosive power of high-velocity concentrated flows.

The velocity of flowing water is a function of the slope of the channel, the resistance offered by the stream bed and banks, and its depth of flow. The steepness of the stream gradient gives flowing water velocity and the power to erode channels. Velocity is always faster in the deepest parts of the channel and away from the sides. A deep river with the same gradient or slope as a shallow stream will have a much greater velocity.

Gravity and friction play important roles. Friction is the resistance to flow or the presence of obstructions that tend to impede the downward flow of water. Friction in streams is not easily modeled or well understood. The resistance to flow is influenced by the stream's roughness. Roughness is affected by the size of materials in the channel that make up the bed and banks, the amount and types of vegetation on the bed and banks, and the amount of curvature in the stream. The shearing action of water running over a stream bed results from the interaction of gravity and friction and causes the erosion of bed and banks. As velocity increases, shear and erosion tend to increase (Fig. 9.7).

Stream obstructions cause increased turbulence and direct flow toward the stream bottom or sides. As a result of turbulence, shear stresses increase on the stream bank or bottom, and the bank erodes or the bottom is scoured.

In the course of forming channels, streams will flood, change channels, scour pools, fill pools, erode banks, and meander (Fig. 9.8) as a result of changes in flow and sediment carried by the stream. To reach dynamic equilibrium, which means the amount of water and sediment that enter a stream are equal to the amount of water and sediment that leave it, the stream will adjust its channel to reflect changing conditions in the watershed. These changes include creating a deeper channel, erosion of the banks for a wider stream, or sediment deposits that create islands and other features. These changes are a response to the stream's tendency toward dynamic equilibrium—that is, to balance the energy of the water with the sediment load. A stream in a state of dynamic equilibrium is called a *graded stream.*

A purely hydraulic system could operate without a gradient because accumulated surplus water can generate its own surface slope and is capable of flow on a horizontal surface. The energy grade line is a graphic representation of the potential energy (head)

FIGURE 9.7 A stream with falls and step pools.

FIGURE 9.8 A natural stream meander.

possessed by the river along its longitudinal profile. The loss in head with distance reflects the amount of energy consumed by resisting elements in the system. Head loss is greater over riffles than through pools; the construction of pools and riffles in a river is probably independent of the channel pattern.

The transport of bed load requires a gradient, and it is in response to this requirement that a stream channel system adjusts to achieve an average steady state of operation year in and year out. In nature the balance between load and a stream's capacity exists only as an average condition: a stream is rarely in equilibrium but is in a constant dynamic change toward equilibrium due to floods, droughts, and manmade changes in the stream or channel. Alternate deepening by scour and shallowing by deposition are responses to changes in the stream's ability to transport its load. This process is known as *degradation*. When a stream has capacity for more bed load, rivers will scour and deepen. When there is too much bed load, stream gradient and velocity increase and channels widen. This process is known as *aggradation*.

Sinuousity

Water does not flow in a straight line. The line connecting the deepest parts of a channel is known as the *thalweg*. Even in channels that appear to be straight, the thalweg will shift from side to side and ultimately create an alternating series of bars. Straight stretches often contain alternate bars—material deposited on the channel bed along the sides alternating down the channel. Deep pools are formed opposite the alternate bars, and shallow riffles are found midway between. Meanders serve to lengthen the channel, which dissipates the stream's energy over longer distances and results in a more stable stream. The distance along the centerline of a channel (channel length) divided by the distance between meanders is used as a measure of stream sinuosity. One effect of meandering is to increase resistance and with it energy dissipation at the pools, making the grade line more uniform; meandering serves to approximate a condition of equilibrium. It should be noted that meandering is synonymous with bank erosion.

Sinuosity refers to the classification of streams into three types of patterns: sinuous, braided, and meandering. These are relative patterns, and there is no bright line distinction between them. Streams with a channel versus valley length of less than 1.5 are considered to be sinuous; those with 1.5 or greater are considered to be meandering; greater than 2.1 the meandering is said to be tortuous. A straight stream would have a sinuosity of 1. Braided streams do not have single main channel. During high-flow conditions, material is deposited in a channel and forms an island. Under lower flow conditions, the accumulated material becomes stabilized by vegetation and resists displacement in later floods, creating two channels.

The process of stream meandering is complex and difficult to accurately model. Stream behavior is a function of gradient, volume, the quantity and character of sediment, channel roughness, and composition. As volume changes, the stream's capacity to do work changes as well, and an accurate model must consider many different conditions. In spite of the difficulties, some practical methodologies have been developed. In general a stream meander radius of 2.7 to 2.8 of the bankful width is recommended.

Stream Assessment

The most commonly used method of stream assessment in the United States today is the Rosgen method. Developed by David Rosgen, this is a fairly sophisticated method that requires specific training or study. It is performed on four prescribed levels, and although the Rosgen method is fairly comprehensive, it contains the necessary flexibility for the assessor to modify the method to the stream.

The first level of assessment is the *geomorphic characterization,* which uses aerial photography and topographic mapping to identify the stream as one of 11 valley types characterized by the gradient of the stream and the topography of the valley. Streams are identified as one of eight general types based on the geometry of their channel and the floodplain.

The *morphological description* is the next Rosgen level and involves a more detailed assessment using actual measurements of the stream. The second level characterizes the stream into one of 94 categories based on the degree of entrenchment, the ratio of width to depth, surface gradient, the stream bed materials, and sinuousity. Stream bed materials include organic and inorganic components and may range from large boulders to fine organic sediments. Organic materials are important to the living members of the stream ecosystem because they provide the basis for the food chain. The ratio of width to depth is considered to be a critical indicator of stream stability.

The third level involves using the findings and experience of the first two levels to summarize the existing conditions and to evaluate the stream's stability potential based on existing riparian vegetation, patterns of in-stream deposition and meander, and the quality of in-stream habitat. From these first three levels of evaluation, preliminary conclusions can be drawn. These conclusions inform the fourth level of inquiry, which utilizes measurements of stream flow, stability, and sediment over time (Fig. 9.9). Not all stream restoration projects require such a sophisticated approach. Very serious stream degradation may require immediate attention. Fairly simple restoration efforts on nominally degraded streams may provide significant improvements.

FIGURE 9.9 A stream restored using the Rosgen method as a guide.

Riparian Zones

Healthy functioning streams are not strictly hydraulic or hydrologic systems. Stream quality is the result of a combination of the hydrologic and biologic landscape processes (Figs. 9.10 and 9.11). Therefore, a key element of stream quality is the health of the contributing watershed. Vegetation and biotic elements of riparian systems contribute to stream quality in the following ways:

1. Roots of trees, sedges, and shrubs bind the soils of banks to increase the stability of stream banks and resist erosion.

2. Overhanging vegetation shades streams, which keeps water along the edges cooler.

3. Biotic debris decays and provides nutrients to water.

4. Biota contribute to the health of riparian and upland soils to increase infiltration and decrease erosion and sedimentation of streams.

5. Animals build dams, wallows, and other features.

Stream Bank Stabilization

The stabilization of a stream bank requires careful consideration of the stream under various flow conditions. For example, wing bars or revetments installed to protect the stream bank under normal flow conditions may increase erosion under flood conditions. Likewise an underdesigned stabilization may not be able to resist the velocities and energy of a flood and be damaged or destroyed. The variability of streams makes prescriptive design impractical.

FIGURE 9.10   A well-developed riparian zone.

FIGURE 9.11   A stream section with dysfunctional riparian zone.

Many early stabilization projects consisted of merely armoring the stream with various materials specified to be heavy enough to resist flood conditions. In heavily developed watersheds with high-velocity frequent floods, the designer may have little choice. Unfortunately, a stream stabilized in such a manner offers little in the way of stream functions other than as a means of conveying runoff away. Armoring eliminates many of the valuable functions of the stream corridor by limiting the biotic and hydrologic interaction between the stream and the riparian zone.

When armor is not necessary, numerous methods and strategies have been successfully applied. Many of these methods have evolved from the experiences of community activists and sportsmen interested in stream quality. In fact, there are watershed interest groups in most communities in the United States today. Many of these groups have acquired a great deal of expertise in watershed and stream corridor protection. The focus of these groups is usually the protection or restoration of stream function.

Restoring overhang and bank conditions that favor improved habitat and riparian function begins with an inventory of habitat areas, debris locations, and stream transects to identify vegetation types, vegetation overhang (Fig. 9.12), measure of shaded area (Fig. 9.13), condition of stream banks (angle and height), undercut banks (Fig. 9.14), channel width and water width, depth and velocity, gradient, substrate composition, and pool to riffle ratio (Hunter, 1991).

The protection and cooling effect of overhanging vegetation and bank angle cannot be overlooked when assessing stream banks. Overhanging vegetation protects aquatic life from observation from above and shades the water from the sun. To be effective as cover, overhanging vegetation should be no more than a foot above the surface of the water. The angle of the bank also contributes to protection and cooling. Overhanging

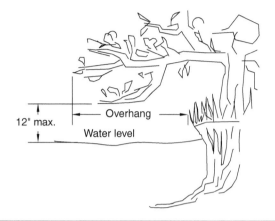

Figure 9.12   Measuring stream overhang.

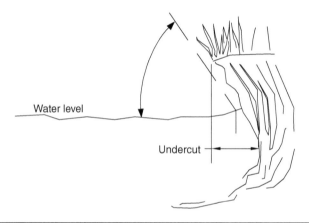

Figure 9.13   Measuring shade.

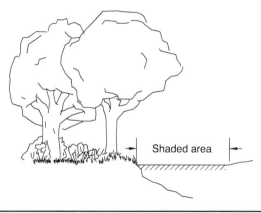

Figure 9.14   Measuring bank angle.

FIGURE **9.15** Stream bank retreating from stream.

banks are particularly important to habitat. Vertical banks or banks with a greater than 90-degree angle offer no protection from predators or the sun. Very often degraded streams have suffered as the bank erodes and the overhanging bank is lost. In urban streams, the stream bank may "retreat" from the stream over time, leaving the stream more and more exposed (Figs. 9.15 and 9.16).

FIGURE **9.16** An impacted stream.

It is important to determine the stream width as opposed to the water width on the day of the assessment. A stream assessor usually measures the stream or channel width as the distance across the channel from the edge of terrestrial vegetation to the opposite edge. In an impacted stream, the channel width may be significantly different from the water surface width. Variations between channel width and surface water may also be attributed to seasonal or annual variations in flow, which must be accounted for.

Bank restoration for habitat purposes involves restoring the relationship of bank angle and height. Many innovative ideas have been employed to re-create this relationship using locally available materials such as timbers or logs (Fig. 9.17). In general, when the logs decompose, the bank has reestablished itself and no longer needs structural support. Fiber fascine—a bundle of live cuttings wired or lashed together and secured, usually at the toe of a bank at or near the water edge—was developed for this purpose as well (Fig. 9.18). The fiber fascine allows a maximum of flexibility, strength, and permeability, much like an established mass of roots might. The materials are lightweight and easily handled and provide an effective medium for encouraging root growth.

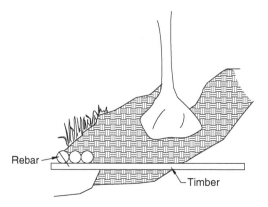

FIGURE 9.17   Timber bank restoration detail.

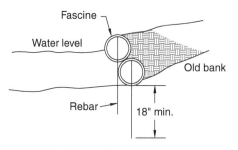

FIGURE 9.18   Fiber fascine bank restoration detail.

The fascine is used in conjunction with other stabilization methods but is an excellent bank protection method for stabilizing the toe of slopes, especially where there is outflow from the bank or where water levels fluctuate. The fascine allows water to pass through it and provides protection and stabilization even before the cuttings become established. Fascines are not used where surface water or drainage will run over them. If cutting materials are locally available, the fascine is fairly inexpensive and is easy to install but requires knowledgeable installers. The flexible, sausagelike character of the fascine allows it to be fitted to the conditions found in the field. Fascines are constructed from plants that root easily such as willows. Cuttings are bundles with all butt ends in the same direction and are wired together every foot to foot and a half. The cuttings are usually 2 to 3 ft long.

Establishing Stream Bank Vegetation

Stream bank vegetation provides mechanical stabilization of the bank by its roots and acts to absorb some of the energy of flooding. If there is substantial traffic (pedestrian or agricultural) or a great deal of shade from overhanging trees, it is sometimes difficult to reestablish vegetation on eroded or damaged stream banks. Of course, the newly planted bank is subject to damage by floods and periods of significant rain until it is established. Generally speaking, the strategies for reestablishing vegetation are limited to planting cuttings or seedling of woody plants or direct seeding. Within the general strategies are a variety of methods, including live stakes and branch packing.

Live Stakes

Live stakes are, as the name suggests, living woody plant cuttings that will tolerate cutting and still be capable of quickly establishing a new root system. They are usually fairly sturdy and will withstand being lightly driven into the stream bank. The live stake is substantial enough to withstand light flooding and traffic and will develop into a fairly robust shrub or tree in short order. Even live stakes, however, will not resist much traffic or active erosion. It is a fairly common strategy because it is inexpensive if cuttings are locally available, it takes little time or skill to install, and, if done properly, it results in a permanent solution. Live stakes often are not sufficient in themselves to stabilize a stream bank or to reestablish effective vegetative cover, and they are often used in conjunction with other methods. Live stakes are most effective on fairly moderate banks with a slope of 4:1 or flatter. They are installed in stabilized original bank soil, not on fill.

Live stakes of 1/2 in. to 1 1/2 in. diameter and from 2 to 2 1/2 ft long are installed during the dormant season and at low water (Fig. 9.19). Stakes are alive with bark intact and branches removed. The butt end is usually cleanly cut at a 45-degree angle. The top end is cut flat to facilitate driving. Live stakes should be cut with at least two bud scars near the top to promise growth and development. All cuttings should be fresh and moist and not stored for more than a day prior to installation. It is preferable that live stakes be installed the day of cutting.

Branch Packing

Branch packing is often used to stabilize small, washed out sections of a bank. Branch packing involves filling a washed out or excavated area with alternating layers of soil and live branches. It requires quite a bit of material and labor. Branch packing is used for relatively small areas, rarely larger than 10 to 15 ft long, 5 or 6 ft in width, and no more than 4 ft deep. The method has been used underwater. Branch packing is done during the

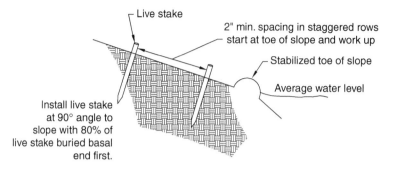

Live stake

2" min. spacing in staggered rows
start at toe of slope and work up

Stabilized toe of slope

Average water level

Install live stake
at 90° angle to
slope with 80% of
live stake buried basal
end first.

FIGURE 9.19   Live stake installation detail.

dormant season and when water levels are low. Branches may vary in size ranging up to 3 in. in diameter. Branch length varies with the size of the washout and the point of installation, but all stakes would be long enough to extend from the stabilized face of the new slope back into the original bank soil as shown in Figs. 9.20 and 9.21.

A cribwall, using logs, is a more robust version of branch packing. This method is used in areas larger than those branch packing might address or in places where strong currents reduce the effectiveness of other methods. The cribwall is a rectangular structure of logs and backfill similar to branch packing, but the materials tend to be larger and heavier. Construction involves preparing a foundation 2 to 3 ft below the existing stream bed. The first logs are placed parallel to the direction of flow, with the second series perpendicular to the first, and so on with each successive layer installed at right angles to the preceding one until the crib is about 60 percent of the finished height of the bank. Each layer of logs should slightly overlap, similar to the construction of a log cabin. Logs should be at least 6 in. in diameter and should be secured in place using rebar driven through drilled holes at the corners. Since the cribwall is used in areas where strong currents or high flows are expected, the leading and trailing edges should be protected with riprap.

As the structure rises, it is filled with a soil and gravel mixture (Fig. 9.22). At the top of each log facing the stream, install live cuttings. The size of the cribwall structure may limit the opportunity to bring the live stake in touch with the original bank material. In that case, the live stake should be securely driven into the fill material at a slightly downward angle.

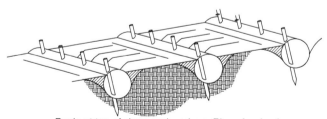

Begin at top of slope and work up. Place fascine in
shallow trenches (approx. as deep as diameter of
fascine). Pin fascine in place using live stakes.
Cover with soil and tamp.

FIGURE 9.20   Branch packing detail.

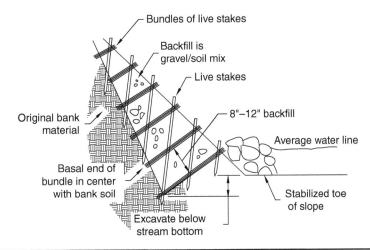

FIGURE 9.21   Branch packing alternative detail.

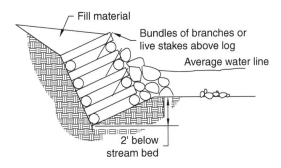

FIGURE 9.22   Cribwall detail.

Nonvegetative Bank Stabilization

Sometimes a vegetative bank is not a practical option, either for natural or anthropogenic reasons. Such cases require stream "hardening" and the use of different strategies. For the most part, this type of hardening does not refer to the capture and channelization of streams into concrete troughs. Gabions and deflectors are two ways to accomplish this task.

Gabions

Gabions are rock-filled wire baskets that are wired together. Although gabions require heavier construction methods than do live stabilization methods, they can provide effective bank stabilization. The great weight of the stone structure creates a gravity mass that is designed to resist expected flows. Once installed, they create a permeable, somewhat flexible, and stabile structure. Live plantings or live stakes can be added to offset the structural, unnatural appearance.

Gabion walls are keyed into place below the stream bed and are installed during periods of low water. For installations using live cuttings, the gabion must be installed during the dormant season as well. Many combinations and dimensions can be specified for gabions, so the designer can select the best combination for a particular site.

FIGURE 9.23   A gabion stabilized stream.

Gabions are usually referred to as baskets or mattresses. Baskets tend to be fairly box-like; that is, they come in lengths of 3 ft and heights ranging from 1 to 3 ft. Mattresses are fairly flat, usually less than a foot high and 2 or 3 ft wide; they come in lengths up to 12 ft.

The installation of the gabion involves keying in the first layers of the structure. The bed is excavated and compacted to prevent settling and slumping. The gabion is set into place empty, then wired together and filled with stone in 1-ft layers (Fig. 9.23). If the filled basket requires a slight adjustment, it is usually winched into place. Baskets usually are filled with 6- to 8-in. stone, whereas mattresses use smaller ballast of 3- to 4-in. stone. Geotextile fabric is placed between the gabion and the backfill when water is expected to seep through the gabion or when erosion might occur. Gabions have been used as walls or as armor on slopes.

Deflectors

Stream flow deflectors are used to divert flow away from an eroding bank or to deepen a channel (Fig. 9.24). They are fairly simple to construct, and many have been installed by local conservation groups to improve habitat and stabilize streams. They can provide protection from bank erosion by directing the stream's energy away from an area. Deflectors can have a negative impact on streams if not carefully designed and installed. Diverting or concentrating too much flow may increase erosion downstream. Many deflectors are built from logs that must be replaced periodically. Deflectors are ineffective or even harmful on narrow or very fast streams or for stabilizing banks at deep pools.

FIGURE **9.24**   A stream flow deflector.

The objective of most deflectors is to direct the current away from a bank and into the center of the channel. The deflector must be substantial enough to resist the energy of the stream at various levels of flow. The most common design involves constructing a triangle with 30-degree, 60-degree, and 90-degree angles, with the short leg facing downstream and the long leg anchored to the bank. Deflectors can be built of logs or stone. In either case the materials must be heavy enough to stand up to anticipated flows. Most deflectors have a fairly low profile, which allows high flows to pass over them. Logs are anchored in place and to each other using 1/2- to 5/8-in. steel rods or rebar driven at least three feet into the stream bed. Log deflectors are usually filled with stone after construction.

Regardless of the type of construction, the deflector should be keyed into the stream bed and bank. The stream bed should be excavated at least 1 to 2 ft, and the deflector should be keyed into the bank at least 6 ft. Gabions may also be used.

Wetlands

Wetlands are areas inundated or saturated by water often enough and long enough to support vegetation that is typically adapted for life in wet soil conditions (Fig. 9.25). Wetlands play an important role in the hydrologic cycle and are very productive environments. Nutrients collect in wetlands, and wetlands generally display a great deal of

Figure **9.25**   A natural wetland.

biodiversity in plant and animal life. Wetlands are identified by the presence hydric soils, the prevalence of hydrophytic vegetation, and the hydrology necessary to support the vegetation. Hydric soils are identified by color and include gleyed soils typical of wetlands (dark clays) as well as rich organic soils. Hydric soils are developed under sufficiently wet conditions to support the growth and regeneration of hydrophytic plants. Hydric soils develop under conditions of saturation in which the soil is flooded or ponded long enough during the growing season to develop anaerobic conditions in the upper part.

Wetland hydrology is usually identified as areas ranging from saturated soils (within 18 in. of the surface) to soils submerged up to 2 ft. The most important source of water for most wetlands is groundwater. Hydrophytic vegetation can live in water or on a substrate that is submerged or at least anaerobic part of the time.

Wetlands can be tidal or nontidal, forested, scrub-shrub, or emergent. More than half of the wetlands in the continental United States were lost between 1700 and the mid-1970s. Approximately 100 million acres of wetlands remain. Coastal wetlands make up only about 5 percent of U.S. wetlands; the remaining 95 percent are inland wetlands. It has been estimated that 43 percent of the threatened and endangered species in the United States rely directly or indirectly on wetlands for survival, and 80 percent of the breeding bird population require bottomland hardwoods for survival. These wooded swamps are found primarily in the southeast. Some 22 states have lost at least 50 percent of their original wetlands, and from the mid-1970s to the mid-1980s wetlands were lost at a rate of 290,000 acres per year (U.S. EPA, 1991).

A study of the Charles River in Massachusetts compared conditions with and without 8422 acres of wetlands within the Charles River Basin and predicted the annual flood damage without wetlands would exceed $17 million (Massachusetts Office of Energy and Environmental Affairs, n.d.). In this case, the Corps of Engineers elected to preserve the wetlands rather than engineer and construct a large flood control facility. Wetlands act to stabilize collected sediment by mechanical action of roots that dampen wave action and retard runoff water velocity.

The Congaree Bottomland Hardwood Swamp acts as a water treatment facility to remove toxic sediment and excess nutrients; the least-cost substitute water treatment plant to replace this swamp would cost $5 million. In the Chesapeake Bay a riparian forest within an agricultural watershed was shown to remove 80 percent of the phosphorus and 89 percent of the nitrogen from agricultural runoff before the water entered the bay. It is estimated that 71 percent of the value is derived from species that use the wetland in some manner during their life cycle. A study in 2004 by the Worldwide Fund for Nature estimated that each acre of wetland generates the equivalent of $5582 per acre in economic value associated with recreation fishing, hunting, and so forth. Waterfowl hunters spend more than $500 million annually. Bird watchers and photography of waterfowl is worth $25 million each year. Results of human impacts are the obvious loss of animals and plants, increases in erosion, loss of water storage capacity, loss of infiltration, and a general loss of water quality as the system is unable to clean water naturally (Forest and Range, n.d.).

Section 404 of the Clean Water Act requires permits for the discharge of dredged or fill material into "waters of the United States" and "wetlands." The 404 program is administered jointly by the Corps of Engineers, which issues permits, and the EPA, which retains oversight and veto power. The program allows for two types of permits: individual and general. Individual permits are provided for special circumstances not covered by the array of general permits and are subject to fairly intense review. General permits, or nationwide permits (NWPs), are provided for many of activities incidental to development that are perceived to represent, collectively, relatively minor impacts. NWPs are available for maintenance (NWP 3), utility crossings (NWP 12), minor road crossings (NWP 14), stream and wetland restoration activities (NWP 27), reshaping existing drainage ditches (NWP 41), recreation activities (NWP 42), and storm water management facilities (NWP 43). It is important to maintain awareness of the current state of public policy on these issues because these regulations continue to be defined and redefined by federal court actions.

Wetlands are mapped by the Department of the Interior using high-level infrared photography; soils maps can also be used to identify hydric soils, but wetlands are delineated in the field. Delineators determine the number and general location of transects through the site to be delineated. Shallow excavations are made to determine whether hydric soil conditions are present. Vegetation around each sample location is surveyed to identify the predominant types of trees, shrubs, and forbs. Delineators keep copious field notes and usually establish a photographic record of conditions. Based on the field conditions, delineators interpolate between nonwetland and wetland areas to find current limits. Hydrologic conditions may vary from year to year, but soils and mature vegetation tend to be reliable indicators of wetland conditions.

Constructed Wetlands

Because much of the hydrology associated with wetlands is groundwater in nature, it is difficult to create wetlands. Key to the long-term success of creating a wetland is the design of the hydrologic element. Choosing a location is critical. Finding a location that has the hydrology or can be adapted to have the hydrology necessary can be a challenge. Likely areas are adjacent to existing wetlands or where significant other earthwork is being undertaken, such as for a highway clover leaf, so that the new hydrology can be designed and built in (Fig. 9.26).

Selected sites should not be subjected to significant grading due to the loss of soil structure associated with those activities. Supplementing the existing soil with hydric soils has been successful in helping to establish vegetation and micro flora and fauna in the built wetland.

Wetlands are natural sinks of surface waters and nutrients that act as natural filters and water treatment systems; these areas may offer important capabilities to designers. When organic matter from livestock waste decomposes in water, oxygen is depleted, potentially suffocating the natural aquatic life. The biological oxygen demand (BOD) of untreated animal waste is about 100 times that of treated wastewater from a sewage treatment plant. Today, wetlands are being built especially to collect and treat wastewater and runoff.

Since 1988 wetlands have been created in the United States to collect and treat runoff from feedlots and barnyards. One experiment in Texas used a series of specially designed wetland cells and a 10-acre-ft, 100-day retention time created wetland to treat

FIGURE 9.26 A wetland created in a highway clover leaf.

all of the wastes from a 400 to 450 cow dairy operation. Solids are collected in a holding tank and the system is flushed twice each day into a primary wetland cell; the water moves via gravity to a second cell in about 10 to 12 days. Clean water is eventually collected into a pond and used to irrigate fields and for gray water uses in the dairy operation. The system can also accommodate a 10-year storm without any impact on operations. Cost of construction was less than $10,000, compared with a minimum of $25,000 for a wastewater treatment lagoon system.

Though the wetlands are characterized by vegetation, it is not the plants in most cases that clean the wastewater. Rather, the plants provide the oxygen and habitat for a variety of bacteria and microorganisms that break down the solids. The plants use the released nitrogen as a primary nutrient.

Constructed wetlands have been notorious for having problems and for failure, and this should be kept in mind during the planning process. Restoration of wetlands has been more successful in practice. In areas where wetlands have been filled or drained, the original hydrology and hydric soils may still be present and able to be restored. In many cases, desirable native plant seeds and materials remain viable as a sort of seed stock in the soil. Careful site evaluation using historic topographic maps can reveal former elevations and drainage patterns to restoration designers, but successful restoration usually requires more than simply removing fill or filling the drainage ditches. In other cases, simply stopping the drainage from a former wetland is all that is necessary to begin the restoration process.

Restoration projects require careful planning, and realistic performance goals should be established. The performance goals provide a clear measurement of project progress and success. Without clear quantitative measures, it may be difficult to determine whether the effort and cost has been worthwhile. The professional should clearly identify benchmarks of progress and success to demonstrate the value of the work to current and future clients. A successful restoration project will ultimately assume a natural appearance, and many may think the restoration was simply a matter of "nature healing itself" when in fact it is the result of careful design and implementation by a restoration professional.

In most cases, the wetland will probably serve multiple purposes in the landscape. Among the functions a wetland can be restored to address are habitat, storm water collection and treatment, flood buffer, stabilization of riparian or littoral zones, water treatment, and recreation. Each purpose adds its own concerns and requirements to the restoration project.

Restoration Planning

A high-functioning wetland is an extremely complex system, which is probably beyond our current ability to design from scratch. Most restoration designs understand and rely on the system's capacity to add complexity to itself as it matures. We may not be able to design or build such a system, but we are able to measure it.

The supporting hydrology is critical to the wetland's success. Wetlands draw water from several sources, including groundwater, tidal water, runoff, and precipitation. Whatever the water source, variations in supply must not be so great as to deprive the wetland of water for too long a period. Understanding the water budget of a restored wetland is a critical part of planning. A careful assessment of the amount, timing, and character of the available hydrology should be the first order of business in a restoration evaluation. Surface waters should be carefully assessed in terms of pollutant and sediment loading. The source of surface water should also be understood. Storm water runoff is generally not considered to be an acceptable sole source for a wetland although exceptions to this guideline exist. Such a project may benefit from lining the project area to reduce infiltration. A rule of thumb is that for every acre-foot of water in the wetland, there should be about 7.5 acres of contributing watershed for projects east of the Mississippi. West of the Mississippi evaporation rates are much higher and precipitation rates generally lower, so more contributing watershed is necessary. Wetlands using only surface water as a source are particularly subject to damage during droughts and other seasonal effects.

A natural spring, a pond, or groundwater is usually considered to be the best source of supply for a wetland restoration. Springs and seeps are often subject to disturbance during construction and should be protected if they are intended to be used to supply the wetland. Seasonal high and low water tables should be carefully evaluated to understand the nature of the available hydrology. Wetland restoration is further complicated by salt content in many western soils. Riparian or littoral zone wetlands enjoy a ready source of water from both the surface water and the interflow of groundwater.

Too much water may be as much a problem as not enough. A project located low in a watershed may have to include control structures to manage high-flow situations and to retain water on the site. The expected water loss must also be considered. Annual and monthly precipitation data is collected from the U.S. Weather Bureau or agricultural stations and compared to evapotranspiration. This comparison is available from the Natural Resources Conservation Service or the National Climatological Center. The precipitation to evapotranspiration comparison is expressed as a P/E ratio. This is simply a measure of the amount of water that would evaporate from an open container; the P/E ratio is sometimes called the pan evaporation ratio. In addition to the P/E ratio, designers should factor in any expected loss from infiltration through the soils. Wetlands typically have soils with a very high organic content and retain a substantial amount of water; as much as 50 percent of wetland soils can be water by volume. This allows the wetland some moisture buffer in periods of low water availability.

Grasses play an important role in most natural wetlands and vary usually in accordance with the depth and duration of flooding. The best source of information for which grasses are best suited for an application is to observe other functioning wetlands in your area. Table 9.6 is a partial listing of plant types according to the preferred depth of water.

Wetland Protection

Regulatory restrictions protect wetlands, but much of the damage to wetlands occurs due to changes in the contributing upland area. To reduce the impacts of development on downstream wetlands, storm water should be managed to retain as much water on a site as possible by minimizing practices that result in runoff and using features to increase infiltration (see Chapter 8). If storm water is going to be discharged into a wetland, it is best to use many small outlets or gabion-type outlets to disperse the concentrated discharge and reduce its velocity. Buffers should be planted between the discharge point and the wetland to filter and provide some "polish" to the discharge. In some cases a wetland might be constructed to act as a filter.

Scientific name	Common name	Distribution
Seasonal Flooding		
Bidens spp.	Beggarticks	Alaska to Quebec to most of the south including most states
Echinochloa crusgalli	Barnyard grass	
Hymenocallis spp.	Spider lily	
Lysimachia spp.	Loosestrife	
Hordeum jubatum	Foxtail barley	
Polygonum lapathifolium	Pale smartweed	Saskatchewan to Newfoundland to Texas and North Carolina
Iris fulva	Red iris	
Setaria spp.	Foxtail grass	
Spatina pectinata	Prairie cordgrass	
Panicum virgatum	Switchgrass	
Calamagtris inexpansa	Reedgrass	
Distchlis spicata	Saltgrass	
Alopecurus arundinaceus	Foxtail	
Scolocarpus fortidus	Skunk cabbage	
Hibiscus moscheutos	Swamp rose mallow	California to Massachusetts, Texas to Florida
Seasonal Flooding to 6 in.		
Leersia orzuides	Rice cutgrass	
Juncus effuses	Soft rush	
Carix spp.	Sedge	
Eriophorum polystachion	Cotton grass	
Cyperus spp.	Sedge	
Iris virginicus	Blue iris	
Iris pseudacourus	Yellow iris	
Dulichium arundinaceum	Three-way sedge	
Beckmannia syzigache	Sloughgrass	
Panicum agrostoides	Panic grass	
Scirpus cyperinus	Woolgrass	
Habanaria spp.	Swamp orchids	
Cypripedium spp.	Lady's slipper	
Hydrocotyle umbellate	Water pennywort	

TABLE 9.6   Wetland Plants According to Preferred Water Depth (*Continued*)

Seasonal flooding to 6 in.		
Calth leptosepaia	Marsh marigold	
Phalaris arundinacea	Reed canarygrass	Alaska to Newfoundland, California, New Mexico to North Carolina
Polygonum coccineum	Swamp smartweed	British Columbia to Quebec, California to South Carolina
Polygonum pensylvanicum	Pennsylavania smartweed	
Flooded from 6 to 20 in.		
Polygonum amphibium	Water smartweed	Alaska to Quebec, California to New Jersey
Cladium jamaicensis	Sawgrass	California to Virginia, southern states
Acorus calamus	Sweetflag	
Calia palustris	Water arum	
Zizania aquatica	Wild rice	Manitoba to Nova Scotia, Texas to Florida, Washington to Alberta, difficult to establish from seeds
Alisma spp.	Water plantain	Southern Canada to southern USA
Glyceria pauciflora	Western manna grass	Alaska to south Dakota, to California and New Mexico
Typha latifolia	Wide-leaved cattail	Alaska to Newfoundland, to the southernmost USA
Typha angustifolia	Narrow-leaved cattail	Washington to Nova Scotia, to southern most USA, most common in northeastern USA
Typha domingensis	Southern cattail	California to Delaware near coasts
Typha glauca	Blue cattail	Washington to Maine, common in central New York and along Delaware and Chesapeake Bays
Scirpus fluviatilis	River bulrush	
Saggittari latifolia	Broadleaf arrowhead	British Columbia to Quebec, to southern most states
Pontederia cordata	Pickerelweed	Minnesota to Nova Scotia, Texas to Florida
Glyceria spp.	Mannagrass	
Nasturtium officinale	Watercress	
Peltandra cordata	Arrow arum	
Vaccinium macrocarpon	Cranberry	
Juncus balticus	Saltmarsh fimbristylis	Coastal salt marsh, New York to Florida

TABLE 9.6 Wetland Plants According to Preferred Water Depth (*Continued*)

Flooded from 20 to 75 in.		
Potamogeton pectinatus	Sago pondweed	
Ranunculus flabellaris	Yellow water buttercup	
Ranunculus aquatilis	White water buttercup	
Phragmites phragmites	Phragmites	Nova Scotia to southern most USA
Deschampsia cespitosa	Tufter hairgrass	Coastal marshes Alaska to California, east to south Dakota and North Carolina
Scirpus validus	Softstem bulrush	Alaska to Newfoundland to southernmost USA
Myriophylum	Milfoil	
Elodea	Water weed	
Zizaniopsis miliacea	Giant cutgrass	Illinois to Maryland, Texas, and Florida
Nuphar luteum	Spatterdock	Alaska to Newfoundland, California to Florida
Floating		
Lemna spp.	Duckweed	Alaska to Quebec, California to Florida
Azolla spp.	Water fern	
Spirodela spp.	Giant duckweed	

TABLE 9.6 Wetland Plants According to Preferred Water Depth (*Continued*)

Erosion Damage

Damage caused by erosion is often difficult to repair because the impacted area is usually subject to repeated episodes of erosive flows of water. Simply replacing eroded materials generally is not sufficient to stabilize the eroded area. In most cases it is necessary to excavate the eroded channel, as shown in Fig. 9.27, and new materials must be tamped in place. For areas with velocities that exceed the ability of the soil to resist shearing, it is necessary to provide at least temporary geotextile protection. Some sites may require permanent protection. Similar steps are required for eroded slopes. It may also be necessary in some cases to divert the runoff from the area disturbed during construction and even for a short time thereafter.

Brownfield Redevelopment

The practice of reusing previously developed sites has become more common in recent years due to a more favorable public policy environment. Often these sites are referred to as brownfields. They are generally thought of as abandoned sites or properties significantly

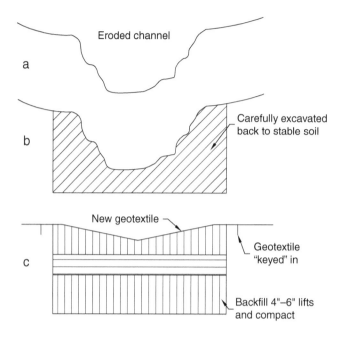

a

Eroded channel

b

Carefully excavated
back to stable soil

c

New geotextile

Geotextile
"keyed" in

Backfill 4"–6" lifts
and compact

FIGURE 9.27   Eroded channel repair detail.

underused and undervalued because of environmental contamination or the general perception of contamination. The definition is ambiguous and can include many sites with little or no significant environmental issues.

The risk associated with owning contaminated property was exacerbated by the Comprehensive Environmental Response Compensation and Liability Act (CERCLA), often referred to as Superfund, which made landowners liable for contamination found on the property whether the landowner had caused the contamination or not. Purchasers became appropriately wary of buying a property that might be contaminated and might elect to purchase an undeveloped site instead (Fig. 9.28). In the past property owners vigorously sought to keep their property from being referred to as a brownfield, but with the advent of financial incentives it is sometimes considered to be a favorable designation today.

In January 2002 President Bush signed the Small Business Liability Relief and Brownfields Revitalization Act (SBLR) into law. This law modified the federal policy on brownfields and increased the resources available for brownfield assessment and revitalization. The law changes the definition of a brownfield to "real property the expansion, redevelopment or reuse of which may be complicated by the presence or potential presence of a hazardous substance, contaminant or pollutant." A number of important changes in the law deal with funding, municipal waste, and support for state programs. Other important changes in the law that may be of immediate interest to site planners and designers include the bona fide prospective purchaser defense and the contiguous property owners' exemption.

FIGURE 9.28   A brownfield site.

The CERCLA statute provided purchasers who could demonstrate they acquired the property without any knowledge of the presence of contamination with the "innocent landowner" defense. As the viability of brownfield redevelopment increased under progressive state laws, the federal laws lagged behind. Although agreements between states and the relevant federal agencies allowed the states to offer various protections to developers of brownfields, these agreements lacked the weight of law. SBLR addresses this directly by providing the bona fide prospective purchaser defense. Under the statute, a purchaser who learns of contamination in the process of performing the prepurchase due diligence may still purchase the property without acquiring CERCLA liability if the purchaser meets the conditions outlined in the law. The contiguous property owners' exemption provides a defense for owners of land adjacent to a contaminated site.

Site development practices sometimes must address residual contamination as part of the site development. The state of brownfield practice is to determine a management and design strategy that will manage the risks associated with the contamination at an acceptable cost-to-benefit ratio. On such sites environmental issues must be accounted for in the construction phase as well as on the built site. Most states have voluntary cleanup programs (VCP) or brownfield programs of one sort or another. Since this is an emerging and developing area of practice, the elements and success of these programs vary significantly. The shift in public policy is to encourage development in communities where these places exist and to bring private money to the cleanup process. The interest from the private development community is based on whether there is a good real estate deal on the table.

A complete analysis of the various state programs is beyond the scope of this book; however, common elements of state programs usually include some form of protection from liability for past acts or contamination, predictability in cleanup standards and processes, risk-based standards for assessment and design, and financial incentives.

Liability Protection

State programs may provide buyers with protection from the liability of the state Superfund program. Since state laws do not offer protection from federal liability, many states have entered into memorandums of understanding (MOU) with the federal agencies. Through the MOU, the federal government essentially acknowledges the state program and agrees to honor its arrangements with developers.

Liability protection from the state program is managed in several different ways. Some states provide a document that acknowledges the state's agreement not to pursue any further action on the site. Letters of cleanup completion may serve the same purpose. Under some programs the state agrees to assume liability for contamination, in essence standing between the property owner and the risk of undiscovered acts of the past. These protections may be restricted to new purchasers and may not be available to existing landowners under some programs.

Planning the Redevelopment of a Brownfield Site

Brownfields present a greater challenge to planners than sites unencumbered by contamination issues. The presence or concern for the presence of hazards on a site may complicate even routine planning decisions involving the use of the soil on the site, grading, storm water management, and construction methods. For example, whereas storm water infiltration strategies might be encouraged on a "green" site, they may be discouraged or even prohibited on a brownfield site to prevent leaching of contaminants. Grading may be restricted to avoid exposing certain areas to weather or require daily stabilization. Each brownfield site will have a unique combination of restrictions and concerns, so planners must seek out a full understanding of the issues early in the program. As long as site assessment continues, there is the likelihood that additional information will come to light that could affect the planner's work. It is not uncommon to continue to learn about site issues even as construction is under way. Planners should be aware that development of brownfield sites usually involves consideration of concerns from a variety of stakeholders ranging from adjacent landowners to state and local regulatory agencies, the larger community, lenders, environmental or community advocates, and of course the client.

Cleanup Standards

Among the concerns of property owners and buyers is the uncertainty of cleanup standards. It is difficult to determine a comprehensive standard for site cleanup that is not so conservative as to be impractical in most cases. The most successful programs have provided developers with a menu of choices ranging from very conservative standards such as the Safe Drinking Water Act's maximum contaminant levels to standards based on risks and specific site conditions. A range of choices allows the developer to prepare a strategy that balances the site issues and the resources. In general, more stringent standards are costlier but result in greater risk reduction. A site with a very small amount of contaminated material might choose to use the most stringent standards available because the liability relief provided is worth the expense. Properties with more contamination may elect to follow a less costly approach but will have to manage the risk of on-site contamination.

In general the faster a remedial action provides results, the more expensive it is. For example, removing contaminated soil from a site and properly disposing of it off site offers a relatively quick and final solution to the contamination problem, but it can be very expensive and the owner retains some future risk. Capping a site is a frequently used strategy; it can be cost-effective and implemented fairly quickly, but all of the contamination remains in place. Bioremediation or phytoremediation may be very effective and have much lower costs, but these processes tend to be much slower, often requiring extended and difficult to predict time frames. Planners must consider the liability risk, the initial and life cycle costs of the remedial strategy, and the resources available to accomplish the task.

Risk and Risk Management

We routinely assess risk in our daily lives by weighing the risks or potential costs of an action against some benefit. We proceed or not based on whether the probable benefit is greater than the potential cost. Determining environmental risk is a scientific process of evaluating adverse effects of lifestyle choice, exposure to a substance, or some specific activity. There is always a degree of uncertainty in risk assessment because our efforts are limited by how much we know or the accuracy of what we know. Uncertainty in this case refers to a lack of precision in the numbers, so risk is most often expressed as a range rather than a specific number.

The risk assessment process for environmental contaminants is fairly straightforward, usually consisting of four steps beginning with a clear definition of the problem. Since all possible issues and risks cannot be simultaneously considered, narrowing the questions is critical to being able to measuring the risk. One source of risk is usually considered at a time, although efforts to evaluate multiple sources or materials have been increasing. The next step is to determine the amount of exposure a person would have to a substance: how much is inhaled, ingested, or absorbed? The length of time of exposure, the pathway of exposure, and how the chemical behaves in the environment are evaluated. The actual toxicity of the substance is known from evidence gathered through animal studies, in vitro studies, comparison studies, and epidemiological studies. Studies of animals are not the same as studies on humans, and for environmental risk assessment purposes extrapolation of such studies is not an acceptable practice.

Site designers are likely to become involved with risk as part of the project review or public hearing process. Understanding the dynamics of risk communication is an important skill in such circumstances. Foremost is the need to understand and expect public outrage and anger. People become angry when confronted by risks imposed upon them by others. The language and concepts of environmental risks are unfamiliar and outside the control of the public in many cases. Confronted with uncertainty, an emotional response is common. People are concerned about the likelihood and the effects of exposure. They will want to know the legal standards and what the health risks are.

Risk must be communicated carefully. Information should serve to help people understand and evaluate risk. Risk communication includes communicating what is not known and providing people with as much information as is available to answer their questions and concerns. There is a tendency to communicate risk in familiar terms to help people understand, but caution should be used when using comparisons. Comparisons of involuntary and voluntary risks, for example, are to be avoided. Lifestyle risks such as smoking or drinking are voluntary and are not valid comparisons with risks that have been imposed on someone. Presumably the person assumes a voluntary risk because of some perceived benefit that is greater than a risk. Involuntary risks are rarely balanced

One part per million	One automobile in bumper to bumper traffic from Cleveland to San Francisco
	One pancake in a stack four miles high
	1 in. in 16 mi
	1 oz in 32 tons
	1 cent in $10,000
One part per billion	One 4-in. hamburger in a chain of hamburgers circling the globe at the equator two and a half times
	One silver dollar in a roll of silver dollars from Detroit to Salt Lake City
	One kernel of corn in a 45-ft high, 16-ft diameter silo
	One sheet on a roll of toilet paper from New York to London
	1 second of time in 32 years
One part per trillion	1 ft^2 in the state of Indiana
	One drop of detergent in enough dishwater to fill a string of rail road cars 10 mi long
	1 in.^{2} in 250 mi^2

TABLE **9.7**   Concentration Analogies

with a benefit. Concentration analogies can help people understand quantitative measures such parts per million or parts per billion (Table 9.7).

Like any presentation, risk communication should be carefully planned and prepared with an understanding of the target audience. Information should be presented in an easily understandable and concise format. It is important that risks be clearly addressed and not downplayed. The presentation should acknowledge uncertainty where it exists. Above all, it is important to be accurate, complete, and honest. The presentation should be sensitive to voluntary and involuntary risks and avoid inappropriate comparisons. All questions should be answered, if not during the presentation then with a follow-up contact. Misinformation is sure to evolve in the absence of accurate information.

General Strategies

The strategies for brownfield projects, listed in a general order of increasing cost and liability relief, are usually limited to doing nothing, using administrative or institutional controls, using engineering controls, on-site remedial action, or off-site disposal or treatment. Although doing nothing may be desirable, it is not often an option on a site that is actually contaminated in some way. Administrative or institutional controls include steps that restrict the use of the property in some way. These include restrictions on what activities may be conducted on the property, restricting access, or other considerations. Owners might have to carry specific insurance or provide some kind of performance bond.

Engineering or technical controls refer to strategies such as caps and active or passive remedial action strategies. Engineering strategies are usually directed toward isolating or containing the contamination or treating it in some way over a period of time that continues after construction. Engineering solutions differ from a remedial action plan that treats the material to acceptable levels before construction begins.

A broad range of technologies and strategies are available for on-site treatment. Table 9.8 lists some common remedial technologies; however, it is not an exhaustive list. Remediation technology continues to be an area of innovation and experimentation. Pump and treat methods are common for addressing groundwater concerns, and improvements in bioremediation techniques promises to increase the use of that approach. Methods such as vitrification, which increases the impermeability of soil either by adding cement or by heating and melting the soil, are less common primarily because of the expense. Phytoremediation and natural attenuation strategies are being used more often and will become more common as our experience with them grows. (See Chapter 10 for more information on bioremediation and phytoremediation.) The least common and most expensive method on a large scale is removing material from the site whether for disposal or treatment. In the case of disposal, the landowner maintains liability for material place in a landfill.

Solidification	Also called *vitrification* or *stabilization*. Removes water and changes the soil or solid media chemically to reduce permeability and transport of contaminants by percolation.
Soil vapor extraction	Used to remove VOCs from soil through the use of vapor extraction wells. Sometimes used in conjunction with air injection systems. Contaminants are volatilized and flushed in the air for treatment.
Incineration	Controlled burning of soil or solids to convert, degrade, or oxidize contaminants. May be done on or off site.
Bioremediation	Microorganisms used to degrade organic compounds in soils or groundwater. May be done in situ or ex situ. Many variations of techniques and methods.
Soil washing	Water is used to flush through soils or medium to flush contaminants out. May involve removing soils and using mechanical agitation. Additives may be used to increase the efficiency of the process.
Solvent extraction	Similar to soil washing but solvents are used to remove contaminant from soils or solid media.
Dechlorination	Chemical treatment to remove chlorine atoms bonded to hazardous chemicals. Hydrogen or hydroxide ions are used to detoxify materials.
Phytoremediation	Use of selected plants to remove or biostabilize contaminants in soil, sediments, or water.
Air sparging	Injection of air into groundwater to flush volatile contaminants, which are collected and treated by the soil vapor extraction processes.
Passive treatment wells	Barriers are constructed of reactive materials and installed in an aquifer to promote a chemical reaction between the barrier and the contaminant in the groundwater. An example might be a limestone barrier used to increase the pH of groundwater.

TABLE 9.8 Types of Remedial Technologies

Design Concerns

Brownfield redevelopment employs all of the techniques and materials normally used in site design. Depending on the site, some extraordinary steps or elements might be required. For most brownfield sites, design issues are limited to dealing with capped sites, installation of utilities in contaminated materials, the use of vegetation on an impacted site, drainage concerns, the risk of exposure to workers and users, and post-construction remediation issues. Soil conditions can be demanding. Many soils on brownfield sites are made land and consist of unconsolidated fills. Many soils have expansive characteristics (Fig. 9.29).

Development on a Capped Site

Development on a capped site includes some challenges for the designer. Constructing a cap on a site isolates and contains contaminated material from receptors and from natural transport mechanisms. Most development involves the installation of underground utilities and infrastructure that by definition penetrate the zone of contamination, so plans requiring the installation of utilities in contaminated materials should be

Figure 9.29   Note the unconsolidated fill and stained soil condition. (See also color insert.)

FIGURE 9.30 A lined foundation excavation. Note that worker protection may be necessary when working in similar soil conditions.

carefully considered. The best practice may be to isolate the utility trench or foundation excavation from the contaminated material by lining the trench with the cap material or another suitable alternative (Fig. 9.30). Caps are constructed of a variety of materials but most common today are the impermeable geotextiles that lend themselves to lining trenches and excavations (Figs. 9.31 and 9.32).

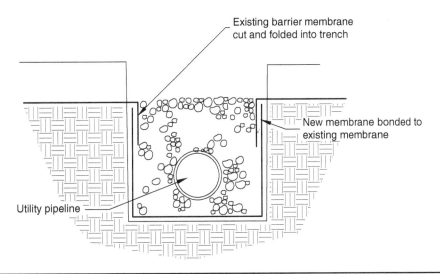

Existing barrier membrane
cut and folded into trench

New membrane bonded to
existing membrane

Utility pipeline

FIGURE 9.31 Lined utility trench detail.

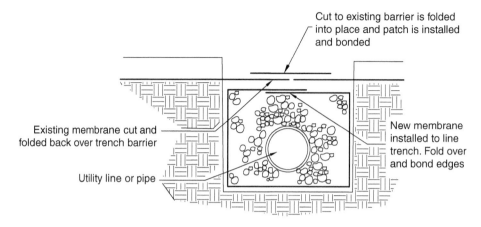

Cut to existing barrier is folded into place and patch is installed and bonded

Existing membrane cut and folded back over trench barrier

New membrane installed to line trench. Fold over and bond edges

Utility line or pipe

FIGURE 9.32 Lined utility trench detail 2.

FIGURE 9.33 A fully revitalized brownfield site, which can be both a source of tax revenues and an economic engine in a neighborhood. (See also color insert.)

Capped sites may restrict penetrations by plant roots as well as requiring the designer to treat the site as if it were, in effect, a rooftop. Rooftop strategies adapt well to capped sites for the most part. Caps are commonly designed and intended to be at least as permanent as the contamination itself. The practical fact of the matter is, however, that caps are under assault from natural processes from the moment they are installed and therefore require maintenance. The life cycle cost of a cap used as a parking lot will be higher than that of a typical parking lot. Potholes and cracks that might occur in the normal wear and tear on a parking lot may not be acceptable on a parking lot over a cap. Sites with clay caps rely on the expansive character of specific clays and require continuous moisture to maintain the integrity of the cap. Paving or introducing impermeable elements to the site with such a cap may have consequences for cap performance.

Managing storm water may also be a challenge. If the site is capped, infiltration methods may not be allowed on the site. In such cases it may be necessary to use less desirable management methods such as a lined detention basin. Pipes conveying storm water will have to be installed using tight, leak proof joints to avoid infiltration and exfiltration. Despite all of these considerations, a fully revitalized brownfield site is well worth the planning necessary to provide for its success (Fig. 9.33).

CHAPTER **10**
Vegetation in the Site Plan

P lants are an integral part of most site plans. Plants contribute to the aesthetics of a site, to its economic value, and to how a site functions. Numerous resources explore design and aesthetic values pertaining to plant use. This chapter focuses on the functional contributions of plants in the landscape rather than on the aesthetic or other intangible values of plants.

Planting Design

Planting plans are shaped by the underlying form of the site plan, but plants are not just window dressing. Plants contribute a great deal to the quality of our experience and to the character of a place. The choice and arrangement of plants can be used to frame views, to accent or to hide features, to direct pedestrian traffic, to create outdoor spaces, to invite, to repel, to provide comfort, to encourage motion or pause, and to modify scale or other environmental elements. Plantings may be formal or informal, simple or sophisticated, according to the objectives of the site.

Effective planting design is a synthesis of texture, color, line, form, and balance. Edges (or lines) can be defined in the landscape using plants, paving, reoccurring patterns, or grading. Landscape form refers to the mass and shape of the planting taken as a whole. Texture refers to the appearance of the form as gradations ranging from coarse to fine. Colors play a variety of roles in the landscape. Warmer colors such as reds, oranges, and yellows tend to appear closer to the viewer; blues and greens are cooler colors and appear to recede. In addition, colors evoke different emotional responses from people. Designers should be familiar with the use and effects of color in the landscape.

These elements are used in combinations to evoke a certain response or to provide a desired character to the project site. Designers employ repeating patterns, use light and shadow, symmetry and asymmetry, and use various materials in conjunction with plants to achieve the desired effect. In nature there are few straight lines, so lines appear to us as inherently human (Fig. 10.1). Planting plans using a symmetrical, balanced form with a central axis are referred to as formal designs. They are highly organized, speak to stability and structure, perhaps even authority (Fig. 10.2). Formal designs were preferred in the past, and many older styles of landscape design are fairly formal. Formal designs are often preferred in important symbolic civic landscapes because they convey a sense of importance to the space or place. Plants can bring an element of informality into otherwise rather formal spaces. The planted median shown in Fig. 10.3 brings an element of informality to this otherwise fairly formal boulevard. This is part of a neighborhood designed by Olmsted in Buffalo, New York. Figure 10.4 is of a common

FIGURE 10.1 These street trees reinforce but also soften the formality of the straight boulevard. The trees also serve to shade and cool the street and neighborhood.

FIGURE 10.2 The reflecting pool and Washington Monument are formal elements of a civil landscape that speak of stability and authority.

FIGURE 10.3   A formal boulevard in a residential neighborhood.

FIGURE 10.4   This formal space between condominiums is softened somewhat by the presence of trees.

FIGURE **10.5**   The formality of this space in a housing development for older persons contributes to orientation and way-finding.

space in a condominium community. The use of trees and shrubs serves to soften the otherwise hard formality of the space and provide cooling shade in the summer months. The formal aspects of the landscape in the housing complex for older adults in Fig. 10.5 contribute to orientation and way-finding by residents. This is highly organized but is composed of smaller, less formal spaces in which residents can meet or, if they choose, spend time alone. In Fig. 10.6 the formality of this site is accented by the strong lines within the pavements and the arrangements of trees and planting beds that direct the eye to the building. Note also that the distance provides for the addition of increased security elements should that be desired.

For most other current applications, less formal asymmetrical forms are more common. The asymmetrical design appears more natural and less austere (Fig. 10.7). Lines in the asymmetrical planting plan are still used to define space and provide way-finding information to pedestrians (Fig. 10.8). Asymmetrical, informal plantings tend to have softer edges and provide less definition (Figs. 10.9, 10.10, and 10.11). It is important to note, however, that asymmetrical designs still require balance. Large masses may be offset by a number of smaller groups of plants or a longer line.

Plantings are particularly good at directing attention and activity and are used in conjunction with other materials to identify a transition from one area to the next. A well-designed transition acts as a subtle signal to the observer and can be used to

FIGURE 10.6   This brick approach to a courthouse provides a fairly formal, highly organized public space clearly associated with the authority of the court.

FIGURE 10.7   This informal landscape at Niagara Falls, New York, contains strong lines and variation of texture and plantings, which provide visual interest, balance, and direction to the pedestrian. The apparent lack of organization adds to the interest of the site, but the underlying organization facilitates the visitor in finding the way.

FIGURE **10.8**   This strong edge provides clear guidance and direction to visitors to the National Zoo in Washington, D.C. Note the use of textures and colors. This restoration remains faithful to the original Olmstead design but serves the contemporary zoo visitor well. (See also color insert.)

"describe" areas as private or public, accessible or out of bounds (Figs. 10.12 and 10.13). Materials can be combined to create masses or lines that provide important signals.

Native Plants

The value of native species of plants and the damage that can be caused by exotics has brought a new awareness to landscape design and an increased interest in working with plants native to the area (Figs. 10.14, 10.15, and 10.16). Using native plants contributes to some degree to biodiversity, reduces or eliminates the need for pesticides and fertilizer, reduces maintenance costs, and may increase or improve habitat. Designs incorporating native species tend to be more natural in context; that is, they tend to use nature as a model and by doing so increase many of the landscape functions missing or

FIGURE 10.9 This residential landscape in South Carolina demonstrates the dramatic effects of texture, light, and shadow in a private space. (*Photo by Brent Baccene*.)

FIGURE 10.10 Plants on an arbor.

FIGURE **10.11** An informal landscape, composed of an eclectic collection of materials from Baltimore Inner Harbor, Baltimore, Maryland, is arranged in an informal fashion but provides visual interest and an inviting place for visitors to meet, sit, and rest.

FIGURE **10.12** Native plants and landscape features are used to separate this residence from the street.

FIGURE **10.13** This street tree signals a change in street width to drivers.

FIGURE **10.14** Native vegetation in a dryscape in El Paso, New Mexico.

FIGURE **10.15** A constructed pond using native plants in Napa, California.

FIGURE **10.16** The Petroglyph Provincial Park in Ontario, Canada, uses native plants to provide a more natural environment.

Figure 10.17   A nonnative species of tree used in a phytoremediation project.

minimized in other landscapes. Once established, native landscapes tend to require less care, less water, and fewer inputs because the plants have evolved to survive and even flourish in the extremes of a particular region or zone.

This being said, it should be noted that what is deemed a native plant versus an exotic pest is anything but precise. As plants extend their range, they necessarily move into new areas. Likewise, once plants are introduced to a new range, they begin to compete with those plants already resident. At what point does an invader become a resident? Many familiar plants are not native, but it would be difficult to imagine the landscape without them. They are as American as apple pie and have flourished in their new environments. Perhaps a species' impact is best measured not only by whether it is native but also by its contribution or function in the landscape (Fig. 10.17).

Exotic and Invasive Species

Awareness of native plants and the undesirable impacts of nonnative or exotic plant species have increased dramatically over the last 10 years. Thousands of exotic species are present in the landscape today, but attention is usually focused on the invasive species that if left unchecked displace native species. The threat from invasive exotic plants is expected to increase, and the damage to native plants will grow accordingly. Different exotic species thrive in different regions, and native plants continue to be displaced, extirpated, and even driven to extinction. Many of these undesirable species were introduced as landscape plants and continue to be sold in nurseries around the country.

Not all introduced plants are by definition undesirable or harmful. Apple trees, for example, are hardly a threat to native forests and have become part of our culture. When selecting plants for the landscape, designers should evaluate the impact of their choice of

Figure 10.18   Here Kudzu vines are enveloping the local vegetation.

materials on the environment (Fig. 10.18). Plants that spread and establish easily by self-seeding or spreading roots should be reconsidered. Groundcovers that establish and spread quickly should not be used where they may "escape" into adjacent open space. Such groundcovers should be confined by paved areas. Table 10.1 lists some common invasive plants and the regions where they can be found.

Using Trees in the Landscape

Trees bring numerous attributes to the site. Tree masses can have significant effects on microclimates by providing cooling shade, acting as filters for dust and particulates, and buffering undesirable sounds and sights.

Landscaping for Energy Efficiency

Energy efficiency can be improved by as much as 30 percent by properly selecting and locating plants. Plants contribute to cooling by shading buildings and cooling surfaces but also by the evaporative cooling associated with transpiration and the latent heat of evaporation. Properly located plants may reduce reflected light from the building surfaces and windows (Fig. 10.19). Sunscreens are most effective when located on the western and southwestern sides of buildings to reduce heat from the summer setting sun. Deciduous trees on south sides of buildings will admit winter sun but block summer sun. Medium to large trees located 15 to 30 ft from buildings are most effective. Trees should be planted one-quarter to one-third of their mature height away from the building (Figs. 10.20 and 10.21). Smaller trees may be planted closer, but dense planting near buildings may reduce desirable summer breezes. Buildings can also be cooled using arbors,

Common name	Scientific name	Region
Trees and shrubs		
Australian pine	Casuarina equisetifolia	southwest
Autumn olive	Eleagnus umbellata	widely distributed
Bradford pear	Pyrus calleryana	mid-Atlantic region
Burning bush	Euonymus alatus	mid-Atlantic region
Brazilian pepper tree	Schinus terebinthifolius	southeast
Camphor tree	Cinnamomum camphora	southeast
Chinaberry	Melia azedarach	southeast
Chinese tallow	Sapium sebiferum	southeast
Downy rose myrtle	Rhodomyrtus tomentosa	southeast
Empress tree	Paulwnia tomentosa	mid-Atlantic region
Honeysuckles	Lonicera spp. (including Belle, Amur, Morrow's, and Tatarian)	mid-Atlantic region
Japanese barberry	Berberis thunbergii	mid-Atlantic region
Japanese spirea	Spiraea japonica	mid-Atlantic region
Mimosa	Albizia julibrissin	mid-Atlantic region
Multiflora rose	Rosa multiflorum	mid-Atlantic region
Norway maple	Acer platanoides	mid-Atlantic region
Privet	Ligustrum species	mid-Atlantic region
Tree of heaven	Ailanthus altissma	mid-Atlantic region
Russian olive	Eleagnus angustifolium	mid-Atlantic region
Sawtooth oak	Quercus acutissima	mid-Atlantic region
Siberian elm	Ulmus pumila	mid-Atlantic region
Winged euonymus	Eounymus alatus	mid-Atlantic region
White mulberry	Morus alba	mid-Atlantic region
Vines and groundcovers		
Air potato	Dioscorea bulbifera	southeast
Bamboo (all)	Pseudosasa, Phyllostachys-Bambusa, Cenchrus ciliaris	southwest
Chinese wisteria	Wisteria sinensis	mid-Atlantic region
Climbing euonymus	Euonymus fortunei	southeast
Creeping bugleweed	Ajuga reptans	mid-Atlantic region
Crown vetch	Coronilla varia	mid-Atlantic region
English ivy	Hedera helix	mid-Atlantic region

TABLE 10.1 Some Common Invasive Plants

Common name	Scientific name	Region
Vines and groundcovers		
Fountain grass	Pennisetum setaceum	widely distributed
Japanese honeysuckle	Lonicera japonica	mid-Atlantic region
Japanese wisteria	Wisteria floribunda	mid-Atlantic region
Japanese climbing fern	Lygodium japonicum	southeast
Eurasian water milfoil	Myriophyllum spicatum	southeast
Garlic mustard	Alliaria petiolata	southwest
Giant salvinia	Salvinia molesta	southeast
Giant sensitive plant	Mimosa pigra	southeast
Hydrilla	Hydrilla verticillata	southeast
Kudzu	Pueraria lobata	southeast
Melaleuca	Melaleuca quinquenervia	southeast
Mint (all)	Mentha spp.	widely distributed
Old World climbing fern	Lygodium microphyllum	southeast
Periwinkle	Vinca minor	mid-Atlantic region
Purple loosestrife	Lythrum salicaria	widely distributed
Skunk vine	Paederia foetida	southeast
Torpedograss	Panicum repens	southeast
Water fern	Salvinia molesta	southwest
Water hyacinth	Eichhornia crassipes	southeast
Water lettuce	Pistia stratiotes	southeast
Wetland nightshade	Solanum tampicense	southeast
Winged yam	Dioscorea alata	southeast
Winter creeper	Euonymus fortunei	mid-Atlantic region

TABLE 10.1   Some Common Invasive Plants (*Continued*)

common throughout the world, and vines. Vines reduce summer heat by absorbing much of the light, and deciduous vines lose their leaves in the fall, allowing winter heat gain.

Planted windscreens also reduce the cooling of buildings in winter by redirecting or blocking winter winds. Evergreen trees located on the north and west side of buildings will screen winter wind. The effective distance of a windbreak from the building to be protected is about 30 times the vertical height of the screen, with maximum protection only within 5 or 6 times the height. A windscreen should be designed to be at least 60 percent dense all the way to the ground, especially on the windward side. Evergreen windscreens should be at least three rows thick, and deciduous windscreens should be up to six rows thick (Fig. 10.22).

An inevitable mixture of land uses results from development. Areas of transition from residential to commercial or industrial often require careful planning to offset the impact of conflicting uses. Using trees and other plantings to screen or buffer the

FIGURE **10.19**   The Moscone center, San Francisco, California.

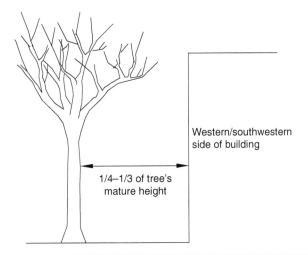

FIGURE **10.20**   Locating trees for building shading detail.

FIGURE **10.21** People have long known the advantages of strategically planting trees around their homes. These deciduous trees allow the winter sun in but provide cooling shade in the summer. (See also color insert.)

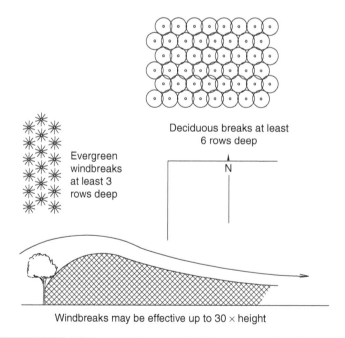

Deciduous breaks at least 6 rows deep

Evergreen windbreaks at least 3 rows deep

N

Windbreaks may be effective up to 30 × height

FIGURE **10.22** Windscreen design detail.

| 1. A visual screen to block unwanted views, to mask glare, or to direct the viewer to a particular feature. |
| 2. A barrier to deflect or absorb sound. |
| 3. A filter to collect airborne dust and particulates. |
| 4. Shade and protection from the sun for purposes of comfort and/or energy efficiency. |
| 5. A wind screen. |

TABLE **10.2**   Applications for Planted Screens

impacts of these areas is a common practice. Buffer plantings can be designed for a variety of purposes or for a combination of purposes (Table 10.2). To be effective, a planted buffer must be designed to accomplish the specific task or tasks required, and the selection of plant types and characteristics is a key element of the design. A poorly located row of trees can make a problem worse; directing a sound or diverting the prevailing wind to conduct a nuisance where it is not wanted.

Providing a visual screen is probably the most common purpose for buffers along residential areas. Blocking an unwanted view is usually accomplished by planting a simple row or rows of shrubs and trees. Care must be taken so plantings do not simply serve to frame the unwanted view rather than hide it. In addition to screening the unwanted view, the well-designed buffer can be used to reduce other intrusive influences such as highway noise or fugitive dusts from adjacent commercial or industrial sites (Figs. 10.23 and 10.24). Through the use of screens and buffers it is often possible to eliminate a negative off-site influence and enhance the desirability of a difficult lot.

FIGURE **10.23**   A planted landscaped buffer between a residential area and a shopping center.

FIGURE 10.24   Here a berm and trees are used as a buffer for an established residential area.

Tree masses have several significant impacts on their immediate environment. The shade from trees will lower temperatures by as much as 10 degrees from surrounding areas. Shade also reduces evaporation from the area affected. The combination of these effects is a localized reduction in the relative humidity. Of particular interest to the design of buffers is the size and location of plants to take advantage of this localized influence.

Plants with compact, tight growth patterns tend to be better screening plants. These plants create a dense, soft collection of surfaces (leaves) that absorb sound and provide for deposition and filtering of dusts. Several rows of trees are more effective than a single row, and several rows of combinations of different plants are more effective still. Increases in the density of the buffer can sometimes be accentuated even further through the use of graded berms to elevate the screen and provide a dense base.

A basic element of the design of buffers is the location of the buffer with regard to the source of the nuisance and the point of observation. Locating the screen is a site-specific consideration, but buffers are usually more effective if located closer to the source of the dust or noise. In the case of energy concerns, such as windbreaks or shade, the buffer should be located closer to the structure.

Sound attenuates over distance, so a sound buffer is more effective when placed closer to the sound source. This is also true of fugitive dusts or airborne particulates. The dimensions of the screen are also important. Width may be constrained by property limits, but ideally screens are not limited to single properties and extend as deep as required to be effective. The height of the buffer is also important. Although there is no formula for precisely determining the exact width and height of a buffer for a specific

FIGURE **10.25**   Plantings as part of a sound screen strategy.

use, careful thought and consideration of the nature of the nuisance should dictate the plan. Sound dissipates at a predictable rate over distance. Dusts and particulates settle out of the air at a predictable rate. By understanding these characteristics, a designer can effectively use the materials and site characteristics to the advantage of the project (Fig. 10.25).

In choosing plants, the design should specify plants that will mature relatively quickly and that will not become a maintenance problem. Plant materials chosen must be able to tolerate the nature of the nuisance, and the buffer must be designed with the impact of the seasons in mind. A solid wall of evergreens is not the only solution to screening issues. Although deciduous trees do not offer significant screening from views, sound, or dust in January, there may be little or no activity to be screened at that time. People tend to remain indoors in winter with windows and doors shut much of the time.

Distance can be used to some advantage by the designer to determine a blend of conifers and deciduous trees to provide sun warming in winter and shade in the summer. The plan might also include planting successive plant types. A combination of plants for a site might include fast-growing plants that would ultimately be removed and be replaced by slower growing but more desirable species over time. Table 10.3 provides some design considerations that should be addressed in the site design when screening is required.

The presence of mature trees on sites is generally considered to be desirable. In residential projects, people often pay a premium for a site with trees, especially mature trees. Designers may enhance the value or desirability of lots by saving existing trees. The decision to save or remove trees should be approached by carefully evaluating the health of the trees and the requirements of the project.

1. Locate the buffer close to a source of noise or dust.
2. The depth of the buffer mass should be relative to the strength or magnitude of the nuisance.
3. Combinations of plants are more effective than single types of plants.
4. Grading can be used to enhance the effectiveness and visual interest of the buffer.
5. Height of screen is as important as width or depth.
6. Buffer should be visually pleasing.

TABLE 10.3   Screening Design Considerations

Tree and Shrub Planting

Contemporary standards are quite different from the old tree pit planting method. Research has led to the modification of techniques and takes site conditions into account. Four different categories of planting have been identified: street, lawn, residential, and pit. These methods each represent a condition that is far different from estate planting, on which the old method was based.

The primary difference in these categories is the amount of soil space available to the tree. A great deal is known about the way trees grow and the requirements of growth. Most roots of trees are very small, ranging in size from a pencil thickness to a hair. These are the feeder roots that absorb and transmit nutrients and moisture to the plant. These roots grow *up* toward the surface to form mats in the first few inches of soil and grow and die back as a reflection of conditions near the surface. Root growth occurs in moist seasons, and dieback occurs in the hot dry summer and in cold winter months.

Whether existing or new, the fundamental need of healthy trees is adequate room to grow. When choosing a location for new trees, consider their size 5, 10, or 25 years from now. Where trees already exist, consider whether the location of proposed improvements may restrict growth or whether the growth of the tree may become a nuisance or cause damage. Landscape plants grow and change over time, and these living site elements should prompt some consideration of the impact of the plant over time in a given location. Selection of specific specimens should be done with a critical eye; look for trees with a straight trunk and well-balanced growth and symmetry throughout the plant. Trees with double leaders or deep Ys should be avoided. Bark should be intact and not swollen, cut, bruised, or cracked. Individual vitality can be quickly assessed by comparing the ball size, tree height, and caliper size.

Urban Trees

The average life span of city trees is less than 10 years. Some lessons can be learned from the causes of these tree losses. The single most common cause of city tree mortality is drainage. Tree pits along city streets or in some compacted urban soils are simply pots that have no drainage. Water collected in these pits does not drain away, and the tree drowns. Tree pits designed for city environments or environments with poor drainage should include a way to drain excess water from the pit (Fig. 10.26).

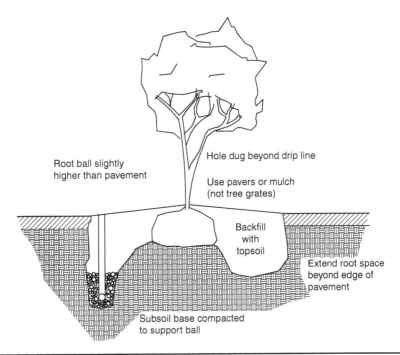

FIGURE 10.26   Urban tree pit detail.

Concerns that may influence your selection include exposure to pollution in urban environments. Even within a city or community, environmental quality can vary widely, so tree selection must vary as well. The surfaces of buildings and pavement absorb and reflect heat, which tends to cause droughty conditions in the urban tree pit. Table 10.4 lists some trees that do well in city environments.

Hedge maple (Acer campestre)
Norway maple (Acer platanoides)
Columnar maple (Acer platanoides 'Columnare')
Ruby horsechestnut (Aesculus carnea brioti)
Lavalle hawthorne (Crataegnus lavelli)
Washington hawthorne (Crataegnus phaenopyrum)
Russian olive (Eleagnus angustifolia)
Modesto ash (Fraxinus velutinum glabra)
Gingko (Gingko biloba fastgiata)
Thornless honey locust (Gleditsia triacanthos enermis)
Golden raintree (Koelreuteria paniculata)
Amur cork tree (Phellodendron amurense)
Red oak (Quercus boreallis)
Little leaf linden (Tilia cordata)

TABLE 10.4   Trees That Tolerate City Conditions

Structural soil can contribute to the health and longevity of urban trees. Structural soil is compacted to a degree that provides an effective subbase for paving, but the soil still allows for the penetration and growth of roots. Various mixes of structural soils have been suggested. One mix includes 25 percent silt from clay, 25 percent organic matter, and 50 percent sand with crushed stone (1/2 to 1 1/2 in.) at a ratio of four parts stone to one part soil mix. Others use less stone or more sand. Structural soil contributes to the health of the plant by providing a volume for the roots to expand into, and it reduces sidewalk heave expected as trees mature. In some cases polymer gels are added to the soil mix to absorb and hold water.

The next most common cause of tree losses is from mechanical damage from wire baskets, wire from staking, tree grates, or tree wrap. All of these devices are intended to support or protect the tree at some point in its move from the nursery to its ultimate location. If installed improperly or left in place too long, these devices can become the cause of tree death. All wire or wrapping around a root ball should be cut away to allow the roots to grow beyond the root ball without restriction. Even biodegradable materials such as burlap may remain in the soil years after the plant is installed.

Tree staking is a practice left over from the time when most planting was of bare root plants, and its usefulness today is debated. A balled specimen should not require staking; however, if stakes are used for plantings on slopes or for security reasons (to avoid plant theft), it should only be necessary for 6 months or so. Tree wrap is used to protect the tree from animals and vandals.

Tree grates are common in urban environments and are used to protect the tree from the damage of pedestrian traffic. The rings are designed to be cut back as the tree grows, providing room for the trunk. However, in today's cities with shrinking maintenance budgets, this is usually not done. One alternative to the tree ring is to install pavers over the tree root zone (Fig. 10.27). The pavers allow some water to penetrate to the roots and can easily be removed as the tree grows.

Creating continuous tree pits or troughs that extend the length of the street can increase the life expectancy of the trees and reduce the cost of replacing dead trees. Each tree root zone is connected to the others, and the pavement over this tree pit could be of pavers. Using pavers over these tree pits is a viable method both from a plant vitality standpoint and a long-term feasibility standpoint. Although some decrease in initial permeability may be noted, the long-term effectiveness of the paver system will only be nominally affected. A dimensionally small paver increases the number of joints and the permeability. A joint thickness of 1/4 in. filled with coarse sand contributes to infiltration. If a base course is used, it should be a mixture of coarse, noncompacting sand over crushed stone. The pavers should be installed with the primary joint running parallel to the contours to intercept more runoff (Fig. 10.28).

Selecting and Planting New Trees

It may be appropriate to remove the existing trees and replace them with new trees. Selecting a tree begins with selecting a site for the tree. Trees for lawns will be selected for different reasons than trees for a city street, and the purpose and desirable attributes of the tree species need to be evaluated. Although shallow rooted trees are ideal for city conditions, they tend to damage sidewalks and curbs and roots exposed to the surface are often damaged by pedestrian traffic. Tall trees may interfere with overhead wires. Some trees are grown for their shape or beauty and appreciation requires that they be viewed from a distance. The characteristics and constraints of the site must be recognized when

FIGURE **10.27**   Pavers over a root zone.

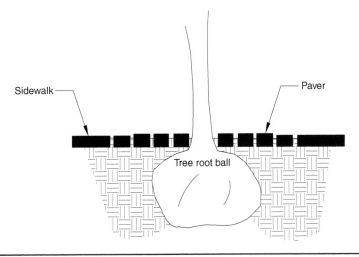

FIGURE **10.28**   Paver detail.

Intolerant	Some tolerance	Tolerant
Sugar maple	Birch	Mulberry
Red maple	Hard maple	Hawthorne
Lombardy poplar	Beech	Red oak
Sycamore	Balsam fir	Tamarix
Larch	Douglas fir	Russian olive
Viburnum	Blue spruce	Black locust
European beech	Green ash	Oleander
Spirea	Pyracantha	White acacia
Winged euonymus	Ponderosa pine	English oak
Black walnut	Arborvitae	Gray poplar
Little leaf linden	Eastern red cedar	Silver poplar
Barberry	Japanese honeysuckle	Osier willow
Rose	Boxelder maple	Bottlebrush

TABLE 10.5   Trees and Shrubs Tolerant of Road Salt

selecting trees. Fortunately there are many species and varieties of trees, and a good fit is usually available for most combinations of site and purpose.

Trees should be chosen with an understanding of the cultural requirements of the tree and the intended impact or value to the site. Nearly every book includes a list of recommended trees, and these lists often have a strong regional flavor, which can be valuable. Consult a knowledgeable local professional such as a local arborist, nursery staff, or landscape architect when selecting trees that will enhance the site and tolerate the conditions on the site. Some common trees that have specific tolerances or intolerance for road salts are listed in Table 10.5.

Preservation of Trees

Experience has taught builders that home buyers will pay a premium for a well-landscaped property. A lot with trees is viewed as more valuable and will bring a higher price on the market, and mature trees are viewed as the most desirable aspect of the residential landscape (Martin et al., n.d.; Wolf, 2007). Trees can increase the value of a residential property from $3000 to $15,000, depending on their size, condition, number, and location. Even the value of existing homes can be increased as much as 15 percent by the addition of trees and landscaping (Wolf, 2007). As home sites are developed, existing trees can add to the aesthetic as well as the economic value of the home.

Mature trees are often destroyed or damaged in the course of construction, and efforts to save a poor quality tree may cost more than the value of the tree. A careful evaluation of the site before construction begins is the first step to avoiding either of these mistakes. In many areas of the country, restrictions on tree removal are very tight. These projects may require a very tight building envelope, leaving the vegetation and

Most effected	Less effected	Least effected
Sugar maple	Birch	Elm
Beech	Hickory	Poplar
Dogwood	Hemlock	Willow
Oak	—	Plane tree
Tulip tree	—	Pin oak
Conifers	—	Locust

TABLE 10.6   Common Trees and Tolerance to Fill

earth outside the envelope undisturbed. These minimum disturbance restrictions are part of the sales appeal, and builders working on these sites are required to meet strict operating guidelines.

Trees are damaged from cuts and fills because the balance of air and water between the roots and the soil is disturbed. In some cases the disturbances weaken the structural base of the tree as well. Tree roots grow and develop partially as a function of the air and water available in a given soil. Soils on construction sites are generally left compacted and nearly impermeable from the trucks and equipment driving over them. Even without removing or adding soil to the base of a tree, the compaction from construction vehicles can damage trees. When a "blanket" of soil is added to the top of a grade, air and water are restricted from the root zone. Generally the deeper the fill, the greater the restriction. Other factors include the type and health of the tree and the type of soil. Some species of trees are more tolerant than others, and a healthy tree of any variety will withstand the stress of a fill better than a damaged or weak tree. Table 10.6 lists some common tree types and their tolerance to fill.

The soil is a dynamic ecosystem in which a complex relationship between microorganisms, organic matter, soil structure, and chemistry takes place. Fill soil texture is at best minimal because of the mechanical action of disturbances. Soil aggregates, or distinct clumps of soil that reflect the organic and mineral content and the beneficial effects of plant life and microorganisms, are an important factor in how a plant is able to grow. Soils with a fine texture or particle size, such as clays, have a greater impact as fills because their fine particle size fills available pore space through which air and water would travel to the tree roots. Even shallow fills of clay can severely damage a tree. Soils with a coarse texture, such as sandy or gravelly soils, cause the least amount a damage to trees because air and water move through the soil more readily. A shallow fill of several inches of gravelly soil, or soils of the same kind as the tree is growing in, generally have no long-term effects as the tree is able to compensate by extending its roots into the new layer. The upward extension of roots is more difficult in a deeper fill because of the loss of water and air and the absence of pore space.

Trees in Fill

Planning and constructing tree wells can save existing trees, but these trees should be chosen for their value and contribution to the landscape to justify the cost and effort of the tree well. Old or damaged trees may not offer the longevity necessary to justify the

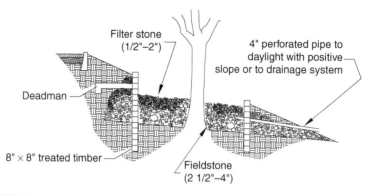

Filter stone
(1/2"–2")

4" perforated pipe to
daylight with positive
slope or to drainage system

Deadman

8" × 8" treated timber

Fieldstone
(2 1/2"–4")

Figure 10.29   Tree well detail.

additional expense; a young tree could be planted at less expense. The number, size, and quality of trees on a given site must be considered in making the decision to construct a fill protection. On a lot with many trees, the cost of saving one or two may not be attractive, whereas the cost of saving a specimen on a lot without any other trees is very attractive.

The site should be prepared before the grades are raised. All vegetation should be removed from the area affected and the soil worked. Fertilizer and soil additives should be added in accordance with specifications provided by manufacturers, nursery personnel, or a landscape architect. Once the soil is worked and the amendments have been introduced, care should be taken not to disturb the area with construction equipment or vehicles. The best method to protect the root zone is to isolate the area with a temporary fence. Tree wells must be designed to provide the tree with air and water and to provide drainage away from the trunk (Fig. 10.29). Some fundamental principles are common to all successful designs. To provide drainage away from the tree trunk and allow air to the area of the root zone, a series of 4- to 6-in. perforated plastic pipes is laid radially from the root zone. The drain tile should be installed with a positive slope *away* from the tree. The drain tiles should extend to or just beyond the drip line of the tree.

Once the drain tiles are in place, the well is constructed. The choice of material for the well can be varied. For shallow wells of 1 to 3 ft, bricks or stone can be used. These should be laid up in an open joint without mortar. This is sometimes referred to as a dry joint. A batter of at least 3 in. per foot should be provided. In deeper wells it may be necessary to construct the well with greater structural stability. In such cases timber tree wells are often used. These structures allow the use of stabilizing features, such as a "deadman" to be incorporated into the design (Fig. 10.30). In either case the well should allow for at least 2 ft of space from the trunk of the tree in all directions (Fig. 10.31).

A means of drainage at the drip line is often provided. This may be a series of drain tiles on end extending into a gravel or stone bed or an actual gravel or stone channel provided to direct water to the root zone. Once the tile and well are in place, a layer of stone 2 to 4 in. in diameter should be installed over the pipe and cultivated soil. This layer should not exceed 18 in., or 25 percent of the depth of the fill, whichever is least. It may be necessary to support the well or the drip line drain pipes with additional rocks. Figure 10.32 shows a tree well on a developed site.

Deadmen on 4' centers or as specified

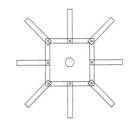

8" × 8" treated timber
5/8" reinforced bar vertical
through all members—5/8" rebar

All members to have
shiplap joint at corners

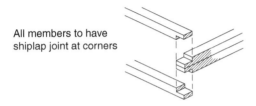

FIGURE **10.30**   Timber retaining wall tree well detail.

FIGURE **10.31**   A timber tree well.

The layer of rocks or stone must be of a material that will not react with the trees or soil chemistry in such a manner as to harm or inhibit the plant. The layer of rocks is covered with a finer "filter" stone to a maximum depth of 12 in., or to within a foot of the ultimate grade. A layer of straw or filter fabric is installed on top of the filter stone. This prevents the soil fines from washing into the spaces between the stones and rocks, at least

FIGURE **10.32** A tree in a tree well.

until the soil can begin to form some structure. Topsoil is then placed up to the finished grade. If vertical drain tiles were used at the drip line, these should be filled with small stones to prevent debris from filling and blocking the hole.

Trees in Cut

It is more difficult to protect a tree from a change in grade that involves removing soil from its base. If soil is to be removed, it is probable that some root damage will occur, including removal of some roots in the process. The roots most likely to be damaged or removed are the smaller roots on which the tree relies for feeding. The rooting characteristics of the tree have some bearing on the degree of impact the disturbance will have. Elms, for example, are deep rooting trees and will tolerate a modest change in grade. Shallow rooted trees, such as conifers, are difficult to save and protect in cuts. It is key to success that soil be removed by hand to minimize damage to the roots. Steps can be taken to reduce the damage by promoting new root growth at a lower level, but this requires at least one full growing season before the removal takes place and is rarely practical (Figs. 10.33, 10.34, and 10.35).

Site management during construction is required to ensure that the decision and efforts to save a tree are successful. Care taken during the construction process can minimize the risk of damage by subcontractors or careless operators. Clearly mark or identify specimen trees in the field using surveyor's tape around trees to be saved and marking trees to be removed with paint on the trunk. The next step is to communicate the plan to save the trees to the field crew so that everyone knows the plan. Other steps that can be used to protect the trees and implement the plan include installing temporary fences

FIGURE **10.33**   A tree in a cut.

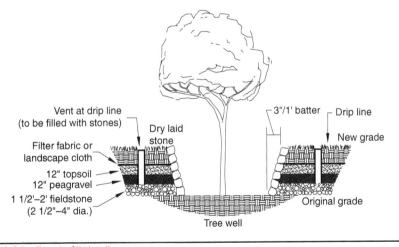

FIGURE **10.34**   Tree in fill detail.

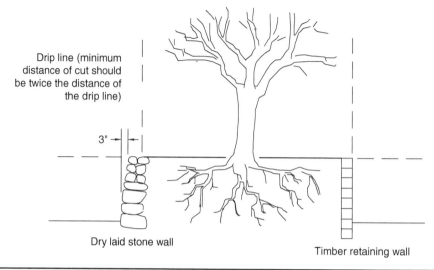

Drip line (minimum distance of cut should be twice the distance of the drip line)

3"

Dry laid stone wall

Timber retaining wall

FIGURE **10.35**   Tree in cut detail.

around the root zone or routing site traffic away from the specimen trees. Trees with low-hanging branches that are likely to be damaged should be pruned or the protective fence extended to encompass the low branches. Disposal and storage areas should be at least 50 ft away from the root zone.

Trees and Carbon Management

As concerns grow over the consequences of global warming, planting trees may emerge among the strategies used to offset the continuing increase in carbon dioxide in the atmosphere. As trees grow, they fix carbon dioxide in their biomass. Early studies indicate that trees can contribute significantly to accumulating carbon dioxide (Northern Institute of Applied Carbon Science, n.d.). If carbon management emerges as a strategy in the United States as it has in other countries, tree planting may represent a source of income in the form of pollution credits. A study of a tree planting program in Kitchener, Ontario, indicates that between 34.5 and 68.8 million lb of carbon dioxide is removed by its trees each year. This represents 20 to 40 percent of the carbon dioxide load of Kitchener (Doherty et al., n.d.). The value of trees and planned woodlands may grow in the next 20 years as a strategy to offset the impacts of development; however, some research indicates that the use of forests as a long-term carbon management strategy may be overestimated (Oren et al., 2001). As carbon dioxide levels increase, plants initially increase growth in response, but as these levels continue to rise, the robust response may level off.

Phytoremediation

Phytoremediation—using plants to clean up site contamination—has become more common as a brownfield remediation strategy. Phytoremediation is an umbrella term that includes several different approaches to cleanup. It is popular primarily because it is relatively inexpensive and can be both attractive and effective. The principal disadvantage lies in the time it may take to be effective.

Phytoextraction, sometimes referred to as phytoaccumulation, is a type of phytoremediation that relies on plants' natural capacity to absorb and incorporate specific materials into their tissues. Some plants are efficient collectors of metals such as lead, mercury, or nickel, and these plants are periodically harvested and either incinerated or recycled. Incinerated material may be recycled or placed in a landfill. The ash from incinerated materials represents a significant reduction in the volume of material that must be stored.

Phytodegradation, on the other hand, relies on the metabolism of plants to decompose certain contaminants once they are absorbed. Some plants produce various enzymes and acids that cause the decomposition of contaminants; other plants are able to absorb organic materials and volatilize the material into the atmosphere through the processes of respiration. Rhizosphere biodegradation occurs around the plant roots rather than within the plant. Substances released into the soil around their root systems encourage the growth and development of communities of microorganisms that biodegrade the contamination. This approach has been shown to be effective against petroleum contamination in soils.

Some 400 plants have been found to be hyperaccumulators; that is, they will absorb and store contaminants, particularly metals. Mustard (Brassica juncea and Brassica carinata) is an effective accumulator of chromium and lead. Poplar, cottonwood, and willow trees have all shown promise in experiments in which the trees have been used to lower local water tables and reduce the degree of contact between groundwater and shallow contaminated soils. Hybrid poplar (Trichocarpa deltoides) has demonstrated the ability to absorb and break down trichloroethylene, as well as some other organic contaminants and some metals. In Europe poplars and willows have been successfully used as biofilters for various organic contaminants (Green and Hoffnagle, 2004). Phytoremediation has significant promise for site remediation, but many of these applications have been studied only under hydroponic situations and not under field conditions.

Other applications involve transgenic plants, which have been designed for the application at hand. This technology may be beyond the typical site development project's budget and schedule, but the products of this research have already begun to appear in the marketplace.

Phytoremediation is an important consideration in those places where it will serve, but much remains to be learned. If a project requires that remediation be completed prior to the redevelopment phase, the rate of improvement using phytoremediation may be too slow. However, if redevelopment and remediation can proceed together, such practices may present an important low-cost strategy. Table 10.7 lists some plants with known phytoremediation capabilities.

Bioremediation

Bioremediation is the use of micro flora or fauna to decompose or stabilize contaminants. Like phytoremediation, living organisms are used to remediate a site. Significant strides have been made in the bioremediation field. The most effective approach has been to identify organisms that exist on the contaminated site that are already at work on the contamination. Some of these organisms are collected and brought into a laboratory to determine the ideal combination of factors such as moisture, air, light, and nutrients to

Plant	Application	Contaminant	Medium
Hybrid poplar	phytovolatilization	trichloroethylene, metals	groundwater, soils
Poplar	phytovolatilization	carbon tetrachloride	groundwater
Willow var.	phytovolatilization	metals	soils
Birch var.	phytovolatilization	metals	soils
Alfalfa	phytoextraction	petroleum hydrocarbons	soil, groundwater
Juniper	phytoextraction	petroleum hydrocarbons	soil, groundwater
Fescue	phytoextraction	petroleum hydrocarbons	soil, groundwater
Clover	phytodegradation	petroleum	soil

Adapted from Milton Gordon, Stuart Strand, and Lee Newmoan, *Finale Report: Degradation of Environmental Pollutants by Plants* (Washington, D.C.: U.S. EPA, 1998), and *A Citizen's Guide to Phytoremediation* (Washington, D.C.: U.S. EPA, 1998).

TABLE 10.7   Plants with Known Phytoremediation Capabilities

facilitate the most ideal environment. Once determined, these conditions are re-created in the field. Bioremediation may take 6 months or more, and the site design may have to accommodate the necessary conditions during construction or perhaps even postconstruction. Table 10.8 lists some plant materials that may be useful for brownfield site cleanup projects.

Type	Characteristics
	Grasses
Bluestem, big, *Andropogon gerardi*, and little bluestem, *Schizachyrium scoparium*	Native to the eastern United States and prairie but has adapted to all regions. Warm season, perennial grass. Slow to develop, but established stands require little maintenance. Will tolerate poorly drained soils. Lower pH limit 4.5.
Buffalograss, *Buchloe dactyloides*	Warm season grass. Prefers loamy and clayey soils. Good drought resistance. Rapidly establishing sod former. Used in western states, Great Plains, and the southwest. Tolerant of saline-alkaline soils.
Tall fescue, *Festuca arundicae*, and cultivars	Adapted to acid or alkaline soils, droughty and wet soils, soils of sandstone or shale origins. Good for channels with intermittent flows, drought resistant. Cool season bunch-type perennial grass. Lower pH limit 4.5. Moderate rate of establishment. Kentucky-31 cultivar widely used to reestablish vegetation and stabilize surface mining sites. Low aluminum tolerance.
Switchgrass, *Panicum virgatum*	Adapted to infertile and saline soils, short lived in northeastern United States. Grows best in mixtures with birdsfoot trefoil; variety "Blackwell" is used widely on mine sites. Moderate aluminum tolerance. Lower pH limit 5.0. Adapted to wet and dry soils.

TABLE 10.8   Plant Materials for Brownfield Sites

Type	Characteristics
Grasses (*Continued*)	
Reed canarygrass, *Phalaris arundinacea*	Good for drainage swales and gullies, tolerates saline-alkaline soils. Cool season, sod-forming perennial grass. Lower pH limit 4.5, moderate rate of establishment. Widely adapted but thrives in northern half of interior United States.
Deertongue grass, *Paricum cladestinum*	Native cool season, perennial grass. Acid tolerant, drought resistant, adapted to infertile soils, strong volunteer characteristics. Moderate to slow establishment. Lower pH limit 4.0. High aluminum tolerance.
Rye, *Secule var.*	Annual cool season grass with rapid rate of establishment. Used as a quick cover with companion grasses with slower rate of establishment. Widely adapted to all regions of the United States. Lower pH limit 4.5.
Annual ryegrass, *Lolium multiflorim*	Annual cool season grass with rapid rate of establishment. Survives well on coarse sandy soils, temporary cover only. May compete with companion species. Lower pH is 4.5. Low aluminum tolerance.
Perenial rye grass, *Lolium perenne*	Perennial cool season grass with rapid rate of establishment but short lived (2–3 years). Does not successfully reseed itself. Used as a companion grass to others with slower rate of establishment. Lower limit pH 4.5. Low aluminum tolerance.
Redtop, *Agrostis gigantean*	Cool season perennial grass with moderate to rapid establishment rate. Sod forming, spreads by rhizomes. Relatively short lived and will give way to companion grasses with slower establishment rates over several years. Lower pH limit 4.5 to 5.0. Low aluminum tolerance.
Timothy, *Phleum pretense*	Cool season perennial with a moderate rate of establishment. Best adapted to cool humid northern half of the United States. Relatively short lived (5 years). Recommended that it be sown with legumes. Lower pH limit 4.0. Moderate aluminum tolerance.
Forbs and legumes	
Alfalfa, *Medicago sativa*	Perennial, cool season legume with a moderate to rapid rate of growth. Best adapted to the northern half of the United States. Adapted to performance on nonacid, fertile soils. Lower pH limit is 5.5 but does best nearer 7.0.

TABLE 10.8   Plant Materials for Brownfield Sites (*Continued*)

Type	Characteristics
Forbs and legumes (*Continued*)	
Crownvetch, *Coronilla var.*	Perennial cool season legume. Lower pH limit 5.0. Slow rate of establishment (3–4 years). Rate of establishment is slowed by lower pH. Will provide continuous, maintenance free cover once established. Moderate aluminum tolerance.
Common lespedeza, *Lespedeza striata var. Kobe*	Warm season annual legume. Tolerant to high levels of manganese in soils. Quick rate of establishment. Limited geographic adaptation, however. Lower pH limit 4.5.
Serica lespedeza, *Lespedeza cuneata*	Warm season perennial legume with slow rate of establishment. Lower pH limit 4.5. Moderate aluminum tolerance.
Trees and shrubs	
Red osier dogwood, *Cornus stoloifera*	Native shrub best suited for moist areas along drainage swales or ponds. Dense root system good for establishing banks. Tolerates light shade. Lower pH limit 4.5. Grows to 6 to 15 ft (1.8–4.7 m).
Silky dogwood, *Cornus amomum*	Native shrub. Tolerates shade better than Red osier dogwood and is more tolerant of acid soils. Lower pH limit 4.0. May be started from direct seeding. Grows to 10 ft (3.1 m).
Indigobush, *Amorpha fruticosa*	Native widely adapted legume shrub with intermediate tolerance to shade. Lower pH limit 4.0. Native to the eastern United States. Used successfully in mine site stabilization. Slow rate of establishment. Excellent soil conditioning characteristics because of nitrogen fixing capability. May be started from seed. Not used above 2500 ft.
Autumn olive, *Elaegnus umbellate var.*	Native legume shrub, intermediate tolerance to shade. Adapted to eastern states. Lower pH limit 4.0.
Viburnum, *Viburnum spp.*	Native shrubs, lower pH limit 4.0. Nanny berry, *V. lentago*, and mapleleaf viburnum, *V. acerfolium*, more tolerant of acid soils than others. *V. cassinodes* and *V. acerfolium* tolerant of dry sites. Low salt tolerance.
Trees	
Loblolly pine, *Pinus taeda*	Native conifer. Lower pH limit 4.0. Fast growing and adapted to a wide range of soils.
Scotch pine, *Pinus sylvestria*	Conifer, greatest natural range of any pine. Grows well in many different conditions, wide variation in appearance and tolerances depending on the source of the plant. Does well in dry to somewhat poorly drained conditions.

TABLE **10.8** Plant Materials for Brownfield Sites (*Continued*)

Type	Characteristics
Trees (*Continued*)	
Black locust, *Robinia pseudoacacia*	Native hardwood tree. Nitrogen fixer, can be seeded directly, adapted to wide variety of soil conditions, good leaf litter, but should be used in mixtures. Good salt tolerance, not desirable near residences, rapid rate of growth.
Red maple, *Acer rubrum*	Native hardwood tree adapted to wide range of soils: wet to dry, fine to coarse. pH limit 4.0 to 7.0. Grows best in well-drained loamy soils. May be multistemmed. Wide range. Low salt tolerance.
Silver maple, *Acer saccharinum*	Native hardwood tree adapted to a wide range of soils: wet to dry, fine to coarse. pH limit 4.0 to 7.0. Grows best in well-drained loamy soils. May be multistemmed. Wide range. Resistant to effects of soot and smoke.
River birch, *Betula nigra*	Native hardwood tree. Adapted to poorly drained soils, may be used where soils are too acidic for other trees. Lower pH limit 4.0.
Hackberry, *Celtis occidentalis*	Tolerates soil pH to 5.0, tolerates soils from poorly drained to well drained.
Gingko, *Gingko bilboa*	Resistant to effects of soot and smoke, tolerates city conditions well.
Red oak, *Quercus rubra*	Tolerates city conditions well. Good salt tolerance.
London plane tree, *Platanus x acerfolia*	Resistant to effects of soot and smoke.
Honey locust, *Gleditisia traicanthos*	Resistant to effects of soot and smoke, tolerates city conditions well.
Norway maple, *Acer platinoides*	Tolerates city conditions well.
Hawthorn, *Crataegus spp.*	Good salt tolerance.
Hybrid poplars, *Populus spp.*	Crosses of native and introduced species. Performance of varieties varies from region to region, local knowledge may be best reference. Lower pH limit 4.0. Some species used in bioremediation.
Gray dogwood, *Cornus racemosa*	Rapid growth, tolerates wide range of soil conditions including wet soils, colony former.

TABLE 10.8   Plant Materials for Brownfield Sites (*Continued*)

Meadows

Natural meadows are preferable to lawns for their function and for their low life cycle costs. Meadows are usually mowed only once in the fall, and they provide important habitat and forage. The meadow functions as an important element of local water quality and is attractive. Nonetheless, sites using natural landscapes have been singled out and criticized by some for their "wild" look. Some communities have taken action to limit or even restrict native meadows. To avoid an unpleasant response, some education of local officials and neighbors may be required when incorporating a meadow in a landscape design.

The popularity of native plants has resulted in an increase in growers and distributors of plant material suitable for meadows. Adequate stock is usually available, and many nurseries offer meadow mixes. It is prudent to understand the seed mixture before specifying or using it as meadows are complex plant communities. Seed mixtures should be evaluated for the number and type of specific species. The mixture should provide a combination of annual, biennial, and perennial plants, including native grasses. If continuous blooming is desired, the species should be assessed for bloom time. Native warm season grasses make up half to three-quarters of the plants in a natural meadow. These are clump-type grasses as opposed to the familiar cool season turf grasses. Warm season grasses tend to grow in the late fall and early spring and do not compete directly with summer germination and seeding of wildflowers. Care should be taken to minimize the use of plants that aggressively spread and that might affect neighbors. Figure 10.36 is a mature rooftop meadow; Fig. 10.37 shows a cross

FIGURE **10.36**   A rooftop meadow. (*Photograph courtesy of Roofscapes, Inc*. See also color insert.)

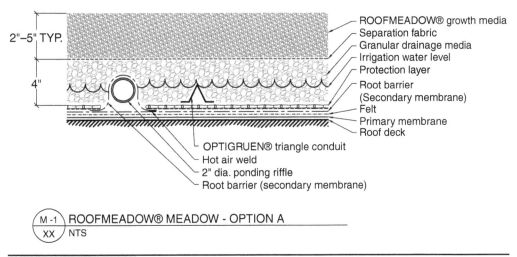

2"–5" TYP.

4"

ROOFMEADOW® growth media
Separation fabric
Granular drainage media
Irrigation water level
Protection layer
Root barrier
(Secondary membrane)
Felt
Primary membrane
Roof deck

OPTIGRUEN® triangle conduit
Hot air weld
2" dia. ponding riffle
Root barrier (secondary membrane)

M-1
XX

ROOFMEADOW® MEADOW - OPTION A
NTS

FIGURE 10.37 A green roof cross section. (*Detail provide by Roofscapes*, Inc.)

section for a green roof design; and Fig. 10.38 provides a look at a rooftop landscape. A meadow designed for a highway right of way is shown in Fig. 10.39.

The first few years of the meadow are the most intensive and costly. Noxious weeds and exotics must be removed by hand during this period and until the meadow can establish itself. For the perennials and grasses, the first years are spent growing extensive

FIGURE 10.38 A rooftop landscape. (*Photograph courtesy of Roofscapes*, Inc. See also color insert.)

FIGURE **10.39**   A meadow designed for a highway right of way. (See also color insert.)

root systems so the annuals will dominate the meadow. By the third year, the perennials and grasses have usually established their roots and begin to flourish.

Meadow site preparation varies. Seeding meadow plants into small prepared areas within an existing landscape will allow the small site to be established and naturally expand over time. Otherwise an area must be cleared of vegetation before seeding is done. An alternative to hand weeding is to water the area for a week or two before an application of Roundup, then repeat the process to collect any resident but newly germinated weeds; after the second round, apply the meadow seed.

Toxic Plants

The trend toward specialized landscapes has increased in recent years along with our appreciation for the natural beauty of landscapes. Specialized landscapes include therapeutic gardens, living laboratories on school grounds, scent gardens, gardens designed for the elderly, and many others.

Many of the plants commonly used in landscape planting pose some risk from toxicity. There are several poisonous plant databases on the Internet as well as Web sites that list plants of particular concern for various animals such as cats, dogs, or horses. Table 10.9 provides a list of common poisonous plants. This list is neither comprehensive nor species specific. Make an effort to become familiar with the toxicity of plants commonly used in your area, especially when working on landscapes or sites for a particular end user such as a day care center.

Common name	Botanical name	Poisonous part
Autumn crocus	Colchicum autumnalle	bulb
Angel's trumpet	Datura (some species)	seeds, leaves
Apricot	Prunus ameniaca	stem, bark, seed pits
Azalea	Rhododendron occidentale	all parts
Baneberry	Actaea spicata	berries, roots, foliage
Bleeding heart	Dicentra (some species)	all parts
Buchberry	Lantana	all parts
Buttercup	Ranunculus (some species)	all parts
Calla lily	Zantedeschia aethiopica	leaves, rhizome
Castor beans	Ricinus communis	seeds are toxic to dogs and cats
Choke cherry	Prunus virginica	leaves, seed pits, stems, bark
Daffodil	Narcissus	bulbs
Daphne	Daphne mezereum	berries, bark, leaves
Delphinium	Delphinium (some species)	seeds, young plants
Eggplant	Solanum melongena	all parts except fruit
Elderberry	Sambucus (some species)	roots, seeds (stones)
Euonymus	Euonymus (some species)	leaves, fruit, bark
Four o'clock	Mirabilis jalapa	roots, seeds
Foxglove	Digitalis purpurea	all parts
Hemlock	Conium maculatum	all parts, root and root stalk
Hens-and-chicks	Lantana	all parts
Hyacinth	Hyacinthus orientalis	bulbs, leaves, flowers
Hydrangea	Hydrangea macrophylla	leaves, buds
Iris	Iris (some species)	rhizome
Jerusalem cherry	Solanim pseudocapscium	all parts, unripe fruit
Jimson weed	Datura stramonium	all parts
Jonquil	Narcissus	bulbs
Larkspur	Delphinium (some species)	seeds, young plants
Lily family	(Many species of the lily are poisonous)	bulbs
Lily-of-the-valley	Convallaria majalis	all parts
Lobelia	Lobelia (some species)	all parts
Lupines	Lupinus (some species)	seeds
Mandrake	Podophyllum peltatum	roots, foliage, unripe fruit

TABLE 10.9 Some Toxic Landscape Plants

Common name	Botanical name	Poisonous part
Mistletoe	Phoradendron flavescens	berries
Monkshood	Aconitum napellus	all parts
Morning glory	Ipomoea violacea	seeds
Narcissus	Narcissus (some species)	bulb
Nightshade	Atropa belladonna	all parts
Oak	Quercus (some species)	acorn, young plant
Oleander	Norium oleander	all parts, including dried leaves
Poinsettia	Euphorbia pulcherrima	leaves, flowers
Pokeweed, inkberry	Phytolacca americana	all parts
Potato	Solanum tuberosum	green seed balls, green tubers
Privet	Ligustrum vulgare	all parts
Red sage	Lantana camara	green berries
Rhododendron	Rhododendron	all parts
Rhubarb	Rheum raponticum	leaves
Sedum	Sedum (some species)	all parts
Snow-on-the-mountain	Euphorbia marginata	sap
Spindle tree	Euonymus (some species)	leaves, fruit, bark
Sweet pea	Lathyrus odoratus	seeds, pods
Tansy	Tanacetum vulgare	all parts
Tulip	Tulipa	bulbs
Virginia creeper	Parthenocissus quinquefolia	berries
Wisteria	Wisteria	seeds, pods
Yew	Taxus	needles, bark, seeds

TABLE 10.9   Some Toxic Landscape Plants (*Continued*)

CHAPTER 11

Preserving Landscapes

Historic preservation is an important area of practice with its own sets of concerns. The value of historic preservation has become more apparent to communities with the rapid expansion of suburban areas and the effort to "renew" older parts of cities. Numerous laws, regulations, ordinances, and programs address historic preservation across the United States. In general these efforts are focused on the preservation of buildings and less often with concern for historic landscapes. Exceptions include areas of exceptional beauty or natural wonders that are preserved as parks or monuments and places of note such as the Gettysburg Battlefield or the birth of the woman's suffrage movement. As with other areas of site planning and design, work with historic landscapes requires familiarity with a set of underlying principles and is an area of expertise in itself.

Investigation of the Historic Landscape

On a typical site, the designer is trying to understand the limitations and opportunities of the site in order to modify the site for the intended purpose. When analyzing a historic site, some elements not normally part of the site analysis phase must be considered. The site analysis is an attempt to understand what has already been done to the site, how and why the site has been altered in the past, what role the landscape played in the past, and ultimately how to preserve, restore, or rehabilitate the landscape. Table 11.1 provides some fundamentals of historic landscape preservation.

A key difficulty of historic work is that historic values are often subjective. For example, finding compatibility between a historic site and the proposed use may be difficult when balancing preservation concerns with the desire to maximize use of a site. Even finding a clear time context can be difficult on a site with a great deal of history or with numerous "periods" of development. Historic landscapes range from the work of well-known designers for historical figures to places that are remembered for a significant event or person, from landscapes of cultural importance to places of natural beauty or ecological significance (Figs. 11.1, 11.2, and 11.3). Although it is recommended that the professionals maintain an objective view and approach to the site, the time context, and the project, this is often difficult. Very often there is no one right answer.

Many organizations and agencies have developed guidance documents to assist and even to prescribe the evaluation and treatment of historic landscapes. Projects utilizing public funding may be required to follow a specific set of guidelines or processes. Other resources may exist in the offices of local and state historic commissions or societies. Many sites have already had cultural or historic landscape reports prepared on them. These resources are valuable sources of information for the designer engaged in work on a designated site.

1. The historic character and nature of the site and the proposed use must be compatible.
2. A clear "time context" of the site must be developed to understand the historic period that is of importance for the site.
3. A comprehensive identification and assessment process must be completed to identify the distinctive elements of the site and how these elements are to be placed in the time context of the site.
4. Changes that have occurred over time and how the site is different now from the time of context should be noted. Care should be taken to determine whether these changes are important elements in their own right.
5. Restoration is preferred over replacement of an element, and stabilization and repair should be undertaken carefully.
6. If new work is to be done, it should be designed so as not to interfere with the character of the site. Any effort to introduce or maintain out of context elements' "fit" should be weighed and considered carefully.
7. The designer must maintain objectivity about the site, the time context, and the project.

TABLE 11.1   Fundamentals of Historic Landscape Preservation

FIGURE 11.1   A formal garden.

FIGURE **11.2**   A formal hedge and garden. (See also color insert.)

FIGURE **11.3**   A formal public garden, Longwood Gardens, Brandywine, Pennsylvania. (See also color insert.)

A fairly thorough history of a site is necessary to understand the appropriate time context of a landscape. Some landscapes may not be time sensitive, but others are associated with a specific period or series of events. Establishing the appropriate time context is critical to assessing the condition of the site from a historic sense. Some sites have fairly obvious time contexts, but others may have multiple contexts, making the selection of just one difficult or even impossible. In such cases the selection of time context may be a matter of some disagreement and involve input from a variety of sources. Determining the time context is rarely the business of the site design professional alone, but the professional should be aware of the site time context before design work begins.

A complete inventory of the site is necessary. Review all available records about the site, including plats and maps, diaries, articles, journals, local records, or any other source of information about the site. Even unsubstantiated "rumors" should be collected. A history of ownership such as a chain of title may be particularly important (Fig. 11.4). On larger sites, aerial photography may be a useful tool (Figs. 11.5 and 11.6). Historic aerial photography may provide important information for the site in the recent past. Current aerial photography sometimes reveals site features not seen from ground level.

Using a topographic map as a base, prepare a site map that includes the significant features of historic significance: show all buildings, foundations, fences, stone piles, tree masses, major or important specimen trees, surface water, outbuildings or appurtenances,

Figure 11.4   A historic home. Formal gardens once found at the site are believed to have been designed by Pierre L'Enfant.

Figure 11.5   Aerial photograph shows the location of the former L'Enfant garden.

road pathways , areas of fill or cut, and visible boundaries. The assessment is an effort to "read" the elements of lost landscape features. Old roads, foundations, unexplained grading, and masses of ornamental trees all tell a portion of the site's history. Trees were planted around houses to shade the house in summer or to provide a windscreen, but it was also common practice in some places to plant a tree to commemorate special events in the life of a family, a community, or the nation. For example, during the United States Centennial in 1876, many communities planted groves of "centennial trees." Landscape elements that sometimes appear disjointed or unorganized by modern standards may represent rational design choices of another time, the underlying form of the landscape hidden from modern sensibilities. During the site investigation, photographs of conditions and features should be collected. Visiting a site in low light conditions (early morning or toward sundown) often reveals patterns in grading and other site features not seen under other conditions. Exotic plants as well as important plant types and species should be noted.

FIGURE 11.6 The L'Enfant garden is no longer present in this contemporary aerial photograph.

The purpose of the site inventory is to identify the site features and to assess the integrity of the site: How much of the historic or important landscape remains, and how has it changed? Do the mature trees of today represent the character of the site in the past? Are the "old" features of the site in keeping with the time context of the site? Integrity must be defined by how much the site retains the character of the historic, natural, or ethnographic character of note. Is the site significant? Are the remaining features significant?

Using Photography in the Site Analysis

Photographs are important to site analysis in a variety of ways. Historical photographs may provide particular insight to past uses of property or help to locate features now lost. Old photographs may be found at local historical societies, libraries, public historical records, private collections, or in local government archives. The difficulty in using old photographs is usually the lack of information about the location being photographed or the location of the photographer. Very often clues can be found in the perimeter of the photograph; physical features like hills, chimneys, or buildings in the distance may still be visible from the site. Old photographs are particularly important if the site has important historical significance.

It may be helpful to use two cameras in the field, one using black and white film and one using color. If an attempt is made to compare current conditions with those shown in the old photographs, black and white film is necessary. Differences in camera equipment should also be considered. Some older cameras provided a wider field of view—as much as 120 to 160 degrees—than the field of view of modern cameras. When using historical photographs, it is important to remember the differences in equipment as well as the time of year and time of day the original was taken.

U.S. Landscape Style: An Overview

Public landscapes in the colonial United States were largely influenced by English and French traditions, but archetypal landscapes reflect the interpretation of the character of their new land through the experience and traditions of the new immigrants. Almost without exception, the planned landscape forms that emerged in colonial America included formal and geometric gardens. As generations came and went, new forms emerged that were adapted to the demands and materials of the new land and climate. Gardens were made to grow food. Land cleared from the wilderness or in town was at a premium, and simple forms were easiest to arrange and manage. More important than the aesthetics of such a landscape was its orientation to the sun, the quality of the soil, drainage, and proximity to water. Plants selected for such gardens were chosen for utility; what could the plant provide to the larder or the home pharmacy? The archetypal landscapes of the United States reveal much about the people who settled here: where they came from, how they embraced the land, and how they adapted to the new land. As much as the form and functions of buildings and architecture reflect the use of materials, adaptation to climate, and aesthetics tastes of their builders, the layout of homesteads and villages speak for the settlers. Buildings and spaces under such conditions were not oriented toward the public highway but toward the things that mattered most: sun, slope, water, and wind (Figs. 11.7 and 11.8).

Early political landscapes such as parks and government properties tended to be small by today's standards and were generally formal. The civic landscape represented the power of man, its formality clearly setting the works of man apart from nature. Private estates ranged from the formal designs favored in the seventeenth century to the more natural landscapes of the eighteenth century. The English first parted from the formality of the seventeenth century through the creation of landscapes portraying an Arcadian ideal; landscapes were designed as three dimensional paintings of scenes from a supposed Roman or Greek antiquity. This style abandoned formal features such as rectangular water forms, formal arrangements of shrubbery and flowers in favor of a more natural, although contrived, appearance. Water features were designed to have a natural, irregular appearance and to serve the landscape as an element incorporated into a whole design rather than as a discrete element such as a formal pool or fountain. This movement away from formal gardens and toward more natural appearing landscapes was championed by Lancelot "Capability" Brown. In Brown's vision, the landscape took on a pastoral

FIGURE **11.7** An early American homestead.

FIGURE **11.8** Another view of the homestead. Note the absence of intentional foundation plantings.

image that blended with the natural landscape but was as much the product of design as the formal gardens he eschewed.

Thomas Jefferson and other gentlemen of the time introduced the European ideas of landscape design to the United States. Pierre L'Enfant worked for many wealthy landowners, designing gardens and estate landscapes using both formal and informal styles and elements. Eventually many of the principles of Capability Brown's romantic landscapes were adopted in the United States. In England the new preference was for the natural sense of the Gothic landscape, using sweeping lawns and natural forms of lakes without an attempt to create a single scene. Although some aspects of the Arcadian tradition such as grottoes and ruins were used, the most notable aspect of the landscape of this period was its inherent naturalism. Frederick Law Olmsted and generations of garden and landscapes architects would eventually be influenced by the work of Brown. The most noted landscapes of this time were often criticized for being indistinguishable from the countryside. Much of the "natural" movement was lost on smaller urban properties, however, where a large expanse of lawn for the development of lakes and such was not practical. Small urban gardens tended toward simpler forms reminiscent of the formal gardens of the archetypal tradition or earlier more formal periods of design.

Andrew Jackson Downing was among the first professional American landscape designers. Downing was concerned that the landscape should improve the look of the house but not be too formal itself. His romantic landscape designs integrated the house and the surrounding landscape by ensuring that flowers and ornamentals could be viewed from within the house and that fragrances from the garden could be smelled and appreciated from inside. Downing's designs were a blend of the formal and informal; he planted flowers and shrubs in circular formal beds but felt that lawns should be bordered by informal curvilinear beds of shrubs and trees (Fig. 11.9). He liked informal arrangements of trees that framed or enhanced particularly good views. Downing influenced landscape and garden design throughout the middle of the nineteenth century, and his *A Treatise on the Theory and Practice of Landscape Gardening Adapted to North America* (1841) and *Victorian Cottage Residences* (1850) were arguably the most important gardening and landscape design books in the United States of their time and are still occasionally reprinted.

In the nineteenth century the design of large private and public landscapes and gardens moved away from the wild and natural forms of the eighteenth century and back toward some measure of formality. Where buildings and homes were placed in the landscape with little to separate the house from the lawn, beds of flowers, terraces, and ballustrades were introduced. Downing continued to advocate for the natural romantic style until his untimely death. Attempts to bring the romantic landscape style into smaller and smaller properties eventually led to its disintegration into random flower beds and specimen trees. About this time the availability of landscape plants increased significantly, and gardens were revised to include specimens from all over the world. This period could be said to have no clear distinctive style of its own, or it could be seen as a period of transition from the romantic to what would become the Victorian garden some years later. Artifice and formality were reintroduced to the landscape, and fountains, fences, and other features of formality were used by designers to make the landscape more inviting. Many large landscape and garden projects in the United States during this period called upon earlier European styles.

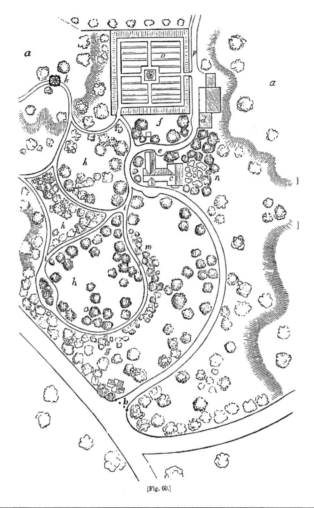

[Fig. 60.]

Figure 11.9 Site plan from *Victorian Cottage Residences*.

Frederick Law Olmsted started his practice in 1856 and was very much a student of the romantic style, but he was not limited to Downing's vision. Olmsted had studied the design of gardens and articulated his own vision of the landscape, firmly grounded in art and science. Olmsted was something of a social activist, with firm beliefs in the values of public landscapes for the quality of urban life. The development of Central Park in New York City, the Emerald Necklace in Boston, and similar park systems across the United States brought important urban open space to the city. Olmsted's designs went beyond the romantic style to produce working landscapes, which were designed to perform functions such as waste treatment and flood control while serving as a visual and social amenity. Public access to green space became an important element of city life because of the vision of many public leaders and the designs of Olmsted, Vaux, and others. Among the important lessons of the best work of this period is that landscapes so well designed and constructed are soon thought to be naturally occurring. It is forgotten that these great landscapes are the product of thoughtful design and that they may require maintenance or that to function properly it is necessary to manage and protect them. Many of the most important parts of these landscapes have been lost because they have matured into such a natural appearance that they are not well understood.

The Victorian garden, although rooted in the principles of Andrew Downing, emerged to embrace elements of many styles. It is an expression of its time—exuberance often expressed as fanciful, busy, even cluttered designs. The Victorian era of the late nineteenth century had the resources and the materials of the industrial revolution at its disposal. Victorian gardens might use one of many commercially available wrought or cast iron fences although wood remained most popular and least expensive. The style of Victorian architecture was to set the house high on a foundation, and foundation planting first became popular during this time. The period is also known for the introduction of many exotic species of plants. Plants were chosen for their textures and colors, and eclectic mixes of plants were common on the borders of lawns and in more formal beds. Exotic plants became fashionable; the more exotic, the more fashionable. Formal parterres, knot gardens, and rose gardens were popular features. In essence the Victorian garden was, like so much of the era, a statement of wealth and class more than anything else.

As with earlier gardening and landscape styles, most homes could not afford the embellishment of a fully developed Victorian garden. However, many homeowners adapted aspects of the fashion so that small formal gardens, statuary, exotic plants, and even fountains or gazing balls might be introduced into the yard. The common practice of shrubbery foundation and border plantings edged with flowers is from this era. During the Victorian era and well into the twentieth century, Gertrude Jekyll conducted her horticultural practice. Much of Jekyll's work reflected her interest in wild, self-sustaining landscapes. She contributed much to restoring the connection between the garden and nature that was lost in the Victorian era and in similar styles of her day. Her influence was felt for many years and is felt again in the current move toward self-sustaining landscapes and the use of native plants.

In *An Introduction to the Study of Landscape Design,* published in 1917, Henry Hubbard and Theodora Kimball observed that landscape design could be divided into two types: romantic or classical. Romantic landscapes were informal and full of contrasts; classical landscapes were formal and restrained. This eclecticism continued into the early twentieth century, but eventually a variety of styles emerged from the enthusiastic Victorian landscape along a continuum ranging from the natural or English landscape elements seen in some of the designs of Beatrix Ferrand to the "architectural" garden styles that employed patios, gazebos, ponds, fences, outbuildings, and other structural elements.

In the post–World War II era, suburban gardens and landscapes flourished, but few important styles or trends emerged from this era. Garrett Eckbo's work extended indoor living into the landscape, but for the most part suburban landscapes tended to mimic aspects of the Victorian or Downing garden. The estate lawn of the nineteenth century became an icon of the suburban good life, and entire industries have grown up in response to the desire for a lawn. Today the lawn is being reconsidered, and more regional and native landscapes are emerging as truly aesthetic and important forms.

Landscape architecture continued to mature and embrace a broader range of practice, from suburban homes and residential development to commercial and public spaces and landscape restoration. Building on its rich past, landscape architecture developed to freely employ formal and informal elements, and natural and more architectural styles, as suited the designer and the site. Site design has become a broad area of professional practice, including engineers, landscape architects, and others. The range of the profession has also grown, from traditional site development to new areas of practice and art. As both the design community and the public have become more aware and concerned with environmental issues, landscape architects and others have expanded the scope of professional practice to embrace landscape restoration in its many forms and to introduce sustainable development practices into their designs.

Planning

Planning for the historic landscape involves many tasks. In addition to the tasks of any site planning effort, concerns for the importance of the site as a subject in itself must be addressed. The historic research may or may not directly involve the design professional, but the inventory of the site features, site analysis, and site plan will. The project may include substantial documentation efforts as the site is disturbed as well as accounting for and avoiding the sensitive elements of the site in the plan. Site professionals will be part of a team in the development of the site plan. Table 11.2 lists the four objectives to be considered in historic landscape site planning.

Developing plans for a historic site requires a fairly thorough understanding of the site history and context. For site design purposes, a map of existing features is important. Confirm the feature map in the field for a first-hand understanding. Addressing the physical characteristics generally flows from understanding the intended use and the philosophy of the project. Preservation projects necessarily proceed differently from rehabilitation projects. It is critical that the underlying philosophy is understood at the outset.

The difficulty in assessing designed landscapes is that the design itself is often difficult to see. Many of the Olmsted firm's parks, for example, are largely seen as natural rather than as designed landscapes. Protecting or preserving these areas may actually be to the detriment of the landscape as elements become overgrown or volunteers are not culled. In particular, the functions of the design may be lost. An important example is the Olmsted design of the Fens in Boston's Emerald Necklace. The original design successfully addressed and accommodated sewage and storm water flows in a beautiful park setting. Users and planners alike forgot the function of the design over time

Preservation	Protect and stabilize site features rather than extensive replacement.
Rehabilitation	Repair or alter a property to be compatible for another use while preserving features of historical or cultural significance.
Restoration	Accurately depict the historic form or features of a property by reconstruction of missing features or removal of later features.
Reconstruction	Depict through new construction the form and features of a nonsurviving landscape or object.

TABLE 11.2   Treatment Types for Landscapes

and saw the Fens only in terms of its beauty. When the Charles River was eventually dammed, the function of the working landscape was destroyed. The designed landscape must be investigated as more than a planting plan.

All too often the landscape of a historic building or feature is not treated as part of the historic character of the site or is sacrificed to parking and providing convenient public access. Such landscapes are sometimes modified to reflect contemporary tastes and standards. Parking, lighting, way-finding, accessibility concerns, liability issues, and the like may not have been present in the original landscape, and finding a balance between these practical necessities and the integrity of the site is challenging. Many of the elements of the restored or rehabilitated landscape are both intrusive and necessary. It is necessary to provide for parking and to stabilize pathways for safety and wear and tear. It might be necessary to introduce lighting and paving to provide for pedestrian or motor vehicle safety. Signs are both intrusive and necessary. The designer is faced with a challenge when balancing these opposing forces in a design that serves the mission and the character of the site.

Way-Finding

Lighting and signs provide safety and enhance the use of the site. An important means of integrating the historic character of the site and a new use is to educate people about the history of the site. Signs are usually of two types: fairly simple signs providing direction and somewhat more detailed signs providing more detailed site information. Signs providing directions should be simple and direct with clear and easily seen lettering or symbols. It is sometimes recommended that such signs use a minimum of letters or characters, but the use of abbreviations or acronyms in off-site signs should be carefully considered.

Signs can provide a simple and direct way of communicating history and increasing the site user's appreciation and awareness. Signs should be designed to minimize intrusion by being both noticeable and subtle. This is accomplished by carefully selecting the size, color, and location of signs. Placing signs very low to the ground, for example, keeps them out of the view but makes them easily found and read. Once visitors or users are aware of the location, they quickly adapt. The use of color or symbols increases visitor familiarity and maximizes the value of signage. Designing content and sign communication is a specialty in its own right.

Adapting the Historic Landscape

Whether the intention is to adapt a historic site to a new use or to restore or preserve the site as it was in an earlier time, the site must accommodate contemporary use by visitors and staff. Walkways may be constructed where none existed, and cars and perhaps buses must be accommodated. Vehicular traffic should be kept a distance from the key elements of the site. Important views or features should be respected and maintained. It may be appropriate to construct unloading areas nearby, but parking and general vehicle circulation should be directed away. The use of plantings and grading to screen parking areas might be considered as well.

Parking areas should be designed to minimize their intrusion and impact on the site. Parking lots may influence the quality of the site visually, audibly, and environmentally. As addressed in previous chapters, a variety of methods are available for screening and mitigating these effects. Vehicle circulation should be simple and smooth. One-way circulation patterns and traffic calming strategies allow for narrower cartways, which reduce vehicle speed and noise. The narrower cartway also minimizes storm water runoff and maintenance issues.

Walkways should be planned to meet expected peak loads. Although narrow walks may be less intrusive, if the walk is underdesigned, damage from foot traffic may result. The impact of wider walks may be minimized by careful selection of paving or path materials. Wherever appropriate, the layout of walks should anticipate the "rounding" tendency of pedestrians and provide for natural and comfortable changes of direction rather than using intersections at right angles. Circulation might benefit if walkways are slightly wider at intersections, rest areas, and points of interest where people might linger or slow down.

Accessibility

Walkway accessibility is also an important consideration. Frequent rest areas and varying degrees of difficulty contribute to the site user's experience. Providing accessible routes in historic landscapes must be considered in the design process. Although providing accessible routes that would threaten or destroy the significance of the site may not be necessary, alternatives should be considered. Determining whether an alteration would destroy the significance of the site or feature may require the input of a local or state official. Americans with Disabilities Act (ADA) regulations require that at least one accessible route be provided. The regulation states a preference for a route that is used by the general public but allows for an alternative if no entrance used by the general public can comply with the accessibility requirements. An alternative access route must be open (unlocked) with signs indicating its location during hours of operation. The alternative location must also have a notification system or remote monitoring system. If the site has toilets, at least one accessible toilet shall be provided along the accessible route. At a minimum an accessible route should provide access to all of the publicly used spaces on the level of the entrance and access to all levels whenever practical. All displays, signs, and other graphic or written information should be positioned so it can be read or observed by a seated person: signs should be placed no higher than 44 in. above a floor surface.

Environmental Concerns

Today the historic character of a community is just as likely to be defined by the former factories and mills as it is by the homes and estates of the former owners of those mills. With this expanded scope comes a greater risk of encountering some form of environmental impairment. Among the challenges to be addressed in the preservation and rehabilitation of historic landscapes is the potential for environmental conditions created by practices or activities in the past. These conditions range from relatively simple issues such as difficult soil quality to an uncomplicated underground storage tank removal to more involved projects involving contaminated soils or active remediation activities. With the new focus on risk-based strategies for dealing with site environmental problems, the site plan may have to accommodate mitigation strategies in a final design.

Redevelopment of urban areas presents new design challenges and opportunities, but urban areas generally are host to a variety of confounding problems not present on "new land" or "green fields." In recent years brownfields have emerged as one new marketplace, and urban "undercrowding" is an emerging challenge. The redevelopment of urban waterfronts has been an important area of practice for many landscape architects, but extending the success of the waterfront into the fabric of cities remains a challenge that clearly has a design component. Many urban landscapes have suffered from neglect or what has been called deferred maintenance. In general urban historic landscape projects are one of four types:

1. Restoration or rehabilitation of an existing urban open space such as a park, campus, or estate.

2. Conversion, reuse, or redevelopment of existing buildings or features of a site from one use to another, such as the conversion of former factories to retail or residential use.

3. Restoration of an environmental function, such as urban stream restoration or urban forestry projects.

4. Redevelopment of new urban spaces by razing existing structures and beginning with new construction.

Each of these project types includes concerns that must be balanced throughout the design and construction process: the character of the site as it is and the risks to neighbors, occupants, or others; the risks to workers during construction; and the risks to the end user. Urban redevelopment requires the design professional to have an understanding of the environmental issues on sites and the implications of design solutions. The historic context of site and an assessment of the environmental legacy of past uses should be included in the typical site analysis. Many tools available for this analysis (see Chap. 3). For example, using the USGS quad map for an area can clearly demonstrate significant changes or land uses over time. These maps show areas of fill or cut and the location of buildings, roads, streams, and other surface features. Aerial photography is also an effective tool when used as a historical reference. Buildings, storage areas, streams, former woodlots, tree rows, alleys, and other features obliterated in later development are often clearly visible in aerial photography dating back to the 1920s and 1930s. Most urban areas have been mapped using aerial photography at least several times since the 1940s.

Soil maps are valuable for identifying the native soils in areas subsequently developed or the soils at the time the area was mapped. In urban areas, soil maps assist in identifying former wetlands by soil type that did not exist at the time the Wetland Inventory maps were produced. Soil maps are also a source of historic aerial photography, though the scale and clarity is sometimes difficult to work with.

Local sources of information such as maps, business directories, photographs, libraries of historical societies, and living memory are often important sources of information. It is often necessary to find corroborating sources for information from newspaper stories, local letters to the editor, or travel letters, which were popular in the late nineteenth and early twentieth century, but these are important sources of information otherwise lost. These materials are preserved and cataloged by local historical societies, or by the historic preservation agency in your county or state, but they often remain unused by designers in the assessment process. Collections may include photographs, paintings, even site maps and diaries that are invaluable in the assessment of a site. An interest in the environmental conditions of a site requires an additional level of effort to find new sources of information during the assessment. If an environmental site assessment (ESA) has been performed, it should be an important source of information. The

ESA should include a look at the historic conditions to determine the presence of any indicators of contamination or conditions that would result from contamination. App. A provides a more detailed discussion of the ESA process.

Activities of Concern

No list can cover all of the possible sources of contamination or activities of concern, but certain rules of thumb can assist you in your assessment. Table 11.3 is a short list of the general types of past activities that should raise concerns. The presence of such an activity is not a definitive indication of environmental trouble, but it is an indicator that a closer look is warranted.

Each of these activities presents its own set of risks and contaminants; types and sources of contamination are summarized in Table 11.4. The "priority pollutants" are a collection of materials used as a general screening tool. In the absence of specific knowledge of contamination, a priority pollutant scan or screening may be done. Knowing the types of contamination that could reasonably be anticipated on an urban historic site will assist the landscape architect in the assessment and design process and assist the client in determining effective strategies for addressing the mitigation concerns. The most probable contamination issues for a given area are best determined by the local history and industries. Among the more common issues found on redevelopment sites are underground storage tanks (USTs) and related petroleum pollution; asbestos containing building materials (ACM), which are outlined in Table 11.5; lead and other metals; polychlorinated biphenyls (PCBs); polycyclic aromatic hydrocarbons (PAHs); and volatile and semivolatile organic compounds.

Printing operations or photography processing
Dry cleaners
Service stations, body shops, fuel depots, and so forth
Industrial operations, particularly plating, chemical manufacturing, metal refining, oil refining, equipment manufacturing, tanning, battery manufacturing, plastics manufacturing, machining, electrical equipment, and dye shops
Pre-1980 electrical substations, transformers, and capacitors (regardless of size)
Old building materials
Industrial suppliers, maintenance shops
Solid waste collection, transportation, or disposal sites
Areas of fill, including "made land" on soil maps
Transportation-related activities, including right of way and railways
Wood preservation operations
Boiler rooms, steam generation plants, or coal gas plants
Nearby activities, particularly those up gradient or up wind

TABLE 11.3   Past Activities of Environmental Concern

Pollutant	Typical sources	Risks/impacts
Asbestos	building materials (see Table 11.5)	asbestosis, cancer
Lead	paint, building materials, fuel additives, old pesticides	chronic health effects, may be found in soils and groundwater
Heavy metals other than lead	metal refining, fuels additives, industrial operations	chronic health impacts
Petroleum, hydrocarbons	storage tanks, fuel storage, improper disposal	carcinogenic
Solvents	degreasing operations, metal manufacturing, painting, semiconductors, dying operations, printing, dry cleaners	carcinogenic
Polychlorinated biphenyls	pre-1980 transformers, capacitors, mastic, hydraulic oil	suspected carcinogen
Semivolatile organic compounds	chemical plants, coal tar by-products, insecticides, solvents	possible carcinogens, skin irritants
Pesticides, herbicides	farms, road sides, railroad siding, golf courses	possible carcinogen, neurotoxins
Polycyclic aromatic hydrocarbons	by-product of incomplete combustion; coal plants, and so forth	possible carcinogen

TABLE 11.4   Priority Pollutants and Typical Sources

Material	Use	Period of use
Surfacing material	sprayed or troweled on	1935–1970
Thermal insulation	batts, blocks, pipe covering	1949–1971
Textiles	fire blankets, lab gloves/aprons, rope, fire cord, tubing, tape, curtains, building felt	1920–1981
Concretelike products	flat, corrugated roof tiles, shingles, pipe	1930–1981
Roofing and construction felt	asphalt materials, caulking, mineral surface of roofing shingles	1910–1980
Asbestos containing compounds	joint compound, dry wall, wallboard, wallpaper adhesive, mastic, tiles, plaster, putty, stucco, spackling	unknown to 1978

TABLE 11.5   Building Materials Containing Asbestos

Land Preservation

The conversion of productive and valuable farmland into residential projects and associated commercial development has been repeated throughout the United States. In general, the loss of farmland is associated with changes of use to urban centers and transportation corridors that allow workers to travel to and from their jobs. A ring of growth, called "suburban" growth, occurred on the urban fringe after World War II. Beginning in the 1970s and blooming during the 1980s, another surge of growth occurred. The earlier suburbs were tied to the original urban fringe because of an undeveloped highway network and a reliance on traditional means of transportation such as urban mass transit and walking. Without the means to quickly and conveniently travel, people chose to live near centers of shopping and work.

The second wave of suburban growth occurred largely on the strength of a developed network of highways and a reliance on the automobile. The development of regional shopping malls and suburban office parks in conjunction with well-developed highways provided the impetus for a new growth wave that would reach much farther into the countryside than its postwar predecessor. Coupled with the significance of the baby boomers to population increases, the development of the countryside outside the traditional urban fringe was unparalleled. The phenomenon known as "edge cities or "exurbs" was a manifestation of this new ring of growth.

The preservation of farmland and the loss of farmland to development is largely a regional issue. In Iowa farmland preservation programs are geared toward community zoning issues and providing "right to farm" ordinances and the like while still encouraging local development. In Ontario, Canada, there are no analogous farmland preservation activities. In primarily rural states and regions, preservation of farmland is less of an issue than the development of rural communities and local economies. The pressure to preserve farmland increases toward the large urban centers. In the fringe of the eastern urban band, traditionally rural areas have seen increasing development pressure as transportation and technology have enabled people to live farther from work and work farther from cities.

Between 1982 and 1992, the amount of developed land in the United States increased by nearly 18 percent, from 78.373 million acres to 92.352 million acres. This increase was an unprecedented surge of expansion, and it prompted, among other things, the concern for our rural heritage and the preservation of farmland. In this same period, the number of family farms decreased, farm foreclosures increased dramatically, and the amount of cropland in the United States dropped from 420.96 million acres to 380.64 million acres, a decrease of nearly 20 percent. Despite acreage lost to farmland, food production continued to increase. The total developed portion of the continental United States in 1992 represented only 4.9 percent of the total land mass.

Some cropland was converted to other uses, such as a commitment to the Conservation Reserve Program (31.8 million acres) or other agricultural activities such as pasture (14.8 million acres), forest (3.1 million acres), or range land (2.1 million acres). Of the 59.7 million acres taken out of crop production, only 4.2 million acres were converted to developed land uses (Kellogg et al., 1994). The amount of land developed from other agricultural activities, in addition to the 4.2 million acres of cropland, include 2.4 million acres of pasture, 2.1 million acres of range land, 5.58 million acres of forest.

In 1981, the President's Council on Environmental Quality and various departments of the United States government jointly published the *National Agricultural Lands Study.*

This comprehensive study looked at development trends and land conversion throughout the United States and reported various methods by which agricultural land could be protected from development. The report was intended to serve as a resource to local officials in the effort to manage the development of agricultural land in their jurisdictions. Although the report has been criticized for errors contained in the calculations that influenced the conclusions, the methods described in the report have been implemented in many places throughout the United States. These methods were classified according to the approach by which they would affect farmland preservation.

The first approach was to reduce the attractiveness of agricultural areas for development through comprehensive regional planning and zoning. By identifying areas for growth and developing infrastructure in those areas, farmland would be less desirable for development. The second approach was to create programs that would reduce the burdens felt by farmers as development encroaches on them. The use of agricultural districts and right to farm legislation, coupled with tax relief for farmland and deferred taxation programs, were among the methods used to reduce the influence of developers. Providing financial and estate planning to assist farm families with the management of their assets was also part of this effort. Finally, some methods were outlined that focused on preventing changes in land use through land use regulations, zoning restrictions, the purchase or transfer of development rights, and the use of restrictive covenants or easements. This class of methods had implications for owners of neighboring properties.

Preventing Changes in Use

Property rights in the United States have been described as a bundle of sticks. An owner of property accrues rights, which are discrete from one another but are taken as a whole, or a bundle. These rights include the right to restrict access, the right to sell all or a portion of land, and the right to use one's land for some economic end. To decide on the disposition of land is one of the "sticks" in the bundle often used to describe the natural rights of landowners. Development of farmland can be prevented if an owner agrees to give up or modify his or her right to develop the land. The owner can decide to encumber the land with a restriction that will "run with the land"; that is, it will transfer with the title. By so doing, the landowner can reasonably be assured that the use of the land by future owners will be constrained in accordance with the restriction; none of the other rights in the bundle is lost.

The difficulty of an institutional approach to encouraging landowners to give up this right is that the greatest asset of many landowners is the value of the land itself. Most farm owners cannot afford to give up the value of the land because it is their largest asset. A wide variety of programs are available to landowners across the United States to restrict the use of land in the future. These programs generally follow or are permutations of one of three types: transfer of development rights, restrictive covenants, or conservation easements. The purpose of each of these is to preserve the farmland either as agricultural land or as open space.

The transfer of development rights (TDR), or a purchase of development rights (PDR), is perhaps the most important of the programs because it involves an exchange of comparable value. The general principle of TDR programs is that undeveloped land sold as farmland has a value less than that of undeveloped land sold for development. The difference in these values is identified as the development value of the land—the price to purchase the development stick from the landowner's bundle. In actuality there is no difference between the PDR and the TDR, but the terms are used exclusively. TDR programs transfer development rights from an owner to another party. In some cases this is done through zoning, growth control restriction, or the outright purchase of these rights. In either case an owner is paid for his rights, and the rights are transferred to another person or body. The method of determining the value differs somewhat from program to program, but in the end the landowner receives cash for his right to develop the land. It is important to note that this right does not vanish but is transferred to another "owner"; the right to develop the property belongs to someone else, usually the state or the county. In some programs the rights are merely "leased" for a specified period of time, and in others the rights are sold outright.

Restrictive covenants are a simpler approach to preservation. A landowner may place a restriction on his or her land at any time and cause that restriction to run with the land. When a restriction is placed on land to restrict a future owner's use, the right remains with the land but is encumbered. With no other party involved except the owner, these restrictions are unenforceable by any third party. If the restrictive covenant is shared because of subdivision or multiple ownership, the restriction is enforceable by any of the other parties that have standing.

The last major type of program is a conservation easement. In this case a landowner assigns an easement to a third party. The conditions of the easement require that activity on the land be restricted to exclude development. The easement is enforceable by the third party in protecting its interest. The easement usually allows some way for the third party to confirm that the landowner complies with the easement agreement. The easement is usually given to a private nonprofit organization and involves some cash payment on the part of the landowner to support the organization's efforts. The easement does not restrict the owner's use in any other way and does not provide the easement holder with a right of use, although some limited right of entry is usually included to allow the third party to confirm compliance. In general, the financial inducement for landowners to participate in such an arrangement is certain tax advantages available to them or some limited cash-for-conservation programs.

In each of these cases the landowner retains all of his rights as an owner except for the development right. The land may be sold, and the restriction passes with the title. The owner may use the land in any other manner save to develop it. Each of these approaches is intended to work best in conjunction with other programs and growth controls, although in practice there is wide variability in the administration of programs and controls.

The preservation of "isolated" farmland refers to the practice of restricting development on farms that are outside of agricultural zoning districts or are not contiguous to other preserved farms. In these cases the land adjacent to the preserved area is still subject to development.

The impacts of growth controls on land use and value have been extensively studied. The role of agricultural zoning is significant in the preservation process for several reasons. The most obvious, and most important, of these is that agricultural zoning reduces development pressure on farms by restricting development. Second, agricultural zoning acts to reduce the value of farmland. It is popularly believed that agricultural preservation raises the value of farms because it eliminates the "interferences" of development, such as complaints from nonfarming neighbors. In fact Vaillancourt and Monty (1985) discovered in a review of more than 1200 land sales that land in agricultural preservation zones lost 15 to 30 percent of its value compared to sales of nonrestricted farmland. In this way agricultural zoning would also help government TDR programs by reducing the development value of properties and therefore reducing the cost of purchasing development rights. In practice it is not clear that this effect is factored into the price being paid to landowners for development rights in areas with agricultural zoning. This may represent something of a windfall for landowners and a programmatic inefficiency in the purchase of development rights.

Similar results were observed in land sold outside the outer growth boundary of Portland. The Oregon land plan called for a 20-year delay in approving development beyond a specific growth boundary. This delay was perceived in the marketplace as a binding constraint on the development of the land and significantly influenced land sales (Knaap, 1985). Some studies indicate that these restrictions may also raise the value of unrestricted properties and, in particular, the prices of single family dwellings (Pollakowski and Wachter, 1990).

The value and effectiveness of growth controls are the subjects of wide-ranging and heated debates throughout the United States. However, in general agricultural preservation is well received by the public and landowners, although for different reasons. Farmers and landowners resist farmland preservation to the extent that zoning and other growth controls are seen to reduce the market value of their assets. Purchase of development rights addresses that concern by paying for the privilege of transferring the private landowner's right to develop his or her land to the public. Ideally there is no loss of value in this arrangement. Inducing landowners to voluntarily restrict their property without compensation can be more difficult. Such landowners often incur significant expense to preserve their land and are motivated by more altruistic purposes. The tax incentives and other programs do not offset the costs and reduction in asset value.

Conservation easements and similar approaches are the tools of private organizations. Public programs usually use cash buyouts or leases of development rights, or try to restrict development through growth controls. Private organizations, such as land trusts and conservancies, approach properties that are not eligible for public programs. In this way landowners interested in preserving farmland or open space, whether or not payment is involved, have a means of doing so, and the public's interests are served. These farms did not score high enough to be considered for the purchase of development rights because they are not prime agricultural properties or because they do not fit the profile of a sustainable agricultural operation. The latter might be the result of proximity to existing development or infrastructure or a zoning district that encourages development. Private groups are under no restriction or imposed guidelines as to the properties on which they accept easements.

Effect of Preservation on Local Revenue

The American Farmland Trust (1992) and the Lincoln Land Institute (Babcock and Siemon, 1985) have both looked at the impact of preservation on local revenue generated from land taxes. Communities often look to the development of open land into commercial or residential uses as a means of increasing the tax base. The American Farmland Trust (AFT, 1992) conducted a cost of community services (COCS) study in the municipalities of Agwam, Deerfield, and Gill in Massachusetts to assess the impact of preservation. The COCS technique is used by communities to assess financial impacts of various land uses, assuming current standards of infrastructure and services are applied. The purpose of the COCS is to compare income to expense for different land uses.

The AFT study found that while farmland did not contribute as significant a return in taxes as the same area developed, the farmland also required fewer services. For example, the study reported that a community can spend as much as $1.15 in services for every new dollar in additional revenue received from residential development. On the other hand, farms were found to require only $0.33 in services for every dollar paid in taxes; a net gain, according to the AFT study. Although commercial and residential properties have different uses, they are inexorably linked in the developed community. This study considered them as having distinct and separate functions. The study did not consider the cost of a community but rather specific elements within the community; perhaps there is a balancing of costs between uses that the COCS method does not identify. The Lincoln Land Institute study did reveal that the cost of commercial or industrial development provided a gain nearly as significant as farmland (Babcock and Siemon, 1985).

The Effect of Growth Controls

Mill (1990) describes zoning as a means of assigning development rights to a community; the right to develop land is a collective right of the community that a potential developer must purchase or be given. This approach essentially circumscribes the Lockean theory of property rights as a bundle of sticks and natural rights, but it may have some value in explaining actual behavior. Essentially, under Mill's theory, a landowner must have the agreement of the community before developing the land. This approval occurs in the form of plan approval and the payment of fees. In effect, the zoning takes a right from the bundle of sticks and then returns it to the developer once the developer agrees with the community's conditions for how it will be used. This restriction on the use of the land serves to devalue the land to some degree.

The adoption of agricultural preservation districts is an adaptation of the classic Euclidian zoning model of establishing zones or districts in which specified activities or uses are permitted. By applying the urban formula for development to rural communities, these communities provided the framework for urban sprawl. Most studies in land use and development behavior use models that assume efficiency in the marketplace, and that efficiency is usually based on the urban center model. In this case efficiency refers to the prudent and effective application of zoning to apply the highest and best use to land, usually taken to mean the most profitable. The urban center model assumes that there is a central business district and that land uses are driven from the efficiencies gained by proximity to that urban center. In its simplest form, the highest valued and most efficient activities are located closest to the center, and the least valued activities are located progressively farther away. Nearly every study on zoning and land value assumes this model to be representative; however, the model is clearly not representative of what our experience tells us is true.

Current development trends reflect our reliance on and preference for the automobile. The automobile and communications technology have eliminated the need for a central business district. Physical proximity is no longer a primary issue; it has been supplanted by time. The development of highway systems, originally conceived after World War II as a national defense system, allowed us to travel farther and faster, and development of networked computers, scanners, and fax machines have accelerated this ability. The need for a central business district is disappearing at an accelerated rate. Public policy and development planners cling to the old center-city planning models but struggle to find the prescriptions to save "downtown." In fact, planners have little influence over growth and the distribution of development in the United States in general. Studies show that the restriction of development does not direct development into the urban center but into the "edge" of cities (Garreau, 1991). Developers are motivated by the ability of a project to pay for itself, and their location decisions reflect the desires of the marketplace rather than public planning models. The growth of King of Prussia, Pennsylvania, and hundreds of similar centers does not reflect a model of planning; rather, it reflects the market forces.

Traditional studies are limited when applied to rural circumstances as well; however, some general trends and behaviors have relevance. The value of agricultural land does reflect the development potential and expectations. The determination of the purchase price of development rights is essentially one manner of accounting for this value. Any influence, particularly zoning, that restricts development on a parcel of land lowers the market value of the effected parcel, but concomitantly raises the market value of adjacent parcels (Hennebery and Barrows, 1990). In one of the few studies concerned only with agricultural issues, Hennebery and Barrows found that agricultural zoning had both positive and negative effects on land prices. Among the measures they addressed were the externalities of agricultural zoning. Externalities are effects of a growth control or land use on adjacent parcels of land. Their study found that agricultural zoning decreased the price of land in the district, but the values of large parcels of land were only nominally affected. They believe this reflects the value in removing development pressure from farmland; farmers are willing to pay more for large parcels that are not threatened by nearby development.

Many studies have considered the effect of growth controls on land and housing values (Pollakowski, 1990). The externalities of zoning and growth controls are well documented. Although growth controls may limit growth and appear to have a positive effect, the spillover effect of restricted growth is often observed in that growth is simply squeezed into another area. This has been described as a balloon; if you squeeze it in one place, it pushes out somewhere else. The growth restriction lowers undeveloped property values and raises developed property values. In effect, growth controls are a windfall for current homeowners. Likewise it will raise the value of undeveloped lands adjacent to the controlled area (Pollakowski, 1990).

William Fischel (1990) conducted a review of the literature on the subject and drew three conclusions:

1. Land use controls, in particular controls that attempt to guide overall growth in an area, are an important constraint in the marketplace.

2. Land use controls do provide some benefits to the public that no other mechanism available can provide.

3. The cost of these controls is probably greater than the local benefits they provide.

In effect Fischel observes that growth controls impose a greater cost, in terms of reduced land values and increased housing costs, than they do a benefit. There is no other mechanism available with which the public can pursue these ends, however.

Another notable element of Fischel's study is that the power to create these controls generally rests with the people who will benefit the most from higher housing prices. As growth controls are implemented, it is the price of existing houses that rise and the value of undeveloped land that falls. As rural areas become developed, eventually a critical mass is reached and the local power shifts from the traditional owners of large tracts of land to the more numerous owners of smaller tracts. The newcomers wish to "protect" the rural character of their community and are willing to do so at the expense of undeveloped landowners.

The Effect of Land Uses on Housing Prices

Numerous studies review the effect of a specific land use on land or housing prices, but the results of these studies are inconsistent and divergent. The lack of concurrence is a result of the elements used in the various models. Without any consistency it is difficult to draw any conclusions from these studies (Pogodzinski and Sass, 1990). In general these studies are concerned with the "disamenity effect" of presumably undesirable land uses on neighboring properties (Gambe and Downs, 1982; Gelman et al., 1989; Nelson, 1981; Pollakowski and Wachter, 1990; Shortle et al., n.d.). The most notable result of these studies seems to be the unexpected minimal effect of undesirable land uses.

These studies attempt to identify the "disamenity margin," or the distance from an undesirable land use to the point where the effect of the land use on land prices is zero. Studies have looked at power plants, nuclear power plants, group homes, solid waste landfills, strip mines, and industrial facilities. The results have often been surprising; for example, undesirable land uses often had a very small effect on housing prices and sales. Two independent studies reported that the Three Mile Island Nuclear Power Plant did not have a statistically significant effect on property values (Gambe and Downs, 1982; Nelson, 1981). Even after the accident, property prices of homes sold nearer the plant did not vary significantly from houses farther away, nor were the frequencies of sales notably different. Even solid waste landfills had a more limited disamenity margin than anticipated (Shortle et al., n.d.). Well-managed landfills were found to have only a very weak effect on local property values. A correlation was noted between the volume of waste accepted and the effect on prices. Landfills accepting less than 300 tons per day were found to have nearly no effect on housing prices, whereas landfills accepting more than 500 tons per day had a weak effect on housing prices. The effects of a given land use on adjacent lands is not always intuitively obvious. Facilities feared to be a disamenity may have a negligible or even positive effect. The presence of group homes in a lower socio-economic neighborhood was found to favorably influence housing prices (Gelman et al., 1989). An "amenity effect" was discovered that attenuated over distance. Clearly these results indicate the possibility of unintended consequences of land uses.

Few discussions with regard to easements can be found in professional journals for real estate appraisers, planners, design professions, and real estate developers. When this subject was addressed, it was primarily in the form of questions from the professional society to its members rather than accounts of actual studies. An exception was an early study regarding the effect of scenic easements on property (Williams and Davis, 1968). This study found that properties encumbered with a scenic easement lost value, and this loss was believed to be the direct result of the owner's loss of his right to use his land unencumbered. The study indicates that these losses were limited to the portion of the land affected by the easement. The unencumbered portion was not observed to suffer a loss. The study did not explore whether the unencumbered portion of the land may have increased in value as a result of the easement. Coughlin (1991) reported that while the use of agricultural zoning programs to protect farmland was a departure from the general use of zoning as a guide for development, agricultural zoning was more effective if used in conjunction with other programs, such as TDR. Agricultural zoning, purchase or transfer of development rights, and an agricultural infrastructure are all different but complementary elements to successful farmland preservation. Coughlin's criteria for evaluating the effectiveness of agricultural zoning did not extend to the consideration of externalities or spillover effects.

The Lincoln Institute of Land Policy published *Assessing Land Affected by Conservation Easements—Resource Manual* in conjunction with a training seminar for real estate professionals (Closser, 1993). The manual observes that sales of land abutting "conservation land" appreciate more quickly than other property. While the land under conservation is reduced in value by as much as 90 percent, the adjacent land quickly increases in value. The manual does not offer a method for evaluating this increase in value.

The American Society of Appraisers (ASA) has also observed, and recommended to its members, that the preservation of land could have "considerable value to an abutter for the additional privacy and seclusion it would afford" (Czupyrna, 1983). To date the ASA does not offer specific guidance or models for making that determination. Federal tax law does consider the positive impact on the value of neighboring properties. The tax code requires that any deduction taken for a conservation easement be reduced by the amount of increase in value experienced on property owned by the donor or a relative to the donor (Small, 1991). The tax law includes what is known as the "enhancement" rule, which is described through the use of examples. Text in the federal tax code states that "by perpetually restricting development on this portion of the land, (the land owner) has ensured that the two remaining acres will always be bordered by park land, thus increasing their fair market value" (U.S. Internal Revenue Service, Federal Tax Code Reg. Sec. 14(h)(3)(i) example 10).

There was significant agreement among those surveyed that the presence of open space or preserved farmland would be expected to raise the value of adjoining properties if the adjoining properties were used for residential purposes (Russ, 1994). There was also agreement that open space would have greater value to adjoiners than would preserved farmland. The presence of open space or preserved lands is viewed as an amenity to potential homebuyers for which they are willing to pay a premium, but these features have little if any value for commercial, industrial, or public uses. There might be some additional value of land adjacent to preserved farmland to farmers as well because the presence of the preserved parcel ensures that the land will remain in agriculture indefinitely. This assurance offsets the "impermanence" concern farmers must weigh when purchasing land or improving leased land. The impermanence factor refers to the risk of a parcel of land next to or near a farm being converted to residential or other nonagricultural uses.

Preserved land, whether open space or farmland, may attract development because of the amenity of the view and the certainty of future land use, but this value is insufficient to attract development without other factors such as location of the parcel, access, available water, and sewage disposal (on site or public). The presence of agricultural security areas and agricultural zoning also serves to discourage development.

Based on the survey results (Russ, 1994), it can be expected that the preservation of farmland or open space will increase the value of otherwise developable adjacent land. Further, this value would be based on the amenity value of the permanent open space or farmland. Homebuyers are willing to pay some premium for permanent visual access to the preserved land.

CHAPTER 12

Landscape and Culture

L and is important as a manifestation of power and wealth, but the landscape is more than simply the space itself. It is perceived emotionally as a source of beauty and solace as well as being a symbol of economic well-being. Land and the landscape form a system of intertwined and related flows of energy and materials upon which we depend in the most fundamental ways. In most discussions, the concept of landscape is limited to gardens or the plants and constructed surface features in a place, but this definition clearly limits the landscape to something superficial, including only those places that reflect the direct, intentional effects of human modification. This idea of the landscape as a reflection of positive human influence is an old one.

Landscape is more than just space. For example, it is four dimensional, it has history and, it is through time that we measure successful landscapes. The common view of landscape is of an unchanging constant, but the biotic elements of a landscape are dynamic—they grow and mature. Olmsted once observed that it is the vision to see a landscape in its future mature state that will occur long after the designer has passed that is the genius of the profession of landscape architecture.

Landscapes are also the media of cultural experience, and human groups have altered the landscape in many ways through history. The 4000-year-old canal system in China, Mayan irrigation systems, and Syrian and Roman water systems are a few examples of human impacts on the environment. It is accepted fact that Native Americans periodically burned woodlands and prairie to manage the environment. Roman aqueducts, which conveyed cool mountain waters to the urban center, changed the landscape in appearance and made Rome a different kind of city. The damming of American rivers bear witness to the will and attitudes of our society as a culture and to our political will. Current efforts toward sustainability and environmental restoration speak of our present attitudes and reflect the qualities and values of our culture today. These efforts will be judged best in historical context with the clarity of time.

As professionals we know that all of our expressions of landscape are simplifications of the natural world. The natural landscape is complex and diverse, and we cannot duplicate it as design. Instead, we direct our attention to what is important to us by eliminating from consideration facets of the landscape we consider unimportant or peripheral to our interests. In this way pieces of the environment are assigned values based on our interests; items of high value are kept, perhaps even enhanced, and items of low value are excluded or ignored. This paradigm of value is so effective that we tend not to see elements that are of low value.

Many complain about the boring sameness of the modern built landscape in which one place is all but indistinguishable from the next place. The universality of the modern landscape and the loss of local significance seem to be practically invisible to most people. Degraded urban streams are invisible to most city dwellers. John B. Jackson (1984) noted that Pausanias's observations of the Greek countryside included reports only of the manmade elements. Jackson referred to this as "political observation" and said that Pausanias "did this because these were the only objects with what to him was visibility" (p. 31). In postmodern society most of us have no direct frame of reference to nature or the environment. At best we see nature through other activities or interests, and we value it according to those interests. Hikers and snowmobilers both value trails but have very different frames of reference. For many, possibly most, nature is observed vicariously, primarily through the media such as magazines and television (Fig. 12.1).

To the degree that the land is influenced by people, it is a landscape as distinct from wilderness. Perhaps the best definition of landscape is to be found in this human aspect of land. Influence can be intentional—that is, by design—or it can be unintended. In either case land that is influenced by human activity is the landscape. It has been estimated that 60 percent of the world is "managed" landscape in that the decisions made by people have the greatest day-to-day systemic influence over the land. We overcome aridity with irrigation, chemically enhance soils for greater fertility, change the shape of land to facilitate our activities, remove forests to create suburbs, divert runoff from soils, and inadvertently overfertilize our surface waters. Humans have been changing the environment for thousands of years, and the character and scope of these impacts have become harmful. This has been called deficit spending in the environment. The

FIGURE 12.1 An editorial billboard.

degradation of natural systems such as air, water, soil, and species diversity are usually externalized from the market costs of products and services. We measure our competence by how fast we move information and transfer energy, but natural systems work slowly, at seasonal, glacial, and even tectonic speeds. Although 76 percent of Americans consider themselves environmentalists, the average American spends only 3 percent of his or her time out of doors.

Landscape values are learned behavior, passed from generation to generation, usually by example. Professional designers produce work based on a cultural ideal or a refinement of traditional values. Exceptions are noteworthy primarily in their differences from the traditional models or because they provide an expanded view of the landscape. Often the degree of change is quite small and could be seen as incremental evolutionary steps toward new values and new cultural norms. Settlers brought what they knew with them as they moved to new places, but within 20 years of landing in Massachusetts, early English settlers were already abandoning the familiar central construct of the "ideal town" for residences in outlying areas. Single dwellings developed without regard for "political" designs or layout. Instead homesteads were built with an orientation to nature, along contours relevant to streams, and so forth. Clergy and village leaders discouraged "outliving" as forsaking god and church and civilization. Within four decades, the original planned towns were abandoned and development began to reflect the abundance of cheap land and the rich agricultural opportunities of the new world. The old world culture adapted to the new world conditions.

The abundance of space in the new world skewed traditional values and roles. Few professional or educated designers worked in early America. Land was developed relating to the landscape, economy, and a practical aesthetic. John Stilgoe (1982) observed that the archetypal landscape and land use "objectified common sense, not the doubtful innovation of professional designers" (p. 10). In 1875 a survey of six counties in New York State reported that about 21 percent of the total cover was timberland. In 1990 a survey revealed that more than three times that area was now in timberland, more than 1.8 million acres. Words changed, meanings changed, and new social roles are created. The New England idyll of a village was transplanted, with varying degrees of success, across the entire United States. Even today, Architect Andres Duany and his innovative "New Town" is an admitted return to these traditional ideals. Perhaps the appeal of this traditional village is the model of a simpler way of life.

Economists, on the other hand, tend to view the landscape as a universal flat plain on which features are obliterated and only markets matter. Nature itself, beyond its resources or its effects on resources, is removed from consideration because it is not valued. Simple surface features such as water expressions or topography may be considered only to account for patterns of distribution. Resources such as minerals or materials are included only as they apply to markets and to the distribution of wealth. Natural resources are thought of as "free goods" and have no inherent cost. Only the costs of extraction or acquisition and distribution are used by economists to determine market value. In this way economies have been subsidized by nature, yet few economic models have ever included the impacts of the markets on the landscape.

The impacts of exploiting natural resources are distributed in the marketplace without regard to benefits; that is, the costs of exploitation are often not borne by those who benefit from the exploitation. The absence of environmental values in the economic system is both a reflection of larger cultural values and, in part, the cause of them. The impacts of degraded environments and damaged landscapes are always felt locally, but the benefits of the destruction may be distributed widely. Forests are dying, most of the river pollution in the United States is from nonpoint sources such as agriculture and urban runoff, we are mining prehistoric groundwater and disturbing basic life systems: the atmosphere, water quality, and soils. These impacts are the externalities of our economic behavior; costs that are not calculated in the market prices of products and services but that must be captured in a sustainable society.

The Use of Land

The Use of Land (Reilly, 1973) is the final report of a task force created by the Citizen's Advisory Committee on Environmental Quality. The Citizen's Advisory Committee was created in 1969 by Executive Order. The "mission" of the task force was to investigate the laws, policies, and trends that existed at the time, to characterize the effectiveness and impacts of these on past and current land use, and to make recommendations as to how land use might be better regulated. The task force undertook its mission with a presumption that land use trends evident at the time of the study were unsatisfactory and unsustainable.

The report observes that "unrestrained, piecemeal urbanization—supported by a value system that has traditionally equated growth with the good life—has produced too many dreary, environmentally destructive suburbs . . . too many bland indistinct city centers; extensive mismanagement of the earth's resources and rising popular discontent" (p. 10). The task force concerned itself with how the process of development might be organized, controlled, and coordinated to protect the environment and the cultural and aesthetic characteristics of land while balancing the needs for housing, manufacturing, public access to open space, and the infrastructure of society such as shopping and highways. The investigators recognized that the laws and institutions, as well as the national psyche were created at a time when development was encouraged.

The seemingly limitless expanse of colonial America resulted in a legal bias in favor of development. American landowners have an expectation that they might use and develop their property as they deem fit, even at the expense of the environment or of the interests of the public. The task force came to the conclusion that the existing laws and public policy frameworks were inadequate for effective planning and control of development; if only because of the pro-development prejudice built into our legal doctrines. The conclusion is qualified, however, by the task force's belief that "with property rights go obligations that society can define and property owners should respect" (p. 16).

This statement appears to be too simplistic a response to such a complex issue, but the report goes on to provide numerous instances in which landowners' use of land had been successfully restricted by law or policy. An entire chapter is devoted to "Adapting Old Laws to New Values." A variety of case law is reviewed in a case study format to illustrate how environmental protection and the interests of the public have been asserted over the rights of the individual landowner. State laws and state constitutions that do not require compensation for "takings" are discussed. The wide variance between states and the federal approach to the regulation of land complicate the issue even further. In spite of the differences, there are many examples of land use restrictions that are sustained in case law as well as common law. These include restrictions on nuisance, activities that clearly endanger the public health and welfare, the right of eminent domain, and the use of zoning ordinances to regulate the use of land for the benefit of the public.

The greatest value of the report might be its exploration of the various methods and approaches that can be used to control and coordinate development. Beginning with the obvious need to restrict development of lands that serve some sort of valuable function (e.g., groundwater recharge areas, particular wildlife habitats, steep slopes that might be unstable or subject to erosion), the report identifies a hierarchy for identifying areas that deserve protection from development. After the environmentally sensitive areas, areas required for future public recreation and areas that would serve as "buffer zones" between urban areas are seen as most important. Unique or highly productive farmland is the last of the identified important areas.

The methods identified to provide protection for these areas include requiring dedication of open space by developers through the use of density bonuses and open space ordinances, outright purchase of the property by government or private entities, requiring environmental impact statements for all "large" developments and encouraging the use of open space easements and transfers of development rights. Today dedication of open space (or cash in lieu of land) and the use of conservation easements have become relatively commonplace. Density bonuses and transfers of development rights have been used as well and experienced mixed results.

The report makes a series of recommendations that encompass various levels of government and private as well as public action. The essence of these recommendations is as follows:

1. A national land use policy that serves the planning and development community in a manner similar to the laws and policies that have addressed air and water quality issues. The task force saw the National Environmental Policy Act as the proper route for development of this policy. Such a policy or legislation would link federal funds to land use actions and regulatory programs at the state and local level.

2. Restructuring tax policy at the state/local level to encourage effective planning and quality development.

3. Noneconomic incentives to promote stewardship such as granting open space easements or land trusts among private parties.

4. Innovative planning considerations such as density bonuses or density transfers that encourage the clustering of housing and commercial development and the protection of larger tracts of open space.

5. Education of the public, public officials, and institutions as to the important links between development, land use, the environment, and quality of life. The task force observed that public policy and the opinions of lawmakers and the courts often follow public opinion; therefore, an educated public will "lead" the lawmakers to new interpretations of the Constitution and legal doctrine or encourage the creation of new laws.

6. Continue the participation of citizen-planners in the process, and encourage the involvement of neighborhood groups.

7. Encourage the broader use of Environmental Impact Statements as part of the development and planning process.

The value of *The Use of Land* as a contemporary reading is its role as a benchmark. The report is a fairly in-depth review of land use trends and planning policy as it had developed up to 1973. From the vantage point of today, we may evaluate the impact of the report and the effectiveness of its recommendations. For example, the task force clearly identified a National Land Use Policy as a priority, but no such policy has been developed. In fact, since the report was published, several administrations have encouraged the sale and development of publicly owned lands. This policy was carried out without the benefit of any development guidelines or restrictions on the buyers.

In spite of the lack of national leadership on these issues, a significant grassroots effort—albeit often unorganized, unsophisticated, and underfunded—has sprung up all over the country. These local efforts have had impacts on the actions of elected officials and caused the development process to include consideration of community impacts. The laws that allow for the transfer of development rights, conservation easements, and preservation of farmland and sensitive areas are largely due to the efforts of private groups. Public policy and regulations have followed the interests and direction of the organized "environmental movement." Whether by design or by accident, the environmental and preservation interests have implemented through private funding or caused public action to implement, in varying degrees and success, aspects or parts of all of the remaining recommendations. The task force was unable to identify any direct method or means by which the federal law may restrict landowners beyond the limits described by the Constitution and defined by the Supreme Court. The recommendations rely on guidelines and on compelling landowner responsibility as a reaction to financial incentives and public opinion.

Public Land and Private Land

Private property is among the most fundamental principles of a free nation, and the rights of the landowner are important considerations in any action that affects private property. Public lands are viewed quite differently, however. Although important distinctions are supposed to exist between public and private organizations, these distinctions begin to blur under examination. In spite of at-large perceptions, public and private landowners may be more alike than different. This is especially true as the size and scope of organizations increase. Public and private land uses share the same objectives of management, and in this way the similarities of the land use, its management, and stewardship may ultimately be more important than the differences that exist between specific landowners and users. The private and public sectors are constantly interacting; there is no private sector organization that is not touched in some way by an element or extension of government. These interactions extend to the use of land and land ownership. In the United States it is private individuals and businesses that most use public lands.

By way of a comparison, these relationships are fundamentally the same in Canada and the United States although in Canada the government's role tends to be more direct and centralized. The Canadian government is an owner or partner in many business organizations. In the United States government/private partnerships exist but usually in a more indirect fashion in the form of financial or other material aid rather than actual ownership. Despite the indirect nature of this relationship, the goods and services of the federal and state governments account for about 25 percent of the U.S. gross national product, so management decisions within the government have an impact on the private sector.

The private sector in both countries is affected by government regulations and policies, adopting what might be viewed as a "public component" into the behavior of the private organization. Landowners and operators in both countries adapt to social demands or public expectations to comply with or to avoid new regulations or the expropriation of rights or use of the land. Interaction between the two sectors is increasing, and they often resemble each other in practice. Governments are judged more often on their ability to respond to constituents and are held to almost "businesslike" accountability for performance. Private landowners and users are held more often to a measure of public accountability for their activities and stewardship.

Ownership of land is a limited concept. Private property in both countries is based on English common law and the feudal doctrine of "fee simple." Under this concept, land is held in ownership at the sufferance of the government. Landowners are subject to the payment of taxes, obligations of use, and eminent domain. In the United States, landowners are protected to some degree by the Fifth Amendment to the Constitution, which requires due process and compensation before the government can "take" private property. In Canada the rights of landowners are protected by statute only, which is subject to change.

The rights and extent of ownership are complicated further by the fact that ownership and interests in the land may be separate. This separation may be by the choice of the owner (as in the case of a lease, where the owner assigns use to a lessee) or by law. An example of the latter would be wildlife held in trust by the government for the people. Under normal circumstances, a landowner may not have the right to take wildlife without the permission of the government. Mineral rights and water rights are examples of an interest in land held separate from the title.

The patterns of ownership in Canada and the United States are different in several ways. In the United States 58 percent of the land is privately held, whereas in Canada the government (federal and provincial) owns 90 percent of the land. A more important and fundamental difference exists in that Canadian property owners do not enjoy vested property rights. The government retains property rights despite the transfer of title. This important difference provides the government with greater latitude in developing and implementing policy. The Fifth and Fourteenth Amendments assign and guarantee property rights and access to due process to private U.S. landowners. In light of these fundamental differences, it is surprising that the policies and results are not more divergent between the two countries.

Government control is more fragmented in the United States than it is in Canada. This fragmentation is considered to significantly inhibit successful management and planning of metropolitan areas or regions. The U.S. political economy and the popular commitment to local autonomy preclude any significant changes or reforms to this situation. Comparisons of planning and managing land use and development in selected American and Canadian cities reveal that in spite of the basic differences in ideological form, planning theories and approaches to development are similar. After World War II the public planning process emerged in a leadership role, directing economic development in the established city centers in both countries. This new role occurred in response to the vacuum left by private enterprise during the war years. Prior to this time, economic development had been almost exclusively a private sector undertaking. With the rise of public planning came the involvement of the public in the planning process. Citizens and neighborhoods became part of the process of development and land use (Feldman and Goldberg, 1987).

The highly centralized form of decision making in Canada did not allow for the process to be changed as easily as in the United States. Although the tools and instruments of policy are similar, implementation remains fundamentally different. The control of growth and land use is managed by government through the use of zoning and the extension of infrastructure; most important of which are sewage, water, and transportation. In the United States, the presence of multiple municipalities, often with conflicting interests and objectives, has served to limit the effectiveness of regional planning to stop "urban sprawl." Development on the edges of cities is beyond the control of those cities in most cases. Cities and those wishing to influence growth have a limited palette of choices with which to control land use. The first and most effective way is to buy land. By purchasing land, the government, as landowner, has the rights guaranteed by the Constitution and can control the use of the land. The second way to control and influence growth and development is through the political nature of the planning and development approval process.

In Canada, the process tends to be less fragmented. Government is more centralized and decision making is less politicized. Although attempts to measure planning and land management success are at best of limited value, Canadian cities seem to be considered more "livable" than their American counterparts by their residents, but the Canadian results are mixed. Management of Canadian forests and rural land development are not equal to their urban counterparts. The uncertain results of the planning and management processes are clear indications that the public's interests may not be best served by government's management and control of the process as it stands in either country. The questions of who should decide how land is used and what community should be considered (a localized view of community or a more regional view) require careful consideration. The landowner's rights and the rights of the public must be balanced.

Attempts to control urban sprawl and development in the United States and Canada reveal that there are as many similarities as there are differences between the two countries. In both countries growth and development are controlled more through political maneuvering and through controlling the approval process than through a deliberate planning and management process. The areas of greatest concern tend to be the areas of weakest control: points of municipal boundaries and edges of growth areas or transition zones.

Recent experiences in siting hazardous waste disposal facilities can serve as an example of how the planning process might be used and adapted. In comparing six case studies of siting projects, the common elements of the two successful projects were the "package" the projects came in (Shortle et al., n.d.). In these cases the disposal facility was only one element, albeit the central element, of a larger package of development including infrastructure and industrial and business development that had value to the community. The "enlightened" self-interest of communities overcame the fractured nature of the process and the organized objections to the projects.

In spite of ideological and constitutional differences between the United States and Canada, the similarities, especially in outcomes, appear to be greater than the differences in the two countries. The differences between public and private enterprise are blurred across international lines. The process of land development and control may differ in context and form, but the outcomes share similar problems and results. The study of successes and failures indicates that different planning and control systems may be appropriate for different regions and cultural areas. The tradeoffs made to satisfy one set of political conditions will differ from the tradeoffs made in another situation. Political influences on the use and management of land are greater than the processes intend or imply, and ultimately it is the political process that dictates much of the actual control.

Growth Controls

Between 1982 and 1992 the amount of developed land in the United States increased by nearly 18 percent, but at the end of this period the total developed portion of the country remained less than 5 percent. Culturally, North Americans have conflicting views of land and property. On one hand, we celebrate and place a high value on natural beauty and the integrity of the environment, and on the other hand, we tend to view land as "property" or as a commodity. These conflicting aspects are built into the system of land use approval and regulation. Although there is a great body of law, public policy, and regulations to govern the use of land and particularly development, under the U. S. Constitution the landowner/developer has generally been given the benefit of the doubt in the process. Government tends not to lead on issues of land use but seems content to follow, reacting to events and trends in the marketplace. While planners, economic development, redevelopment authorities, and federal and state programs all attempt to direct development, ultimately builders respond to their own perception of the marketplace and challenge the public planning effort to meet their needs.

Throughout the literature the message is the same: the final authority in determining the nature of land use is the community and the consumer. Political influences on the use and management of land are greater than the formal process recognizes or intends. Case study after case study shows the power of public interest in determining the short-term decisions governing land use and the long-term influence of the marketplace in influencing the definition of "public interest." Examples of successful government-directed development are uncommon. The lesson appears to be that government cannot compel a project to be successful; ultimately government projects must meet the same tests as private projects to be successful. Housing developments to replace substandard housing fail because they are located in undesirable sections of the city. No private developer would build there because *no one* wants to live there. The success of some projects since the 1990s may be driven by more than location. Where such public efforts have been successful, inducements have included mortgage programs, home ownership programs, the engagement of local institutions and businesses, and the development of supporting commercial and institutional development.

Communities are motivated by the interests of the individuals that make up the community. The interests of the majority often are in conflict with public interests, and in these cases the interests of the majority tend to prevail. In the Mount Laurel, New Jersey, cases the court allowed the town to resolve its unfair housing practices in one of two ways: build low-income housing throughout the city (including in the upscale areas) or provide density bonuses and incentives for the development of better housing in the urban areas, to be paid for, in part, by the more affluent areas. The city chose the latter. The power of community influence in preventing the development of projects that serve a broader base than the "host" community alone (NIMBY's) clearly demonstrates the power of a community's interest over a larger public interest. Equally important is the ability of municipalities to affect adjacent communities through the use of various growth management efforts. By restricting development, communities force development and the extension of infrastructure into adjacent communities.

In the 1960s and 1970s a surge of zoning and land development regulation was widely experienced across the United States for the first time. As sprawl has continued, so have the attempts to control it. Local and state governments have proceeded from the presupposition that growth controls do work. It is widely accepted that the effect of regulating growth through local regulations is to increase the value of developable land and the prices of existing housing. Obviously, owners of property that is valued higher after growth controls would tend to favor such controls, and buyers wishing to acquire property would not favor such controls. Still, does controlling growth through regulations have the desired effect?

Higher prices for existing housing could simply be a reflection of supply and demand; regulations restrict or reduce the supply of available housing and cost rises in response to an unfulfilled demand. Another explanation for the higher prices is the buyer's willingness to pay for what may be perceived to be an amenity resulting from the restriction (Fischel, 1992). The amenity may be in the form of preserved open space or reduced density, which result in a more attractive environment.

Many studies have asked various questions pertaining to the effect of zoning on land use and value. Unfortunately, they have not produced a conclusive answer regarding whether growth controls work. The complex nature of the relationship between a zoning ordinance and a property makes the design of a comprehensive analysis a mind-numbing proposition. Variances in location, political influences on the formation and administration of the ordinance, as well as the necessity to combine land uses into "common" types all serve to reduce the resolution of the studies. For example, in one study open spaces included swamps and floodplains as well as golf courses and public parks (Williams and Davis, 1968). Evaluating the impact of zoning on property values without making a distinction between the qualities of the land is an exercise with limited value.

Generally studies seemed to confirm what might have been intuitively obvious. For example, land located near public sanitary sewer collection systems is valued higher than land farther away. A moratorium on sewer connections increases the value of sites that have secured the right to connect to the publicly owned treatment works. Land zoned for higher density residential development is valued greater than land zoned for lower density residential development. It is interesting to note that the rate of increase in value is not linear; that is, doubling the density allowance increases the property value but does not double it. One study noted property located next to city limits and zoned 20 units to the acre was valued seven times higher than similar property zoned for only one unit to the acre (Fischel, 1992). This same study looked at a site 15 mi from the city limits with the same density allowances and found only a threefold difference between the 20 units per acre site and the one lot per acre site.

Fischel (1992) observes that of all the studies done "almost all of them conclude that growth controls raise housing prices." One effect of controls is the spillover effect: a zoning or other land use restriction has an impact on areas outside the prescribed boundary. Studies in Montgomery County, Maryland, found that in the 17 planning districts in the county, areas adjacent to districts with more restrictive controls had higher property values (Fischel, 1992). It was concluded that the property near these restricted areas was seen as more valuable because of the restriction. When the growth management program was coupled with conventional zoning restrictions, a maximum number of new units were allowed each year. It is not a surprise that one effect of this arrangement is higher property values for existing housing. Another perceived value is the amenity value of a growth restricted community. The cost of these values is shifted almost entirely to owners of undeveloped land and, ultimately, to buyers of new homes. A spillover effect of these restrictions was found in areas adjacent to the areas of restricted development where property values were "slightly, but significantly" increased. Fischel (1992) notes that growth controls are in effect a transfer of "entitlements to develop from the landowner/ developer to the community." Extending this thought, Fischel suggests that fees charged by the community for reviews and impacts are really the developer buying back the entitlements from the community. High impact fees merely represent a community's "unwillingness to accommodate development, or it may represent a change of heart . . . allowing some development if it pays its own way (and perhaps a little more)." If this were true, under federal legal guidelines this might be a taking because no overriding public health or safety interest is being protected and the individual's right to "use" of his or her land is completely compromised without due process.

Developers do not like impact fees but reluctantly support them as a cost of doing business, even more so when they are tied to performance criteria. Impact fees must be supported by justification and a fair share measurement to be legal in more than 20 states. In general, the research reviewed by Fischel indicates that growth controls impose a net cost on society. He concludes that (a) land use controls impose constraints on the land/real estate marketplace, which in turn affect the cost of housing and land; (b) land use controls do provide a benefit to the public; and (c) the cost of growth controls are greater than the benefits that they provide. Fischel's work does not consider the environmental impacts of development and does not allow that perhaps higher costs caused by growth controls have an unintended consequent of "greener" development.

The development of growth controls is a reflection of attempts by legislatures and the courts to limit local exclusionary zoning. Affluent communities that do not want to accept low-income housing, for example, are able to restrict all housing. These types of controls have not been undone through the courts, presumably because they are "democratic"; that is, they exclude everyone, not just low-income residents. Citizen ballot initiatives have also encouraged growth controls. Many growth control ordinances are the result of such direct democracy, which precludes the normal give and take of compromise. The resulting controls tend to restrict a voting minority (owners of undeveloped land and business interests) in favor of providing the gains of restricting land use to the majority of voters. Could it be argued, in such cases, that the growth control is in fact a transfer of land rights from the owner to the public? If the answer is yes, at what point does the loss of private rights (in this case the right to develop or use property) become a public taking of private land for a public benefit (the amenity of no growth)?

Growth controls also cause development to spread out; as developers and buyers seek opportunity, they move to new areas. The net effect is to encourage the urban sprawl that the growth control efforts were organized to combat. A municipality that passes strict development restrictions causes at least a portion of the development that would have occurred within its boundaries to be pushed into the next "ring" of municipalities. The political power of the community shifts from the original residents to the newcomers as these outlying areas become more populated. The newcomers adopt growth controls to restrict further development and to maintain the character that attracted them in the first place. The long-term effects of this cycle are a lower standard of living (more time spent commuting, more income required to sustain a lifestyle, more pollution and attendant costs), continued flight from the central business district, and a loss of the economies of established "agglomerations" of business.

Growth controls fuel sprawl and unsustainable growth as businesses leave the urban center for the developing rings around the cities. In *Edge City,* Joel Garreau (1991) recognizes the appearance of commercial centers on the fringes of traditional cities as a logical extension of city-building and as a reflection of modern transportation (automobiles) and the limiting factor in modern life—time. Garreau pronounces the edge city to be the third wave of urban development. The first wave was the post–World War II flight to the suburbs; "home" was removed from the city. This new freedom was made possible by the affordability of the family automobile. The second wave was the move of the marketplace from the central business district to the suburbs in the form of shopping centers. Garreau observes that the third wave is a predictable response to the success of the first two: if the home and the marketplace were in the suburbs, it was only a matter of time before the workplace would join them.

Although cities evolved as a response to the need for protection, they remained largely independent marketplaces. Even within cities trade occurred throughout the city, without a single business center or district. This remained true, according to Garreau, until the industrial revolution when inexpensive power and mass production brought a number of changes. In the early days of industry, factories required large numbers of workers. The available transportation at the time was either foot power or, somewhat later, steam locomotives. The natural limits of the mode of transportation led to high concentrations of residential areas around what became central business districts.

Ironically, Garreau points out, the first predictor of the edge city was probably General Motors. In 1919 construction started on "New Center," which at the time would be the world's largest office building. This huge complex was not built in downtown Detroit but rather at a busy intersection about 10 mi from downtown. This new complex was accessible only by "personal" transportation; that is, the automobile. Ford soon followed suit, after all a downtown location did not provide enough parking for all of Ford's employees. In 1928, the year Henry Ford began to build the Model A, and only 2 years after building the millionth Model T, Ford moved its first plant out of Detroit to Dearborn, and according to Garreau, the edge city was born.

Like all trends, the edge city has certain characteristics that are replicated, albeit in different degrees, in each new city. Edge cities are developed along or near important intersections of highways, are anchored by a regional shopping mall of at least 600,000 ft^2 (one that serves a population of at least 250,000 people), have 5 million ft^2 of office space, more jobs than bedrooms, and an identity as a place. The underlying influences driving the growth of edge cities are the effects of technology. The automobile and the information age (computers, communications) have combined to shift the limitations of urban development from issues of distance and proximity to issues of convenience.

According to Garreau, an unintended consequence of the development of edge cities has been the lack of recognition given to them by the design and planning community. It would be fair to say that the edge city is viewed as a blight upon the landscape by most architects, planners, and many citizens as well. In the 1980s building boom, 80 percent of development dollars were spent outside of the old central business districts to build elements of new edge cities. The planning and design community has largely resisted recognizing these developments as any form of urban development at all. The development of edge cities has been led by developers, who have responded with an almost intuitive sense of what the public wants and the most desirable form of what "should" work. The developers viewed the edge city as a product of the culture and society, and viewed themselves as providers of what people desire. The edge city is a result of the forces of the marketplace.

Designers and planners continue to believe that the central business district must be the focus of our planning efforts and that despite all evidence to the contrary the public really wants to be "downtown." While professional planners and designers continue to decry the form and trend that is the edge city, developers are going about building the urban form that best reflects our society and technology. Garreau provides ample argument to demonstrate that, in fact, the public does not want to be downtown and despite the best efforts by planners is not going to change its behavior. Reinvented downtowns actually support Garreau's observations; these revitalized and saved central business districts have been remade into tourist and entertainment nodes that serve several outlying edge cities or become edge cities themselves. The requisite 5 million ft^2 of office space required to be an edge city, according to Garreau, is larger than all but the largest central business districts.

The form is in its youth and not without its own problems, but it has been legitimized by the marketplace. It would seem it is here to stay. The disagreement over the "sprawl" of edge cities is rooted in the two faces of the American people. On one hand, our history is a history of building and developing the wilderness: we have a constitutional predisposition toward a landowner's right to use his or her property. On the other hand, as a people we value the land for itself: we identify with natural beauty and the land. To preserve the land, Garreau believes conservationists would be best served by working with developers and the public to do two things: (1) identify important specific features or attributes of an area that should be protected and work to protect them, and (2) work to improve the quality of life in existing urban centers. Until people see no advantage to living "out" and no disadvantage to living "in," they will continue to move out.

An interesting aspect of this is the concern that edge cities are developed indiscriminately and without the benefit of good planning. In fact the underlying design and development criteria are very specific and concrete. Based on economies of scale and the expectations and limitations of the users and residents, the development of an edge city is a very deliberate undertaking. Garreau observes that the sense that they are uncontrolled stems from their unfamiliar form. We simply are not used to cities with such a low density of buildings, ample parking, and greenery. The classic planning expectation that the "right plan" or restrictions will bring everyone back downtown is doubtful, and the desire of preservationists to stop all development is equally unrealistic. Developers must recognize the importance of landmarks, however, and adhere to appropriate environmental planning as part of the edge city development. Edge cities often include open space and provide an opportunity to introduce the principles of sustainable design, even at retrofit sites. Instead of resisting the trend, we should find ways of incorporating new design principles into it. In the end the interests of the public and the requirements of sustainability must find common ground. Growth controls and zoning are neither good nor bad, but they represent development paradigms of the past. As such they may need to be replaced with a new vision.

Takings

The political theories of John Locke were important to the framers of the U.S. Constitution. Locke held that man had certain "natural rights"; that is, rights that were intrinsic to the individual and were not derived from the sovereign or the government. Representative government is based on the premise that state's rights are no greater than the sum of the rights of the individual; the state has no independent set of entitlements or rights. The natural rights of the individual were equal to the rights of the government; the government was not entitled to any privilege or greater consideration than the individual. Locke believed that such natural rights included an individual's right to "own" himself; that is, individuals own the fruits of their labor and are free to determine the disposition of such fruits. When the interests of the people (many individuals) encroach upon the rights of the individual, the individual is entitled to compensation. In fact the return on any government encroachment or taking must be greater than the cost to the individual. In such a situation, the value of the public good must be greater than the value of the right to the individual, and the compensation paid to the individual must also be greater!

Takings are public or private encroachments on the property rights of a landowner without the agreement of the owner. Takings are fairly complex legal issues and subject to ongoing definition between legislative and judicial actions. Common law states four conditions for establishing a taking:

1. The property must have equal value to defendants and the plaintiff.

2. The taking is conscious and deliberate.

3. The taking is accomplished without third party or natural events.

4. The entire thing is taken, not just a part or a portion of the thing.

If any of these elements is missing, the event is not a taking. The individual may have recourse under tort law or under strict liability, but under common law this is not a taking. In any case, the plaintiff's options for recovery lie with the courts.

Takings may be public or private. In private takings, the taker is liable for the cost of replacement or the cost of mitigation for the taking. In public takings, the government pays for the value that has been transferred to the government, not necessarily the value to the owner, or even the market value. This is illustrated in *Kimball Laundry Co. v. U.S.* (1949) where the government, under eminent domain, condemned property that included the Kimball Laundry Company business. The owner of the business sued the government for the value of his business. The government had paid for the value of the real estate (the laundry was in a modest residential area), but the compensation paid by the government was insufficient to relocate and reestablish the business. The Supreme Court ruled that the government must only pay for the value of the resource it has taken, and not attributes that the government does not use, such as the laundry business.

The U.S. Constitution is not designed to protect the thing that is owned but to protect the owner of the thing. The rights associated with ownership of property have several aspects: possession, use, and disposition. These elements are fully and completely the rights of owners. There can be no "degrees" of ownership and no abridgement of the rights of the owner. Within the limits of public protection, police powers, and common law principles any encroachment on the rights of ownership is a taking. To be found to be a taking, the U.S. Supreme Court has determined that the following must be shown:

1. A "nexus" or direct relationship between the action and a legitimate public interest.

2. An invasion of the property or that an owner is denied the right to control access.

3. A legitimate public interest that has greater value or benefit than the cost to the individual.

4. The individual is denied the use or other economic value of the property.

Property rights have been described as a bundle of sticks, and ownership consists of a number of unique rights. For land ownership such rights might include the right to control access to one's land or to sell a portion of it or to lease it to another, to make improvements on it, or to leave it fallow or unimproved. The loss or modification of one stick does not affect the others.

In *Penn Central Transportation Company v. City of New York* (1978), the owner of the Grand Central Terminal building was denied a permit to build an office tower over the top of the terminal because of the historic value of the building. The Supreme Court held that the state might restrict the use of a portion of a property or a particular use of the property. It is a "fallacy" to assume, according to the Court, that the loss of any particular right of easement constituted a taking of property. This has stood as a cornerstone of preservation efforts for many years.

Takings by regulation are common. Although the state has the right, and arguably, the duty to regulate land use under the police powers, many land use regulations are not justified under the police power and might therefore be considered takings. The central purpose of government is to maintain peace and order. To do so, the government must have certain powers; the rights retained by the citizens must not be so broad as to prevent the government from discharging its responsibilities. These justified encroachments on the rights of the citizen are the police powers. The form and structure of government is designed to limit police powers and jurisdictions of authorities within the government.

Land use regulations that go beyond the justifiable police powers are subject for consideration as takings. Much environmental and land use regulation is within the police power, but when the justification is not clear, we need to answer the following question: Is the regulation an attempt to control the defendant's wrong or to provide a public benefit? In some views, if a public benefit is the goal, the regulation is a compensable taking of private property, but there is a need for police powers and the forced exchange of property (eminent domain) only for public use. In any case, the result of the taking should be for everyone's use or enjoyment; the displaced owner and the public must each receive something greater than the cost of the exchange. A "public good" must not merely provide a benefit.

This approach to the police powers raises several interesting questions. The U.S. Constitution does not explicitly include any environmental rights, but many state constitutions do. In Pennsylvania, for example, Article 27 of the Commonwealth Constitution identifies a right citizens of Pennsylvania have to the protection and enjoyment of environmental, cultural, and historical features of the state. This explicitly extends the police power and responsibility of the state to include the protection of the environment. In Wisconsin similar constitutional language has caused the Wisconsin Supreme Court to hold that the environment is clean and pure and that pollution is a result of human activities. Based on the environmental rights of Wisconsin's citizens, therefore, an individual's property rights do not automatically include the right to change the land from its natural use or state, and such changes are subject to regulation under the state's police powers (*Just v. Marinette County,* 1972). A similar argument could be made (although I am not aware that it has been) under Pennsylvania's constitution. In effect, what is a taking under federal law may not be under state law.

Sustainable Development

Humans have had and continue to have a significant impact on the world environment. It has been said that 60 percent of the world land surface is under the management of people, but that 100 percent of the world is affected by the practices of that management. Whether we are aware of it or not, our activities have an effect on our world. Practices and methods that contribute to reducing our impact have been discussed throughout this book. In February 1996 the President's Council on Sustainable Development published *Sustainable America—A New Consensus for Prosperity, Opportunity and a Healthy Environment for the Future.* The report adopted the World Commission on Environment and Development definition of sustainability as "the ability to meet the needs of the present without compromising the ability of future generations to meet their own needs." The President's Council outlined 10 goals for the nation to become sustainable, but all 10 can be subsumed in the first three: (1) health and the environment, (2) economic prosperity, and (3) equity. Beyond the rhetoric, these goals represent a substantial challenge because we have tended to see these things as antagonistic or mutually exclusive. To become sustainable, we must create a society that embraces all three.

One theory of sustainability holds that as long as there is a fair exchange of value the loss of environmental quality is acceptable. We can afford a less diverse environment, or a lower air or water quality, in exchange for an improved infrastructure. Future generations are compensated for lower environmental quality by this same improved infrastructure. This is known as *weak sustainability,* or the constant capital rule. Others believe there can be no exchange: that environmental values or quality cannot be offset by infrastructure, that the functional aspects of the environment cannot be equated to the values of, say, a mile of new road. In this view functional values must be preserved and development must occur within the constraints. This is known as *strong sustainability.* Actual practice will necessarily lie somewhere in between, and we will learn to make decisions on a continuum between strong and weak sustainability.

Building the Postindustrial Landscape

The move from builder/expansionist thinking toward stewardship is a shift in values more than it is simply adopting new techniques or standards. It is an intellectual shift away from the fiction of landscape control, from simply stabilizing the land, and toward a point of natural social satisfaction and conservation because it makes sense. As greater values are placed on nature and environmental quality, these elements become part of our sense of satisfaction.

On March 26, 1996, Interior Secretary Bruce Babbitt turned a valve in the Glen Canyon dam to release a flood into the Grand Canyon. The flood was intended to mimic the natural floods that no longer occur seasonally because of the dam. Periodic flooding is believed to be necessary for the renewal of soil nutrients and temporary pools that serve as habitat. The experimental flood was to determine whether "natural" flood cycles can be mimicked. Perhaps turning that valve is the most tangible example of the subtle changes taking place in the attitude of people and conventions toward the environment. Thomas Berry (1988) correctly observed that the argument is usually framed as the good of nature against the bad of society, or the bad of society against the good of society. Berry suggests each side has good and bad points and that we should compare the good with the good and the bad with the bad.

Aldo Leopold (1949) wrote of the first ethic as the relationship between individuals (the Golden Rule) but found "no ethic dealing with man's relation to land and to the animals and plants which grow upon it" (p. 203). Leopold noted that the relationship between people and the land was strictly economic. People saw no obligation to the land or to nature. Since Leopold's death in 1948, the population of the world has more than doubled, from 2.75 billion to more than 6 billion. Our impact has grown even faster. Part of the move toward sustainability must be the recognition that property rights include obligations that society defines and property owners must respect. Aldo Leopold is famous for writing, "A thing is right when it tends to preserve the integrity, stability and beauty of the biotic community. It is wrong when it tends otherwise" (p. 224). Leopold himself underwent a profound change in values through his experience and observations, a dynamic shift in his perception of quality.

The postindustrial landscape must embrace the processes of nature as the model on which we base our activities and as the context in which we carry them out. This requires a new expression of landscape. The picturesque landscape based on the idyll English pastoral landscape and estate has been degraded into strange configurations of single story offices with huge lawns and three-quarter-acre exurban pseudo-colonial villages. We know inherently that there is an imbalance but feel that there is little an individual can do. In spite of our technology and economic resources, there is a sense of dissatisfaction as we learn there is a limit to what can be consumed. The cycle of production, consumption, and disposal that has come to characterize "modern" living is not satisfying; there is no end point.

We have become so competent and numerous that our day-to-day activities have global impacts. In the past we worked to survive; today we work to consume. While we have traditionally resisted the "tyranny" of nature for survival, we cannot deny its value to our own existence.

Landscape Ecology and People

Landscape ecology recognizes the integration of humans in the environment as both cause and effect. The discipline has grown from work undertaken primarily in Europe to understand the ecological role of humans in shaping the land itself but also in the relationships within the ecosystem. Much of our interaction is guided by a mixture of values that vary widely in application. Attempts to quantify the impact of values on individual and social actions and decisions have improved our understanding of motivations and self-interest, but little research has focused on the relationship between the environment and values, where the environment is the cause and the value the effect. If humans are indeed a part of the landscape ecology, it must be presumed that they are influenced by that same environment.

Humans act and interact based on complex relationships that have evolved to promote the development and survival of the group. Individual actions are directed and assessed by the culture at large: in general, actions that are good for the individual and good for society are encouraged; actions that are good for the individual but bad for society are discouraged.

Cultural and political infrastructure has been developed to support these tendencies. For example, society requires children for its long-term survival; therefore, elaborate mechanisms evolved to encourage families. Some of these are basic and perhaps are biologically based (the nearly universal sense of protecting children from harm), and at the extreme are more elaborate, purely political constructs (tax benefits to married couples). In fact, these are reflections of the values of the culture at large.

Values are in one important sense recognition of an important commitment and responsibility to the future. As guidelines, they serve to modify individual and cultural behavior in ways that contribute to the good of the group but do not benefit the individual directly. These values are often unrecognized as discreet moral choices but stand as a bundle of underlying, usually unarticulated, principles that serve as the foundation of both social and individual behavior. Planners sometimes find a disconnect between what is considered "good" planning within the profession and what is "good" for the communities in which they work.

Change occurs incrementally and is typically based on the pursuit of what is deemed a circumstance of higher quality by the members of society at large. Individual values tend to reflect the larger social fabric of values and the definition of quality. As individuals form opinions about the form and content of quality, these choices are reflected in the principles they adopt to guide their own behavior. Though perhaps not a cognitive process, each person adopts a model of quality and the underlying principles to support and advance toward this model. Values are indeed an assessment of importance and quality for the individual as well as for a cultural group.

As circumstances change, individuals may test their principles against new information and adapt to the new information. Change may be expressed as small "course corrections" or as fundamental changes in individual principles. As the number of individuals with like feelings increase, these new values are expressed in the culture at large at the political and social levels. Predictably, such changes are slow to occur, but evidence of the process abounds. Design professional and professions, in view of their knowledge and experience, have an obligation to educate communities and to advocate for sustainability.

In 1991, the 22 largest environmental advocacy groups in the United States reported 11,533,818 members, a more than 100 percent increase over their rolls in 1980. By 1999, 20 of the largest environmental advocacy organizations in the United States combined in a new effort called "Save Our Environment," with the intent to leverage their power in a more focused attempt to influence public policy. More Americans identify themselves as environmentalists as time passes. Surveys since 1990 have reported that 58 to 85 percent of those asked considered themselves to be environmentalists (Hendee and Pitstick, 1992). By 1995 membership in environmental groups had grown to 19 million and doubled again by 2000 when the IRS estimated membership in such groups to be 41 million. Since 2005 major environmental organizations have reported robust growth in membership.

Individuals identify with the principle of being environmentalists rather than identifying with a particular environmental issue. In a survey taken within the Chesapeake Bay watershed in 1994, 85 percent of those surveyed said they were somewhat or very concerned about pollution in the bay, 68 percent said they were active or somewhat active in helping to reduce pollution in the bay, but less than 10 percent could identify the most significant sources of pollution to the bay (Chesapeake Bay Program, 1994). A study conducted by the Times-Mirror organization in 1992 also found that most Americans identified strongly with environmental issues. In several surveys conducted in 2007, more than 90 percent of the people asked were concerned about environmental quality. When asked which was more important, 71 percent felt that protecting a wetland was more important than a developer's right to build 50 new homes. In the same group, however, only 48 percent felt protecting the wetland was more important than a broke homeowner's right to sell his land for new home construction. Although generally encouraging, these surveys all show similar kinds of uncertainty. In the Chesapeake Bay survey, most respondents identified themselves as concerned and active but only 10.5 percent belonged to an environmental group. Agriculture, construction, and suburban and urban runoff represent the greatest sources of pollutants affecting the bay, but those surveyed did not rank them in the top four reasons. Only 8 percent surveyed thought farming was the most serious source of pollution, 7 percent thought individuals were, and 2 percent considered construction a major source. The overwhelming majority believed business/industry (32 percent), sewage treatment (16 percent), and commercial shipping (15 percent) were the most serious sources of pollution. In general, most people have little difficulty assigning problems to large corporations or to the government for solution, but they are less committed in expecting the same involvement from individuals.

Individual values are learned through cultural and personal experience in both formal and informal circumstances. Formal experience generally conveys a standard of behavior, concepts of right and wrong, and cultural standards based on fact and myth. These are the concepts that underlie the social contract and political fabric of the community at large. To varying degrees, each individual is a version of the cultural model under process of modification via firsthand experience.

We recognize intuitively that values do not operate in isolation from other influences; most choices are an amalgam of factors and motivations. This is particularly true for environmental values: high environmental values can be expected to meet a high degree of conflict with competing motives such as economic opportunity, personal advancement, and lifestyle values. Environmental values have been studied at length, and Kempton et al. (1996) identified three sources of environmental values: (1) religious or spiritual values, (2) anthropocentric or human-centered values, and (3) biocentric or life-centered values. Although there is debate among scholars as to the quality of the different sources, Kempton et al.'s study concludes that the source is less important than the cultural model through which the values are expressed.

The cultural model is the order in which values are ranked. If most people identify themselves as having high environmental values, the differences between them are the order in which they rank environmental values with other values. This order is the cultural model of the individual. Each individual thinks his or her order is the correct one. The cultural model is a reflection of the individual's understanding of how nature works. As the public has come to understand the interconnectedness of nature and the impact of human activity, the sense of responsibility has increased and the need to protect nature has grown. The Kempton et al. study looked at how different groups responded to questions regarding environmental values, and how they ranked these values. A shared set of beliefs was found among a diverse set of groups ranging from Earth First! and Sierra Club members to laid off sawmill workers, dry cleaners, and the general public.

When differences are noted, they are found primarily in the cultural model—that is, in selecting one value over another. For example, as a group, laid off sawmill workers (70 percent) expressed caring for their families as more important than the environment, whereas few Earth First! members (13 percent) did. It is interesting to note, however, that more Sierra Club members felt this way than did sawmill workers. The values of the individuals range from religious/spiritual (the environment should be respected and protected because of God/Nature), to human centered (the environment should be protected and preserved for our use and the future of humans), to life centered (nature has intrinsic value and should be respected and protected for that reason alone). The study concludes, among other things, that while the sources of values may differ, the values themselves are very similar. Although the source of the motivation may be different, the expressed environmental values have more in common than they do differences, and it is through the cultural model that these differences are expressed.

Individuals tend to hold values that reflect experiences they view as high quality and that do not conflict with other learned values. In general, things valued as being of high quality are sought out, and things of low quality are ignored or discouraged. To some extent, low environmental values or expectations of environmental or landscape quality can be correlated to the corresponding poor environmental and landscape quality of places. The sameness from place to place, the universality of the American city, and the loss of environmental quality in the built environment are reflections of the low value and expectations of builders and users in the past. We tend not to see things of low value, and we tend not to provide for them in our construction.

If we are to embrace sustainable development, the value of the environment must be appropriately reflected. Moving toward a model of sustainable development is not simply a matter of adopting new design standards, otherwise sustainability is a luxury, something only high-end projects can afford, the first thing lost when budget is an issue. Developing a sustainable culture will require a greater awareness of development and a more sophisticated approach to design.

Science and Design

To begin with it is important to understand what we mean by design; Victor Papanek (1995) expresses it best: "In the broadest sense a designer is a human being attempting to walk the narrow bridge between order and chaos, freedom and nihilism, between past achievements and future possibilities" (p. 7). Papanek expresses a telesistic view of design; that is, a view in which the processes of nature are put to good use to meet a social or individual goal. Christopher Alexander (Alexander et al., 1977) wrote about assessing design within its context, and William McDonough and Michael Braungart (2002) discuss design as being about our intentions.

Good design is an intellectual process oriented toward a desired outcome, whereas nature is a reflection of dynamic processes that follow certain immutable laws. Snowflakes, the shapes of leaves, and ripples in the sand are not design, they are patterns. People design to achieve some outcome. Design is intelligent, conscious, and intentional and represents the application of knowledge, insight, and intuition. Designers work on several levels at once: the objective (technical knowledge, geometry, and the laws of nature), the subjective (individual insight, creativity, and experience), and the intersubjective (one's cultural view or social paradigm). It could be argued that design that proceeds on only one or two fronts is by definition incomplete. Good design is always thoughtful.

Science is a way of knowing. It is both a process and a body of knowledge. Other ways of knowing may include knowledge stemming from traditions, faith, intuition, and experience. Our objective view is firmly rooted in science. From the fifteenth century until well into the twentieth century, western science proceeded on what has been called the Newtonian paradigm, the objective science of Newton and Bacon, to the near exclusion of other ways of knowing. In this view, sometimes called reductionist science, things can be known by reducing them to their essence and understanding, through observation, the parts and relationship between the parts. Things are said to be known if they can be observed. The resulting objective knowledge is not good or bad; it is simply knowledge. The objective view has larger implications for our view of nature and how we have perceived our role in the environment. Design of all types is more or less applied science, and until recently the reductionist objective view has been the only significant view of science.

The twentieth century has been described as the Century of the Engineer, among other things. It is an apt description inasmuch as modern society placed much of its faith in the ability of engineers to solve problems. Beginning in the nineteenth century and throughout the twentieth century, engineering design was reduced to its most objective form. Engineering economics emerged as a means of studying and expressing objective efficiency in design. In this expression, efficiency is narrowly defined, usually in economic terms. Much good was accomplished using this objective, efficient approach, and much harm was done as well. The Newtonian paradigm and engineering efficiency simply were unable to consider other values. As engineering expertise and capabilities grew from this knowledge, our efforts grew to maximize them in architecture and design. The finistrations and beauty increasingly became something added at the end of the design process, not inherent to it. Exceptions to this trend are fairly common but notable because they stand apart.

Science is a way of knowing, but it is only one way. Science has moved past the rigidity of reductionism; for example, chaos theory and complexity consider the implications of simple actions within complex systems. Science has discovered synergy, processes in nature that are greater than the sum of their parts. When Frank Lloyd Wright countered Louis Sullivan with the remark that form is function, he was more correct than even he knew. Today McDonough and Braungart (2002) are leading us to a new iteration and to realize "form follows evolution."

The twenty-first century finds us more able to appreciate the complexity of the world and the need for a deeper, more thoughtful approach to design of all types. The preservation of landscape function and the creation of beautiful and functional places are complementary and require a holistic approach to design. A sustainability paradigm will emerge from what is learned and done by professionals working today. It is called sustainable design, regenerative design, and other things, but it embodies a deeper understanding that comes from knowing both how things work and how they relate to other things. Sustainability cannot ignore aesthetics. Human beings desire beauty. To be sustainable, the environment must offer us opportunities for individual as well as cultural fulfillment. In *Zen and the Art of Motorcycle Maintenance* Robert Pirsig (1984) contrasts what he calls the romantic and classical views; essentially it comes down to do you want to look good or do you want it to work? The classical view is concerned with functionality, and the romantic view is concerned with the appearance of a thing. Sustainability requires both.

Today it has become inadequate to simply collect storm water and convey it away in the most efficient manner possible. We must consider the wider role of water on the site and its place within a broader region. We must begin to design within the natural system, recognizing that precipitation is an asset and a resource. The definition of quality in design has expanded to consider the natural system. As this recognition continues, these parts of the landscape will become more visible because they will begin to have value for us. The role of science is to help us understand, but in the end it is only one part of the designer's voice.

Principles of Sustainability

Nature evolves to become more diverse and more complex. Living things adapt to many niches, creating pathways and links through which energy and materials pass. Our approach to design has been to focus on efficiency and uniformity; concentrations of energy and materials that by definition reduce the pathways of energy and materials. Nature is redundant, finding many ways to accomplish energy and material transfer.

Where nature recycles everything, modern industrial and postindustrial systems are one-way systems of consumption. Although there have been significant improvements in pollution control and prevention, the quality of air and water in the United States continues to decline because the underlying system of cleansing and assimilation has been minimized while the generation of wastes has increased. If pollution is defined as the presence of a substance in quantities that exceed nature's or the ecosystem's ability to process it, then we have been inhibiting natural systems in two ways: increasing the presence of pollutants while decreasing the natural capacity to absorb them. Sustainability requires replacing or improving these processes of assimilation and natural cycling of materials.

The strategies for design should be fairly straightforward, but we are too often practiced in ignoring the ecologic underpinnings of design. Site design professionals should be students of nature and look for ways to let nature do the work on a site. By using existing landscape elements or enhancing them, the development of a site can occur while preserving the landscape functions both on site and as part of a regional fabric. For example, expanding existing on-site wetlands to treat the anticipated runoff from a development preserves the integrity of the landscape system and reduces the impact of the site. By preserving or developing riparian zones in green ways, designers can preserve the hydrologic, habitat, and assimilative capacities of the landscape and provide a site amenity.

By looking to nature and understanding how nature works, improvements can be planned in such a way that maintenance and life cycle costs are reduced and environmental values are increased. Natural communities are diverse because diverse communities thrive. Instead of a few species of plants, there are many. In this way the plants are better able to resist disease and predation. Planning for diverse plant communities may involve some greater initial costs, but operation and maintenance costs are much lower as the community is established and matures in comparison to a more formal and monotonous plant scheme. Less natural elements have their place, but natural plant communities also belong to the developed site. The best models for designing a functional site are found in nature.

Efficient design is epitomized by minimizing development costs, and costs are kept low by minimizing the amount of material and labor required to develop a site. For design to be effective, however, we must go beyond efficiency and look to the impacts of our choices and the effects of our products. Through efficient development, we decrease the infiltration on sites and increase runoff. We then collect and concentrate runoff into pipes designed to maintain an effective scour velocity, and deliver all of this sediment and pollutant laden water in a concentrated dose to a collection facility or, worse yet, directly into some natural surface water. Nature also concentrates runoff, but water in most overland flow occurs only after much has soaked into the ground. Surface runoff is filtered as it courses through and around vegetation and is absorbed into riparian and littoral zones. By observing nature we have learned to encourage infiltration rather than concentrating runoff into pipes and to use many small infiltration systems rather than one large one.

We should use information and intellect to replace power. Throughout the world are examples of architecture and site planning that were based on understanding the character of the place. Designers, for the most part not professionally trained, accomplished design goals by understanding and taking advantage of the character of the places in which they lived. In New England buildings were located to take advantage of the winter sun and to shut out the cold winds from the north and west. In the southeast houses were built with tall ceilings and large windows to encourage air movement through the house, eaves were built to shade the house from the summer sun, and houses were oriented to collect the evening breezes. In the southwest Native Americans built thick-walled houses to insulate from the heat and cold and developed xeric forms of agriculture. The examples are as plentiful as the places and the people that lived in them.

The availability of inexpensive energy and building systems has resulted in a lack of sophistication in design; time-tested models are ignored. Buildings once reflected an elegance of design, a thoughtful construction based on an awareness of the environment. Buildings in this tradition were active working machines. With cheap energy and systems engineering, buildings have become mere decorative boxes, containers for people and activities managed by complex systems. Complexity does not imply sophistication or elegance. There is a price for this lack of sophistication; energy and building operation costs are higher for one thing. In a deeper way, such buildings contribute to our separation from the natural world; we do not have to understand the seasons if all we have to do is push a button for heat or for cool air. Intelligently designing buildings and sites to reduce energy requirements is an important strategy for sustainable design.

We should look for ways to use resources for multiple purposes. Wet ponds may be used to enhance cooling systems or provide habitat as well as treating and storing runoff. Parking lots might be designed to be shared between complementary uses. Building materials could be selected with recycling in mind and so on. Table 12.1 lists some elements of a sustainable economy. The key to sustainable design is to incorporate the principles of sustainability in every design decision.

Emerging Trends

Much is happening in the transition toward sustainability. It is sometimes difficult to have a sense of progress, but a designer by nature must be an optimist and believe that

Decrease our reliance on nonrenewable energy.
Increase material efficiency through recycling and reuse and better design (doing more with less).
Improve functionality through design and a reduction in the use of energy.
Reduce the use of toxic materials.
Recognize the environmental costs in accounting procedures.
Repair damaged or lost environmental functions.

TABLE 12.1 Elements of a Sustainable Economy

what may be done will make a difference. Smart growth has become the focus of much attention in recent years. The essence of smart growth is to slow down suburban sprawl by encouraging development in places where it can be best supported by existing infrastructure. Many interests have attached themselves to smart growth and tried to refocus its intent, but for the most part smart growth appears to be a fairly effective approach to addressing development concerns. Smart growth promotes environmentally friendly and community-oriented development. Among its concerns are transportation, community equity and health, environmental quality, and economic prosperity. It is difficult to determine how many individual smart growth community organizations there are in the United States, but the network of interested people and organizations continues to grow.

Smart growth at the state level usually involves directing public funding to identifiable growth areas that have existing utilities, adequate public and highway transportation, and civic infrastructure. In this way public funds (taxes from those living in the existing communities) are used to support existing communities rather than subsidizing communities that do not yet exist. Growth is directed in such a way as to encourage the use of public transportation, the development of open space, the stabilization of communities, and to contribute to the quality of life.

States are necessarily going beyond smart growth as growing populations and development begin to exhaust limited resources. In the arid southwest, for example, the population of Nevada, the fastest growing state in the nation, doubled in the last decade. Arizona, second only to Nevada, has seen its population increase by 40 percent. California, the most populated state in the nation, expects to add 15 million more residents to the 34 million that already live there. Water has long been a contentious matter in the west, and increases in population promise to make it even more so. In the fall of 2001, California law began to require that any residential project of over 500 dwelling units must conclusively demonstrate that a sufficient supply of water exists for at least 20 years' use. Failing such a demonstration will prevent the project from breaking ground. Limiting development may be one component of smart growth, but it cannot be the only solution. People will continue to locate in the desirable sunshine states, and stopping development for whatever reason will serve to limit the housing supply, resulting in higher prices and limiting housing affordability still more. Development of some form will continue because it must. It is the form and related practices that will change.

The National Association of Home Builders (NAHB) has made a series of commitments to smart growth and to improve the practices of home development. Some have complained that NAHB brings a self-serving view to its articulation of smart growth and green building practices, but perhaps the differences are a matter of degree rather than substance. There will always be room for disagreement in sustainable development practices. Sustainability is not a one-size-fits-all or a unified field theory of development; it is a new paradigm replete with its own problems, trends, and rewards.

The Chesapeake Bay Foundation announced "Builders for the Bay" in December of 2001, a program to bring environmental activists and builders together to develop sustainable building practices in the Chesapeake watershed. Another encouraging trend has been the shift in the purchasing practices of the federal government. In requests for proposals (RFPs) for buildings and site work, various federal agencies have started to include sustainability in the evaluation criteria. The BEES system (see Chap. 2) provides a method for evaluating the embodied energy and life cycle impact of materials. The federal government is the largest buyer in the U.S. marketplace, purchasing more products, materials, goods, and services than any other single entity. With the purchasing power of the federal government, design and construction firms have had to become more expert in sustainable and green development practices as a matter of good business.

The private sector has also begun to respond. The Leadership in Energy and Environmental Design (LEED) is a method of building assessment developed by the U.S. Green Building Council that provides professionals with a consensus-based set of practices to guide design decisions (see Chap. 2). This self-assessment process is based on life cycle considerations and accepted energy and environmental design principles and practices. The LEED rating system recognizes the values of redevelopment and steering development to existing urban areas. Designers are encouraged to meet fairly specific performance standards with regard to storm water management, minimizing disturbed areas, reducing the amount of water required for the landscape, reducing the heat island effect, minimizing light pollution, and encouraging alternative transportation. In addition to LEED, other important sources of information have emerged such as the Center for Watershed Protection and the Green Building Network.

Industry has also started to change its behavior. Many large corporations are rethinking their approach to the environment. In the past environmental compliance had been the target, which consisted largely of treating or managing wastes after they were produced. The cost of compliance was significant; the consequence, if not the objective, of many environmental regulations was to increase the costs of producing wastes, particularly hazardous wastes. In the 1980s businesses began to realize that cost avoidance was a better strategy: if they never produced the waste, they would not have to manage it, thereby avoiding the costs and liability altogether. The so-called pollution prevention, or P2, movement was the result. By the early to mid-1990s, businesses began to move past P2 toward an industrial ecology. Bradley Allenby, a vice president of AT&T, has been an important promoter of this concept.

Industrial ecology is an approach to business that uses the model of an ecosystem as its guide. Recognizing the principles nature employs such as recycling, multiple pathways for energy and materials, and system redundancies, industries have started to look for ways of developing similar relationships among themselves. In such a system one firm's waste might become raw material for a second firm; waste heat from one operation may be used to power the process of another, and so on. In principle everything is used, there is no waste. While real-world obstacles must be overcome, successful efforts have demonstrated that such an approach is more than simply cost avoidance; there is a positive contribution to the bottom line.

Challenges

Although there is much already under way, much remains to be done. This period of change provides the opportunity for design professionals to assume leadership roles not only within their profession but within their communities also. The site planning and development profession is among the few professions in which trained and experienced practitioners find their reasoned and well-founded work subject to review by people with no training. Sustainable design issues present a challenge to design professionals to lead and teach through the design and planning process. More design professionals should participate on local planning and zoning commissions. There should be greater political involvement on the part of design professionals beyond simply protecting or renewing practice acts every so many years. In the absence of such leadership, we must be content to be led by others.

Sustainable design requires a greater awareness of the underlying science of site design. It also will probably require working in more interdisciplinary teams. There is not a significant existing body of research or criticism that addresses the practices of landscape and site planning and design. With notable exceptions, most of the literature of planning and design is directed toward recounting historic or contemporary successes, and most criticism among professionals is focused on aesthetics. Effective means of criticism and review between professionals would strengthen the state of practice. Understanding what has not worked and why is at least as useful as celebrating another success. Colleges and universities are the best places to promote this type of thinking. Thankfully many have embraced this responsibility and have completed projects that demonstrate the practicality and wonder that may emerge from sustainable development. Although much research may be done, there are few places where this research is made available or disseminated within the profession. Much of the research that is promoted tends to be conducted by manufacturers, and although some of it is interesting, there is rarely any review or criticism. Site planning and design is an interdisciplinary profession of applied science, technology, and art. This should serve to increase the opportunities for research.

In addition to the science of sustainability, designers and planners should reach out to communities to understand the interests of the people. It is insufficient to remain apart and criticize poor design. Recently in the Washington, D.C. area a well-respected author of innovative community design was shouted down in a presentation he was invited to make to a community because his talk encouraged higher densities and more public transportation. The audience was unprepared to listen to these ideas, which may very well be core principles in the future of sustainable design in communities like theirs. We must assume they were unprepared in part because they did not have all of the facts at hand. It is incumbent upon design professionals to listen to what the public is saying so we can consider their interests as important stakeholders in our work.

The site design professional has a unique place among the design professions in that site design work is almost always subject to the review and approval of citizens who frequently do not have either the expertise or knowledge of the design professional. That can be frustrating, as anyone who has worked in the field will attest, but it is a fact of our professional life. It is in our own self-interest to work with communities and citizen planners to develop a deeper understanding of the impacts of our collective work and to provide leadership as advocates for sustainability.

CHAPTER **13**

Professional and Project Management Issues

Failure

One way of viewing the planning and design process is as a process of avoiding failure; design proceeds by weighing solutions in terms of what will work. Henry Petroski (2000) observed that design is always evaluated in terms of failure, and success is celebrated in terms of failure avoided. Failure is most often perceived as the antithesis of success, but in fact failure can be seen in several ways.

Failure is sometimes a matter of perception: one person's failure is another's success. The old saw that the operation was a success but the patient died is an expression of this.

Sometimes failure is an event. The elevated walkways in the Kansas City Hyatt Regency were a successful design. The design was sound, but when the walkways failed due to an ill-advised contractor's modification, it was an event. A bridge could be said to be a successful design until the day it suddenly falls down. Success in this case is a condition or a state. Once a thing is seen to have failed, it cannot be seen again to be otherwise.

Some failures are related to economics. Economic failure may be a result of poor financial planning, a change in the marketplace, unexpected developments, or spiraling operating costs.

Engineering failures are almost always limited to projects or designs on the cutting edge of design and materials. Catastrophic failure in site planning is rare, primarily because standards of care and practices have emerged, been tested, and refined over its long history. This vast experience has led to safety factors or practices of overdesign that are routinely employed to avoid risk and reduce liability. These safety factors and design practices have evolved from trial and error as much as from rigorous engineering and scientific study. These practices may be so familiar to us that they are followed without question.

Some failures are related to changed circumstances. All responsible designs and designers proceed on the basis of what they have learned either firsthand or as students. There are very few truly inspired new solutions to problems; solutions tend to be iterations of solutions that have worked in the past. Failure may occur because the design problem or circumstance changes, requiring new applications for familiar methods or an entirely new consideration.

As students or practicing professionals, we rarely study failure in any meaningful way. No one likes to dwell on mistakes, particularly one's own, but it is the lessons learned from mistakes that make our experience valuable. Failure is rarely discussed openly, and its causes are often dismissed as ineptitude, poor judgment, or misadventure. The literature of site planning and design is primarily a catalog of practical methods and a library of success stories. Expositions on failure are uncommon, but we readily acknowledge that there is more to learn from understanding failure than from mimicking past successes. To study failure is to gain understanding of the underlying principles and forces at work in a situation, but it is also to gain an appreciation for the choices that were made and why.

Design failure is usually divided into technical and nontechnical causes. Technical causes are addressed directly in the practice of overdesign and safety factors. Most technical problems can be discovered in the quality assurance process through repeated checking and multiple reviewers. Nontechnical causes of failure may be more difficult to identify or address. The nontechnical threats to project success usually fall into one or more of these categories:

1. Inadequate capitalization through design and construction and into the future.
2. Regulatory resistance or apathy in the form of a lack of interest, a lack of authority, or a lack of will.
3. Community resistance and image issues.
4. Client infatuation or the honeymoon syndrome, in which clients proceed with a vision but without a well-defined plan or the fiscal and management discipline required. Often the client's vision is visible only to the client.
5. Designer infatuation or the Taj Mahal syndrome, in which design professionals pursue their goals without regard for project limitations.

It is the role of the project manager to avoid all of the causes of failure, whether technical or nontechnical.

Effective management of a project is as important as any of the other various design and planning skills. Firms are often distinguished as much by their abilities to successfully manage the project as they are by any of the other individual parts of the project. Experience suggests that more clients are lost due to management issues than to design concerns, and firms struggle to find, develop, and keep effective project managers. Project management is often treated as a skill one is destined to acquire with time and experience. This is as true for management skills as it is for design skills. Experience improves our skills and burnishes our judgment, but our experience is more productive when supported by training and a sound understanding of the underlying principles and practices. The fundamental objectives of project management are simply stated: to manage cost (within budget), time (on schedule), and quality (meet specifications or expectations). Actually doing it, however, can be a challenge.

In most contemporary environments, working with qualified and creative professionals requires an interactive and fairly open style of management. Many firms are organized around key people who direct the project and staff. Harold Kerzner (2009) makes an important distinction between project managers and project champions (Table 13.1). Most of us have attributes of both manager and champion. Certainly most organizations have people of both types and benefit from their relative strengths. Still, the project

Project managers	Project champions
Prefers to work in groups	Prefers to work individually
Committed to management and technical responsibility	Committed to technology
Committed to organization	Committed to profession
Seeks to achieve objective	Seeks to exceed objective
Willing to take risks	Unwilling to take risks; must test or study everything
Seeks what is possible	Seeks perfection
Thinks in terms of short time spans	Thinks in the long term
Manages people	Manages things
Committed to pursuit of material values	Committed to the pursuit of intellectual values

From Harold Kerzner, *Project Management, A Systems Approach to Planning, Scheduling, and Controlling*, 9th ed. (Hoboken, NJ: John Wiley & Sons, 2009).

TABLE 13.1   Differences between Project Managers and Project Champions

manager is better suited to the levels of interaction required to work with project teams and stakeholders.

The Project Manager

Firms are organized in many different ways, and how the project management role is organized reflects the culture of the organization. Differences also exist between private for-profit organizations and public organizations. Several principles seem to contribute directly to the success of the project manager, however, and some common strengths and roles are required of project managers. In general, project managers are effective communicators, good problem solvers, technically knowledgeable, effective advocates, and articulate representatives of the project, the firm, and their profession. Firms organize the role of the project manager in different ways, and it is difficult to choose one as the most effective. A project manager in a small firm may have quite different responsibilities from a project manager in a large firm.

Project managers are responsible for the successful outcome of the project, and success is comprised of design quality, financial performance, and schedule compliance. Meeting these objectives requires the coordination of in-house resources, subcontractors, scheduling, managing the client, estimating, establishing and meeting budgets, and recognizing and resolving problems in addition to site planning and design responsibilities. Table 13.2 outlines the scope of the project manager's many roles.

Communication

The project manager's role is primarily one of communication. The project manager is the clearinghouse for information both inside and outside of the organization. To be effective, the project manager must be an advocate and balance the sometimes conflicting

Who is the client?
Is there a contract?
What is the objective of the project?
Who are the stakeholders?
Determine the scope of work:
What is it you are going to do?
What is your objective?
Who are you doing it for?
What resources will you need?
Project organization
Subcontractors
Equipment
Where are the decision points in your project?
What regulatory involvement is required? Permits?
What are the deliverables?
When is the job finished?
Project schedule:
How long will it take?
What needs to be done first?
What is the critical path?
When must it be done?
Who sets the pace and the standards?
What regulations will affect the project?
What problems should be anticipated?

TABLE 13.2   Scope of Project Management

interests of the firm, the project, and the client. It is the project manager who articulates the project objectives and controls the design and planning process within the organization. To do this, the project manager must be an effective communicator.

Effective communication is always a challenge. Language is not precise, people tend to hear different things, and the ambiguity of memory all work to muddle the message and the information. An effort beyond casual communication is required to be effective in this role. The project manager must establish a record of communication from the outset of the project and maintain this practice throughout the life of the project.

Project managers soon learn that communication requires preparation. Project information should flow in a consistent form and pattern between staff and subcontractors. Communication is more effective when used in the same fashion and in the same way. Although it is best to provide clearly written communication, if less formal methods are preferred, there should be a consistent format. The consistency alerts the listener that this communication is different—it is more formal and has more weight than casual conversation. Managers should avoid verbal directions to staff as much as possible; when verbal directions are given, they should be supplemented with written confirmation. In the modern office environment, there are numerous tools to provide such written interaction.

Meetings should be organized with a written agenda. Managers should control the meeting as to content and time but be sensitive to new information that might indicate problems or unexpected concerns. All meetings should be summarized in a brief set of minutes, establishing a record of formal communications. The purpose and the value of the agenda/minutes process is in the consistency and expectation created in those being communicated with. Project records that include meeting minutes are often valuable later in the project to re-create the decision-making process. It is also highly recommended that project managers keep a project journal of some form.

External communication to clients, regulatory agencies, and other stakeholders should be carefully prepared. Written communications often have a life well beyond the intention of the author and must stand alone. Every written document must contain all of the relevant facts discussed or provide a reference to another document where the facts can be found. This provides a future reader with the ability to understand or re-create the writer's intent and purpose.

Public communication requires even greater care. Public presentations require planning. When preparing for a public presentation, identify the objectives of the presentation: What is the purpose of the presentation? What is to be accomplished? Articulating the objective provides clear guidance for how to prepare and for how to assess the results. After establishing a clearly stated objective, identify the key points and supporting arguments. Site planning is fairly unique in that trained and experienced professionals are responsible for planning and design, but project approvals are made by individuals who may have no training or experience. Presentations should be carefully prepared to educate the public and public officials. The quality of the presentation and the credibility of the presenter are critical components of the successful presentation.

Project managers may also consider preparing routine project reports. These reports may not be appropriate for small or short-term projects, but larger projects often benefit from periodic summaries. Quarterly summaries to the client and key staff provide updates on progress, identify issues that require attention, and describe performance measures. They provide a reference for correspondence and establish a project history. These reports may have little value once the project is complete, but for those few times when they are needed they are very valuable. During the project, they serve as important internal and external communication tools.

Finally, project managers should consider a project or personal diary. The diary provides an ongoing record of decisions and contacts. Project managers can use the diary to prepare summaries, letters to the file, and similar documents. Many tools exist today to assist the project manager in managing all of these communication demands. Personal communication assistants (PCAs) and similar devices that are compatible with computers can provide valuable assistance to the project manager.

Leadership

Much has been written about leadership, and the various leadership styles and methods are topics of many books and seminars. Project managers must provide leadership by setting objectives and motivating staff to meet those objectives, but leadership style is usually fairly individualized. Most leaders develop a style that is an amalgamation of their own personality, skills they have learned either formally or informally, and the circumstances. That being said, some characteristics of leadership seem to be more effective in professional design environments.

Working with creative, highly trained people requires that a leader be able to direct people through influence perhaps even more than through authority. Often a project manager is responsible for outcomes that rely on the performance of people who do not work for him or her. The project depends on the timely and precise performance of people often working apart from one another and coordinated by a project manager who is not their supervisor. The project manager must find an effective method of communicating and influencing that relies as much on informal influence as it does on formal lines of authority.

Consensus needs to be built in multidisciplinary project teams. The project must proceed on many fronts with confidence that each team member is progressing and that each role is properly informed and coordinated. The project manager must find the means to generate consensus through leadership, facilitation, and influence. The design professional in today's marketplace is highly trained and motivated and requires a participatory role or understanding in his or her work. It is unrealistic to try to build a staff of competent and reliable professionals without developing a sense of project ownership and responsibility in every individual. This sense of professionalism is a reflection of the individual character of each staff member and the degree to which each feels engaged by the organization. This feeling or perception of involvement can be difficult to establish and nurture, but it is a cultural element of many truly successful and innovative firms. It may be the firm owners and senior folks who empower this creative culture, but it is the project managers who breathe life into it through their methods and behavior.

Leadership is most effective when it acts to empower others and when followers feel they can use their own judgment and initiative within the context outlined by the leader. Leaders must be patient, persuasive, recognize the value of followers' contributions, and be active learners.

Managing Change in the Organization

There are four ways to consider the future: (1) things will go on as they have been but get better, (2) things will go on as before but get worse, (3) something serendipitous and wonderful will happen and things will be great, or (4) we will think and plan to influence the future as best we can. Designers and planners intuitively value the last view; projecting a vision into the future is the essence of design. The historian Alexander Toynbee described what he called the challenge-response formula of success: when a response is equal to the challenge, the response is defined as successful, and this remains true until the challenge changes. Warren Bennis, a noted leadership researcher, observed that success is by definition the seed of failure because the challenge will inevitably change. Project managers must provide leadership for the project, but firms require innovators as well.

Change in the firm is inevitable. Resistance to change is natural but is the most significant roadblock to innovation. Within the professional environment, individual experience is comprised of three aspects: skill, knowledge, and attitude. These elements act as both cause and effect. They are honed by experience, but they also influence our behavior and perception. Abraham Maslow once observed, "A man who is good with a hammer tends to see everything as a nail." To become and remain successful, a firm and an individual must avoid the trap of success and intelligently embrace change.

True change occurs in organizations in one of three ways: it is imposed by outside influence, it is the path of least resistance, or it is sought. Change may be imposed on the organization from the outside by changes in regulations, new ownership coming into the firm, or a change in market conditions or competition. The path of least discomfort or pain may lead to change because it is easier or more comfortable to do something different from the way it has always been done. Such change is undertaken to avoid something unpleasant. The last form of change is embraced because it feels good, because it is rewarding or because it promises to be rewarding. Only this kind of change provides a positive experience that can be said to be a function of leadership and management.

Project Management Software

Relatively inexpensive and powerful computers have made significant contributions to project management. The contributions come at a price, however, and many project managers find the maintenance of project information systems to be a time-consuming effort focused more on measuring outcomes than on managing projects. Project management software should serve to manage projects not just collect accounting information.

Good software programs are available to assist the project manager in organizing and tracking project elements. Such programs use a high degree of integration and cross utilization of information, allowing multiple reports from a single set of data. Project management software should be able to track project performance in terms of costs, milestones, and schedules. It should provide forecasting and cost control tools but not be limited to accounting functions or reports. Project management information systems should be designed and implemented to support project management and so should address the needs of project managers primarily. A wide variety of software programs is available, ranging from modestly priced software for creating schedules to expensive network programs. There is a package for every firm and situation. Project managers should evaluate software in terms of what they need or desire, not in terms of what the software company says it can do. Many firms have invested in elaborate packages only to find that project managers use only limited capabilities of the software. Ultimately project management software is project tracking software: no matter how sophisticated, these programs are not truly creative and cannot make decisions or solve problems.

Contracting

The simplest contracts require only that there be an agreement for exchange of value for consideration. Formal contracts are documents that acknowledge the conditions and limits of the exchange, the nature of the value to be exchanged, and the nature of the consideration. The contract language and standard clauses commonly used by design professionals include a description of limits of liability, indemnification clauses, ownership of drawings and reports, and payment. Some contracts include the schedule and the specific scope of work; other contracts refer to documents that contain this information.

Most design professionals include a limitation of liability clause, which limits the liability of the firm, principles of the firm, licensed design professionals, or staff to a sum no more than the sum of fees paid to the firm. In fact, most firms view this language as negotiable and are often persuaded to increase the limits of liability in exchange for increased consideration. Another form of limits on liability is the exclusion of work done by others or effects caused by the actions of others. This limits the firm's liability to work actually done by the firm and excludes liability that might arise from actions of others, such as labor stoppages, or from substantial changes to the scope of work.

Typically contracts for design services include a clause that clearly states that the firm makes no warranty of its work, implied or otherwise. In general, this clause requires the work of the design firm to be judged by a standard of reasonable care; that is, the degree of care generally observed by other design professionals under similar circumstances.

Most design professionals have worked without a contract at one time or another. Over time many firms establish close working relationships with clients and subcontractors. In many cases this arrangement is mutually satisfying and profitable. Most design professionals have also experienced difficulties getting paid or resolving unhappy situations without a contract. Many professional liability insurance carriers require project-specific contracts for projects that are equal to or of greater value than the firm's out-of-pocket deductible.

Professional Liability

Risk management begins with knowing what you are being paid to do and what client expectations are. One of the most important aspects of formal written contracts is the exercise that is necessary to describe the work and the outcomes. Firms should never assume greater responsibility than they contracted for and shouldn't contract for work they are unprepared for. Professional liability usually stems from negligence, omissions, and/or errors.

Professional liability insurance, sometimes called E&O insurance, is purchased to protect firms and individuals from suits and costs arising from omissions and errors, but it may not address negligence. Furthermore, professional liability insurance may limit the activities that fall under the professional design umbrella. For example, firms that choose to act as a contractor, even for a moment, may not be covered by insurance for claims arising out of such action. Most professional design liability insurance policies include a "pollution exclusion." This clause has been interpreted differently by various companies.

Protecting yourself from claims is generally referred to as risk management. Some providers of E&O insurance provide training for staff to learn about risk management and to recognize problems while they are still manageable. Such firms sometimes offer discounted insurance rates for firms that complete such training. The basic principles of risk management (Table 13.3) are fairly straightforward, but they are often found to be difficult to practice.

1. Know what you are being paid to do.
2. Do not assume greater responsibility that you have contracted for.
3. Formally recognize changes in the scope of work.
4. React immediately to problems that may be potential claims.

TABLE 13.3   Basic Risk Management Principles

Ambiguity in project scope or in objectives is fertile ground for later difficulties. A tight scope of work provides a clear set of tasks and deliverables and significantly less room for misunderstanding. Once the scope is established, the project manager must be on guard for "mission creep"; that is, taking on more work or tasks than originally called for. More work is usually welcome, but not if it is going to be difficult to get paid for it later or if it is the seed of client discontent. Additional work should be formally recognized and incorporated into the agreement between the firm and the client.

Professionals with a good relationship with their clients are often called upon to assist the client when trouble arises. Occasionally the professional may be asked to assume a management role in construction activities. Such opportunities may be exciting and demonstrate the firm's value to the client, but the professional may be moving from a professional relationship to a contractor relationship in terms of liability. Although there may be business advantages to taking on these tasks, they are not without costs. Professionals must be careful to never unintentionally cross the line from recommending and observing to directing and supervising.

Finally, perhaps the most difficult part of risk management is to recognize and react to the earliest warning signs of a problem. This is difficult because few of us enjoy dealing with problems, especially if they result from our decisions. The fact of the matter is, however, that problems identified and addressed early are most likely not to progress to insurance claims or suits. If nothing else, costs are contained by early action. In many situations recognition and swift action makes the relationship between the firm and the client much stronger. We all make mistakes eventually, but only those who manage mistakes effectively can actually profit from them.

Problem Solving

A critical project management skill is to be able to recognize and solve problems. Much time can be spent in seminars and training trying to acquire this skill. For many project managers the capacity to deal with problems effectively is their defining skill. No single approach is best, and different sorts of problems may require different skills. If experience can be considered a guide, an unscientific survey of successful project managers suggests the following strategies:

1. Address causes of a problem not merely the symptoms.

2. The earlier the problem is addressed, the less impact it will have.

3. Problems are solved quicker and better in an environment of openness and communication.

4. Understand the scope of the problem in the context of the project.

It is not always easy to identify the causes of problems. Problems in projects may be rooted in anything from materials to management, from poor design to poor training, from acts of God to acts of incompetence. The project manager owns the problem without regard to its cause, but understanding and addressing the cause is critical to success. Successfully anticipating problems is as good as a project manager can hope for, but in the absence of that, reacting quickly once a problem is identified is nearly as good. An early intervention usually reduces the impact problems inflict on schedules, lost or wasted materials, and on personnel. Problem solving requires effective communication; an environment of openness and cooperation is better suited to problem resolution. Problems left in the dark usually make it to the light of day, often with otherwise avoidable consequences.

Finally, problems in site design and planning occur within the context of a project. Most project managers are members of a larger group of people working for the success of the project, and problems that occur in the course of the project may "belong" to the group at large rather than to an individual member or firm on the team. It is important to understand problems in this context as issues of both standard of care (obligation to the client and stakeholders) and professional liability. Effective communication is the key to successful problem solving within a project team.

Quality Assurance in the Design Process

Quality assurance is a critical element of the design and planning process, but it remains an elusive and ambiguous objective: defining quality is perhaps more difficult than achieving it. There are many approaches to quality assurance, but in general quality is achieved through communication, technical competence, and a commitment to the work. These are the necessary attributes of the firm and the individuals who make up the firm. Quality is not accomplished through checklists, though for some people checklists are a helpful tool. Pushing responsibility down to the lowest level of the organization does not achieve quality if the staff is unqualified or the project is poorly defined. A competent staff cannot produce quality work without effective leadership, communication, and resources. Quality often seems to be as much a part of an organization's culture as it is any distinct effort. Some firms seem to operate in a paradigm of quality guided by the unspoken character of the members and leadership of the firm. Others seem to rely on the leadership or supervision of key personnel.

Getting Paid

Getting paid can be a challenge. Unpaid invoices are important warning signs that every project manager should be aware of. A client who is slow to pay may be unhappy with some aspect of the firm's performance, be underfinanced, or be reevaluating the project. The project manager must determine why the invoices are not paid and what, if anything, to do about it.

In an unscientific survey of project managers, the most common reason for lack of payment was related to communication. Although other reasons may have been given by the client, the underlying reason was a perceived lack of attention on the part of the client. Whether there was an actual lack of communication was less important than this perception. Many project managers have discovered an effective tool for getting paid is to make a special call to a client after the invoice has been received to confirm that it has been received and to inquire if there are any questions about the invoice. If there is a problem, it surfaces early instead of a month or two later.

Once a problem is identified, it is critical that some action be taken in fairly short order. In many cases the quick and effective response strengthens the relationship between client and the professional. In cases of untrustworthy clients, the sooner the problem is identified, the sooner the action can be taken.

Dealing with unpaid invoices is among the least favorite tasks for many project managers. Unpaid invoices leave both the client and the firm unhappy with the circumstance. It is important that the manager remains objective. The firm is entitled to be paid for work contracted and performed. The client is entitled to receive the benefit of work performed and fairly paid for. There must be a win-win, and it is the manager's role to balance these interests and solve the problem.

Payment terms and conditions should be part of every contract. Firms should bill and expect to be paid in accordance with the contract. Exceptions should be dealt with immediately and in person. Clients who refuse to pay or do not meet payment promises should not expect continued service, and the relationship should be formally terminated.

Early and frequent contact with clients is the best way to ensure payment or to identify a problem with a client.

Greening Up the Design Practice

Many of the suggestions in this book are common practices, but the standards and the reluctance to change in some communities and even in some design firms is evident from the types of projects still being produced. Design professionals are not the only party in the design process, but they are best suited to educating and bringing change to the built environment. Firms engaged in land planning and design should seek opportunities to provide access to public transit and create linking pedestrian corridors and bicycle paths. The character of communities is more that the eyewash of clever plantings and curvilinear roads; it is ultimately how they work, and transportation is a critical feature of the modern community.

Design professionals should encourage zoning ordinances to permit mixed-use development so homeowners can walk to the store, to school, or to work. It is necessary to advocate for these changes when not representing the interest of a client so the motivation is clearly the quality of the design. Buildings should be situated to maximize energy efficiency, allow for pedestrian access, and reduce development impacts. The cost implications are generally favorable because of narrower and shorter roads and reduced lengths of utilities.

Plans should incorporate the protection of trees and topsoil during site work. When backfilling a foundation or grading around a building, specifications should require that construction debris be removed rather than buried. Contractors should be encouraged to minimize jobsite waste by centralizing cutting operations to reduce waste and simplify sorting. Clearly marked bins for different types of usable waste (wood scraps for kindling, sawdust for compost, etc.) should be set up. Salvaged materials can be recycled or donated to low-income housing projects or community groups.

In addition to introducing more green design practices to the site, firms should consider finding ways to "walk the walk" and improve the environmental performance of their own businesses. Reducing the environmental impact of the firm contributes to the firm's credibility and serves as a model for other firms. Simple strategies such as the type of vehicle used in the company fleet, encouraging employee carpooling, and the use of mass transit are important steps. The use of recycled paper or rebuilt office equipment and using recycled materials in office furniture and decorating speaks volumes to clients and the public. The well-designed and appointed office could serve as a calling card for the firm's values and commitment. Make the daily routine in the office a reflection of the values brought to bear in your designs.

The "greening" of design and planning becomes more of a reality as time passes. This is probably a reflection of a wider recognition in our society of the importance of responsible design, but it is also the result of many individual professionals moving toward greener design with each new project and opportunity. The environmentally sensitive site plan is no longer the work product of a few boutique firms; in a matter of only a few more years, it will be expected and required by everyone.

Dealing with the Public

The work of site design professionals is always under scrutiny and subject to change and approval by nonprofessionals. This can cause frustration due to required changes to plans that contribute nothing to the project or, worse yet, undermine the design in some fashion. Nonetheless, it is a tenet in the United States that land use is a public process and locally controlled. Professionals must learn to work effectively with citizen-planners and local authorities. Much of what an effective designer does is to educate the public in the value and values of the project. Good presentation skills are critical to this process.

Presentations

Preparation is the key to every presentation, and preparation begins with understanding what your presentation is to accomplish. Articulate a clear and concise objective, and build your presentation around that. It has been said that for every 5 minutes of presentation you should plan on an hour of preparation time. Some presentations take more preparation and others take less. Articulating your objective should help you to determine the preparation effort required. By clearly stating what the presentation is meant to achieve at the outset, the preparation will be more focused.

Preparation

Once an objective has been stated, the next step is to understand to whom the presentation is being made. In a public meeting, is the presentation being made to the members of the community or to the members of the planning commission? Depending on the circumstances, it could be one or the other, or both. It is necessary to understand why the members of the public are there: What is their interest? How will they be affected by the project? By addressing key issues in the presentation, you will address their concerns directly. Develop a strategy for the presentation.

There is a tendency among some design professionals to project a casual, laid-back manner of dress and behavior. This might work for some groups, but not for others. If your ideas are to be taken seriously, you must be taken seriously. If your casual attire and manner is taken as a reflection of your work or the quality of your ideas, your presentation may have to overcome this perception before anyone listens to you.

Know how much time is allotted to your presentation, and plan to end early. By intentionally running short, you will allow time for questions and any overrun. No one enjoys listening to a 10-minute presentation for half an hour. Also, know what you will leave out if pressed for time. Spending the bulk of the presentation on one or two points and forcing several more into the last 2 minutes undercuts the credibility of the presentation.

If you are going to use visual aids, plan them to support your presentation, not to replace or compete with it. Every visual should have a purpose that directly supports what you are saying. Do not put too much information on the visual; you do not want your audience reading while you are talking. If there is reading to be done, provide a handout at the end of the talk. Every visual should have a purpose, but it should not contain too much illustrative information. Data presented on visuals should be as simple as possible. Complex charts and tables generally do not work well and serve to confuse the listener and muddle the presentation. A visual should be shown for a maximum of 3 minutes. This keeps the information per view limited and keeps the presentation on a good pace.

Prepare notes to guide the presentation, but do not read directly from the notes or from the slides. Do not memorize the presentation, but use notes as a prompt and a guide. If you are using equipment during your presentation, arrive early to set it up and test it. Always be familiar with the equipment you are about to use. If there is an equipment failure, do not spend time working through the failure while the audience waits. Instead move on to your presentation without the equipment. The key is to minimize disruption and display confidence and aplomb. Remember, you are the presenter, not the equipment. Finally, always arrive on time. It allows you to set up your equipment, learn the room, and assess the formal and informal leaders present.

The Presentation

Introduce yourself or acknowledge an introduction made by another. Demonstrate an open and objective approach to your subject. Assume a comfortable posture, but avoid sitting, leaning on furniture, hands in pockets, or other casual body language. The use of stories and jokes is generally to be discouraged. First, few people tell jokes well, and second, the choice of a joke or a story is difficult to manage without offending someone. Face the audience. Stand straight and emphasize your points with natural gestures. An occasional big gesture may help make a point, but too often done big gestures are a distraction. Use your voice to make points; speak louder or softer, faster or slower to give emphasis or to underscore a point. Use a pause to draw attention to an important point and give it a moment to sink in. The key to the presentation lies in your eyes. People are more likely to like and trust a person who makes direct eye contact. Look at each person you are speaking to; make eye contact at least once with every key person. Always make eye contact with a person who asks a question.

In many public presentations the audience is sitting before a panel of members and the presentation area lies between them, making it difficult to face both the audience and the board members. In such a circumstance, it is best to assess the purpose of the meeting and the objective. If it is a public presentation, ask permission of the board to face the audience. If the presentation is to the board to request an action, face the board and apologize to the audience.

Open the presentation by stating your objective and what you want them to know. Many trainers instruct presenters to find a way to describe how the project benefits the listener. In many cases when a development project is being presented, the public is not interested in the benefits. It may be best not to antagonize them with benefits if you are unwilling to address the impacts as well. Report hard data, and tell the audience how these issues are addressed in the plan. Demonstrate the thinking and problem solving that has gone into addressing their concerns.

When questions are asked, be sure to listen; avoid shuffling papers, looking at your notes or adjusting the equipment. Acknowledge the question somehow and provide a direct answer to it. If you do not know or do not have an answer, say so, but be sure to promise to follow up. The language of the presentation should be conversational and simple. Avoid the use of technical jargon unless you are talking to a group familiar with the jargon. Avoid the use of acronyms. Keep track of your time.

Closing

It is better to leave out part of your presentation than not to deliver your closing. At the end of your presentation, remind your audience of your objective and recount the reasons that support your objective. If you want a specific action or decision, ask for it. Do not leave it to someone else to parse together your request; simply and directly ask for what you want.

Not in My Backyard

A common experience of developers and site professionals is community resistance to a proposed project; the so-called NIMBY effect, or "Not in My Backyard." The typical NIMBY reaction is based on the community's reaction to the project's impact on property values.

A number of studies speak to the negative impact of specific projects on property values (Gelman et al., 1989; Kenyon, 1991; Nelson, 1981; Shortle, n.d.). Some studies of the impacts of NIMBYs on neighboring properties provide policy makers with additional data with which to develop plans and public policy, but many consider only the negative impacts of the unwanted project and ascribe no value or benefit to the public or society. If a power plant in a small town devalues property by $200,000 to $18 million, is there no offset in value to the town and its residents? Would the property in this small town be of greater value without electricity?

To deal with the expected NIMBY reaction, designers should consider how the project might be sited or prevented and offer three approaches to minimizing the impacts. Some NIMBYs might be prevented by redefining the parameters of the solution. For example, instead of building a large low-income housing project, why not offer housing vouchers to eligible citizens? In fact, the Section 8 housing program of HUD does exactly this for eligible residents or eligible housing units. Other options include the use of recycling to reduce the need for landfills and transfer depots. However, if the residents perceive the cost of avoidance or loss of convenience to be greater than the negative impact, these approaches to preventing the NIMBY are unlikely to succeed. NIMBYs fail or are prevented by grassroots action when the costs (loss of property value) are greater than the perceived benefits.

NIMBYs are a problem to communities that fear a loss of property value and/or a loss of quality of life without any offsetting value or return. Contemporary communities place a high value on quality of life issues that require a significant return. The "carrot" of jobs and lower taxes are not adequate offsets to these impacts. Siting issues should be left to the marketplace, but the NIMBY should survive on its own economic merit.

Most land use decisions are ultimately local decisions, and this consideration fails to recognize the regional nature of many NIMBYs. A power plant or a landfill, even a group home, might service an area and provide a benefit to a much larger population than the local population within the scope of its immediate impact. The solution to the considerations of local populations is to provide compensation for impacts. Compensations must be in a form that will be capitalized in the affected community to support the continued viability of the community. These compensations may be in the form of tax relief, host fees, or some other offsetting value that neutralized the NIMBY for the locally affected population, not that gives the benefit to the larger population to be served.

APPENDIX A

Environmental Site Assessment

Brownfields are lands or buildings that are abandoned or underutilized, and redevelopment or reuse is complicated due to the perception or presence of environmental contamination. The number of brownfield sites in the United States ranges from tens of thousands to more than 450,000, and the total acres of impacted land is unknown. The industrial heritage of many cities has left them with acres of properties deemed valueless because of the potential environmental liability associated with the former industrial practices. These abandoned sites are largely the unintended consequence of federal and state laws enacted to force cleanup of contaminated industrial sites. Federal and state laws have often required that significant cleanup and mitigation efforts be undertaken before these properties can be used to their fullest potential. To avoid the expense and environmental risks, former industrial centers have experienced deeply eroded tax bases, a loss of urban development, a loss of employment, underutilization of existing infrastructure, and the sprawl of industrial development into suburban and exurban green fields. The resulting spread of industrial and commercial resources has had its own consequences, which include the increased use of automobiles, reduced environmental quality in outlying areas, and increased pressure on the limited resources of suburban and rural communities.

Historical Perspective

At the heart of the issue is liability and the uncertainty created by the Comprehensive Environmental Response, Compensation and Liability Act (CERCLA) passed in 1980, widely known as Superfund. CERCLA mandates, among other things, the cleanup of contaminated sites. Sites are submitted for consideration and placed on the Comprehensive Environmental Response, Compensation and Liability Information System (CERCLIS) list. Sites that rank high enough on a point system are placed on the National Priority List, or the NPL. Sites are selected for cleanup based on their rank after scoring.

Who Is Liable?

Under Superfund legislation, liability is assigned under the concepts of strict liability and joint and several liability. Simply put, *strict liability* is the assignment of liability without fault, and *joint and several liability* asserts that any responsible party can be held liable for the entire cost of a cleanup. Under Superfund, a responsible party may be liable for costs incurred by the EPA and state agencies for assessment, removal, and remediation; costs incurred by other persons; damages to natural resources; and the costs of health and environmental assessments. Superfund goes on to extend liability to any of the following entities:

Current owners

Current operators

Any prior owner or operator who owned the property when hazardous substances were disposed of

Generators of hazardous substances

Transporters that brought substances to the site

Superfund Defenses

Landowners or prospective buyers can protect themselves from the onerous liabilities that might be imposed under CERCLA by invoking one of the following defenses:

Acts of God or war

A substantiated claim of minimal involvement

The innocent landowner defense

To be considered an innocent landowner, a person must be able to demonstrate that he or she acquired the property through no fault of his or her own (inheritance) or acquired the property in an action to secure a loan or other fiduciary actions (but did not act as an operator). To be innocent, the landowner must further show that he or she did not know, or have reason to know, of contamination on the site. To meet this test, a purchaser or lender must show that he or she attempted to protect him- or herself through the exercise of "good commercial or customary practice." A purchaser who acquires property or becomes the operator of the property after contamination is present is not liable if at the time of acquisition the individual made a commercially reasonable investigation and as a result had no reason to believe the site was contaminated (42 USC Sec 9601 (35) (A) and 9607 (b)).

Further, CERCLA requires that persons make "all appropriate inquiry into the previous ownership and uses of the property consistent with good commercial or customary practice in an effort to minimize liability" (42 USC Sec 9601 (35) (A)). When a court is evaluating the sufficiency of a person's inquiry, the judge is to consider "any specialized knowledge or experience on the part of the defendant, the relationship of the purchase price to the value of the property if contaminated, commonly known or reasonably ascertainable information about the property, the obviousness of the presence or likely presence of contamination by appropriate inspection" (42 USC Sec 9601 (35) (B)).

The congressional history of CERCLA has been important and has been used by the courts to further expand the definition of acceptable "due diligence." In part the congressional history reads as follows:

The duty to inquire under this provision shall be judged as of the time of acquisition. Defendants shall be held to a higher standard as public awareness (grows), as reflected by this Act, the 1980 Act, and other Federal and state statutes. Moreover, good commercial or customary practice with respect to inquiry in an effort to minimize liability shall mean that a reasonable inquiry must have been made in all circumstances, in light of the best business and land transfer principles. Those engaged in commercial transactions should, however be held to a higher standard that those who are engaged in private residential transactions. (H.R. report No. 962, 99th Congress, 2nd Session 187, 1986)

In other words, lenders, commercial real estate developers, and the like will be held to a higher level of inquiry. The higher level is undefined. Over the years various efforts have been made to provide a definition in law or regulation, but to date none has survived. "Good commercial or customary practice" has come to mean a Phase I Environmental Site Assessment, at a minimum.

State Programs

In addition to the concern of cleanup liability, owners were faced with uncertainty because there were no guidelines for the cleanup of non-CERCLIS, or permitted, hazardous material generation/disposal sites. Since the early 1990s, more than 32 states have initiated their own programs to provide cleanup guidance. State brownfield programs are discussed in general in Chapter 9. More than 20 states have entered into "memorandums of agreement" (MOA) with the EPA. This provides some assurance that the EPA will not override the state programs, but other important federal initiatives may affect the state programs.

The EPA issued a policy statement in 1995 that said it would not take action against the owner of a property where hazardous substances are present solely as a result of subsurface migration in an aquifer from sources outside of the property. This is commonly referred to as the Off-site Contaminated Aquifers Policy.

The Comfort/Status Letters Policy has been developed in the absence of a federal brownfield statute. Under this policy the EPA has established a practice of providing "comfort letters" to eligible prospective owners. The purpose of these letters is to provide information about the site and about EPA's intention to exercise Superfund authority. These letters do not provide a liability release or assurance that EPA will not pursue the landowner for cleanup costs if additional information or contamination is found. The comfort letters are based on existing and known information only.

Also in 1995, the EPA issued guidance for entering into agreements with prospective purchasers of contaminated properties if there is to be a substantial direct benefit to the agency in terms of cleanup or a substantial indirect benefit to the community. Essentially the agreement is a covenant between the purchaser and the EPA that states that in return for the benefits, the EPA agrees not to sue the purchaser.

Environmental Site Assessment Methods

A number of site assessment protocols are available in the marketplace from various professional associations, private interests, and public agencies. However, the predominant protocol, and ostensibly the measure of professional practice most widely used, is the American Society for Testing and Materials (ASTM) Standard Guidelines. The ASTM is a volunteer organization made up of representatives from government, industry, and academia and organized around technical subjects for the purpose of establishing standards and protocols. ASTM E50 Committee is responsible for environmental assessment. The ASTM standards are very carefully crafted, and that language is important. At various times ASTM has been criticized for developing "standards" that limit the discretion of practicing professionals. The E-1527 standard identifies its purpose as follows: "to define good commercial and customary practice in the United States for conducting an environmental site assessment of a parcel of commercial real estate with respect to the range of contaminants within the scope of CERCLA and petroleum products. As such this practice is intended to permit a user to satisfy one of the requirements to qualify for the innocent landowner defense to CERCLA liability."

Terminology

The language of the ESA practice is fairly precise, and users should be aware of the meanings of particular key words and phrases as they are used in the reports. A "recognized environmental condition" means the presence or likely presence of any hazardous substances or petroleum products on a property under conditions that indicate an existing release or a material threat of a release of any hazardous substances or petroleum products. The term includes hazardous substances or petroleum products even under compliance with the law but is not intended to include de minimis conditions. Conditions that might be considered de minimis are incidental contamination such as oil stains from parked cars in small quantities that do not represent a material risk of harm to people or the environment.

ESAs are conducted to a large degree on the basis of existing information. The protocol says the information used in the ESA is limited to what is "practically reviewable." This refers to information that is available in such a form that substantive analysis of the data is not necessary. Records that cannot be retrieved by reference to the property location or geographic area are not generally considered practically reviewable.

All ASTM standards include a section called Significance and Use, which describes the application of the standard and its limitations. Section 4.5 of the E-1527 standard guideline lists the principles under which a site assessment is to be undertaken and used. E-1527 clearly acknowledges that Phase I ESAs are not sufficient in scope to eliminate uncertainty and that, by definition, Phase I is not an exhaustive investigation. The nature of the Phase I assessment and the range of properties that might be subject to and ESA requires that the practice be flexible.

Section 6 of the protocol describes the scope and depth of the Phase I investigation. The typical Phase I process consists of four parts: a review of existing records of activity and site conditions, interviews with knowledgeable persons, a firsthand site reconnaissance, and a report that summarizes these activities and the relevant findings. The typical Phase I investigation does not include collection or analysis of samples. Section 6 also describes who may conduct an environmental site assessment under the ASTM protocol and the duties of the professional. The professional is required to conduct the interviews and the site reconnaissance, but he or she is not required to independently verify all information. The professional may rely on information provided by others unless there is actual knowledge that the information is incorrect or unless it is obvious that it is incorrect.

The objective of the records review is to obtain and review records that will help identify recognized environmental conditions in connection with the property. Information pertaining to environmental permits, actions, activities, or events may be found in a variety of databases. Minimum search distances to be used in accessing these databases are described in the standard as approximate and may be reduced at the discretion of the environmental professional in consideration of the local density: the distance hazardous substances might be expected to migrate based on geology, hydrogeology, or other conditions. The minimum search distance is called "property only." The recommended minimum search distances in the ASTM standard are as follows:

NPL	1 mi
CERCLIS list	0.5 mi
RCRA TSD list	1 mi
RCRA generators' list	property and adjoining property
ERNS list	property only
State NPL/CERCLIS	1 mi
State landfill	0.5 mi
LUST	0.5 mi
Registered UST	property and adjoining properties

Accuracy and completeness varies from record to record and from site to site. The user or environmental professional is not obligated to identify mistakes or to confirm information provided except that a reasonable effort will be made to compensate for mistakes or insufficiencies that are obvious or in conflict with other information. Further, the search is limited to records and information that is "reasonably ascertainable" from standard sources. The environmental professional is not required to identify, obtain, or review every possible record that might exist; only sources and data that are reasonably ascertainable from standard sources. The standard describes reasonably ascertainable as information (1) that is publicly available, (2) is obtainable within reasonable time and cost constraints, and (3) is practically reviewable. Reasonable time and cost are considered to be a nominal cost within 20 days of a request. "Practically reviewable" means that the information pertaining to the site is accessible without excessive analysis. Information should be accessible for a limited geographic area by address, zip code, county, and so forth. If information is not reasonably ascertainable or available, the environmental professional will attempt to find information from other sources such as by interviewing owners, neighbors, or local officials. Sources of information shall be documented: name, date, last update of database, and so on.

In addition to interviews, existing records are used to provide historical information. Typical sources may include the following:

Department of Health/Public Safety
Fire Department
Planning Department
Zoning/Building Permit
Water Department
Local utilities
Lists of local landfills, hazardous waste sites, spills, fires, and public or private wells
USGS Geological Survey Maps—groundwater, bedrock geology
USGS Geological Survey topographic maps
Soil conservation services soil maps
Department of Interior wetland maps
Historical USGS topological maps
Aerial photography
Recorded land title records
Standard historical sources

   Insurance maps
   City directories
   Property tax files
   Street directories
   Building department records
   Zoning and land use records

   The degree to which historical information is sought and used is usually based on what is reasonably ascertainable and its appropriateness. For example, land records may go back to 1700 for a property. However, if the property was undeveloped until 1960, there is usually little point in going back that far. Long periods of the same use do not need further investigation (e.g., if an apartment building built in 1940 is still an apartment building in 1960, no interim check is required).

   The purpose of firsthand site reconnaissance is to visually and physically observe the property and any structures to the extent that the investigation is not obstructed by bodies of water, adjacent buildings, or other obstacles. Exterior areas are viewed from all adjacent thoroughfares. The purpose of roads or access points is determined. Areas of stressed vegetation, stained soils, areas of fill, disposal areas, material storage areas, adjacent property uses, and general housekeeping are observed and noted. Building interiors, including accessible common areas, hallways, utility areas, boiler rooms, maintenance and repair areas, and a representative sample of occupied areas are inspected.

   In this process the current use of adjoining properties, and to the extent possible the past uses of subject property and adjoining properties, are determined. The physical characteristics of the site such as topography, aspect, drainage, existing water bodies, roads, descriptions of structures, paved areas, water supply, sewage disposal, existing material storage area, presence of drums or tanks, odors, pools of liquid, heating/cooling methods, stains or corrosion, floor drains, sumps, pits, ponds, lagoons, solid waste disposal, and wells are observed and noted.

   The purpose of the interview is to acquire more information about current and historic uses and conditions observed in the site reconnaissance or found in the records search. Interviews may be conducted in person, over the phone, or in writing and may be done before, during, or after the site visit. Typical candidates for interview include the site manager, occupants, the owner, local officials, and neighbors. Persons interviewed should be asked to be as specific as possible to the best of their knowledge, but, of course, they are under no obligation to answer questions. If possible, the environmental professional should acquire copies of documentation that may support the interview. Typical documents include the following:

   Previous site assessment reports
   Environmental audit reports
   Environmental permits or records
   Registration of tanks
   Material Safety Data Sheets
   Right to know or emergency plans
   Site-specific reports, drawings, and so forth
   Correspondence

The recommended report format is described in Appendix X2 of the ASTM Standard Guide. Briefly, the report should consist of an Executive Summary, supporting documentation (including references, copies, records of conversations, photographs), a professional résumé and/or the credentials of the environmental professional(s), opinions, findings, and conclusions.

Phase II ESAs

Phase II Environmental Site Assessment is intrusive; samples are collected and analyzed. Phase II assessments are performed when common sense or a Phase I investigation indicates the potential for or an actual environmental contamination. Phase II is usually directed to a specific finding: an area of stained soil, a known underground storage tank, a chemical storage area, an area of suspected contamination, and so on. The purpose of the Phase II assessment is usually to confirm the suppositions of the Phase I investigation: to identify the limit and extent of contamination in three dimensions. It may be necessary to conduct an expanded Phase II investigation to meet the requirements of a state voluntary cleanup program. It is by definition also a reiterative process.

Sampling Plans and Methods

Some suspected areas can be preliminarily identified using historic topographic maps, aerial photographs, or firsthand observation. These resources assist the environmental professional in developing a sampling strategy and plan. Sample collection should be undertaken only after an understanding of the objectives of the sample collection are established and the limitations of the plan are agreed upon. Samples have limited value. Depending on the nature of the site and the objective, the sampling plan can vary widely from a very few samples to a complex three-dimensional sampling plan. A sampling plan may include a list of the sample collection methods, equipment to be used, the rationale for each choice, the number of samples to be collected, the depths and location where they will be collected, and whether the samples will be composited.

Composite samples are made by mixing individual samples of equal weight thoroughly before performing a single analysis. The results are typically multiplied by the number of individual samples for comparison sake. The advantage is that the cost of sampling is reduced, often substantially. When there is a positive result, however, a fair amount of uncertainty exists as to where the problem may be. Other elements of the sampling plan include a site plan showing the sample location (approximate), the equipment decontamination procedures to be used, the analytical methods to be used, the name and location of the laboratory, the QA/QC methods, chain of custody, a demonstration of compliance with regulatory requirements or practices, a plan for the disposal of wastes generated by the sampling plan, and a health and safety plan for field staff.

Sample locations may be obvious from the work done in the Phase I portion of the investigation; however, there are protocols to be observed. Sampling programs may be divided into four groups: judgmental, random, systematic, or a combination of the first three. Samples are categorized into three types: grab, composite, and integrated. Judgmental sample programs are based on specific information about a release or contamination, such as observed areas of stained soils or an area known to have been affected by a spill. The advantage of this approach is that it tends to be cost-effective and efficient;

however, it is definitely biased toward the worst case situation and marginal areas may be missed.

Random sample programs are developed to evaluate all areas of a site by dividing the site into a grid and using a random selection of grid intersections to choose sample locations. Each location has an equal chance of being selected for evaluation and results are said to be indicative of an average condition. This technique is used when statistical analysis is appropriate or when information is to be used for "legal" purposes. Such sites might include areas of widespread contamination. Advantages of this approach are that it is a low-bias, sitewide approach. Its disadvantage is that grid design is often restricted by inaccessible areas, or areas where sampling isn't feasible (street surfaces), and random selection of location can result in clustering of samples. The number of samples to be collected in a random sampling process is determined using the formula provided in EPA SW-486. In general, a grid is established that will provide enough sample locations so that 10 percent of the site is covered by the requisite number of samples.

Systematic sample programs are similar to random samples to the extent that the site is divided into a grid, but in this case samples are collected at each grid intersection. Grid patterns do not have to be square; they could be rectangular or circular (around a tank), depending on site shape and geometry. Difficult or inaccessible locations can be eliminated. The advantage of the systematic system is the low-bias, sitewide coverage and the ability to eliminate inaccessible areas. Disadvantages lie in the judgment used to select the grid frequency and the limited application for statistical analysis. Results are easily challenged, and this method can be expensive.

Combination sample programs are a blend of random and systematic sampling. Limited judgment is used to eliminate or at least minimize bias. It can be used to eliminate the biggest disadvantages of systematic or random sampling, but it is not completely random, and the results can easily be challenged if the selections are not carefully documented.

Grab samples are individual samples taken from a specific location at a specific time. This is an appropriate choice when the size, shape, location, and nature of a suspected release are defined.

Composite samples are made up of a combination of samples. It is used to make up a "representative" sample or to produce enough material for analysis. Analysis represents average conditions; that is, sample locations could have higher results individually than are found in the composite. These are used for initial assessment purposes in which the worst case values can be extrapolated from the results.

Integrated samples are a composite of material taken from the same location over a period of time, such as effluent discharges or waste streams.

The collection of the soil sample is a function of the homogeneity of the soil, the ease of collection, the ease of decontamination, and the construction of the sampling equipment. Shallow soil samples are typically collected with a hand auger that is manually rotated into the ground. Hand augers can be used up to 6 feet or so in depth in soft soils without interference. Power driven hand augers can go a bit deeper. Sample material is collected into a tube (usually brass but sometimes plastic) that fits inside the auger tube. Other shallow soil sampling equipment could include shovels, trier (a hollow rod used to collect a core sample), a thief (a hollow tube within a hollow tube that is closed until a particular depth or material is reached, at which time it is opened and inserted into the material to collect a sample), and trowels.

Deeper soil samples are collected using truck-mounted equipment such as a well drilling rig or direct push technology. Depths of from 10 to several hundred feet are possible. Hollow stem augers and split spoon augers are commonly used to produce undisturbed samples. Soil sampling devices can be inserted into the core at particular depths to gather samples. The core is evaluated for color, smell, moisture, and composition at the time the sample is taken.

Liquid samples can be collected from drums, tanks, and surface water using dippers, glass tubes, and composite liquid waste samplers (COLIWASAs). Pumps can be used to assist in the collection, but pumps should be of a type and quality that do not introduce air into the sample.

Groundwater samples are collected by drilling a well and installing a monitoring well. Temporary groundwater sampling stations are those in which a well is not installed. These are often discouraged because the results are not repeatable. Monitoring wells are always purged before a sample is taken. A well is purged by removing from 3 to 5 well casing volumes (determined by multiplying the total depth of the well from the ground surface to the bottom of the water column by the cross-sectional area). The purpose of the purge is to obtain a representative sample of the groundwater rather than a sample that has been sitting in the well. Temperature, pH, and conductivity measures are taken of the sample. Purge water is collected into drums or another receptacle and handled according to the analysis results.

Quality assurance is a necessary part of the sampling process. There are established procedures and methods for meeting the quality assurance necessary for a responsible sampling process. These methods include matrix spikes, laboratory blanks, and field duplicates. Matrix spikes are duplicate field samples that are spiked in the laboratory with measured quantities of the contaminant; the volume of the added material can then be subtracted from an analyzed result to get an accurate analysis. Laboratory blanks are laboratory-grade samples that are analyzed the same way as the field samples. Generally speaking, a laboratory blank is used for each 10 samples per round of samples. Field duplicates are extra samples of the same material used to check analysis accuracy. Duplicates are usually selected from areas suspected of having the highest concentrations.

Information found during the Phase II assessment could indicate that the owner of a property is out of compliance with a federal or state environmental regulation. This may have significant economic repercussions, either in the form of additional work or cleanup or in the devaluation of the real estate. Reporting must always be factual and limited to what is known.

Redevelopment Strategies

It is critical to understand the project objectives as well as the character of the site when evaluating redevelopment strategies. The strategies for an urban redevelopment project that is strictly a real estate development undertaking may be very different from a project undertaken with additional economic or social development aspects. The existing condition and the degree of effort and expense necessary to mitigate conditions must be considered in terms of the intended use. A project that has a social outcome may not involve the same concerns with economic return as a straightforward real estate project.

Understanding the site character is the focus of the Phase I and II environmental site assessments. Site issues that influence redevelopment planning include the physical characteristics (Phases I and II site evaluation issues such as storm water, slope, and floodplain), the real estate characteristics (location, utilities, site access, adjoining uses, zoning, and so forth), and the market characteristics (location, proposed use, antici-pated future use, and bankability). Successful redevelopment and response action plan-ning must consider all of the facets of redevelopment.

Based on these investigations, site conditions are identified and data are analyzed to determine the risks associated with redevelopment of the site. These risks are evalu-ated to identify the most effective and appropriate development response. Although choices may differ from state to state, a redeveloper generally must choose from several standards for cleanup of a site: a pollutant-specific, uniform, risk-based standard, local background levels, federal or state standards (water quality standards are often used), or site-specific risk-based standards. Once the standard is chosen, a response method for meeting the criteria is selected. The possible responses include the following:

No action required
Avoidance
Administrative controls
Design controls
On-site remediation
Off-site remediation

In some cases the degree of contamination is so low that specific action steps are not necessary. Small areas of contamination often can be left in place and undisturbed in the redevelopment process so that no specific mitigation is required. By locating site fea-tures such as storm water management facilities away from areas of marginal contami-nation, or by locating impermeable surfaces such as parking over these same areas, more expensive controls or mitigation can be avoided.

Administrative controls are used to manage risks associated with contamination by limiting access through the use of deed restrictions. These controls generally limit the use of the site to a specific application or to a specific maintenance performance. Design con-trols are site redevelopment features designed to reduce exposures to contamination or to provide passive treatment of contamination. Such features may include the coordination of impermeable surfaces to isolate contamination, the selection of contaminant resistant vegetation, and the installation of fences or landscape barriers to isolate areas.

Remediation technologies are wide ranging. Remediation is usually undertaken in the early phases of a project, and typical brownfield sites will have relatively predict-able remediation demands. As a general rule of thumb, the more short-term and expen-sive the remediation, the greater the liability reduction it offers.

The purpose of the public policy shift is to encourage the investigation and to accel-erate the cleanup of eligible properties. The public agenda is not concerned with the development program beyond the issues of public health and safety and the protection of the environment. To succeed, the redevelopment program must have a wider range of concerns than strictly the cleanup aspects of a site or building. The site must work for the proposed program. The redevelopment plan and the environmental action plan must be inclusive. In designing a response plan that accomplishes the site program, designers must consider these issues:

Remediation costs (initial costs and life cycle costs)

Impact on current and future users

Future impacts (changes in regulations, potential of exacerbation, and so forth)

"Bankability"

The developer or landowner must also consider the business and risk management aspects of the plan:

Remediation costs (initial and life cycle costs)

Impact on users (effect on potential buyers or tenants)

Future impacts (changes in regulations, potential for exacerbation, and so forth)

Impact of property restrictions on the marketability of the property

Reopeners

Nearly every state program includes "reopeners"; these are conditions under which the state may revoke the letter of no further action or certificate of completion. Reopeners usually include the following:

Imminent and substantial endangerment to the public health and environment

Certificate obtained through fraud or misrepresentation

Remedial response action failed to meet criteria

Use of land is out of compliance with restrictions

Previously undiscovered contamination (may cause the liability to reopen for the responsible party)

New contamination or a change in condition that exacerbates contamination

Maintenance commitments not met

Environmental Insurance

Landowners and developers may choose to purchase "environmental insurance" as part of the redevelopment and risk management strategy. Although there is a great deal of flexibility in the marketplace in terms of specific insurance, the environmental insurance market is comprised of basically two types of insurance: stop-loss insurance and real estate insurance. These insurances cover specific types of insurable risks such as instances where environmental restoration can exceed anticipated costs primarily due to preexisting but previously unknown contamination, excessive remediation costs due to changes in regulations, greater than anticipated contamination, or other causes. Insurance could also cover third party or postremediation liability (migration off site, bodily harm, stigmatization and loss of market value, and so forth).

Stop-loss insurance is purchased by the owner to provide a guarantee of the proposed cost of the remediation project. Generally it covers an exposure equivalent to 100 percent of the remediation cost estimate, although variations of this can be underwritten. Some insurers require approval of the response action plan; others do not. However, some do not cover costs increased due to regulatory change. Stop-loss insurance is usually priced from 8 to 20 percent of the policy limit value and remains in effect until the work plan is completed or to a specific policy limit. There is no standardization for this type of insurance.

Environmental real estate insurance is written to protect current and future land-owners. These policies may cover remediation costs incurred due to the discovery of previously unknown contamination, third party claims for cleanup or injury, and costs of cleanup required after a letter of no further action has been issued. Environmental real estate insurance typically has a five-year renewable term and may be renewed annually to insure five years of future coverage. Policy premiums range from $25,000 to $250,000 for a $5 million policy limit with a $50,000 deductible.

A Sample Preparedness, Prevention, and Contingency Plan

As the NPDES rules on construction sites mature, it should be expected that a Preparedness, Prevention, and Contingency Plan (PPC Plan) will be required on all construction sites. The following sample plan provides an example and an outline for developing such plans.

General Site Layout and Site Conditions

Property boundaries, loading/unloading areas, truck wash areas, storage areas for materials, location of drainage appurtenances, sediment removal devices, and site entrances/exits are to be shown on a site plan titled "Preparedness, Prevention, and Contingency Plan." Sources of additional information regarding the site, such as the Erosion and Sediment Pollution Control Plan and Report, can be included by references or be attached to the plan.

The Emergency Response Plan

The Emergency Response Coordinator for the site should be clearly identified and an outline of the Emergency Response Organization should be included with this report as Attachment A. Alternate emergency coordinators should be listed on the attachment as well. All listed personnel should be authorized to commit the necessary resources that might be required to carry out and fulfill the objectives of the PPC Plan although it is the responsibility of the Emergency Response Coordinator to complete the PPC Plan for the site and oversee and confirm the installation and maintenance of control and containment equipment or structures in accordance with the plan.

The coordinator shall arrange and provide training to all appropriate personnel on the site, including subcontractors reporting to the operator or responsible to the operator. Training will consist of the elements of the waste disposal plans for the site, emergency response procedures for spills and releases, material storage requirements, the location of safety and emergency response equipment, and the location of material safety data sheets. The coordinator and the site superintendent shall oversee and confirm the location of emergency response and safety equipment, the installation of PPC Plan elements such as waste disposal locations, material storage locations, and security devices or equipment to confirm compliance with the plan. If appropriate, local emergency response services (fire, police, etc.) should be contacted regarding the project and the PPC Plan, and copies of the plan and site drawing should be provided to these agencies. Periodic site inspections should be conducted to confirm operational compliance with the elements of the plan and to revise/adapt the plan to changes in site conditions or circumstances as required.

All appropriate personnel should be trained and authorized to initiate emergency response procedures to control and mitigate spills and releases on the site, including but not limited to employing equipment and materials available on site. A qualified contractor should be on retainer to contain, cleanup, and remove contaminated soils or water or other materials as required. The Emergency Response Coordinator shall contact the appropriate authorities in the event of a spill or release. The Emergency Response Coordinator may delegate some of these responsibilities to other staff or to contractors. Employees and subcontractors should know that in the event of an imminent or actual emergency situation, alarms should be activated and key personnel should be notified. The Emergency Response Coordinator must assess the character of the spill or release as to the nature of the material, the source of the spill, and the amount and extent of the spill. This assessment must include an evaluation of the threat to human health and safety or risk to the environment. This assessment must consider direct and indirect effects of emissions, discharge, fire, or explosion. If the Emergency Response Coordinator determines that a threat to health and safety or to the environment exists or will exist as a result of the event, the local authorities should be contacted. If appropriate, evacuation of the area should be discussed at this time. If a reportable quantity of a material has been released, it may be necessary to contact state authorities and the National Emergency Response Center at (800) 424-8802.

Contacts to the National Emergency Response Center require the following information:

1. Name of the person reporting the incident.
2. Name and location of the site.
3. Phone number of the person reporting the incident.
4. Date, time, and location of incident.
5. Brief description of the incident, nature of materials/waste involved, nature of any injuries, and possible hazards to health or safety for people and/or the environment.
6. Estimated quantity of materials/waste released.
7. Extent of contamination of land, water, or air.

During an emergency, the Emergency Response Coordinator must take all reasonable measures to ensure that fire, explosion, emission, or discharge do not occur. These measures may include stopping construction operations while a spill is controlled and cleaned up. Once control is established, the Emergency Response Coordinator must provide for the collection, treatment, storage, and disposal of residues, contaminated soils, or materials that may have resulted from the emergency.

Employee Training Program

The Employee Training Program may consist of all employees working on the site receiving instruction regarding the PPC Plan and its elements from the Emergency Response Coordinator at the start-up of the project. This training meeting will be held at the earliest stages of the project, at about the same time the erosion and sediment control facilities are being installed and the earthwork is beginning. Employee training should include the following information:

1. The purpose and legal basis for the PPC Plan.

2. The steps being taken on the site to comply with the requirements of the law and to protect the environment from spills.

3. The location of waste disposal, material storage, and emergency response equipment and facilities, and the methods to be followed for waste disposal.

4. Definition of spills and minor spills, the steps to be taken in either case, including notification of the Emergency Response Coordinator or alternate, and location of call list.

5. Employees will be trained in the use of equipment, materials, and personal protective equipment required to respond to an emergency.

6. Training will include required housekeeping procedures, techniques, and responsibilities, as well as routine maintenance of control and containment facilities; specific housekeeping and maintenance assignments may be made at this time.

A record should be kept of all training sessions. The record will include the date and time of the training as well as the names of those who attended, the name of the trainer, the subject matter covered, and copies of all materials distributed.

Emergency Equipment and Procedures

The project site must have equipment required to respond to routine spills and to emergencies of a manageable nature as determined by the plan and the judgment of the Emergency Response Coordinator. This equipment shall be maintained in an accessible and clearly marked location. This location should be kept locked to maintain the supply and integrity of the equipment and materials required by this plan. The location of the keys or the personnel with keys should be well known. The Emergency Response Coordinator shall inspect the emergency response equipment at least monthly to confirm supplies and equipment are accessible and in working order. A permanent inventory list shall be maintained and permanently mounted on the inside of the locker door. The inventory list shall include a complete compilation of the contents of the locker as required by this plan. The Emergency Response Coordinator shall maintain a record of these inspections and any replacement materials required. These inspection records shall be maintained in the project file.

The Emergency Response Equipment could include the following items:

- 50-lb bags of absorbent sweeping compound
- 2 coarse push brooms

- 2 flat, long-handled shovels
- 1 box 8 mm plastic minimum 10 by 100 ft
- 2 sealed beam flashlights, with one extra set of batteries for each (batteries should be marked with the date at the time of installation)
- sets of disposable coveralls
- gloves, including at least one pair impermeable "acid" type gloves
- 1 roll of duct tape (250 ft)
- overboots
- 1 copy of the EMERGENCY RESPONSE PROCEDURES from this plan
- 1 copy of the CALL LIST hung in sight but removable from the locker
- first-aid kit
- chemical fire extinguisher
- disposable flash camera
- 1 copy of the INCIDENT REPORT form
- 1 set of nonsparking tools to include a hammer, adjustable wrench, pliers, pump pliers, and flat shovel

Fuels and Petroleum Products

Fuels and volatile petroleum products shall be stored in approved containers out of doors in a secure, covered area or indoors in a properly ventilated area. Bulk storage of these materials (55 gal container or larger) shall be in a containment area sized to contain 110 percent of the largest single vessel within it.

In the event of a spill or a ruptured or leaking vessel, the material will be caught in the containment area. In the case of small spills, absorbent material will be used to collect the material. Contaminated absorbent material will be collected into an open barrel that is stored in a well-ventilated area. The material will be properly disposed of in accordance with applicable environmental regulations.

If spills are too large to be collected by available absorbent material but are within the containment area, the integrity of the containment area should be assessed. If the containment area shows signs of stress or imminent failure, steps shall be taken immediately to secure and support the containment. Where the containment is secure, the Emergency Response Coordinator shall contact an oil recovery contractor to remove the spilled fuel. In the example of gasoline or other highly volatile materials, the local fire department shall be called to assess and secure the situation, including the use of foam to suppress the volatiles and reduce the risk of fire/explosion.

For spills from smaller vessels outside of the containment area, absorbent material will be used to collect the material. Steps should be taken immediately in the case of such spills to minimize the spread of materials over soils and to water. Such steps might include diverting the direction of flow or containing the spill with available materials.

In the event spills reach soils, the soils shall be removed and placed on plastic sheets and covered. Removal of contaminated soils shall proceed as soon as possible.

In the event spills reach a drainage facility, the situation should be assessed to determine if upstream drainage facilities can be diverted. In all cases, the first step is contain the spill.

If a fuel oil/gasoline/kerosene spill that is not contained reaches the soil or water and is greater than the allowable maximum spill quantity, the incident should be reported to: the NATIONAL EMERGENCY RESPONSE CENTER (800-424-8802), sewer authority, natural resources agency, fire department, police department, and local government.

Construction Chemicals

All construction materials shall be stored, used, and disposed of in accordance with manufacturers' instructions, safety and health regulations, and solid waste disposal regulations. All on-site storage and disposal of materials shall conform to this plan. Construction materials shall include paint, acids, cleaning materials, solvents, fertilizers, soil conditioners, and building materials. Bulk storage of these materials in a liquid form (55 gal container or larger) shall be in a containment area sized to contain 110 percent of the largest single vessel within it.

In the event of a spill or a ruptured or leaking vessel, the material will be caught in the containment area. In the case of small spills, absorbent material will be used to collect the material. Contaminated absorbent material will be collected in an open barrel that is stored in a well-ventilated area. The material will be properly disposed of in accordance with regulations.

For spills that are too large to be collected by available absorbent material but that are within the containment area, the integrity of the containment area should be assessed. If the containment area shows signs of stress or imminent failure, steps shall be taken immediately to secure and support the containment. Where the containment is secure, the Emergency Response Coordinator shall contact an environmental cleanup contractor to remove the spilled substance. For solvents or other highly volatile materials, the local fire department shall be called to assess and secure the situation, including the use of foam to suppress the volatiles and reduce the risk of fire/explosion.

For spills from smaller vessels outside the containment area, absorbent material will be used to collect the material. Steps should be taken immediately in the case of such spills to minimize the spread of materials over soils and to water. Such steps might include diverting the direction of flow or containing the spill with available materials.

In the event spills reach soils, the soils shall be removed and placed on plastic sheets and covered. Removal of contaminated soils shall proceed as soon as possible.

In the event spills reach a drainage facility, the situation should be assessed to determine if upstream drainage facilities can be diverted. In all cases, the first step is contain the spill.

Dry, granular, powdered, or other materials shall be stored in a covered secure area. Releases and spills of these materials shall be cleaned up immediately. Care shall be taken to avoid the contamination of soils or surface water.

Cleanup methods may include the collection of these materials by sweeping, shoveling, or other means. Contaminated materials unable to be used in the operation will be disposed of according to the manufacturers' instructions and in accordance with regulations. Spilled materials that are collected and deemed to be hazardous waste will be labeled and stored in a secure, properly identified, and protected area. Such materials are subject to hazardous waste storage, transport, and disposal requirements.

Personnel involved in the containment and clean up of materials that pose a health risk or hazard are required to wear proper personal protective equipment. The Emergency Response Coordinator shall evaluate each event to determine the presence and nature of risk as provided for in the Material Safety Data Sheet.

Solid Waste

Solid waste shall include wood, concrete, scrap metal, plastic, masonry products, roofing materials, and other building materials. These materials shall be collected in portable dumpsters located on the site and properly disposed of according to the solid waste regulations of DER. There shall be no burning or burying of waste materials on site.

Miscellaneous materials that may be encountered on the construction site include wash from concrete trucks, waste asphalt, pesticides/herbicides, tar, demolition wastes, and other materials.

An area shall be designated for washing concrete trucks. The rinse water from these trucks can be extremely hazardous to fish. The wash area shall be located well away from surface water or drainage paths. The area may be arranged in a sump condition to contain the washed material and allow it to dry.

Waste asphalt shall be collected away from drainage paths, consolidated, and disposed of as construction wastes.

Pesticides and herbicides represent a significant risk to health and safety of site personnel as well as to the environment. All such materials shall be used by trained and knowledgeable personnel wearing the proper safety and personal protective equipment, and in accordance with the manufacturers' instructions. At such time as the application is complete, the materials shall be removed from the site. There shall be no bulk storage of herbicides or pesticides on the site. In the event of a spill or release from smaller vessels outside of a containment area, absorbent material will be used to collect the material. Steps should be taken immediately in the case of such spills to minimize the spread of materials over soils and to water. Such steps might include diverting the direction of flow or containing the spill with available materials.

In the event spills reach soils, the soils shall be removed and placed on plastic sheets and covered. Removal of contaminated soils shall proceed as soon as possible.

In the event spills reach a drainage facility, the situation should be assessed to determine if upstream drainage facilities can be diverted. In all cases, the first step is contain the spill.

Care should be taken to assure that all cleanup personnel are wearing impermeable gloves and clothing and properly equipped respirators.

Inspections

The Emergency Response Coordinator is responsible for maintaining routine inspections of all facilities, equipment, and devices described by this plan as part of the Prevention, Preparedness, and Contingency efforts. Attachment C includes an inspection report form. The Emergency Response Coordinator or his/her trained delegate shall complete the inspection at least once per month, commencing within the first 30 days of the start of work. The record of these inspections and actions taken shall be maintained in the project file.

The nature of the construction site makes denying access to the site impractical. Vehicular access is limited to the defined entrances and exits on the plan. Material storage and containment areas shall be secured by locked doors, tanks and drums shall have valve locks, and the emergency response equipment locker shall be locked. A copy of the Call List and the Emergency Response Coordinator's phone number shall be posted in a weather resistant cover.

APPENDIX C

Internet Resources

AASHTO
The website of the American Association of State Highway and Transportation Officials
www.transportation.org

ADA Standards
Changes to the ADA standards had been proposed but not yet approved at this writing.
www.ada.gov/NPRM2008/ada_standards/proposedadastds.htm#pgfId-1006245

ADAAG
"Americans with Disabilities Act Accessibility Guidelines"
http://www.ada.gov/stdspdf.htm

Aerial Photography
An online source for archived aerial photography of the United States
http://terraserver-usa.com/

American Society of Civil Engineers
www.asce.org

American Society of Landscape Architects
www.asla.org

American Planning Association
www.planning.org

ASTM
The American Society for Testing and Materials is a nonprofit organization that produces consensus-based standards and protocols for industries.
www.astm.org

Association for Community Design
www.communitydesign.org

Brownfields
The Small Business Liability Relief and Brownfields Act
www.epa.gov/brownfields/html-doc/hr2869.htm

Building Materials Reuse
The Building Materials Reuse Association site has current news about the trend, some case study stories, and links to local resources for information and available materials.
www.buildingreuse.org/

Community Design
The Association for Community Design is a resource for professionals working in community design.
www.communitydesign.org

Complete Streets
Complete the Streets is an organization promoting a universal design approach to streets. The site includes valuable case studies, sample ordinances, studies, and reports.
www.completestreets.org

Constructed Wetlands
This link is to a general database of information on a variety of topics, including constructed wetlands- http://www.toolbase.org/Technology-Inventory/Plumbing/constructed-wetlands
http://www.epa.gov/owow/wetlands/pdf/design.pdf

Consumer Safety
The U.S. Consumer Product Safety Commission website has links to a wide range of standards and practices of relevance to site planning.
www.cpsc.gov

Deconstruction
See "Building Materials Reuse"

Flexible Zoning
This link to the Bucks County, Pennsylvania, ordinance is used as a "model ordinance."
www.smartcommunities.ncat.org/codes/bucks.shtml

This link provides an overview of different zoning approaches within a community. Several case studies are included
http://nirpc.org/environment/pdf/Chapter%203%20Subdivision.pdf

This link is to a study that complied the experience and parameters of flexible or performance zoning in a number of municipalities.
http://www.pioneerinstitute.org/municipalregs/pdf/cluster_flexible_zoning.pdf

Green Buildings/Green Sites
The Building Green site from the National Resources Defense Council provides an excellent overview of the argument for green buildings and tools for helping with life cycle assessment of costs.
www.nrdc.org/buildinggreen/default.asp

The University of Colorado Environmental Center is good resource for green buildings.
http://ecenter.colorado.edu/events/index.html

The Building Green site is aimed for builders but is a good resources for designers too.
www.buildinggreen.com

The U.S. Green Building Council is among the best resources for green building and the home of the LEED protocols.
www.usgbc.org

Green Building Codes
This site provides links to many existing building and development codes that are in use today.
www.smartcommunities.ncat.org/buildings/gbcodtoc.shtml

Low Impact Development Center, Inc. is concerned primarily with sustainable site design and management practices that protect water quality. Valuable information for site design elements and region-specific information on design and plants is available here.
www.lowimpactdevelopment.org

National Resources Defense Council site focuses on low-impact development.
www.nrdc.org/water/pollution/storm/chap12.asp

A Sourcebook for Green and Sustainable Building
www.greenbuilder.com/sourcebook

Sustainable Sites Initiative Guidelines and Performance Benchmarks is a report outlining how to build and measure a sustainable site. This link is to the 2008 edition, but additional reports are anticipated in the next few years.
www.sustainablesites.org/report/

LEED
This is the home of the LEED protocols.
www.usgbc.org

Low Impact Development
See "Green Buildings/Green Sites"

Performance Zoning
See "Flexible Zoning"

Phytoremediation
This EPA Web site provides general information on phytoremediation and links to specific applications and methods.
http://www.clu-in.org/techfocus/default.focus/sec/Phytoremediation/cat/Overview/

Plant Hardiness Zone Map
The new interactive map by the USDA is accessible via the website
http://www.usna.usda.gov/Hardzone/ushzmap.html

Plant References
This site is a clearing house of a number of online plant references.
http://filebox.vt.edu/users/jodaniel/plants.html

This site is a searchable image gallery of plants.
http://www.noble.org/WebApps/PlantImageGallery/ForbsSearch.aspx

Another clearing house for plant references.
http://www.dclunie.com/eshelton/wildflow/plntlnk.html

Porous Paving
Portland Cement Association has an excellent overview of porous concrete.
www.cement.org

Rain Gardens
This link is to the Rain Garden Network and is a primer and good resource for information on rain gardens and similar strategies.
http://www.raingardennetwork.com/

Low Impacts Development Center, Inc. has excellent information on the design and specifications for the construction of rain gardens.
www.lowimpactdevelopment.org/raingarden_design/construction.htm

Recycled Building Materials
A resource for finding recycled building materials.
www.ecobusinesslinks.com/links/sustainable_building_supplies.htm

Building Materials Reuse Association
www.buildingreuse.org

SCS certified recycled materials
www.scscertified.com/ecoproducts/materialcontent/index.html

Retirement
A study discussed in Chapter 5 regarding the relative degree of preparation for retirement by baby boomers.
http://www.bls.gov/opub/cwc/cm20050114ar01p1.htm

Roundabout
An excellent primer on the modern roundabout, how it differs from the traditional traffic circle, and its advantages.
www.roundaboutsusa.com/intro.html#types

A link to the Federal Highway Administration research center web page about roundabouts.
http://www.tfhrc.gov/safety/00068.htm

Smart Growth
Smart Growth contains a good deal of information on smart growth and links to more sites.
www.smartgrowth.org/

Soil Maps
Soil maps are available online.
websoilsurvey.nrcs.usda.gov/app/

Storm Water
This EPA document provides information on storm water infiltration and water temperature.
www.epa.gov/nps/natlstormwater03/08Dorava.pdf

This article reviews best management practices in storm water infiltration.
http://www.water-research.net/Waterlibrary/runoffeq/stmwt_infil.pdf

This article is concerned with evaluating a site for infiltration strategies.
dnr.wi.gov/Runoff/pdf/stormwater/techstds/post/dnr1002-Infiltration.pdf

The Center for Watershed Protection offers many publications regarding sustainable design and water resource protection.
www.cwp.org

Streams
The EPA site describes the Rosgen method of stream assessment.
www.epa.gov/watertrain/stream_class

Streets
Institute of Transportation Engineers has links to many resources regarding street design and research associated with street design.
www.ite.org

Topographic Maps
The USGS home page for topographic mapping.
http://topomaps.usgs.gov/

The USGS site for the National Map has maps and aerial photography.
nationalmap.gov

This site has historical topographic maps available online. Unfortunately the coverage is limited to only some eastern states.
http://historical.maptech.com/

A source for purchasing topographic maps for the United States and Canada.
http://www.topozone.com/

A source for topographic maps from around the world.
http://www.digital-topo-maps.com/

United States Botanical Garden
A worthy source of information on conservation and a partner in the Sustainable Site Initiative.
www.usbg.gov

Urban, James
"Growing the Urban Forest" by James Urban, is an excellent paper on the issues and methods for urban tree planning and maintenance.

Woonerf
This article is a good introduction to the Woonerf concept.
http://www.livablestreets.com/streetswiki/woonerf

References

Chapter 1

Anthony, J. 2004. "Do State Growth Management Regulations Reduce Sprawl?" *Urban Affairs Review* 39(3): 376–397.

Butrica, B., and Uccello, C. 2004. "How Will Boomers Fare at Retirement?" *AARP*, p. 93.

Currens, G. 2004. "Urban Housing Trends." National Association of Home Builders, http://www.nahb.org/generic.aspx?genericContentID=36678

DeVaney, S. A., and Chiremba, S. T. 2005. "Comparing the Retirement Savings of Baby Boomers and Other Cohorts." *Compensation and Working Conditions.* Washington, D.C.: U.S. Bureau of Labor Statistics.

Ehrlich, P. R., and Holdren, J. P. 1971. "Impact of Population Growth." *Science* 171:212–217.

Goetz, S. J., Shortle, J. S., and Bergstrom, J. C. 2004. "Land Use Problems and Conflicts." In *Causes, Consequences and Solutions.* New York: Routledge.

Intergovernmental Panel on Climate Change. 2007. *IPCC Fourth Assessment Report: The Physical Science Basis.* http://www.ipcc.ch/ipccreports/ar4-wg1.htm

Irwin, E. G., and Bockstael, N. E. 2007. "The Evolution of Urban Sprawl: Evidence of Spatial Heterogeneity and Increasing Land Fragmentation." *Proceedings of the National Academy of Sciences* 104(52): 20672–20677.

Kolankiewicz, L., and Beck, R. 2007. "100 Largest Cities." http://www.sprawlcity.org/studyUSA/index.html

Pendall, R. 2003. "Sprawl without Growth: The Upstate Paradox." http://www.brookings.edu/reports/2003/10demographics_pendall.aspx

President's Council on Sustainable Development. 1996. *Sustainable America—A New Consensus for Prosperity, Opportunity and a Healthy Environment for the Future.* http://clinton2.nara.gov/PCSD/Publications/TF_Reports/amer-top.html (accessed May 1999).

Sewell, C., Ahern, L-K., and Hartless, A. 2007. "Yellow School House Blues." *1000 Friends of Maryland.* http://www.friendsofmd.org/reports.aspx

Woods Hole Research Center. 2007. "Land Use Change and the Chesapeake Bay Ecosystem." http://www.whrc.org/midatlantic/modeling_change/SLEUTH/maryland_2030/md_scenarios.htm

Chapter 2

Battles, S. J., and Burns, E. M. 2000. "Trends in Building-Related Energy and Carbon Emissions: Actual and Alternate Scenarios." Presented at the Summer Study on

Energy Efficiency in Buildings, August 21, 2000. http://www.eia.doe.gov/emeu/efficiency/aceee2000.html#carbon_trends (accessed November 2, 2006).

Cockram, M. 2006. "Saving Concrete Energy." *Architecture Week*, February 22. http://www.architectureweek.com/2006/0222/environment_1-1.html

Davis Langdon International. 2004. *Costing Green: A Comprehensive Cost Data Base and Budgeting Methodology.* http://davislangdon-usa.com/publications.html (accessed November 17, 2006).

Fahet, V. 2005. "Building Green Always Made Sense—Now It's Beginning to Pay Off." *The Chronicle*, September 11. www.sfgate.com/cgi-bin/article.dgi?file=/c/a/2005/09/11/REG4DEKFQD1.DTL&ty

Heschong Mahone Group. 1999. *Daylighting in Schools, an Investigation into the Relationship between Daylighting and Human Performance, Condensed Report.* Prepared for The Pacific Gas and Electric Company. Fair Oaks, CA: Author.

Irwin, E. G., and Bockstael, N. E. 2007. "The Evolution of Urban Sprawl: Evidence of Spatial Heterogeneity and Increasing Land Fragmentation." *Proceedings of the National Academy of Sciences* 104(52): 20672–20677.

Kats, G., Alevantis, L., Meran, A., Mills, E., McQueen, J., and Stevens, J. 1998. "Disposal of CCA-Treated Wood." *Forest Products Journal* 48(11/12).

Steven Winter Associates. 2004. "GSA LEED Cost Study, Final Report." General Services Administration. http://www.wbdg.org/ccb/GSAMAN/gsaleed.pdf

The Weidt Group, Minnesota Office of Environmental Assistance. 2005. "Top 6 Benefits of High Performance Buildings." http://www.moea.state.mn.us/publications/highperformance-brochure.pdf

Woods Hole Research Center. 2007. "Land Use Change and the Chesapeake Bay Ecosystem." http://www.whrc.org/midatlantic/modeling_change/SLEUTH/maryland_2030/md_scenarios.htm

Chapter 3

Brown, D., Hallman, R., Lee, C., Skogerboe, J., Eskew, K., Price, R., Page, N., Clar, M., Kort, R., and Hopkins, H. 1986. *Reclamation and Vegetative Restoration of Problem Soils and Disturbed Lands.* Park Ridge, NJ: Noyes Data Corporation.

Griggs, G. B. 1983. *Geologic Hazards, Resources and Environmental Planning*, 2nd ed. Belmont, CA: Wadsworth.

Chapter 4

Arendt, R. 1991. "Cluster Development: A Profitable Way to Save Open Space." *Land Development* (Fall).

Graycar, A. 1998. "Safer Communities: Strategic Directions in Urban Planning." Paper presented at the Conference for Safer Communities, Melbourne, Australia, September 10–11.

Harris, C. W., and Dines, N. T. 1988. *Time-Saver Standards for Landscape Architecture.* New York: McGraw-Hill.

Hylton, T. 1995. *Save Our Lands, Save Our Towns.* Harrisburg, PA: RB Books.

Kreager, W. 1992. "Building Small Lot Homes in Your Community." *Land Development* (Winter).

Martin, D. 1997. "Research Summary: Preventing Crime: What Works, What Doesn't, What's Promising." A Report to the United States Congress, Washington, D.C.

National Association of Home Builders. 1986. *Cost Effective Site Planning: Single Family Development.* Washington, D.C.: Author.

National Association of Home Builders. 2008. "Research Weighs Consumer Preferences in Soft Market." *Nations Building News,* March 17. http://www.nbnnews.com/NBN/issues/2008-03-17/Front+Page/index.html

"Technical Note 29. Brick in Landscape Architecture—Pedestrian Applications." www.bia.org/BIA/technotes/t29.htm

White, R. 1998. "Public Places and Community Crime Prevention." Paper presented at the Conference for Safer Communities, Melbourne, Australia, September 10–11.

Yaro, R., Arendt, R. G., Donaldson, H. L., and Brabec, E. A. 1988. *Dealing with Change in the Connecticut River Valley: A Design Manual for Conservation and Development.* Lincoln, MA: Lincoln Institute of Land Policy.

Chapter 5

Carstens, D. Y. 1985. *Site Planning and Design for the Elderly.* New York: Van Nostrand Reinhold.

"Child's Play—Specifying Safety on the Playground." 1985. *The Construction Specifier* (October).

DeChiara, J., and Koppelman, L. E. 1984. *Time-Saver Standards for Site Planning.* New York: McGraw-Hill.

Harris, C. W., and Dines. N. T. 1988. *Time-Saver Standards for Landscape Architecture.* New York: McGraw-Hill.

Minnesota Department of Natural Resources Trial Planning Classification 2007. *Sustainable Trial Development Guidelines.* http://www.dnr.state.mn.us/publications/trails_waterways/index.html

Pennsylvania Department of Environmental Resources, Office of Program Planning and Development 1986. "Pennsylvania's Recreation Plan 1986–1990."

Chapter 6

American Association of State Highway and Transportation Officials (AASHTO). 1994. *A Policy on Geometric Design of Highway and Streets.* Washington, D.C.: Author.

Appelyard, D., and Lintell, M. 1972. "The Quality of Streets: The Resident's Viewpoint." *Journal of the American Institute of Planners* 38(2).

Baranowski, B. 2009. *Roundabouts USA.* http://www.roundaboutsusa.com/design.html

Burley, J., Dr. Rogness, R., and Burley C. 1993. "Edge Scour: Developing and Repairing a Grassed Roadway Shoulder." International Erosion Control Association, Proceedings of Conference XXIV.

Center for Watershed Protection. 1998. *Better Site Design: A Handbook for Changing Development Rules in Your Community.* Prepared for the Site Planning Roundtable. Ellicott City, MD: Author.

Daisa, J. M., and Peers, J. B. 1997. *Narrow Residential Streets: Do They Really Slow Down Speeds?* ITE 6th Annual Meeting Compendium of Technical Papers.

Hornberger, W. S., Deakin, E. A., Bosselman, P. C., Smith Jr., D. T., and Beukers, B. 1989. *Residential Street Design and Traffic Control.* Englewood Cliffs, NJ: Prentice-Hall.

Markowitz, F. 1995. *Shared Parking Planning Guidelines.* Washington, D.C.: Institute of Transportation Engineers.

Metropolitan Area Planning Council. 2009. *Low Impact Development Fact Sheet.* http://www.mapc.org/regional_planning/LID/permeable_paving.html

Ridgway, M. 1997. *Residential Streets—Quality of Life Assessment.* Lafayette, CA: Fehr & Peers.

Sacramento Transportation and Air Quality Collaborative. 2005. *Best Practices for Complete Streets.* Sacramento, CA: Author.

Chapter 7

Goldman, S.J., Jackson, K., and Bursetynsky, T. A. 1986. *Erosion and Sediment Control Handbook.* New York: McGraw-Hill.

Chapter 8

Booth, D., and Levitt, J. 1999. "Field Evaluation of Permeable Pavement Systems for Improved Stormwater Management." *Journal of the American Planning Association* 65(3).

Booth, D., and Reinelt, L. 1993. "Consequences of Urbanization on Aquatic Systems: Measured Effects, Degradation Thresholds, and Corrective Strategies." In *Proceedings of Watershed 1993.* A National Conference on Watershed Management, Alexandria, VA.

Brewer, W. E., and Alter, C. P. 1988. *The Complete Manual of Land Planning and Development.* Englewood Cliffs, NJ: Prentice-Hall.

Chow, Ven Te. 1988. *Open Channel Hydraulics,* 2nd ed. New York: McGraw-Hill.

Fahet, V. 2005. "Building Green Always Made Sense—Now It's Beginning to Pay Off." *San Francisco Chronicle,* September 11. www.sfgate.com/cgi-bin/article.dgi?file=/c/a/2005/09/11/REG4DEKFQD1.DTL&ty

Landphair, H. C., and Klatt Jr., F. 1988. *Landscape Architecture Construction,* 2nd ed. New York: Elsevier Science.

Miller, C. 1998. "Vegetated Roof Covers—A New Method for Controlling Runoff in Urbanized Areas." Proceedings of the 1998 Pennsylvania Stormwater Management Symposium, Villanova University.

Maryland State Department of Education. 1999. *Conserving and Enhancing the Natural Environment: A Guide for Planning, Design, Construction and Maintenance on New and Existing School Sites.* Baltimore MD: Author.

Metropolitan Washington Council of Governments. 1992. *A Current Assessment of Urban Best Management Practices: Techniques for Reducing Nonpoint Source Pollution in the Coastal Zone.* Publication 92705 (March).

Schueler, T. 2000. "Comparative Pollutant Removal Capability of Urban BMPs: A Reanalysis." In *The Practice of Watershed Protection.* Ellicott City, MD: Center for Watershed Protection.

Tourbier J., and Westmacott, R. 1981. *Water Resources Protection Technology: A Handbook of Measures to Protect Water Resources in Land Development.* Washington, D.C.: Urban Land Institute.

Chapter 9

Brown, D., Hallman, C. L., Skogerbee, J., Eskern, K., and Price, R. 1986. *Reclamation and Vegetative Restoration of Problem Soils and Disturbed Lands.* Park Ridge, NJ: Noyes Data Corporation.

Darmer, G. 1992. *Landscape and Surface Mining—Ecological Guidelines for Reclamation* (edited by Norman L. Dietrich). New York: Van Nostrand Reinhold.

Dramstad, W. E., Olson, J. D., and Forman, R. T. T. 1996. *Landscape Ecology: Principles in Landscape Architecture and Land-Use Planning.* Washington, D.C.: Island Press.

Forest and Range. n.d. *Wetlands Management.* http://forestandrange.org/new_wetlands/wetland_types.htm

Hunter, C. J. 1991. *Better Trout Habitat.* Washington D.C.: Island Press.

Massachusetts Office of Energy and Environmental Affairs. n.d. *Climate Change and Preserving Water Resources.* http://www.mass.gov/?pageID=eoeeaterminal&L=4&L0=Home&L1=Air%2c+Water+%26+Climate+Change&L2=Preserving+Water+Resources&L3=Massachusetts+Watersheds&sid=Eoeea&b=terminalcontent&f=eea_water_charles&csid=Eoeea

Naveh, Z., and Lieberman, A. 1994. *Landscape Ecology: Theory and Application,* 2nd ed. New York: Springer-Verlag.

Rogoshewski, P., Bryson, H., and Wagner, R. 1983. *Remediation Action Technology for Waste Disposal Sites.* Park Ridge, NJ: Noyes Data Corporation.

Sobek, A., Sknuller, W. A., Freeman, J. R., and Smith, R. M. 1976. *Field and Laboratory Methods: Applications to Overburden and Minesites.* Park Ridge, NJ: Industrial Environmental Research Laboratory.

U. S. Environmental Protection Agency. 1991. *Wetlands.* http://www.epa.gov/owow/wetlands/

Vogel, W. G. 1987. *A Manual for Training Reclamation Inspectors in the Fundamentals of Soils and Revegetation.* Prepared for the Office of Surface Mining and Enforcement. Berea, KY: U.S. Department of Agriculture.

Chapter 10

Doherty, T., Murphy, M., and Lalani, R. n.d. *Carbon Sequestration in Trees in City of Kitchener Parks.* http://www.watgreen.uwaterloo.ca/projects/project_records/carbon.html

Green, C., and Hoffnagle, A. 2004. *Phytoremediation Field Studies Database for Chlorinated Solvents, Pesticide, Explosives and Metals.* Washington, D.C.: U.S. EPA Office of Superfund Remediation and Technology Innovation.

Martin, C. W., Maggio, R. C., and Appel, D. N. n.d. *The Contributory Value of Trees to Residential Property Value in the Austin, Texas Metropolitan Area.* http://joa.isa-arbor.com/request.asp?JournalID=1&ArticleID=2275&Type=2

Northern Institute of Applied Carbon Science. n.d. *Forests Absorb Carbon Dioxide.* Washington, D.C.: U.S. Department of Agriculture. http://www.nrs.fs.fed.us/niacs/forests/

Oren, R., Ellsworth, D. S., Johnsen, K. H., Philips, N., Ewers, B. E., Maier, C., et al. 2001. "Soil Fertility Limits Carbon Sequestration by Forest Ecosystems in a CO_2 Enriched Atmosphere." *Nature* 411 (May).

Wolf, K. L. 2007. "City Trees and Property Values." *Arborist News* (August).

Chapter 11

American Farmland Trust. 1992. *Does Farmland Protection Pay? The Cost of Community Services in Three Massachusetts Towns.* Northampton, MA: Author.

Babcock, R. F., and Siemon, C. L. 1985. *The Zoning Game Revisited.* Cambridge, MA: Lincoln Institute of Land Policy.

Closser, J. E. 1993. *Assessing Land Affected by Conservation Easements—Resource Manual.* Cambridge, MA: Lincoln Institute of Land Policy.

Coughlin, R. E. 1991. "Forumalting and Evaluating Agricultural Zoning Programs." *Journal of the American Planning Association* 57(2, Spring): 183–191.

Czupryna, J. J. 1983. *Newsletter of the American Society of Appraisers* (March).

Fischel, W. A. 1990. *Do Growth Controls Matter?* Cambridge, MA: Lincoln Institute of Land Policy.

Gambe, H. B., and Downs, R. H. 1982. "Effects of Nuclear Power Plant on Residential Property Values." *Journal of Regional Science* 22: 457–478.

Garreau, J. 1991. *Edge City: Life on the New Frontier.* New York: Doubleday.

Gelman, S. R., Epp, D. J., Downing, R. H., Twark, R. D., and Eyerly, R. 1989. "Impact of Group Homes on the Values of Adjacent Residential Values." *Mental Retardation* (June): 127–134.

Hennebery, D. M., and Barrows, R. L. 1990. "Capitalization of Exclusive Agricultural Zoning into Farmland Prices." *Land Economics* 66(3): 250–258.

Hubbard, H., and Kimball, T. 1917. *An Introduction to the Study of Landscape Design.* New York: Macmillan.

Kellogg, R. L., TeSelle, G. W., and Goebel, J. J. 1994. "Highlights from the 1992 National Resources Inventory." *Journal of Soil and Water Conservation* 49(6).

Knaap, G. J. 1985. "The Price Effects of Urban Growth Boundaries in Metropolitan Portland, Oregon." *Land Economics* 61: 28–35.

Mill, D. C. 1990. "Zoning Rights and Land Development Theory." *Land Economics* 66(3): 285.

Nelson, J. P. 1981. "Three Mile Island and Residential Property Values: Empirical Analysis and Policy Implications." *Land Economics* (57): 363–372.

Pogodzinski, J. M., and Sass, T. R. 1990. "A Review of Zoning Theory." *Land Economics* 66(3): 294–313.

Pollakowski, H. O., and Wachter, S. M. 1990. "The Effects of Constraints on Housing Prices." *Land Economics* 66(3): 315–324.

President's Council on Environmental Quality. 1981. *National Agricultural Lands Study.* Washington, D.C.: U.S. Department of Agriculture.

Russ, T. 1994. "Impacts of Land Preservation on the Value of Adjacent Land." Unpublished study, Kutztown University, Kutztown, Pennsylvania.

Shortle, J., Downs, R. H., Epp, D., and Gamble, H. B. n.d. "Effects of Solid Waste Disposal Sites on Community Development and Residential Property Values." Unpublished paper prepared by the Institute for Research in Land and Water Resources.

Small, S. J. 1991. *The Federal Tax Law of Conservation Easements.* Washington, D.C.: Land Trust Alliance.

Vaillancourt, F., and Monty, L. 1985. "The Effect of Agricultural Zoning on Land Prices, Quebec 1975–81." *Land Economics* 61(February): 36–42.

Williams, H. L., and Davis, W. D. 1968. "Effect of Scenic Easement on the Market Value of Real Property." *The Appraiser Journal* (October): 15–24.

Chapter 12

Alexander, C., Ishikawa, S., and Silverstein, M. (with M. Jacobson, I. Fiksdahl-King, and S. Angel). 1977. *A Pattern Language*. New York: Oxford University Press.

Berry, T. 1988. *Dream of the Earth*. San Francisco, CA: Sierra Club.

Chesapeake Bay Program, Communications Subcommittee. 1994. "The Chesapeake Bay Attitudes Survey." College Park: University of Maryland, Survey Research Center.

Feldman, E. J., and Goldberg, M. A. (eds.). 1987. *Land Rites and Wrongs: The Management, Regulation and Use of Land in Canada and the United States*. Cambridge, MA: Lincoln Institute of Land Policy.

Fischel, W. A. 1992. *Do Growth Controls Matter? A Review of Empirical Evidence on the Effectiveness and Efficiency of Local Government Land Use Regulation*. Cambridge, MA: Lincoln Institute of Land Policy.

Hendee, J. C., and Pitstick, R. C. 1992. "The Growth of Environmental and Conservation Related Organizations 1980–1991." *Renewable Resources Journal* (Summer).

Jackson, J. B. 1984. *Discovering the Vernacular Landscape*. Cambridge, MA: Yale University Press.

Kempton, W., Boster, J. S., and Hartley, J. A. 1996. *Environmental Values in American Culture*. Cambridge, MA: MIT Press.

Leopold, A. 1949. *A Sand County Almanac*. New York: Oxford University Press.

McDonough, W., and Braungart, M. 2002. *Cradle to Cradle*. New York: North Point Press.

Papanek, V. 1995. *The Green Imperative*. New York: Thames and Hudson.

Pirsig, R. 1984. *Zen and the Art of Motorcycle Maintenance*. New York: Bantam.

President's Council on Sustainable Development. 1996. *Sustainable America—A New Consensus for Prosperity, Opportunity and a Healthy Environment for the Future*. Washington, D.C.: Author.

Reilly, W. K. (ed.). 1973. *The Use of Land: A Policy Guide to Urban Growth*. New York: Thomas Y. Crowell.

Shortle, J., Downs, R. H., Epp, D, and Gamble, H. B. n.d. "Effects of Solid Waste Disposal Sites on Community Development and Residential Property Values." Unpublished paper prepared by the Institute for Research in Land and Water Resources.

Stilgoe, J. R. 1982. *Common Landscape of America*. New Haven, CN: Yale University Press.

Times Mirror Magazines. 1992. "Natural Resource Conservation: Where Environmentalism Is Headed in the 1990s." *Times Mirror* Magazines' National Environmental Forum Survey. Survey conducted by The Roper Organization, Los Angeles, CA.

Williams, H. L., and Davis, W. D. 1968. "Effect of Scenic Easement on the Market Value of Real Property." *The Appraiser Journal* (October): 15–24.

Chapter 13

Gelman, S. R., Epp, D. J., Downing, R. H., Twark, R. D., and Eyerly, R. 1989. "Impact of Group Homes on the Values of Adjacent Residential Values." *Mental Retardation* (June): 127–134.

Kenyon, D. A. 1991. *The Economics of NIMBYs*. Cambridge, MA: Lincoln Institute of Land Policy.

Kerzner, H. 2009. *Project Management: A Systems Approach to Planning, Scheduling, and Controlling,* 9th ed. Hoboken, NJ: John Wiley & Sons.

Nelson, J. P. 1981. "Three Mile Island and Residential Property Values: Empirical Analysis and Policy Implications." *Land Economics* (57): 363–372.

Petroski, H. 2000. *Design Paradigms, Case Histories of Error and Judgement in Engineering.* Cambridge UK: Cambridge University Press.

Shortle, J., Downs, R. H., Epp, D, and Gamble, H. B. n.d. "Effects of Solid Waste Disposal Sites on Community Development and Residential Property Values." Unpublished paper prepared by the Institute for Research in Land and Water Resources.

Index

Land use (*Cont.*):
  rate of sprawl, land consumption growth and, 20
  site design and, 20–23
  task force recommendations for, 419–420
  in U.S. and Canada, 420–422
Landowners
  defense of "innocent," 63
  risks for, 63, 65
  takings and, 428–429
  taxes and, 421
  use of land and, 418–419
Landscape(s)
  building postindustrial, 430–434
  culture and, 415–440
  definitions of, 415–416
  editorial billboards and, 416
  energy efficiency and, 360
  growth controls and, 423–429
  intellectual shift away from fictional control of, 430
  investigation of historic, 389–395
  nighttime, 94
  overview of U.S. style of, 395–400
  planning, 400–405
    accessibility, 402
    activities of concern, 404–405
    adapting historic landscapes, 401–402
    environmental concerns, 402–404
    treatment types, 400
    way-finding, 401
  plants and informal, 356
  preservation of land and, 406–413
  preserving, 389–413
  science, design and, 434–440
  toxic plants and, 387–388
  use of, 418–423
  using trees in, 360–368
  values, 415–417
Landscape ecology
  people and, 431–434
  site planning and, 299–300
Landscapes, historic
  adapting, 401–402
  aerial photograph of former L'Enfant garden and, 393
  aerial photographs and, 394
  early American homesteads and, 396
  formal gardens and, 390, 391
  fundamentals of preservation, 390
  historic houses and, 392
  investigation of, 389–395
  photography in site analysis of, 394
  site plan from *Victorian Cottage Residencies*, 398
Landscapes, postindustrial
  building, 430–434
  changing attitudes toward sustainability and, 432
  ecology and people, 431–434

Landscapes, postindustrial (*Cont.*):
  economic relationship between people, 431
  environmental surveys and, 432–433
  mimicking natural flood cycles and, 430
Landscapes, restoration of, 299–347
  Brownfield redevelopment and, 337–347
  characteristics of selected trees and shrubs with, 309–312
  criteria for selecting plants for, 306
  cultural operations and, 304–305
  enhancing slope stabilization with trees and, 307–313
  erosion damage and, 337
  nitrogen fixing trees and shrubs on, 308
  planning and collecting soil samples with, 303
  selecting plant materials for, 305–307
  site planning and ecology of, 299–300
  site preparation for, 301–304
  stair-stepping and, 304
  streams and, 313–329
  tracking on slope and, 305
  trees planted on slopes and, 308
  using sod and, 307
  vegetative cover restoration and, 301
  wetlands and, 329–337
Landslides, 50
LCA (*See* Life Cycle Assessment)
Leadership in Energy and Environmental Design (LEED), 31–32, 439, 475
  certification, 33
  program, 41
LEED (*See* Leadership in Energy and Environmental Design)
L'Enfant, Pierre, 397
L'Enfant Gardens, 393
Leopold, Aldo, 431
Liabilities
  Brownfields and protection from, 340
  contracting, 447–450
  ESA historical perspectives and, 455–456
Life Cycle Assessment (LCA), 35
Lighting
  maintenance factor and, 96
  moonlighting, backlighting and, 97
  performance characteristics of light sources and, 97
  point distribution calculation dimensions and, 96
  point illumination method and, 94, 96
  recommended levels of illumination and, 95
  security and, 94–97
Lincoln Land Institute, 410, 413
Lintel, Mark, 173
Liquefaction, 55
Live stakes, 325, 326
Loading areas, 93
Locations
  building, 44
  site analysis, 48

Printed in the USA
CPSIA information can be obtained
at www.ICGtesting.com
JSHW050735240724
66864JS00001B/4